Racine

Racine

The Power and the Pleasure

edited by
EDRIC CALDICOTT
and
DERVAL CONROY

University College Dublin Press
Preas Choláiste Ollscoile Bhaile Átha Cliath

First published 2001 by University College Dublin Press,
Newman House, 86 St Stephen's Green, Dublin 2, Ireland
www.ucdpress.ie

ISBN 1 900621 56 8 (hardback)
1 900621 57 6 (paperback)

British Library Cataloguing in Publication Data
A catalogue record for this title is available from the British Library

Typeset in 11/13 Baskerville in Ireland by Elaine Shiels, Bantry, Co. Cork
Printed in Ireland by ColourBooks, Dublin

Contents

Acknowledgements

This book has its origins in the international conference which was organized jointly in Dublin, in October 1999, by the French departments of Trinity College (Dublin University), University College (National University of Ireland, Dublin), and the Alliance Française of Ireland. Without the conference there would not have been a book, and without the assistance of a number of institutions, agencies, and colleagues there would not have been a conference. In conjunction with the conference, a concert of seventeenth-century French music was held, featuring for the first time in Ireland the performance of choral parts written for Racine's *Esther* by Jean-Baptiste Moreau. It is therefore with great pleasure and gratitude that the editors acknowledge the material contribution of the following to the organization and promotion of the Dublin conference and concert: André Raynouard, Conseiller Culturel of the French Embassy in Dublin, with his able *adjoints* Anne-France Badoui and Dominique Suquet, of the Service Culturel of the French Embassy; The Ireland Fund of France; Marie-Christine Vandoorne, director of the Alliance Française, Dublin; the Arts Faculty and the French Department of University College Dublin; the Department of French, the Faculty of Arts (Letters) and the Visual and Performing Arts Fund of Trinity College, Dublin.

Finally, for their assistance in the production of *Racine: The Power and the Pleasure*, we would like to thank the Board of Funded Research of University College Dublin; the Provost's Academic Development Fund of Trinity College, and the Trinity College Dublin Association and Trust. All our participating authors, having been as convivial as Dublin demanded at the conference, were punctual and precise in the preparation, return and correction of their respective contributions, and we thank them for their practical help, as well as for so much else. It is also a quite particular pleasure in the terrain of the 'frères ennemis' for the two editors representing the separate Dublin universities of Trinity and UCD to turn to each other, and say 'Merci'.

C.E.J.C.
D.C.
Dublin, July 2000

Notes on Contributors

Jean-Louis Backès, Professor of Comparative Literature, University of Paris–IV (Sorbonne): an authority in many fields, whose publications include *Racine* (Editions du Seuil, COLL. 'Ecrivains de Toujours', 1981, republished 1999); *Musique et Littérature* (PUF, 1994); *Pouchkine* (Hachette, 1996); *La littérature européenne* (Lettres Belin sup, 1996), and *Les Vers et les Formes Poétiques* (Hachette, 1997). Jean-Louis Backès's *Racine* had the distinction of being one of the first critical works to reconcile the positions of the irreconcilable Roland Barthes and Raymond Picard.

Christian Biet, Professor of Theatre Studies, University of Paris–X (Nanterre): bringing a specifically theatrical focus to the work of Racine, his considerable output includes such radically new works as *Œdipe en monarchie. Tragédie et théorie juridique à l'âge classique* (Klincksieck, 1994); *Racine ou La passion des larmes* (Hachette, 1996); *Racine* (Hachette, 1996); *La tragédie* (Armand Colin, 1997).

Edric Caldicott, Professor of French, University College Dublin, has written widely on the social and material setting of the writer's career in seventeenth-century France. For his many publications on Molière, he was awarded the Grand Prix du Théâtre of the Académie française in 1989, and subsequently wrote *La Carrière de Molière – entre protecteurs et éditeurs* (Rodopi, 1998).

Derval Conroy, Lecturer in French at Trinity College, Dublin: her research interests are in the area of gender studies, women's history, women writers and political thought. She has published several articles on the representation of women and is currently completing a study on gender and sovereignty in the *Grand Siècle*.

Jane Conroy, Lecturer in French, National University of Ireland, Galway: active in a number of scholarly fields and author of an important pioneering study of seventeenth-century French perceptions of English and Scottish history as filtered through the theatre, *Terres tragiques. L'Angleterre et l'Ecosse dans la tragédie française du XVIIe siècle*, coll. Biblio 17 (Gunter Narr, 1999).

Jean-Michel Delacomptée, Professor of French, University of Bordeaux–III: his most recent work, a sensitive reconstruction of Racine's life observed through close scrutiny of contemporary sources, *Racine en majesté* (Flammarion, 1998), was published to great acclaim, as were *La Princesse de Clèves, la mère et le courtisan* (PUF, 1990); *Madame, la Cour, la mort* (Gallimard, 1992), and *Qu'un seul soit l'ami: La Boétie* (Gallimard, 1995).

Georges Forestier, Professor of French Literature, Paris–IV (Sorbonne): a prolific commentator on seventeenth-century French theatre, with an active interest in the practical application of his work to stage production. His books include *Esthétique et Identité dans le théâtre français, 1550–1680. Le déguisement et ses avatars* (Droz, 1988); *Molière en toutes lettres* (Bordas, 1990); *Introduction à l'analyse des textes classiques* (Nathan, 1993); *Essai de génétique théâtrale: Corneille à l'œuvre* (Klincksieck, 1996); *Racine. Œuvres*, 1, *Théâtre et Poésie*, coll. la Pléiade (Gallimard, 1999).

Gráinne Gormley, Teaching Fellow in the Department of Music at University College Dublin: director of the Tercentenary Concert of Moreau's music for *Esther*, heard for the first time in Ireland on 2 October 1999. Well known to Dublin music lovers as conductor of the University of Dublin Choral Society, University College Dublin College Choir, the choir of St Teresa's, Clarendon Street, and Tallaght Choral Society. She conducted performances of Handel's Messiah at St Etienne du Mont, Paris, in context of *L'Imaginaire Irlandais*. Concerts in Dublin have included Fauré's *Requiem*, selections of Poulenc and Duruflé, Haydn's *Creation*, and Beethoven's *Mass in C*.

Susanne Hartwig, professorial assistant in Romance languages at the University of Münster, Westphalia. She and her associate, Berthold Warnecke, have explored the music of Jean-Baptiste Moreau to discover not only the degree of his cooperation with Jean Racine in the 'tragédies sacrées', but the true musical originality of the score of *Esther*.

Robert McBride, Professor of French at the University of Ulster, Coleraine: specialist of seventeenth-century theatre, Molière, and currents of scepticism, on which he has written several books, most notably *The Sceptical Vision of Molière: A Study in Paradox* (Macmillan, 1977). Co-founder of the annual review *Le Nouveau Moliériste*.

Ireland

Marc Serge Rivière, Professor of Cultural Studies at the University of Limerick: an eighteenth-century specialist who has published widely on Voltaire, and in whose work he has discovered commentaries by and about the women, patronesses and actresses, in Racine's career.

Ireland

Louis van Delft, Professor of French Literature, University of Paris–X (Nanterre): editor and commentator on the work of La Bruyère, new edition of *Les Caractères* (Imprimerie Nationale, 1998); author of a pioneering study on national identities in literature, *Littérature et anthropologie. Nature humaine et caractère à l'âge classique* (PUF, 1993). He is also drama critic for the review *Commentaire*, with reviews anthologized in *Le Théâtre en feu* (Gunter Narr, 1998).

Paris

Alain Viala, Professor of French Literature, University of Oxford and University of Paris–III (Sorbonne Nouvelle): editor with Jacques Morel of the theatre of Racine (Editions Garnier, 1980); biographer of Racine, *Racine. La stratégie du caméléon* (Seghers, 1990); a household name with the publication of his thesis, *Naissance de l'Ecrivain: Sociologie de la littérature à l' âge classique* (Editions de Minuit, 1985), he has continued his extended analysis of French literary forms with *La Littérature galante* (Editions SLC, 1989) and other works.

Paris

Berthold Warnecke, technical adviser to the City of Münster Symphony Orchestra and to Münster Opera.

Münster

13 contribs,
14 scholars < France + Ireland + Germany
(check!)

Translators' Note

All our overseas contributors, from France and Germany, wrote their
papers in French. With the prior permission of the contributors
concerned, the editors translated their articles into English, but
retained the French text of quotations from Racine, and from French
critical sources. Translations have been added in square brackets after
all quotations in French prose, but we have not attempted translations
of French verse. There are a number of terms in the language of
seventeenth-century France which defy easy translation, for example,
'galant', 'gloire', 'généreux', or 'bienséance'. Rather than expand into
long glosses on these terms, we have assumed that they are widely
known and have left them in the original, occasionally adding an
explanatory parenthesis in the text. Translators'/editors' interventions
are always signalled by square brackets.

Bibliographical Summary

This is intended as no more than an explanation of the abbreviations of most commonly recurring titles in the book; all contributors have offered extended bibliographies of works most useful to them in their own footnotes.

The two most widely used working instruments to appear in the course of the tercentenary year were the new editions of Racine's complete works by Georges Forestier and Jean Rohou:

Georges Forestier (ed.), *Racine. Œuvres Complètes*, 1, *Théâtre–Poésie*, coll. de la Pléiade (Paris: Gallimard, 1999).

Jean Rohou (ed.), avec la collaboration de Paul Fièvre, *Racine. Théâtre Complet*, coll. Classiques Modernes (Paris: Librairie Générale Française, 1998)

Forestier's edition reproduces the first editions of Racine's plays, and Rohou's the final revised versions of Racine's lifetime. They are referred to respectively as:
Forestier, *Œuvres*, and Rohou, *Théâtre*.

It should be added that Forestier's edition replaces the previous Pléiade edition of Racine's theatre by Raymond Picard. Picard's was the original volume 1; his volume 2 in the Pléiade series, *Racine. Œuvres Complètes*, 2, *Prose*, remains the companion volume to Forestier's new edition, and is referred to as Picard, *Œuvres*.

The admirably complementary editions of Forestier and Rohou have not used all the additional material available in the edition of Paul Mesnard in the collection Grands Ecrivains de la France, 9 vols (Paris: Hachette, 1865–73). This is referred to as G.E.F., with the appropriate volume number added.

Abbreviations

The abbreviations used for standard editions of Racine's theatrical works are: Forestier, *Œuvres*; Picard, *Œuvres*; Rohou, *Théâtre*; G.E.F.

Where work from Corneille and Molière is quoted, references are drawn from the following editions of their complete works:

Corneille, *Œuvres complètes*, Bibliothèque de la Pléiade, 3 vols (Paris: Gallimard, 1980, 1984, 1987)

Molière, *Œuvres complètes*, Bibliothèque de la Pléiade, 2 vols (Paris: Gallimard, 1971).

These are abbreviated respectively to:

Couton, *Corneille* (with appropriate vol. no. attached); Couton, *Molière* (followed by vol. no).

In addition the following abbreviations are used for journals and publishers:

CAIEF	*Cahiers de l'Association Internationale des Etudes françaises*
CMR 17	*Centre Méridional de Rencontres sur le 17ᵉ siècle*
CNRS	Conseil National de Recherches Scientifiques
NRF	*Nouvelle Revue Française*
PFSCL	*Papers on French Seventeenth Century Literature* (coll. Biblio 17)
PUF	Presses Universitaires de France
SEDES	Société des Editions D'Etudes Supérieures
STFM	Société des textes français modernes

Aristotle's *Poetics* is always referred to in the edition by D.A. Russell and M. Winterbottom, *Ancient Literary Criticism: The Principal Texts in New Translations*, translated by Margaret Hubbard (Oxford: Oxford University Press, 1972). This is abbreviated to: *Poetics*, ed. Russell.

Introduction

EDRIC CALDICOTT AND DERVAL CONROY

Racine's tercentenary

Jean Racine died in April, 1699; as was the case with the previous anniversaries of Molière (1973) and Pierre Corneille (1984), the occasion of the tercentenary was marked by a number of commemorative activities, including new editions and new theatrical productions of his work, and by literary conferences. The contributors to this book were the original participants at the Dublin tercentenary conference which was held in early October, 1999. Other Racine conferences were organized in Nice, Paris, London, Oxford, Manchester, Santa Barbara (California), Turin, and Tel-Aviv. Some of these conference proceedings have appeared in print, others have still to do so, but the volume of work published in the tercentenary year has already ensured that for the second time in the last half century, following the celebrated controversy between Roland Barthes and Raymond Picard, Racine has been propelled to the fore in literary debate. With so many conferences taking place, is there anything different about the Dublin approach?

Within the international community that investigated these issues in the course of 1999, there were a number of common concerns. The most obvious of these concerns was the interrogation of Racine's theatre, which requires today as always, and whether in France or elsewhere, an examination of his work on stage. This is not as trite as it may seem, because the theatrical event also takes account of synchronic factors such as reception, language, taste, patronage, and political symbolism of the time. The Dublin conference addressed the work of Racine on stage in two specific ways: (a) it provided one of the first complete concerts outside France of the choral parts written for *Esther* by Racine and Moreau; (*b*) it developed a line of study of the nature of pleasure in Racine, pleasure in performance as well as the complex nature of pleasure within his work, and in his time. Given that William of Orange was already permanently settled in England (while James II was in the audience at Saint-Cyr) when Moreau's music was first performed, the choral performance in Trinity College Chapel on 2 October 1999 was probably the first time that the music had ever been performed in Ireland. It was a memorable event, enjoyed by a large and appreciative audience. With her presentation in this volume of the conclusions to be drawn from the performance, Gráinne Gormley, director of music for the occasion, has ensured that the experiment need never be as nerve-wracking again. Organized by her, with the soloists and instrumentalists named by her in the notes to her analysis, the Dublin concert also owed much of its success to the meticulous work of transcription for choral and instrumental parts which had already been completed by M. Emmanuel Mandrin, who originally performed extracts of it in the parish church of La Ferté-Milon (Racine's birthplace) with the Maîtrise of Radio France and La Symphonie du Marais on 30 May 1999. With the work of Mandrin, we now have indispensable access to a hitherto unknown aspect of Racine's work, and he will be encouraged by all Raciniens to publish the musical score that he has so attentively restored. As a number of studies in the book will show, the proper appreciation of Racine's last two plays depends upon access to that music.

Our second point of focus at the conference has become one of the principal themes of the book. The question of pleasure in Racine is so absorbing that several chapters in the book examine the issue, while others explore the nature of power and its victims in a synchronic scrutiny of Racine's world. It is often the case that the tragic dilemma in Racine's theatre stems from the constantly misleading confusion by his characters of power with pleasure, and this spectacle offers in turn a darker kind of pleasure to the spectator/reader. Through this focus, while seeking to make its own contribution, *Racine: the Power and the Pleasure* is also the product of wider international debate.

The divisiveness of the Barthes–Picard battle of the 1960s allowed no foreign intrusion: it was as much a debate about being French as about Racine. With the arrival of the tercentenary, critical attention in the form of publication has proved to be as lively as it was in the 1960s, but much less divisive. It will be apparent that Racine has never been so well served by his editors and commentators, but it can also be added that in terms of theatrical production, the semiology of the

stage, and performance in English, not to mention the recovery of
the music that Racine wrote for, the situation is much more promising. *benefitted from contemp. stage*
Constructive, informed, stage experiment is in the air, and part of *experiments -*
academic debate. Within the pages of this book, the drama critic of *constructive + informed.*
Commentaire, who is also our academic colleague Louis van Delft,
presents a selection of critical reviews of productions on the Paris
stage. Not all the productions are memorable (and some may have
been listed for their incongruity), but among them is one of the most
exciting fusions of scholarly research and stage production of recent
times, unfortunately the object of a dismissive review by Marc Fumaroli
in the selection proposed, *viz.* the staging of *Mithridate* 'en déclamation'
by Eugène Green, with every gesture rigorously synchronized in har-
mony with a studied rhetorical delivery. Like it or hate it, it remains a *incl. Mithridate*
brave and thought-provoking model for future experiment. What is the *'en déclamation'*
point of exploring the theory of rhetoric if it is never to be tested in
practice? Premiered in the chapel of the Sorbonne in May 1999, it was
produced by Georges Forestier who, as everyone knows, also doubled
as editor of the new Pléiade edition of Racine's verse and theatrical
works. Outside France, a renewal of wider interest in Racine's theatre
was stimulated by the last poet laureate, Ted Hughes, whose translation *+ Ted Hughes'*
of *Phèdre* was produced to great acclaim by the Almeida Theatre in *Phèdre*
1999.[1] It was, in every respect, a satisfying riposte to an earlier poet
laureate, John Dryden, who argued in *An Essay of Dramaticke Poesie*
(1668) that French plays in translation would never succeed on the
English stage. The Irish poet Derek Mahon also translated the same
play in 1996.[2]

   The Dublin contribution to the Racine year owes an immeasurable
amount to the wider academic community, and to none more than
our visiting contributors, who ensured the transition from a conference
to a book. Susanne Hartwig came from Münster to present a new
and absorbing appreciation of the novelty of Moreau's music, but her
co-author was unfortunately unable to travel. Of our six French
contributors it is safe to say that their engagement in critical debate
and their prodigious published output over the last decade have
placed them among the principal agents for a fuller understanding of
the French seventeenth century. It is very satisfying in this regard to
note the element of continuity provided by Jean-Louis Backès whose
book, *Racine* (Editions du Seuil, 1981), was the first in France to reconcile
the indispensable contributions of the warring Barthes and Picard, by

1 *Jean Racine, Phèdre: A New Version by Ted Hughes* (London: Faber, 1998).
2 Derek Mahon, *Racine's Phaedra* (Oldcastle: Gallery Press, 1996)

drawing upon the work of both of them. If they are all well-known figures in the French literary world, it is also the case that almost none of their work has ever been translated into English. It was for this reason that an early decision was taken in advance of the conference to publish the proceedings in English, therefore translating the French contributions into English, and our French colleagues were informed of this. None demurred. The work of translation was done by the editors, and it was done in the confidence that introduction of the work of these scholars to readers in the English-speaking world who might not otherwise have access to it was part of the process of bringing Racine to a bigger audience.

These, then, were the circumstances in which this book was born; it is aimed at anyone with an interest in the theatre of Racine, whether as a student, casual amateur of French theatre, or an academic specialist. Turning to presentation of the contents of the book, and some of the general points arising from them, we now face the challenge presented by the brilliantly polemic work of the doyen of Racine studies, Jean Rohou, *Avez-vous* lu *Racine?*, in which he reminds us that 'la difficulté n'est pas de trouver des livres, mais de se limiter à ceux qui valent d'être lus'.[3]

The Power and the Pleasure

Playing on the concluding words of the Lord's Prayer, the title of the book was suggested by the example of Racine himself, who so often invests an apparently new turn of phrase with echoes of a significant past. The fact that when taken together our two principal themes, power and pleasure, evoke the oldest prayer of the Church seems only appropriate in the case of Racine; after all, the concluding 'Eternité' of Esther is a reprise of what we translate in English as 'for ever and ever'. From the passions, pleasures, and eventually power, of Solomon and David, Racine derived an insight for his time, which is, as Jacques Morel put it, that 'l'homme tragique par excellence, c'est le prince. L'œuvre de Racine est un long dialogue avec Louis XIV' [the essence of tragic man is the the prince. The work of Racine is a long dialogue with Louis XIV].[4] Jean-Michel Delacomptée reached similar conclusions in his persuasive psychological portrait *Racine en Majesté*, which traces Racine's doomed veneration for the monarch who was the

3 Jean Rohou, *Avez-vous* lu *Racine?* (Paris: L'Harmattan, 2000), p. 403.
4 Jacques Morel and Alain Viala, *Racine. Théâtre Complet* (Paris: Garnier, 1980), Introduction, p. xxxi.

intro not terribly well org'd?.

same age as him, and to whom he bore an increasingly striking resemblance. 'Aimer le roi, le glorifier, il n'a jamais fait rien d'autre' [Loving the King, and glorifying him, is all that Racine ever did].[5] Converging in their most exemplary manner in the person of Louis XIV, power and pleasure also result in tragedy if confused with each other.

The thirteen contributions to this volume all focus on Racine's tragedy, and range from his dramaturgy to the recurring topoi of his theatre, from plot design and text to dominant themes. In between, the notion of pleasure is explored with many of its complex ramifications, not all them purely pleasurable. Close to the concept of pleasure is the enjoyment of power, which opens further avenues of exploration: the role of women, their access to authority, or the consequences of their disempowerment. There is an excursion into Racine's prose which investigates his defence of theatre in his letters to Nicole, and not the least interesting aspect of this study is the portrait of the man which emerges from it, particularly in contrast with Molière. It also raises the question of reception, a subject which is explored in the following chapter, more specifically in the eighteenth-century perception of Racine as 'le poète des femmes'. At a time when the growing vogue of opera expressed a specific form of audience pleasure in the 1680s, Racine's cooperation with the composer Jean-Baptiste Moreau was a logical development, but it has its own particular interest. The shift from 'l'antiquité païenne' to 'l'antiquité chrétienne' again raises questions of dramaturgy. The inevitability and finality of divine intervention, and the opportunity of redemption (manifested and reinforced through music in Racine's biblical plays), are not necessarily compatible with the earlier classical canon of composition. Does the concept of tragedy itself not therefore undergo a change? In this light, the penultimate sequence of chapters which deal specifically with Moreau's music constitute a totally new and henceforth indispensable addition to the study of Racine's tragedy. In juxtaposition with the analysis of Moreau's music, itself a manifestation of divine intervention in Racine's theatre, the full impact of the concluding exploration of the theme of 'vanitas' in Racine's work is better appreciated, perceived as a developing momentum in an *œuvre* which concludes in a sense of the inevitable. Many chapters range across the whole spectrum of Racine's tragedy, others deal with specific plays. Coverage was not a condition of contribution, so some plays are treated more fully than others; this is particularly true of the first two and the last two plays, a welcome development even if it is at a relative cost to *Phèdre* and *Iphigénie*.

all on R's tragedy·

dramaturgy, recurring topoi plot design dominant themes

pleasure ↓ power ↓ role of ♀?

defense of theater

portrait of R (vs. Mol.)

reception (R poète des ♀?)

collab. vol / Moreau

tension: antiquité ♀ vs. classical comp'l rules

vanitas

5 Jean-Michel Delacomptée, *Racine en Majesté* (Paris: Flammarion, 1999), p. 181.

French tragedy, with its full corpus of classical antecedents, has its own strict protocols. So tightly does Racine adhere to these protocols that in order to offer a coherent account of his method this volume is obliged to concentrate on his eleven tragedies, excluding, therefore, his one comedy, *Les Plaideurs*. It is the technical craft of the tragic writer which provides the subject for the first two contributions, by Georges Forestier and Jean-Louis Backès respectively. Forestier looks at Racine's innovative dramaturgy, i.e. the mechanism of plot structures and the concept of character, while Backès scrutinizes the quite specific way in which the apparent authority of the maxim is used to infuse local colour and character difference. It is entirely appropriate that the first chapter should be presented by the editor of the new Pléiade edition of Racine's verse and theatrical work. In his introduction to the new edition, Forestier has revised and rewritten the old story of the rivalry between Corneille and Racine. In a tight and systematic analysis of their complete theatrical works, he shows how Racine was able to introduce meaningful change to the principles and practice which had governed Corneille's work. This is not the point at which to rehearse Forestier's masterful examination of the question: he does it himself, by drawing upon his own material to show how, in the specific case of *Andromaque*, Racine inaugurated a new phase in the history of French tragedy. By redefining and realigning the prescriptive notions of 'vraisemblance', 'ressemblance', and 'bienséance', he was able to take account of a new sensitivity in new audiences, with a different emotional range from his illustrious predecessor. From this study emerges a much clearer synchronic picture of what, exactly, the fashionable novelty of Racine in his own time, and the rearguard resistance he encountered, consisted. Modern, fluid, and intimate, he was able to foreground the role of women in a way which the social pressures of the time dictated. Needless to say, the fidelity to Holy Scripture required of his biblical plays created a different set of priorities; these are explored in the chapters on *Esther* and *Athalie*.

The second chapter also deals with the technical craft of the writer, not in this case with the design and mechanisms of plot structure, but with the quite specific exploitation of the maxim by Racine. Commonly assumed to be an expression of universal truth, brilliantly executed by writers like La Rochefoucauld and La Bruyère, and eagerly read in seventeenth-century France, the maxim is exploited in Racine's theatre in a subtle and novel way. It is shown by Backès to take on a more elusive inflexion of relativity, but is no less persuasive for that. In an attentive reading of the texts, and particularly of *Bajazet*, Backès illustrates the way in which the maxim is exploited to enforce acceptance of a different 'Other'. In the case of *Bajazet*, the 'Other' is, of course, Turkish, but the control exercised by the square-hewn form of the maxim at the level of audience reception maintains the illusion of truth, thus allowing the psychological credibilty of the 'Other' to hold Racine's French audiences. The subjective identity of the 'Other' is given objective weight by a set of maxims which express 'Turkish truths'. In this way, the 'otherness' of Turkish truths, clearly expressed in the content of the maxim, is redeemed by the traditional perception of its form as an expression of universal truth. The studies of Peter France, Michael Hawcroft, and Gilles Declercq[6] have all allowed us to appreciate Racine's mastery of rhetorical devices, and this new study of the maxim, prising open the apparently hermetic interstices which divide meaning and form in the maxim's clear-cut symmetry, adds finesse to our understanding of a meticulous writer's technical craft.

In his study of the dramatic and psychological study of tears, Christian Biet takes us beyond questions of composition into the territory of emotional expression, as communicated by the actors, and as shared with the audience, in the startling semiology of women's tears. If the exploitation and impact of tears on stage were startling in Racine's time, Biet draws out implications which are startling in our own time, too. Developing the ideas he first presented on the subject in his *Racine ou La passion des Larmes* (Hachette, 1996), he confronts us with a sensitive and disturbing reflexion on the nature of cruelty on stage, and the pleasure that we can derive from it. Tears, pleasure, beauty, and the physical vulnerability of women, are offered, with particular reference to *Britannicus* and *Bérénice*, as a theatrical ritual of striking modernity and cruelty. It is the *Théâtre de la Cruauté* of Antonin Artaud which comes to mind as Biet draws us compellingly into his bold reflexion. It is a reflexion, however, which takes us through a state of acute unease to the processes of redemption. It is in this way that Biet is able to show that Racine's tragedy is of its time, in its Augustinian preoccupation with redemption; but in finding redemption – the quasi-religious redemption beyond self that lies, literally, beyond the veil of tears for Junie and Bérénice – tragedy also reaches a non-tragic universality. It was Biet himself who, in his admirable *La tragédie*,[7] reminded us that tragedy is not necessarily tragic, but if we are invited to believe that redemption through tears can bring us to a transcendental level beyond tragedy, we are bound also to raise a few

---

6 Peter France, *Racine's Rhetoric* (Oxford: Clarendon, 1965); Michael Hawcroft, *Word as Action: Racine, Rhetoric, and Theatrical Language* (Oxford: Clarendon, 1992); Gilles Declercq, *Racine. Une rhétorique des passions*, to be published by PUF.
7 Christian Biet, *La tragédie*, coll. Cursus (Paris: Armand Colin, 1997).

questions. Are tears a physiological accident, or do they really have a real spiritual significance? The example of Esther and her entourage of 'jeunes lévites', who weep buckets between them, seems to reinforce Biet's point of view, although he does not pursue his topic into the biblical plays. Alternatively, Jean-Michel Delacomptée shows in his study of *Bérénice* that it is in the proper assumption of authority that Titus finds his particular form of grace. But Biet's main point is secure: the use of tears in Racinian theatre is a device of disturbing and unsuspected complexity. At this stage, the major themes of the book have been broached, the critical words uttered: 'power', 'pleasure', the 'otherness' of women, the responsibility of sovereignty, and the nature of redemption in tragedy.

The idea of power is again a central concern in Derval Conroy's analysis of the dynamic of gender, power, and authority in *Alexandre le Grand* and *Athalie*. Conroy's chapter, like Jane Conroy's below, presents a wealth of new bibliographical material, summarized in their respective footnotes. Conroy's analysis introduces a different element into Racinian research, by focusing not on the figure of *le souverain* but rather *la souveraine*, in two plays where the issue of female sovereignty, rather than solely queenship, is at stake. In the France of Louis XIV, the exclusion of women from the throne was an established and justified fact. In an approach drawn from Foucault's ideas on discourse and power, Conroy examines to what degree Racine's plays can be read as upholding or subverting the epistemological paradigms of the time, arguing that the representation of the power and authority of Axiane and Athalie highlights the ambiguities, in a patriarchal society, of female exclusion from the throne.

Central to Jane Conroy's thoughtful contribution on the relationship between alterity and identity, the Occident and the Orient, are notions of 'otherness'. In reading Racine's plays as cultural narratives, Conroy examines the representation of origins and race, of both the collective and the individual 'Other' (predominantly although not exclusively woman), and analyses how issues of identity are constructed in Racine. Through her focus on *Bajazet*, Conroy illustrates how, in a France increasingly preoccupied both with the Orient and with its own national identity, the construction of the 'Other World' as a dark universe, a world of inverted political and religious values, of enclosure and darkness (associated with the 'sérail'), of disorder and barbarity, of illusory power, serves not only as a representation of the Orient (of dubious verisimilitude moreover), but more importantly as an inverted reflection, the polar opposite, of the glorious, absolutist France of Louis. Definitions of the 'Other' necessarily define the 'Self', just as ideas of what we 'are' are shaped by our perception of what we 'are not'. In flattering national pride, such representations also serve to justify France's intervention abroad, and may well have appealed to Louis in his role as 'Mars Christianissimus'.

Louis XIV is again the central figure by implication in Edric Caldicott's reassessment of existing historical interpretations of *Esther* and *Athalie*. History is, in a sense, answered by history, as he draws upon the edited correspondence of the Comte d'Avaux, French ambassador to James II in Ireland, to tilt at the flattering preconceptions which still prevail about the Jacobites. The true significance of Racine's biblical plays lies, he argues, in Racine's remarkable transcription of biblical themes and biblical style, particularly of the Psalms. As befits a treatment which is inspired by the Psalms, *Esther* and *Athalie* are also accompanied by music. Racine himself comments in his preface to *Esther* on the degree of collaboration between himself and the composer, but the two studies below by Hartwig and Warnecke, and Gormley, underline in comprehensible technical terms just how remarkable this is. Significantly, Caldicott shows how, in the choral passages of *Esther* which are inspired by the Psalms, Racine alludes specifically to the original Psalms and to the circumstances in which they were written; this is a a particularly striking theatrical innovation which underlines how, in the movement from 'l'antiquité païenne' to 'l'antiquité chrétienne', the writer's freedom to create new effects, indeed to create 'tout court', remains uninhibited. The lessons of rhetoric inherited from a corpus of non-Christian work thus remain valid, even for a devout Christian, in works of Christian inspiration. This then raises the question as to how a play wholly derived from the Bible may be called a tragedy.

Racine's biblical plays were the only ones he was to write subsequent to his appointment as 'historiographe du roi' in 1677. It is therefore not surprising to note how effectively he promotes the ideals of kingship in them. His sensitive adaptation to modern music of the Psalms and other biblical sources masks the work of a skilful and combative political apologist. One of the many points of interest in the comparative study by Robert McBride, the well-known Moliériste, of the strategies of self-defence used by Molière and Racine in the 'querelle du théâtre', is the raw and cutting aggressivity of the young Racine in his correspondence with Nicole, his former mentor at Port-Royal. Racine has often been criticized for the ferocity of his attack on Nicole, but McBride's study shows how right he was to defend the unjustly maligned Desmarets de Saint-Sorlin. It was, perhaps, a reckless sense of justice which drove him, but reread today, his letters can be identified with positions which are modern, generous, and fair. Racine's skill in argument is shown up even more in contrast with Molière's mild-mannered rearguard action in defence of *Tartuffe*. Showing a courtly, accommodating attitude to most of the objections raised against his play, Molière did not perhaps believe his own argument himself. Was this an accident of education or of temperament? Certainly the contrast between the Jesuit-educated Molière and the Jansenist-educated Racine could not be more striking. This fleeting glimpse of the temperament of the two men is the reward for a careful scrutiny of the texts involved, and an insight to be remembered in the appreciation of their respective theatrical works.

Serge Rivière approaches the idea of reception and the role of women in Racine from another angle, in his examination of the reception of the great dramatist both by contemporaries and by an eighteenth-century public. Examining comments gleaned through painstaking examination of Voltaire's *œuvre*, Rivière traces the development in the *philosophe's* attitude towards Racine, often in comparison with Corneille, which moved from an emphasis on the treatment of themes and characters to an emphasis on style. Rivière also examines how Voltaire treats the commentaries of two of Racine's female contemporaries, Mme de Sévigné and Mme de Caylus, on the work of Racine as the 'poète des femmes', before examining how eighteenth-century women treated both Racine and Voltaire. He indicates to what extent not only did both dramatists appeal specifically to female sensibilities, but that Voltaire's championing of Racine was not entirely disinterested. It is particularly interesting to note how Voltaire was able to disregard (when he chose) such valuable contemporary testimony to artistic life at the court of Louis XIV. Mme de Sévigné attended in person one of the limited court performances of *Esther*, and Mme de Caylus, the niece of Mme de Maintenon, actually performed in it, singing the role of la Piété in the Prologue. Hers was not, perhaps, as challenging a role as those of the five singers identified by Gráinne Gormley, despite the indirect flattery of her kinswoman, Mme de Maintenon, which was addressed to her, but she was an eyewitness who deserved a better hearing.

Adopting deliberately the stance of a working theatre critic, Louis van Delft, Professor of French at the University of Paris–X (Nanterre) and editor of *Les Caractères* of La Bruyère, rolls up his sleeves and thoroughly enjoys himself in an uninhibited challenge to his readers to reflect on what exactly one expects of a modern production of a canonical (or 'classical') French play of the seventeenth century. Is it to be judged by the fixed and firm rule of orthodoxy (and thus risk condemnation by more adventurous spirits), or should it innovate and adapt to modern times (so incurring the wrath of entrenched traditionalists)? It is the specific status of the notion of 'classicism' which is at stake here. How is it to be defined, and what is the nature of the pleasure we can derive from this corpus of work? A specific point of focus in his answer to these questions is 'la tristesse majestueuse' of Racine's preface to *Bérénice*. Taking issue with the definition offered by Forestier in his Pléiade introduction to the play, van Delft works his way towards his own sense of what 'tristesse' and 'majestueuse' can mean; this offers him an opportunity to illustrate the musical qualities of the alexandrine, so often neglected in a thematic exploitation of Racine's work. Modern in his concern for contemporary stage production, traditional in his defence of the perennial qualities of the literary canon, and constantly stimulating in his wide-ranging consideration of theatrical values, van Delft is a theatre critic at play; it is in this role that he offers us a wonderful, if controversial, panorama of Parisian theatre life at the end of the twentieth century, and also exposes other kinds of pleasure deriving from the theatre, which can be enjoyed before and after taking one's seat in the parterre.

Jean-Michel Delacomptée also chooses 'la tristesse majestueuse' as a point of focus, and this, too, is seen as a critical criterion in the present-day reception of *Bérénice*, but his mode of approach is not so much aesthetic as political. For the author who explored so sensitively the relationship of Racine and Louis XIV in *Racine en Majesté*, the emphasis lies on the politicized 'majestueuse' rather than on any sentimental interpretations of 'tristesse', and he explicitly argues that the play is more convincing if shifted from a focus on love to a political examination of the responsibility of kingship. In a close and rewarding scrutiny of the rotating roles of the triangular relationship of Antiochus, Titus, and Bérénice, 'ami', 'amant', and 'amante' respectively, he shows how the two apparent rivals in love continue to support each other in renewed loyalty as their unhappiness deepens. It is when their moral stamina flags, that Bérénice herself finds an unsuspected heroic role to rally their spirits, transcending their suffering and her own to offer them an example to follow. From a play in which so little appears to happen, and which was criticized by the abbé de Villars for that, the spiral of moral ascendancy extends with increasing complexity and deepening irony to the point where the Latin source, 'dimisit invitus invitam' is shown to be no more than a superficial explanation of events. Behind the historical record, and this misquotation of Suetonius from the preface, Racine is seen to explore a sequence of actions in which it is Bérénice who, to ensure that Titus remains on his throne, banishes herself; 'fugit invita invitum', so to speak. This differs from the interpretation proposed by Christian Biet insofar as the solidarity of friendship appears to offer solace in this world. But if the political dimension is to weigh more heavily, as Delacomptée appears to wish, then the spotlight shifts slightly to focus on the weighty responsibility, and gratification, of power assumed unselfishly.

From power and kingship in 'l'antiquité païenne', the study of Moreau's music for *Esther* by Hartwig and Warnecke brings us to kingship in 'l'antiquité chrétienne'; as has already been suggested, the subject of kingship becomes even more explicit in the biblical plays, and invested with even greater dignity by Moreau's music. As one of the first modern analyses of Moreau's music, studied in conjunction with Racine's treatment of the Bible story, this is an invaluable contribution to our understanding of *Esther* today; it is made even more valuable by its full exposure in the footnotes of the abundant corpus of German work on the subject of royal music of homage. In a highly technical but accessible study of Moreau's composition, they show how he is able to respect both traditional patterns of musical homage to the monarch and to reinforce in a highly lyrical, individual way the moments of dramatic intensity created by Racine. Respecting certain musical traditions, Moreau's music for *Esther*, as the authors persuasively demonstrate, is innovative enough to contain already the features of the oratorio which was to be so successfully developed by Handel. As they point out, one of Handel's first compositions in England was his own version of *Esther*.

The second contribution to this volume on the music of *Esther* comes as a welcome and highly appropriate complement to the study of Hartwig and Warnecke above. The two chapters present different but supportive approaches to the rarely performed work of Moreau. The Hartwig/Warnecke chapter analyses the musical language and points out its longer-lasting impact in the Handelian oratorio. The study of Gráinne Gormley focuses on the practical considerations that would have influenced Moreau's composition and which, Gormley argues, should inform performance practice today. Having produced and conducted Moreau's *Esther* in 1999, Gormley initially provides in her chapter a welcome summary of the career of Moreau, of whose life little is known, before turning to a stimulating and highly original analysis of the interaction between Moreau's role as teacher and his music. By distinguishing between five main voices, which Gormley labels A to E, in terms of the demands of the music (range, tonality, intonation, rhythm etc) rather than as they are actually labelled in the text (such as 'Une autre' 'Une des Israélites'), Gormley illustrates how Moreau probably composed his music for specific pupils. Such an approach, Gormley argues, would have allowed him to exploit the different strengths and weaknesses, the different timbres, of his pupils' voices, so as both to protect these young teenage voices, and also to sketch individual musical personalities which reflect the dramatic conflict of the plot of *Esther*. This fascinating piece of musicological detective work also provides valuable source material on the technical, as distinct from the social and hierarchical, criteria for selection of the young singers for performance before the king.

The final coda in this suite of reflexions on the tragedy of Racine is delivered by Alain Viala, whose thought-provoking analogy of Racinian topoi with the realm of fine art, and with the form of still-life (or 'vanitas') in particular, is given even more weight by the musical studies which precede it. As we have seen, the music of Moreau was used in Racine's biblical plays to enhance the might of God's intervention. The majestic crescendo of 'l'Eternité' at the end of *Esther* brooks no response: this may only be the beginning for some of the protagonists, but it is definitely the end, the 'dies irae', for others. That this is the end, and that the end will always come, defeating all minor aspirations, is as much the message of Moreau's music as of the still-life tableaux evoked by Viala. But Viala's analogy with the 'vanitas' does not stop, of course, in the realm of fine art; it extends into a moral dimension, and it is here that the full resonance of Racinian irony makes itself felt. So rarely mentioned, it is all important. The 'vanitas' may be low key, but it is also a supremely compressed expression of the pervading irony of unworthy human endeavour. This is not a message which is restricted to the biblical plays; the extended intimacy of the classical world, so sensitively evoked by Roberto Calasso in his *The Marriage of Cadmus and Harmony*, is also the climate in which Racine's nine earlier tragedies unfolded, giving rise to the same sense of secret complicities in which irony thrives. The choric song of Tennyson's 'The Lotos-Eaters' denounces the gods who 'find a music centred in a doleful song'. This strangely haunting music of impotence and 'vanitas' is also found in Racine's 'tristesse majestueuse quit fait tout le plaisir de la tragédie'.

I

The Racinian Hero and the Classical Theory of Characterization

GEORGES FORESTIER

It is evident from a reading of Subligny's *La Folle querelle ou la Critique d'Andromaque* (1668) that the debate surrounding *Andromaque* immediately provoked contention regarding whether or not Racine was worthy of being considered Corneille's equal.[1] As far as is known, it was never seriously considered that Quinault, despite his success, should even be compared to Corneille. In the case of Racine, however, the public genuinely felt that the young author had opened up a new path between Cornelian tragedy and *la tragédie galante*. Racine's new form, based on the tragedy of passionate love, was superior to *la tragédie galante* and could reasonably be compared to Cornelian tragedy. It is this aspect of passionate love that the first part of the preface to *Andromaque* (the extract from the *Aeneid*) set out to defend, and it does so by evoking the highest authority, Virgil. However, the second part of the preface, i.e. the preface proper, written by Racine, is entirely and exclusively devoted to the manner in which tragic roles are recreated for the stage, proving that contemporaries had clearly recognized that *Andromaque*'s revolutionary quality also lay in its conception of characterisation.

Twentieth-century criticism of Racine, however, has generally concentrated on the preface purely as a basis for analysing and examining Racine's insincerity and his adroit deflection of charges against him by discussing issues that may not even have been controversial. Consequently, it is felt that Racine pretends to ignore the main reproach against him, namely that Pyrrhus's conduct towards

---

The editors would like to thank Aedín ní Loingsigh for her assistance in the translation of this chapter.

1. Subligny, Preface to *La Folle Querelle*, in Forestier, *Œuvres*, p. 259.

Andromaque is no different to that of a courteous hero of a
fashionable novel of the time. Instead, Racine deals with a niggling
objection, one that may indeed never have been raised, and defends
himself for having portrayed Pyrrhus as a little too brutal. Whence the
argument judged to be supremely polemical:

*instead, R. focuses
on Pyrrhus'
brutality —*

> J'avoue qu'il n'est pas assez résigné à la volonté de sa Maîtresse, et
> que Céladon a mieux connu que lui le parfait Amour. Mais que faire?
> Pyrrhus n'avait pas lu nos Romans. Il était violent de son naturel. Et
> tous les héros ne sont pas faits pour être des Céladons.

> [I must admit that he is not sufficiently submissive to the wishes of his
> Mistress, and that Celadon was better versed than [Pyrrhus] in Perfect
> Love. But what can be done about it? Pyrrhus had not read our
> [French] Novels. He was of a naturally violent temperament. And not
> all heroes are cut out to be Céladons.][2]

To which it is easy for one of the characters of *La Folle Querelle* to retort:
'Je lui soutiens, moi, que *Pyrrhus* avait lu la *Clélie*' [But I insist that
Pyrrhus had read *Clélie*].[3] It is true that Racine was accused of having
portrayed a Pyrrhus for whom, 'l'*amour* est l'âme de toutes ses actions'
[love is the motive for all his actions], a quality judged to be 'indigne
des grands caractères' [unworthy of great characters].[4] But he was *also*
accused of the opposite, as the preface to *La Folle Querelle* illustrates:

*too focused on love?
not enough?*

> M. Corneille, dis-je, [. . .] aurait conservé le caractère violent et
> farouche de Pyrrhus, sans qu'il cessât d'être honnête homme, parce
> qu'on peut être honnête homme dans toutes sortes de tempéraments: et
> donnant moins d'horreur qu'il ne donne des faiblesses de ce Prince
> qui sont de pures lâchetés, il aurait empêché le spectateur de désirer
> qu'Hermione en fût vengée, au lieu de le craindre pour lui.

> [I maintain that M. Corneille [. . .] would have preserved the wild and
> violent character of Pyrrhus, without him failing to remain an 'honnête
> homme' because one can remain an 'honnête homme' with different
> kinds of temperament; and by giving less horror to the role than he
> accords to the weaknesses of this Prince, which are morally reprehen-
> sible, he would have avoided the spectators' desire to see Hermione get
> her own back on him, instead of fearing for his safety.][5]

2 Preface to *Andromaque*, in Forestier, *Œuvres,* p. 197. [The reference to Céladon is to
the 'héros galant', and model of the 'parfait amant' in the famous novel *Astrée* (1607–28)
by Honoré d'Urfé (1567–1625), completed by his secretary Balthazar Baro.]
3 Subligny, *La Folle Querelle*, Act II. 9, in Forestier, *Œuvres,* p. 280. [The reference to
Clélie is to Madeleine de Scudéry's ten-volume novel, published between 1654 and
1660.]
4 *Ibid.* (All italics are in the original).
5 *La Folle Querelle*, in Forestier, *Œuvres,* p. 262.

Thus it is evident that Pyrrhus was accused of being excessively 'violent et farouche' [violent and wild], qualities entirely inappropriate for a king, who must remain an 'honnête homme'.

The first question raised by these contradictory criticisms concerns their interpretation. Can Pyrrhus be at once too *galant* and too violent? In effect, the contradiction is invaluable, as it prompts us to reflect upon Racine's work and to understand his innovative contribution to the portrayal of tragic heroes. Secondly, why does his argument deal only with one of the two criticisms levelled at him? Is it simply the manœuvre of a good polemicist? In fact, the question of whether it is necessary or not, in Racine's words, to transform 'tous les héros de l'Antiquité pour en faire des Héros parfaits' [all the heroes of Antiquity to make shining Heroes of them all],[6] touches on one of the essential points of the poetics of tragedy: the relationship between *bienséance* (propriety) and the *ressemblance* (verisimilitude) of characters, a point which had proved to be an encumbrance for Corneille, but which Racine completely revolutionizes. In this way, the two issues become so closely linked that they form a single question.

In the seventeenth century, bringing a tragic role to the stage meant adhering to a complete series of criteria relative to his/her *caractère* (or what was referred to in the seventeenth century as his/her *mœurs*). These criteria had been defined by Aristotle and had been unanimously espoused by dramatists of the modern age, including Corneille.[7] Based on the rhetorical typology of *caractère*, this series of specifications had proved itself over two thousand years, in judicial prosecutions as well as in the major literary genres, and none would have thought to question it. Three of these conventions were considered essential: *convenance* or *bienséance*, *ressemblance* and *constance* (consistency).[8]

Firstly, a tragic role must be *bienséant*, that is to say it had to conform to the human or social type to which it belonged. In chapter eight of his *Poétique* (1639), La Mesnardière wrote that it was necessary to

faire les Héros généreux, les Philosophes prudents, les Femmes douces et modestes, les Filles pleines de pudeur, les Ambassadeurs hardis, les Espions téméraires et peu soucieux de la vie, les Valets grossiers et

---

6 Preface to *Andromaque*, in Forestier, *Œuvres*, p. 197.

7 Aristotle, *Poetics*, Ch. 15, ed. Russell, pp. 110–11. For a French edition, see R. Dupont-Roc and J. Lallot (eds), *La Poétique* (Paris: Editions du Seuil, 1980), pp. 84–5; Corneille, *Discours de l'utilité et des parties du poème dramatique*, in Couton, *Corneille*, 3; see especially pp. 129–33. Ch.15 of the *Poetics* is the one which Racine translated with most diligence. See Picard, *Œuvres*, 2, pp. 927–9.

8 The fourth criterion, *la bonté*, will not be discussed here. For an analysis of its characteristics, see my *Essai de génétique théâtrale: Corneille à l'œuvre* (Paris: Klincksieck, 1996), pp. 222–3.

fidèles: et ainsi des autres personnes, chacune selon sa fortune, son âge et sa condition.

[make Heroes magnanimous, Philosophers cautious, Women gentle and modest, Maidens full of modesty, Ambassadors bold, Spies hardy and reckless of life, Valets ungainly and faithful; and so on with other characters, according to their wealth, age, and condition.][9]

Tragicomedy had progressively yielded to this convention since the controversy over *Le Cid* and criticism of the character not only of Chimène, whose conduct in front of Rodrigue was deemed inappropriate for a 'fille pleine de pudeur', but also of King Fernand whose perfunctory reaction, when informed of the threatened attack by the Moors, was considered unkingly. Consequently, in *Andromaque*, Oreste and Pyrrhus, respectively King of Argos and King of Epirus, must act in accordance with their royal status, which in the seventeenth century meant assuring the welfare of their kingdom, being *généreux*, and also being *galant* in love. As for Hermione, daughter of Ménélas and betrothed to Pyrrhus, she must act in accordance with the dignity pertaining to the status of princess. Secondly, a character must resemble the image which tradition has bestowed upon him/her. Thus, Oreste must be melancholy; Hermione, Racine's major borrowing from Euripides' *Andromache*, must be jealous and vindictive; and Pyrrhus, as Racine indicates in his preface, referring to Horace's *Ars poetica*, must be 'farouche, inexorable, violent' [wild, unyielding, violent].[10] Needless to say, the ideal situation was one where a character was both *bienséant* and *ressemblant*, a situation which allows Andromaque to act freely both as a dignified and submissive captive princess, and also as the loyal and tearful widow of tradition. However, the extent to which these two conventions may prove to be contradictory in the case of the other three roles soon becomes evident. How can Pyrrhus, for example, a character on whom contemporary critics of Racine concentrated, be at one and the same time *généreux* and unyielding, *galant* and violent?

In his first *Discours*, Corneille had underlined the contradictory nature of *bienséance* and *ressemblance*, and judging it impossible to render them compatible, the only solution he found was to establish a system whereby these conventions were adhered to differently according to the type of subject:

Ainsi ces deux qualités, dont quelques interprètes ont beaucoup de peine à trouver la différence qu'Aristote veut qui soit entre elles sans la

9 La Mesnardière, *Poétique* (Paris: Antoine de Sommaville, 1640; repr. Geneva: Slatkine, 1972) p. 140. [First edition 1639].
10 Preface to *Andromaque*, in Forestier, *Œuvres*, p. 197.

désigner, s'accordent aisément, pourvu qu'on les sépare, et qu'on donne celle de convenables aux personnes imaginées qui n'ont jamais eu d'être que dans l'esprit du poète, en reservant l'autre pour celles qui sont connues par l'histoire, ou par la fable, comme je le viens de dire.

[And so these two requirements, between which several interpreters are unable to distinguish despite Aristotle's uninformative insistence that a distinction should be observed, can easily be reconciled, but on the specific condition that they are separated from each other, and that the seemly roles be given to imaginary characters, whose existence was only ever in the mind of the poet, with the other requirement being matched by those who have been identified by history, or legend, as I have said.][11]

Corneille's clever solution which, as we shall see, he did not apply in his own work, seems, in fact, to be the only possible solution. This is because the third Aristotelian convention, which demands that a character also be *constant*, or consistent, for the duration of the play, usually makes it impossible to solve the contradiction by alternating between *bienséance* and *ressemblance*. On this subject the most influential European theorist, the Dutch thinker Daniel Heinsius, explains: 'If one begins by portraying a character as hard, cruel and volatile, he must remain in this disposition until the end of the tragedy', unless, as he adds, the dramatist introduces a character who is by nature inconsistent, or unless, as in the case of Ajax, the character, during the course of the play, should temporarily lapse into madness before returning to reason.[12]

With all the above in mind, the extent of Racine's daring in the writing of *Andromaque* becomes obvious and the criticisms levelled at him much clearer. He dared to portray a Pyrrhus *généreux* and *galant* like a king of French tragedy, yet inexorable like his classical model. His Hermione is dignified and proud and never demeans herself by wishing for Andromaque's death, unlike the sterile, neglected and jealous matron in Euripides' play. However, like the Euripidean model, Racine's Hermione is also vindictive and jealous. Racine's Oreste conforms to his royal status and hesitates until the very end before assassinating another sovereign, but he also conforms to the *tristis Orestes* of legend, caught up in the throes of violent melancholy, which leads him ultimately to accept the idea of murder.[13] Far from

11 Couton, *Corneille*, 3, p. 132.
12 Daniel Heinsius, *De Tragœdiae constitutione* (Leiden: Jean Baudoin, 1610), Ch. 1.
13 Even when his passion has led Oreste to accept the idea of murder, Cléone's account of events in Act V. 2 reveals him to be unresolved until the very end. Furthermore his own account of events indicates that the Greeks set upon Pyrrhus before Oreste himself could intervene.

favouring *bienséance* over *ressemblance*, as most of his contemporaries did
and which he himself had done in *Alexandre le Grand*, where few of the
historical characteristics of Alexandre are evident, Racine did not
hesitate to combine these two conventions despite their glaring contradiction. However, this was only possible by representing the third
criterion of *constance* in a novel way. Given that the nature of passionate
love is its irresistibility, its function becomes akin to that of Ajax's
madness in that it permits a temporary rupture in the character's
consistency. Thus Pyrrhus can be alternatively *généreux* and inexorable,
galant and violent, in other words, *inconstant*, or inconsistent as dictated by
the rhythm of passion's aberrations.

With his success in staging two-sided characters (i.e. variable and
contradictory), Racine had forcefully challenged one of the pillars of
dramatic poetics, the principle of *bienséance*, undoubtedly the most
important remaining principle at a time when the question of the rules
of unity had been resolved. Consequently, as he himself took pleasure
in underlining, Racine had also run headlong into Cornelian and
courtly conceptions of the perfect hero, which had derived from the
epic and the heroic novel, and to which he had conformed in his first
two tragedies:

> Quoi qu'il en soit, le Public m'a été trop favorable, pour m'embarrasser
> du chagrin particulier de deux ou trois personnes, qui voudraient qu'on
> reformât tous les Héros de l'Antiquité, pour en faire des Héros parfaits.
> Je trouve leur intention fort bonne, de vouloir qu'on ne mette sur la
> scène que des hommes impeccables. Mais je les prie de se souvenir, que
> c'est n'est pas à moi de changer les règles du Théâtre. Horace nous
> recommande de dépeindre Achille, farouche, inexorable, violent, tel
> qu'il était, et tel qu'on dépeint son Fils.

> [Whatever the case may be, the Public has been too indulgent to me for
> me to be seriously concerned by the distress caused to two or three
> particular people, who would like all the Heroes of Antiquity to be
> reformed into shining Heroes of today. I find their intention to put
> only perfect examples of behaviour on the stage entirely laudable, but
> I beg them to remember that it is not for me to change the rules of the
> Theatre. Horace urges us to portray Achilles as fierce, unmerciful, and
> violent, as he really was, and as his own son portrayed him.][14]

While the Cornelian conception of the perfect hero is directly inherited
from the hero of the epic (and of the novel and tragi-comedy),
following the controversy over *Le Cid*, it was nevertheless validated by

14 Preface to *Andromaque*, in Forestier, *Œuvres*, p. 197. The reference to Horace is to
his *Ars Poetica*, ll. 120–2. See Horace, *The Art of Poetry*, in D. A. Russell and
M. Winterbottom (eds), *Ancient Literary Criticism. The Principal Texts in New Translations*,
trans. by Donald A. Russell (Oxford: Clarendon, 1972), p. 282.

the pre-eminence accorded to the principle of *bienséance* of character. For a long time prior to his elegant 1660 theoretical solution to the articulation of *bienséance* and *ressemblance* (quoted above), Corneille had, in practice, privileged the principle of *bienséance* over *resssemblance*, whilst at the same time pushing the convention of *constance* to its limits. In addition, it was only in the case of historically virtuous or historically monstrous characters that Corneille applied his proposal for a theoretical distribution of conventions. However, each time one of his plots required a hero whose character was based on a doubtful past, *bienséance* took precedence over *resemblance*. The most striking example of this is the case of Nicomède, the parricidal king, whom Corneille depicts as a perfect prince, and who, contrary to historical fact, chooses to be led to his death rather than revolt against his father.[15] As regards the manner in which he justifies his portrayal of Sophonisbe in the *Avis au lecteur* of the play of the same title, it is extraordinarily ambiguous (whilst at the same time revealing the same tendency).[16] It is clear that alone amongst his predecessors and contemporaries, Corneille respects the principle of *ressemblance*. But in the name of what? In the name of what a seventeenth-century image of a Carthaginian heroine might be, in other words, in the name of *bienséance*!

In order to understand fully the extent of the break with the Cornelian and *galant* aesthetic, one need only examine the character of Hermione in *Andromaque*, in particular in the scene at the end of Act IV where Hermione and Pyrrhus meet. Hermione appears firstly as a typical Cornelian princess, not only in her refusal to lower herself by offering the slightest reproach to him who announces her rejection, but also in her constant ironic tone; she seems to have been directly modelled on the character of Éryxe from Corneille's *Sophonisbe*. However, from the moment that Pyrrhus answers her as though she were a Cornelian heroine (in summary, 'forgive me for having being presumptuous enough to think you loved me'), Hermione breaks down and becomes reminiscent of another model: i.e. that of Ovid's *Heroides* which is evoked in the informal address, insults, degradation, honest admission, jealousy, ultimate supplication, and veiled threat.[17] More tellingly, when

15 See also the elegant solution proposed in *Cinna*. The tyrannical and bloodthirsty image of Auguste is rejected in the accounts of the past that the conspirators give: each time Auguste is on stage (in fact from the moment he appears on stage), he presents an image of a perfect sovereign. For further analysis of the characteristics of Cornelian heroes, see my *Essai de génétique théâtrale*, Ch. 4, pp. 198–270. (For Auguste and *Cinna*, see pp. 212–15 and 225–9).

16 Couton, *Corneille*, 3, pp. 382ff.

17 See my article, 'Écrire *Andromaque*. Quelques hypothèses génétiques', *Revue d'histoire littéraire de la France*, 1 (1998), 43–63. See also my introduction to *Andromaque* in the Pléiade edition, pp. 136–8.

Hermione learns of Pyrrhus's death, Racine denies her any sense of avenged *gloire*, even if it were only to temporarily assuage her extreme distress. Subligny was precisely sensitive enough to this fact to criticize it by comparing it with the Cornelian model:

> Enfin, [Corneille] aurait modéré l'emportement d'Hermione, ou du moins il l'aurait rendu sensible pour quelque temps au plaisir d'être vengée. Car il n'est pas possible qu'après avoir été outragée jusqu'au bout, qu'après n'avoir pu obtenir seulement que Pyrrhus dissimulât à ses yeux le mépris qu'il faisait d'elle: qu'après qu'il l'a congédiée, sans pitié, sans douleur du moins étudiée, et qu'elle a perdu toute espérance de le voir revenir à elle, puisqu'il a épousé sa rivale; il n'est, dis-je, pas possible qu'en cet état elle ne goûte un peu sa vengeance

> [At least [Corneille] would have moderated the frenzy of Hermione, or rendered her vulnerable for a short time to the pleasure of being avenged. Because it is simply not possible after being insulted to the limit, after succeeding only in having Pyrrhus mask his contempt when actually talking to her; after being rejected by him without pity or remorse, after she has lost all hope, for her to see him return to her as the spouse of her rival; I repeat that it is simply not possible for her in this state not to savour to some extent her revenge.][18]

It is clear from the first staging of the play that critics mooted the question of divergence from the Cornelian model, and therefore from the dominant norms, of the tragic heroine.

All this brings us to an analysis of the preface to *Britannicus*, where Racine continuously shelters behind Tacitus and at the same time justifies his portrayal of the character of Néron by the fact that 'il ne s'agit pas dans [ma] Tragédie des affaires du dehors. Néron est ici dans son particulier et dans sa famille' [my Tragedy is not about external matters. Nero is here in his private capacity, in the intimacy of his family].[19] This has usually been perceived as bringing us to the crux of the rupture between the Cornelian and the Racinian aesthetic, not in relation to the concept of character, but in relation to the question of history and politics, as if Racine wished to underline that he was not trying to paint vast historical frescoes or to depict major political conflicts. Needless to say, if I deem it necessary to return to this well-worn interpretation it is because it seems to me to be based on a misinterpretation.

There is no doubt that there is a break with Corneille, but not in regard to the question of history and politics, not at least in *Britannicus* which is the play under consideration here. Once again, it is the

[handwritten margin note: many have said R's break w/C = move to personal from historical / polit.]

18 *La folle Querelle*, in Forestier, *Œuvres*, p. 262.
19 Preface to *Britannicus*, in Forestier, *Œuvres*, p. 372.

conception of the tragic character which is at stake. This is immediately obvious when one compares *Othon*, Corneille's most recent tragedy, with *Britannicus*, its exact counterpoint. In both cases, according to Corneille 'ce ne sont qu'intrigues de cabinet qui se détruisent les unes les autres' [they are only closet conspiracies, which are mutually destructive].[20] Also, in both cases power has been usurped, while clearly the place attributed to the 'épisode amoureux' is less 'épisodique' in *Othon* than it is in *Britannicus*. In short, a comparison of the two plays illustrates that maintaining the endless opposition between the two authors cannot be justified. The difference between the two poets, therefore, lies elsewhere.

Corneille constructed his characters from the image created by external circumstances. Othon, a debauched character of some notoriety, who had shared his wife with Nero, had subsequently presented an outward impression of being a virtuous provincial governor and also (for a short while) of being a righteous emperor. This allowed Corneille to apply the principle of *bienséance* without hindrance and to represent Othon as a perfect hero. Racine, however, constructs his heroes in the opposite way. Like Othon's final years, the early years of Nero's rule had created the image of a good emperor. But it was an outward appearance based on actions inspired by good counsellors, and the sequence of events tragically revealed that it was, in fact, just an image. Racine obviously uses this image, but he does so in order to contrast it to Néron's 'true character', which he could only reveal in his private surroundings, and the lengthy description of which in Tacitus provides the starting part for Racine.

As we have said, far from ignoring Néron's external image, inspired by Sénèque and Burrhus, the virtuous governors of the young emperor, Racine uses it as a counterpoint when Néron's 'true' character (the character as revealed through his 'actions') is revealed. The admirable scene in Act IV, where the tyrant, on the brink of committing a crime, yields to the tears of Burrhus, undoubtedly constitutes the most perfect illustration of the way the Racinian ethic works. The exceptional power of the scene derives from the fact that the 'true Néron' is placed face to face with his external image, which Burrhus tries to reflect, like a mirror, as though it were the true image of Néron's private self. Hence the ambivalence of this two-sided character, whom Racine characterizes in his celebrated formula: 'c'est ici un monstre naissant'. This represents the essential characteristic which posterity has described as Racinian 'psychology': the dramatic principle of the two-

20 Corneille, Preface to *Othon*, in Couton, *Corneille*, 3, p. 462.

sided character (which of course conforms to the 'psychology' of the latter half of the seventeenth century, based on the dialectic of mask and face).

We therefore have good reason to take seriously the conclusion to the preface to *Andromaque*, where Racine confirms his desire to apply to the letter the Aristotelian theory of the tragic flaw, which is linked to the conception of the imperfect hero. The tragic hero must be a virtuous man but capable of weakness. He is thus susceptible to committing an error, which provokes a calamity, and thus arouses fear and pity in the spectator. Clearly a subtle argument: Racine justifies his bending of the Aristotelian system of 'character' in the name of Aristotle. It is as though abandoning the perfect hero in favour of the two-sided character had allowed him to access the secret of the perfect tragic hero. Perhaps this preface was an *a posteriori* justification destined to silence all those who had criticized the behaviour of his principal characters. Whatever the explanation, the accidental merging of the two-sided character with the imperfect tragic hero would subsequently be exploited deliberately by Racine. From *Britannicus* it would become one of the bases of his formula for tragedy.

The subject of *Britannicus*, which is based on the subjugation of an innocent victim by an omnipotent tyrant, was the type of subject for which Aristotle had posed the problem of the tragic hero. According to Aristotle, pity is unquestionably the emotion elicited when the spectator is confronted with the undeserved suffering of an individual. However, at the same time, the vision of misfortune suffered by a completely innocent victim creates such an impression of injustice that it prevents all identification, on the part of the spectator, and gives rise to feelings which surpass fear and pity: repulsion and horror, that is to say a feeling that completely destroys the tragic pleasure. When Corneille dramatized the executioner versus victim plot (as in *Rodogune*, *Héraclius*, *Théodore*, *Attila*, for example), he had surmounted this difficulty by means of his dramatic art of the perfect hero. The heroic (and stoic) response offered by his heroes to oppression managed to replace repulsion by the modern feeling of admiration, in itself a combination of terror and pity. For Saint-Évremond, this was one of the reasons for modern tragedy's superiority over Greek tragedy.[21]

21. 'J'aime à voir plaindre l'infortune d'un grand homme malheureux; j'aime qu'il s'attire de la compassion, et qu'il se rende quelquefois maître de nos larmes; mais je veux que ces larmes tendres et généreuses regardent ensemble ses malheurs et ses vertus, et qu'avec le triste sentiment de la pitié nous ayons celui d'une admiration animée, qui fasse naître en notre âme comme un amoureux désir de l'imiter. [I like to see the misfortune of a great man pitied; I like to see him draw compassion and tears from us, but I want those generous and understanding tears to take account of

Having turned his back on the Cornelian principles of dramatic art in *Andromaque*, Racine was necessarily led, in choosing the subject of *Britannicus*, to reflect upon the way in which to oppose the executioner and the innocent victim. The technique of the two-sided character, introduced for the first time in *Andromaque*, allowed him firstly to mitigate the horror aroused by an outright tyrant, such as Tristan L'Hermite's Néron in *La Mort de Sénèque*. Hence the irony of his preface to *Britannicus*, in which Racine dismisses, one after the other, criticisms which held that his Néron had been depicted as too good or as too cruel. Hence the role he attributes to passionate love in the progressive unveiling of the monstrous nature of a character, who until then had carried out only virtuous actions, even if under the guidance of his good counsellors. At the same time, however, it was also necessary to moderate the extreme innocence of Britannicus: his excesses of love, fervour, candour and blindness result in him carrying out actions which, although innocently motivated, provoke the murderous wrath of the 'monstre naissant'.[22] In short, Britannicus is a hero who does not deserve his misfortune, but who is nonetheless partly responsible for it.

Apart from the specific experiment of *Bérénice*, this idea of the victim's part in his/her tragedy would consequently determine the representation of a significant number of Racine's heroes. It explains why, at the end of *Bajazet*, the innocent Atalide assumes complete responsibility for the tragic catastrophe before killing herself. It also explains, in the same tragedy, the variant which emphasizes Bajazet's guilt in his attitude towards Roxane. In the first performance of the play (1672), before he even considers himself 'barbare, injuste, criminel' (Act III. 4, l. 995), Bajazet declares:

> Et je serais heureux, si je pouvais goûter
> Quelque bonheur, au prix qu'il vient de m'en coûter
> (*Bajazet*, Act III. 4, ll. 943–4).

Later, in the 1676 and subsequent editions this became:

> Et je serais heureux, si la foi, si l'honneur
> Ne me reprochait point mon injuste bonheur.

21 *cont.* his misfortune and his qualities, and that with the melancholy feeling of pity we also have that of admiration, creating within us something like an affectionate desire to emulate him], Saint-Évremond, *De la tragédie ancienne et moderne* (1674), in *Œuvres en prose*, ed. by R. Ternois, 4 vols (Paris: S.T.F.M., 1962–9), 4, pp. 179–80.

22 Love, fervour and blindness are among the main characteristics of the behaviour of the young, according to the traditional typology; these same characteristics, when excessive, can be the source of the 'tragic flaw', as Racine explains in his preface. For further detail, see my introduction to *Britannicus*, in Forestier, *Œuvres*, p. 1418.

This notion also explains why Mithridate, one of Racine's most admirable two-sided characters (apart from Phèdre), perishes because of the flaw of his own blindness. It explains the tragic nature of Agamemnon's role in *Iphigénie*, and finally, it explains the intense satisfaction of the poet who, in his preface of 1677, would describe Phèdre as the character 'le plus raisonnable' that he had put on stage.

However, in order to gauge exactly what Racine meant by 'reasonable',[23] one must read what comes next:

> Je ne suis point étonné que ce Caractère ait eu un succès si hereux du temps d'Euripide, et qu'il ait encore si bien réussi dans notre siècle, puisqu'il a toutes les qualités qu'Aristote demande dans le Héros de la Tragédie, et qui sont propres à exciter la Compassion et la Terreur. En effet Phèdre n'est ni tout à fait coupable, ni tout à fait innocente.

> [I am not all surprised that this character had such success in the time of Euripides, and that it should have succeeded in our own time, because it has all the qualities that Aristotle demands of the tragic Hero, and which are conducive to the emotions of pity and terror. In fact, Phèdre is neither completely guilty nor completely innocent.][24]

Phèdre effectively marks the end of a quest, a quest for the ideal tragic hero, who allows for the representation of the entire gamut of tragic emotions within the context of a tragic conflict. In short, Phèdre marks the accomplishment of the two-sided character, who emerged from the break with the system based on the rhetorical conception of 'character'. And at the same time, Phèdre marks the apogee of the 'Racinian psychology' of contradiction, which for three centuries has been considered more natural than its Cornelian equivalent.

In conclusion, it is possible now to understand why, in his preface to *Andromaque*, Racine ignored criticism of Pyrrhus's *galanterie* – after all, this was only criticism regarding the degree of *galanterie*, since all tragic kings, as we saw, need to be courteous and *galant* according to the laws of *bienséance*. It also becomes clear why most of this preface is exclusively devoted to the problem of *ressemblance*. In fact, this issue sums up all the implications of Racine's revolution. It was a risk he could justify only in the name of the principle of fidelity to sources:

> Mais véritablement mes Personnages sont si fameux dans l'Antiquité, que pour peu qu'on la connaisse, on verra fort bien que je les ai rendus tels, que les anciens Poètes nous les ont donnés. Aussi n'ai-je pas pensé qu'il me fût permis de rien changé à leurs mœurs.

23 Here 'reasonable' means appropriate (for tragedy).
24 Preface to *Phèdre*, in Forestier, *Œuvres*, p. 817.

[But to tell the truth, my characters are so well known from Antiquity, that if one is already familiar with them, it will easily be seen that I have presented them just as the poets of old did. Therefore I felt it was not legitimate to change anything in their behaviour.][25]

In this respect Racine had support, dangerous support, which before long would be at the centre of another more general debate, known as the *querelle des Anciens et des Modernes*. But that is another story.

25 Preface to *Andromaque*, in Forestier, *Œuvres*, p. 197.

2

Racine's Use of Maxims

JEAN-LOUIS BACKÈS

> Ma foi, sur l'avenir, bien fou qui se fiera.
> Tel qui rit Vendredi, Dimanche pleurera.
> Un Juge, l'an passé, me prit à son service,
> Il m'avait fait venir d'Amiens pour être Suisse.
> Tous ces Normands voulaient se divertir de nous,
> On apprend à hurler, dit l'autre, avec les Loups
> (*Les Plaideurs*, Act I. 1, ll. 1–6).

Three maxims in six lines. But are they really maxims? Should we not say proverbs? And what is the connection between the word maxim itself and the 'sentence', as in 'sententia'? Jacques Scherer speaks of 'la sentence ou maxime', as if he thought the words were synonyms; and he observes in a footnote, 'nous préférons le terme de "sentence", parce qu'il est plus usité au XVIIᵉ siècle' [we prefer the word 'sentence' because it is more frequently used in the seventeenth century].[1] Later on, he suggests that for him a proverb like 'La façon de donner vaut mieux que ce qu'on donne [the style of giving matters more than what one gives], which comes from *Le Menteur* (Act I. 1, l. 90), is really a form of 'sentence'.[2]

The semantic fog which covers these three words does, in fact, have a central focus: the sentence / sententia, or maxim, also called a proverb, can all be defined as an affirmation which is detachable from its context, and adaptable for use elsewhere without loss of meaning. This possibility exists because it is an affirmation containing at least one grammatical sentence, without any explicit reference to the

---

1 Jacques Scherer, *La Dramaturgie classique en France* (Paris: Nizet, 1950), p. 316.
2 *Ibid.*, p. 321.

circumstances of the utterance: there are no proper names; no second or first person pronouns; no adverbs or complements specifying a time or place, and the verb is in the present tense. There are, however, some stylistic considerations to be noted: in a line such as 'Un Bienfait reproché tint toujours lieu d'offense' (*Iphigénie*, Act IV. 6, l. 1413), there is what Greek scholars would call an 'aoriste gnomique', the gnomic past tense. This past historic tense does not stand in opposition either to a present or a future. It has a universal value which can be found in certain uses of the definite article, as in 'Le Peuple aime un Esclave, et craint d'avoir un Maître' (*La Thébaïde*, Act II. 3, l. 572). This is not so much about the people of Thebes as about all peoples; 'peuple' here, then, is taken universally. The question is sometimes complicated by rules of prosody, as in 'Mais enfin le succès dépend des destinées' (*Bajazet*, Act I. 1, l. 58). In order to isolate the maxim for quotation elsewhere, the first word (the conjunction 'mais', which cannot be used elsewhere) would have to be deleted.

In consequence, the counting or identification of maxims / sentences, a task which we thought was easy, becomes quite complex. The results can vary according to our criteria, whether we consider only those maxims which coincide with the line of verse or, alternatively, we choose to compromise with the rules of prosody.[3] An even greater disparity emerges if we accept implicit maxims. Unable to count the occurrences mathematically, the best result we can get is an order of magnitude. We can, however, use a statistic, approximate as it may be, to illustrate an observation of Scherer's: that towards 1660 there occurred the 'crépuscule de la sentence' [the waning of the maxim].[4] We are in a position to specify that Corneille, for one, remained true to himself: there are about twenty maxims in *Attila* (1667). And there are as many to be found in *La Thébaïde* (1664), but Racine then quickly changed his approach, with only five or six maxims in *Alexandre le Grand* (1666). But there are, of course, fifteen in *Phèdre* (1677).

The last brilliant illustration of this technique was seen in *Astrate roi de Tyre* (1665), which made Quinault's fame and fortune. The maxims (or 'sentences') of Astrate are agressive, resonant, sometimes excessive. They are not at all 'sententious'. The strutting hero who declaims them bears no resemblance to those down-to-earth moralizers of the Spanish theatre of the time, ironically known as 'barbas'. Astrate himself knows how exceptional his expressions are: only an exceptional being could live up to them. It was in commenting on this play that

3 Le cadre normal de la sentence est le vers entier' [the usual platform for the maxim is the whole line of verse], Scherer, *La Dramaturgie classique*, p. 329.
4 *Ibid.* p. 322.

the *Journal des savants* reported: 'L'on y remarque [. . .] plusieurs
maximes nouvelles de politique et d'amour, qui sont poussées dans
toute leur étendue' [There are several novel maxims on politics and
love to be noted in it, and they are extended to their limits].[5] But let
the hero speak for himself:

> Lorsque, par un transport dont on n'est plus le maître,
> On devient téméraire, on ne saurait trop l'être,
> Et dès qu'on a pu mettre un feu coupable au jour
> C'est l'excès qui peut seul justifier l'amour
>
> *(Astrate, roi de Tyre*, Act IV. 4).

Is the maxim particularly novel? One would hesitate to say so, but it
is certainly the case that this praise of hyperbole lends an entirely
appropriate splendour to the 'waning of the maxim'.

So, at this stage, two questions have been asked: Are all maxims
universal? Can the maxim be adequately defined by its form?

The comment of the *Journal des savants* seems to construe 'maxim' in
a way which would make the notion of 'sentence', as in 'sententia',
inappropriate. Sabine, in other words Poppée, says to Néron, in *La
Mort de Sénèque* by Tristan L'Hermite:

> Pour s'assurer d'un Trône, il faut être capable
> De confondre parfois innocent et coupable,
> Et ne discerner point ce qu'on doit immoler
> Quand notre impunité nous peut faire ébranler
>
> *(La Mort de Sénèque*, Act I. 1).

adding immediately afterwards:

> Mais tu pratiques mal cette bonne maxime.[6]

There is a maxim here, or a sentence, in the sense proposed. But the
word 'maxim' conveys better than the word 'sentence' the idea that
the universal truth, expressed in a square-hewn form, will lead to a
specific application. This extract from Tristan is very interesting in
the way that it operates as a transition between, on the one hand,
texts where maxims are to be found, but without the word maxim
being used, and, on the other hand, other texts where the word itself
is to be found, but without a specific example being demonstrated.
The word occurs with an equally Machiavellian meaning in *Bajazet*:

---

5 Quoted by Jacques Truchet in *Théâtre du XVIIe siècle*, Bibliothèque de la Pléiade, 3
vols (Paris: Gallimard, 1986), 2, p. 1549.
6 Tristan l'Hermite, *La Mort de Sénèque*, in *Théâtre du XVIIe siècle*, 2, p. 335.

Mais moi, qui vois plus loin, qui par un long usage
Des maximes du Trône ai fait l'apprentissage [...]
(*Bajazet*, Act IV. 7, ll. 1393–4).

It is, of course, Acomat who is speaking. As in Shakespeare, there is a long cast in French classical theatre of unscrupulous political figures, emerging like premature parodies of a theatrical Bismarck. In this way, in Corneille's *Attila*, Honorie says to Attila (who is planning to marry her to a man beneath her rank):

Va, ne me tourne point Octar en ridicule
(*Attila*, Act IV. 3, l. 1249).

She concedes that the same Octar will go far, particularly in the light of the example he has followed:

L'exemple y peut beaucoup: instruit par tes maximes,
Il s'est fait de ton ordre une habitude aux crimes
(*Attila*, Act IV. 3, ll. 1257–8).[7]

Later in the same play, the beautiful Ildione says to the same tyrannical master:

Seigneur, ensanglanter cette illustre journée!
Grâce, grâce du moins jusqu'après l'hyménée.
A son heureux flambeau souffrez un pur éclat,
Et laissez pour demain les maximes d'Etat
(*Attila*, Act V. 4, ll. 1661–4).

In either case, these maxims are the expression of political principles, and frequently cynical ones, assuming, in effect, the canonical style described above.

In the real world, too, outside the theatre, these theorists of Realpolitik can be found. And they were widely condemned. In Racine's time, Algernon Sidney (1623–83) secretly compiled a text which was not published until 1996, under the title *Court Maxims*. It is no more and no less than a violent attack on absolutist political theory. The author quotes and refutes thirteen maxims of the royal court, of which this is the fifth: 'La monarchie n'est pas assurée à moins que la noblesse soit réprimée, efféminée et corrompue' [The crown is safe only when the nobility is suppressed, emasculated, and corrupt].[8] Acomat does not content himself with mere reference to the existence of court maxims.

7 Couton, *Corneille*, 3.
8 Algernon Sidney, *Court Maxims*, ed. Hans X. Blom, Eco Haitsma Mulier, Ronald Jansen (Cambridge: Cambridge University Press, 1996); French translation, *Les Maximes de cour*, Introduction by Paulette Carrive; trans. and notes by Lucien Carrive (Paris, 1998), p. 100.

He pronounces and creates several himself, all of which have a universal application, despite their Turkish trappings:

Un Vizir aux Sultans fait toujours quelque ombrage.
A peine ils l'ont choisi, qu'ils craignent leur ouvrage
(*Bajazet*, Act I. 1, ll. 185–6).

This is a bitter observation, entirely at one with the style of our own courtly La Rochefoucauld, a bleak assessment which matches the moral of several of La Fontaine's fables:

Selon que vous serez puissant ou misérable
Les jugements de cour vous feront blanc ou noir
(La Fontaine, *Fables*, Livre VII, 1, 'Les Animaux malades de la peste').

What is extraordinary in Acomat's maxim is that it does to some extent dictate his behaviour. His observation is also a prescription. The faithful servant of prince Bajazet plans to cultivate 'un appui' [an ally] to support him against his master, and takes action accordingly.

When the maxim, or sentence, is presented as it is by Jacques Scherer, as a manifestation of dramatic writing, the reader is naturally sensitive to what isolates it from its context, even if it is only a question of diction. And it is also possible to ignore the function of the maxim in its context, as, for example, in *Phèdre* when Thésée exclaims: 'Toujours les Scélérats ont recours au parjure' (Act IV. 2, l. 1134). Scherer is understandably insistent upon the emotional value of these lines addressed to a departing son by a father who curses him, 'cette sentence tire [. . .] sa valeur, non de l'idée générale qu'elle exprime, mais du témoignage qu'elle apporte sur les sentiments de Thésée au moment où il la prononce' [this sentence derives its force, not from the general truth which it expresses, but from the evidence it provides about Thésée's mood when he utters it].[9] It will be recalled that at that particular moment the speaker interrupts his interlocutor. Hippolyte has just begun to formulate an oath of truthfulness, but he is unable to finish it. Yet twenty lines earlier, the same Hippolyte was in the process of piling up maxims in great numbers: there are no less than eight lines full of them, 'Quelques crimes toujours précèdent les grands crimes' (ll. 1093–1100). As we can see, the recourse to universal terms had as its goal the construction of an argument by syllogism. Thésée's exclamation has exactly the same potential: 'Toujours les Scélérats ont recours au parjure', or in other words, 'you are resorting to perjury'. So you, my son, are a villain. In terms of strict logic, the inference is invalid, but that is not the point: the maxim served a

9 Scherer, *La Dramaturgie classique*, p. 318.

purpose in building an argument, no matter how specious the argument actually is.

It would be easy to find other examples of this process in Racine; given that a universal proposition may always be part of a deductive chain, it is only to be expected. And this leads us to an important consideration. It is often the case that a maxim assumes a canonical form of implication. The chapter which Jacques Scherer devotes to the question concludes with an impressive inventory of maxims, all built on the model of famous proverbs, such as 'qui vole un œuf vole un bœuf' [to steal an egg is as bad as to steal an ox], or 'qui veut voyager loin ménage sa monture' [he who would travel far spares his mount], or again, 'sur l'avenir bien fou qui se fiera' [it's a foolish man who trusts the future].[10] The word 'implication' can be taken here in the strictest sense: if one proposition is given, it is necessarily taken that another necessarily follows (by implication). 'L'inimitié succède à l'amitié trahie' (*Bérénice*, Act I. 3, l. 91).[11] The terms can also be transposed: si l'amitié est trahie, alors l'inimitié lui succède [if friendship is betrayed, hostility will follow]. In Monime's cry, 'La Mort au désespoir ouvre plus d'une voie' (*Mithridate*, Act V. 1, l. 1500), the further, narrowing, implication, is that a person who is desperate enough can choose several different ways of meeting death. Similarly, Hermione's 'L'Amour ne règle pas le sort d'une Princesse' (*Andromaque*, Act III. 2, l. 825) can be construed as 'si quelqu'un est princesse, l'amour ne règle pas son sort' [even if you are a woman of noble birth, love does not necessarily provide an answer].

In this form, the maxim clearly shows us how it can lead to an application. Whoever is a princess should know that love will not determine her future. Hermione even follows this up by saying 'La gloire d'obéir est tout ce qu'on nous laisse' (l. 826) [the honour of obeying is all we are left with]. And this first person pronoun, normally misplaced in a maxim, demonstrates that we are moving towards a specific case. This 'nous' speaks simply for the collectivity of princesses of which I, Hermione, am one. In fact, the specifically singular 'je' is used in the following line, ' Cependant je partais [. . .].'

A little later, Oreste says:

> Chacun peut à son choix disposer de son âme.
> La vôtre était à vous. J'espérais. Mais enfin
> Vous l'avez pu donner sans me faire un larcin
> (*Andromaque*, Act III. 2, ll. 830–2).

10 *Ibid.*, Ch. IV, 'La Sentence', pp. 316–33.
11 The use of the definite article is ambiguous: 'l'inimitié' and 'l'amitié' could apply to Antiochus in particular, or more universally to the world at large.

[margin annotation: maxims also suggest practical applications]

Pronouncement of the maxim is followed by its application. To quote it is to recognize in it a sound basis, and consequently to comply with it. The maxim of Oreste is absolutely universal, and therefore applies to all of humanity. Hermione's maxim is universal only within certain narrow limits, concerning only princesses. But it does touch them all, whether they be Greek or pagan.

It can therefore happen, and it does happen frequently, that by its very form the maxim indicates the idea of a subsequent sequence of events. It suggests a consequence; either it imposes a duty, or it justifies the realization of a desire. In *Phèdre*, Œnone announces that 'La faiblesse aux Humains n'est que trop naturelle' (Act IV. 6, l. 1301). More decorously, Aricie, does something similar, 'Et la fuite est permise à qui fuit ses Tyrans' (Act V. 1, l. 1384). In this way we end up with some curious paradoxes. Destined to be isolated from surrounding discourse, marked off by quotation marks, used as an extract, quoted elsewhere, the maxim nonetheless contributes effectively to the linking of words and actions. Furthermore, although designed to express eternal truths, it appears to have the capacity to provoke or accompany specific events or, in other words, a change in the state of the world. And we should even add that, because it is proferred as information to the interlocutor, the maxim is in itself an event. It serves to condition the person to whom it is addressed.

It is time now to look for a link between the sequential nature of the maxim and the wider aspect of implication which it also has. This would help us to understand the complex function of imagination in intellectual activity. The operation in logic which we call implication is imagined as a succession, or consequence. Is this why we first represent to ourselves a person's character, turning only after that to his or her actions? Many are the maxims in Racine which have as their subject 'cœur' or 'un grand cœur'. It is a given that the character is of good breeding, not in a social sense, but in the moral implications of the term. What the characters do comes as a natural consequence of their 'qualité d'âme', or their moral and human stature:

> Au travers des périls un grand Cœur se fait jour
> > (*Andromaque*, Act III. 1, l. 791).

> > cette défiance
> Est toujours d'un grand cœur la dernière science,
> On le trompe longtemps
> > (*Britannicus*, Act I. 4, ll. 339–41).

> > Que ne fait point un Cœur
> Pour gagner ce qu'il aime, et plaire à son Vainqueur?
> > (*Bérénice*, Act II. 2, ll. 509–10).

Un cœur noble ne peut soupçonner en autrui
La bassesse et la malice
Qu'il ne sent point en lui
(*Esther*, Act III. 9, ll. 1218–20).

Of all that has been said about maxims, perhaps none of it is specific to Racine. All the examples given here come from his theatre. Could we not have found some elsewhere in his work? But this long approach was needed in order to pose in clear terms the question of his exoticism. Everyone is familiar with the last paragraph of the second preface to *Bajazet,* a paragraph which inexplicably disappeared in the edition of 1697: 'Je me suis attaché à bien exprimer dans ma Tragédie ce que nous savons des mœurs et des maximes des Turcs' [I strove in my tragedy to communicate what we know of the customs and maxims of the Turks]. We know that various grudging souls have taxed Racine with a fanciful portrayal of these customs: 'Les mœurs des Turcs y sont mal observées; ils ne font point tant de façons pour se marier' [The customs of the Turks are poorly observed in the play; they are not so fastidious in their preparation for marriage], wrote la marquise de Sévigné on 16 May 1672. She might well have squealed in shock had Racine staged the version of events related by contemporary diplomats: 'Le prince Bajazet [. . .] devint amoureux d'une belle fille favorite de la [. . .] sultane, et la vit de si près qu'elle se trouva grosse' [The Prince Bajazet [. . .] fell in love with a beautiful woman, the Sultana's favourite, and got so close to her that she found herself pregnant].[12] Not so fastidious, indeed.

Racine's preface to *Bajazet* was written to answer malevolent comments such as these. It relies upon printed accounts and sources, but its connection with the tragedy is no less specific for that. On the subject of the prince, it mentions that: 'Si l'on trouve étrange qu'il consente plutôt de mourir, que d'abandonner ce qu'il aime, et d'épouser ce qu'il n'aime pas, il ne faut que lire l'Histoire des Turcs. On verra partout le mépris qu'ils font de la vie' [If people find it strange that he should prefer death to the loss of the one he loved, and to obligatory marriage with a woman he did not love, they only have to read the History of the Turks. Everywhere it illustrates their contempt for human life].[13] The terms seem ambiguous, or would be, if taken out of context. Here they clearly mean that a Turk would accept death without a qualm rather than yield to an obstacle to his love. Zaïre calls on all the customary stupidity of confidantes when she

12 Dispatch from the comte de Cézy, 10 March 1640. This quotation, like the previous one, can be found in Forestier, *Œuvres,* pp. 1496–7.
13 Forestier, *Œuvres,* p. 626.

replies 'Quoi'? [What?] to Atalide's announcement that she intends to die, 'J'ai cédé mon Amant, Tu t'étonnes du reste' (Act III. 1, l. 830). The implicit maxim is evident. More lucid, Osmin declares that 'Bajazet veut périr' (Act IV. 7, l. 1388). He was able to identify this unspoken resolve in the news that he has just been given: the revelation of Bajazet's love for Atalide. The prince attached no importance to the risk of death.

But it is evident that if a Turk attaches no importance to his life, the life of others will appear no more important to him. This is the clear implication of the anecdote with which Racine concludes his preface to *Bajazet*, and with which his public was already familiar: 'Témoin un des fils de Soliman, qui se tua lui-même sur le corps de son Frère aîné, qu'il aimait tendrement, et que l'on avait fait mourir pour lui assurer l'Empire' [Let us cite as evidence one of the sons of Sulieman, who killed himself on the body of his eldest brother, a brother whom he loved deeply but who had been murdered in order to ensure the succession of the Empire to the younger sibling].[14] The young prince preferred to die rather than to live without the object of his affection. A further point for consideration is that somebody who remains anonymous coldly committed murder (or instigated a murder) in order to resolve in his own way a problem of succession. As Georges Forestier rightly observes: 'Après *La Thébaïde* et après *Britannicus*, *Bajazet* présente donc une nouvelle variation sur cette structure tragique fondamentale qui voit, dans le cadre d'une rivalité pour le pouvoir suprême, un frère tuer son frère [After *La Thébaïde* and *Britannicus*, *Bajazet* offers a new variation on the basic tragic structure which, in the context of rivalry for ultimate power, had shown a brother killing a brother].[15]

There is, however, a subtle difference to be noted here. The murder of Britannicus was an inconceivable crime, and the two sons of Œdipus still generate feelings of revulsion three thousand years after the alleged events. And yet, the political execution of a potential political rival in the near-contemporary Ottoman empire, as seen through the eyes of Racine and his contemporaries, was presented as a commonplace event. Fratricide had been elevated in these foreign parts to an institutional status, protected by maxims of the state and government. Racine's preface of 1676 speaks of the custom as if it could be taken for granted. And the two themes are encountered in a passage of the play where the implicit maxim can be easily detected. The Sultan Amurat, it is naturally assumed, represents the whole Turkish race when Zatime says of him:

14 *Ibid.*
15 *Ibid.*, p. 1492.

Des cœurs comme le sien, vous le savez assez,
Ne se regagnent plus, quand ils sont offensés,
Et la plus prompte mort dans ce moment sévère
Devient de leur amour la marque la plus chère.
(Bajazet, Act IV. 5, ll. 1291–4).

His behaviour may not perhaps appear extravagant in comparison with the passionate exchanges of stage lovers in a safely policed western state, who bravely declare that they will kill or be killed, but the play still ends with a marriage.

What is so surprising in *Bajazet* is that this hyperbole apparently converges with reality. And the audiences are ready to believe it all because their heads are full of stories of oriental practices of strangulation. The detour into exoticism accommodates the introduction on stage of passionate excesses which were found only in novels. Boileau chortled over the 'excès' of Quinault's *Astrate*, but he appears not to have understood how *Bajazet* also played off what the Spanish called at the time 'extremos'. To study the maxims of the Turks is therefore to gain access to a world in which, more than ever, the full flood of the passions can be released.

Would it have been because he had so closely studied the maxims of the Turks that Racine was then able in *Iphigénie* to evoke the fanatical ferocity of the Greek army? Calchas is an uncommon soothsayer, accused by Eriphile of imposture. Racine knew the opinion of Euripides on this assertive profession. And because he had become familiar with the 'maxime d'Etat' and happened to be plunged into an exotic setting, he had written some years previously, the following two verses (which contain a maxim):

Je sais combien crédule en sa dévotion
Le Peuple suit le frein de la Religion
(Bajazet, Act I. 2, ll. 235–6).

One could persuade an uninformed reader that this couplet was written by Voltaire, but that would be to miss the point. It is not, in fact, evident that Racine wanted to attack the ministers or priests of any particular religion at all. Perhaps the lines express Racine's attempt to understand from within, as an actor, just what goes on in the mind of a Grand Vizir. We can find supporting evidence in a detail which dictates the action of *Bérénice*. The word 'maxim' is used in the play, and it is Paulin who pronounces it:

Elle a mille vertus. Mais, Seigneur, elle est Reine.
Rome par une Loi, qui ne se peut changer,
N'admet avec son sang aucun sang étranger,
Et ne reconnaît point les fruits illégitimes
Qui naissent d'un Hymen contraire à ses maximes

(Bérénice, Act II. 2, ll. 374–80).

[margin note: in Bérénice, maxim dictates B's conduct]

A Roman may not marry a foreigner; and so a Roman may not marry
a queen [necessarily a foreigner]: with this double weighting, the
maxim assumes the form of a canonical, imperative, implication. In
clear terms, if a person is Roman, then he does not, may not, marry
a queen. We are all familiar with the wild flights of fancy to which contemporaries resorted in order to identify anecdotal origins for the plot
of *Bérénice.* Given that *dimisit invitus invitam* ('the male host dismissed his
female guest', as expressed by Racine in an epigraph to his preface to
the play), the next step was to identify the *invitus* and the *invitam.* If the
invitus was Louis XIV, well the *invitam* could have been . . . take your
pick! And contemporaries also found fault with the text of the play;
Bérénice, for example, uses the expression 'Dieux' [Gods], in the
pagan plural. Who would have thought that in the France of His
Most Christian Majesty it would have been possible to perform a play
which was based on the hatred of monarchy, and which articulates
that belief? In the foreground we have an exotic maxim: kings are
hateful. But how could this be so? Corneille was wary of the question;
in his *Tite et Bérénice,* he systematically rhymes 'reine' and 'haine', but he
goes no further. He avoids such specific terms as 'la haine des rois avec
le lait sucée' [the hatred for kings communicated with their mother's
milk]. It is in Racine's *Bérénice* (Act IV. 4, l. 1015) that the expression is
to be found. In a climate of such free speculation and criticism, the
collective blindness of audiences, readers, critics, and commentators is
truly phenomenal. And did the writer himself know what he was
doing? A little more, perhaps, than those who criticized him for not
portraying real Turks in *Bajazet,* or for merely putting on stage in
Bérénice 'courtisans français' [French courtiers].

[margin note: (so chars in Bérénice are not just "français")]

Curious to note, in *Esther,* a religious play which abounds with
maxims, it is the pagans who pronounce the greatest number in
dialogue. From Assuérus we hear:

[margin note: in Esther, pagans pronounce maxims]

De soins tumultueux un Prince environné
Vers de nouveaux objets est sans cesse entraîné.

(Esther, Act II. 3, ll. 543–4).

And from Zarès, 'Il est des contretemps qu'il faut qu'un Sage essuie' (Act III. 1, l. 841). In *Athalie*, the balance is different. Here there are superb maxims which exalt the splendour of the Almighty, as for example, 'Le bonheur des Méchants comme un torrent s'écoule' (Act II. 7, l. 688): these words provoke a stunned silence because they fall from the mouth of the innocent Eliacin, like a little Tom Thumb. It is also given to the same child to recite (with some reference to Deuteronomy), the Holy Law:

> Un Roi sage, ainsi Dieu l'a prononcé lui-même,
> Sur la richesse et l'or ne met point son appui
>   (*Athalie*, Act IV. 2, ll. 1278–9).

We have already mentioned that, in order to find the pure, clear-cut maxim, it is sometimes necessary to juggle with the versification, as in:

> les plus saintes Lois,
> Maîtresses du vil peuple, obéissent aux Rois.
> [. . .] un Roi n'a d'autre frein que sa volonté même
>   (*Athalie*, Act IV. 3, ll. 1391–3).

Here, in turn, the High Priest recites maxims, but he obviously does not believe what he is saying; he momentarily lends his voice to the infidel wrong-doers in order to deceive them. What he does say in maxim form could find expression in the mouth of Mathan, or even Narcisse (*Britannicus*). As it happens, Mathan and Narcisse are remarkable actors. They disguise their intent, and hide their true identity. But whoever learns their true maxims (which, unlike Astrate, they never pronounce) will be able to slip into their shoes.

In Racine, then, the maxim, that weapon of the wisdom of nations, that absolute truth which is universally applicable, becomes the instrument of alienation. 'Banal', says Jacques Scherer about the maxims of Racine. Banal, sure, but the banality of the Turks is not ours. If we scrutinize the maxim, drawing closer to the implications for those who express or create it, we become ourselves a little bit Turkish for the duration of a performance. In the same way, we could also become criminal, 'On apprend à hurler, dit l'autre, avec les Loups'.

3

Women and Power in Britannicus *and* Bérénice: *The Battle of Blood and Tears*

CHRISTIAN BIET

In a previous study on Racine, with a focus on the 'passion of tears',[1] I was struck by the fact that the dramaturgical and emotional principle of tears was of primary importance in the majority of the Racinian tragedies, particularly in *Britannicus*, *Bérénice*, and *Andromaque*. Similarly, theatrical effects and their ideological consequences were connected in such a way that the tears of women, heroes and kings, and also the tears provoked by tyrants, constituted not only a significant issue but were also polysemic signs linking all Racine's plots. Although tears were initially characterized by an *aspect galant*, intended to attract a particular public, they rapidly outstripped this professional concern and came to signal ways of acting, of writing and thinking the body, of naming the passions, even of proposing access, albeit uncertain, to the divine. In this chapter, I want to develop my earlier analysis and attempt to understand the issues surrounding the aesthetic, anthropological and ideological motif of tears by focusing on the tears of Racine's female characters, and in particular those of Junie and Bérénice.

---

1 Christian Biet, *Racine ou La passion des larmes* (Paris: Hachette, 1996). [See also parallel treatments in Christian Biet, '*Mithridate*, ou l'exercice de l'ambiguïté: "Que pouvait la valeur dans ce trouble funeste?"', pp. 83–98 and Suzanne C. Toczyski, 'Two Sisters' Tears: Paralinguistic Protest in *Horace*', pp. 221–9 both in Claire Carlin (ed.), *La Rochefoucauld, Mithridate, Frères et Sœurs, Les Muses Sœurs, Actes du 29ᵉ congrès annuel de la North American Society for Seventeenth-Century French Literature*, coll. Biblio 17, no. III (Tübingen: Gunter Narr, 1998)].

The Pleasure of Experiment

It is evident that, in his plays, Racine constructs the image of tears according to the public he seeks to attract. Racine is a great experimenter and, with almost every successive tragedy, changes or broadens his objective through his choice of subject and the aesthetic mode he adopts. His first play, *La Thébaïde*, allowed the young poet to gain a foothold in theatre by referring firstly to Greek tragedies (particularly those of Sophocles and Euripides), then explicitly to Aristotle (who, in his *Poetics* maintains that *Œdipus Rex* is the only truly tragic play),[2] to Rotrou, and also, implicitly, to Corneille (*Œdipe*, 1659). Focusing *La Thébaïde* on the story of the entire house of Œdipus, Racine reveals how the Theban family is subject to a devouring *libido dominandi*, particularly between the *frères ennemis*, a theme to which he often returns. At the same time, the play succeeds in its aim of establishing the two essential tragic passions as recognized in the *Poetics*: terror and pity. In *Alexandre le Grand* and *Andromaque*, the two plays which followed *La Thébaïde*, pity takes on a more genteel aspect. With *Alexandre*, Racine seeks the approval and recognition of his sovereign by striking the right note of *émotion galante* so favoured by the 'young court'. With *Andromaque*, he finds what would become his most faithful public, the socialite *mondains*, by adopting a plot borrowed from mythology and structured like a pastoral romance (A loves B who loves C who loves D . . . , in Barthes's now-famous formula), in which tears are the essential vector of the aesthetic developed. This prompted the *galants* and the *mondains* of a social élite, a considerable number of whom were women, to weep upon seeing the play thereby giving it all the appearance of success. Later, *Britannicus* provided Racine with an opportunity to convince an even wider public, more or less successfully, that his own weapon of sensitivity, allied to the technique of tears, matched Corneille on the latter's territory of Roman history. However, Racine's notion of pity, which he willingly acknowledged should feature in theatre, diverged somewhat from strictly held contemporary theories. For if the couple Junie–Britannicus is destined to arouse pity, the other couple, Junie–Néron, seems to be playing an entirely different game. Although this is centred on tears, the pity elicited is sometimes overwhelmed by a distinct sense of *Schadenfreude*, a point I shall return to below. Finally, with the creation of *Bérénice*, the significance of pity and tears changes once again. This time it seems Racine is anxious to rework his choice of a Roman setting for his tragedy. He also appears

2 Aristotle, *Poetics*, Chs 13 and 14, ed. Russell, pp. 106, 108.

to want to push the question of dramatic simplicity even further, and to guide the spectator on a deeper, more complete, more troubling journey as regards pity and tears. Hence, he writes a tragedy of 1518 lines, adjusted to 1506 lines,[3] with very little action, bloodshed or death, and with only the tears we find inventoried in the words of the three main characters. Indeed, all three express an 'hélas!' which is destined to become the play's emblem and which, in Antiochus's final line, is the very last word of the play.

If Racine's experiments in tragic dramaturgy are a bid for professional success, and designed to conquer an ever-wider audience, he also uses tears as a technique; similar to that used frequently by the religious in their intercessions, it is aimed at uniting the stage and the theatre, that is to say the characters and the audience, through a shared spirit of emotion. The sorrow and the chagrin of the stage character arouse the spectators' pity and move them to tears. The resulting elegiac tone reflects at once the characters' affliction and the spectators' compassion, allowing both to share in a compelling theatrical experience. Tears thus become a genuinely rhetorical effect and, in this case, a genuinely theatrical effect, a means of uniting the fictional characters with those watching them in the same physical, moral and aesthetic emotion. This process takes place firstly within a sort of courtly ceremony, but consequently, through the emotion aroused, achieves a moral effect which surpasses both pity and the pleasure of crying. In other words, from Aristotelian pity is elicited compassion, a moral and Christian emotion.

As eighteenth-century theorists noted, in particular Luigi Riccoboni in his *Discours sur la comédie à l'impromptu* (1721), Racine foregoes applause by exploiting silence and tears. In other words, by ensuring that the audience do not appreciate the aesthetic to the point of showing their pleasure, he guarantees that compassion, i.e. the link uniting the sorrow of the characters to that which the spectator might feel, is not compromised. Through the interplay of their glances and facial expressions, the actors create and maintain this link, and allow the public to participate in the experience of regret. The therapeutic function of tears can thus give rise to a sense of suffering which, paradoxically, is pleasurable and thereby provides a means of physically and morally tempering passions. Tears, however, are also signs; in this function they can indicate the extent to which both the idea of sin and the will to take the narrow and uncertain road to salvation are simultaneously present in the modern tragic system. Tears, in effect, can lead both to

---

3 The edition of 1671 has 12 lines more than that of 1697.

sin and to conversion, and it is mainly through his female characters that Racine represents this double aspect.

In *Britannicus*, Néron effectively attains the sweet and dark pleasure of making an innocent victim cry, and in this instance suffering can be viewed as a beautiful theatrical spectacle. But these same tears can also be transformed into the suffering which leads Junie to conversion when, in tears, she decides to enter the Vestals' temple and devote her life to God in an act of triple motivation: escape from the tyrant's threat, vengeance against Néron, and a gift of self to God. For *Bérénice*, tears lead to a decision to leave for a remote and pious life, and indicate the emergence of a divine emotion, when reason and the passions have failed. Consequently, from their tears as social signals to the divine tears of conversion, women are at the centre of the Racinian dramaturgical and ideological mechanism; by their very nature, they illustrate humanity's profound sensitivity more forcefully than men. Where Néron represents the cruel face of tyrants who revel in their power to make the innocent cry, where Titus is uncertain as to whether he should follow in the tradition of saintly kings and hesitatingly confines himself to regret and spontaneous, 'natural' tears, Junie turns to God through the sensuous and emotional vehicle of tears, while Bérénice takes a less defined route where tears will be the only way possible. The question remains, however, whether the characters can find salvation through tears, or whether they can only desire it without any real hope.

Junie's flight and Néron's Pleasure

In the well-known example of *Britannicus*, Junie is physically at the centre of all attention. It is through her that the crisis begins insofar as Agrippine drops everything to present herself at her son's private apartments in the early morning in order to question him about Junie's imprisonment. Agrippine has waited for four acts to see him, just to see him, trying in vain to impose her lost power on him, and by-passing the grand protocol of formal entries, departures, and exits. It was the sight of Junie which was at the origin of Néron's superb phantasm: seeing a naked Junie arriving in the middle of the night, surrounded by the guards, he describes her as 'Triste, levant au Ciel ses yeux mouillés de larmes', and later adds, 'J'aimais jusqu'à ses pleurs que je faisais couler' (Act II. 2, ll. 387 and 402). It is precisely because of Junie and the phantasm he creates of her that Néron converts his political passion into a devouring amorous passion:

originally he had intended to imprison her for political reasons but now he keeps her in his power for emotional reasons. Under his spying scrutiny (*libido sentiendi*), Junie finds herself moved to centre-stage, where he forbids her all discourse, wanting to manipulate her mind, body and soul in his favour. Throughout all this, the only resistance Junie can offer is her tears. In *Racine ou La passion des larmes*, I suggested how Néron-as-author, with recourse to traditional theatrical sequences and aesthetic rules, and by playing on diversity and tragic combinations, subjects all the other characters to his will and proves himself unassailable.[4] He highlights, directs and tries to impose on Junie, a role *he has composed* for her by limiting her freedom. He thus obliges the most innocent character, the most external to the tragedy, to abandon everything which is authentically her or hers except her silence, which he also knows how to penetrate. However, through her suffering, Junie quickly learns the secrets of the theatre, to the extent that she manages to play Néron at his own game by making him suffer. This allows her ultimately to defend herself through her tears, and Néron, writer, author and actor, is powerless against God. He can enslave, poison, exile or destroy her loved ones, but he cannot counter Junie's free will to seek refuge with God.

To escape the confinement imposed on her by Néron, she can only choose that offered by God. Junie neither can, nor wants, to disguise her own tears, so much so that this Christian *femme forte*, as Racine's contemporaries fully recognized, imposes her virtue by embracing the Absolute. In one day she has learned the reality of the world and the theatre. She has learned that she was unable, or did not want, to play a role, even under duress, and could bear suffering but without being able to hide it ('Je trouvais mes regards, trop pleins de ma douleur' (Act III. 7, l. 1010)). She knows, therefore, that she must go even further with her newly found insight, and that she must leave this theatre and choose God instead of the persona that Néron offers her. More than death, her decision, taken in tears at the foot of the marble statue of Augustus (Act V. 9, l. 1749), to exile herself in the divine world, defeats Néron. Only then do the tyrant's 'regards égarés' (Act V. 9, l. 1778) become powerless, as does Narcisse's profane gesture, punished by the people in his guilty blood: the tears of the blessed confront the blood of the impious. Like a Christian heroine in communion with the people, Junie is protected by them in her desire to worship the Lord and escape from Evil. Her flight leaves an empty dramatic space for political, moral and religious questions. The final

4 Biet, *Racine ou La passion des larmes*, pp. 67–79.

in the end, there still ∃ hope that Néron will reform <J's piety

outcome remains unresolved, allowing Burrhus to say that it is still possible for the monster to mend his ways if he can be moved and show remorse. Consequently, the audience is enthralled and likely to be moved by Junie's piety, and even to show proof of Christian charity in the hope that Néron will redeem himself, thanks to the sacrifice of the innocent. Junie's character has, therefore, resisted both violence and the imposition of inappropriate trappings. This resistance to playing a role translates naturally into the exit of a character whom Néron had forced upon his stage in the intention of keeping her there. Hence, the Evil represented on-stage is contrasted with the Good off-stage.

but not all has moral explanation –

we enjoy seeing J cry –

dark pleasure

<

seductive power of cruelty

But the theatre remains what it is, a contradictory representation which, through its exploration of cause and effect, seeks a complexity which frequently defies moral explanation. In fact, if Junie escapes from absolute evil, from the villain of the play and bloody tyrant which Néron is, it must be said that her tears are not simply an opportunity for the audience to sympathize. It would be naïve to deny that, even in the seventeenth century, the sight of Néron taking pleasure in seeing Junie cry is not without interest. Indeed, could it not be said that enjoying the sight of an innocent woman cry is not in itself a theatrical pleasure? For there is a dark pleasure in watching Racine's tragedies, an indignant horror mixed with a particular sweetness when, for example, we see Athalie resist to the death, or witness Néron impose his cruelty on all around him; it is a pleasure which is opposed to the pleasure of pitying, through tears, the victims' misfortunes. If we are saddened at Britannicus's death and reassured to know that Junie has taken refuge with the Vestals to live in tears and prayer for the rest of her life, we cannot but doubt both Agrippine's final hope and the wish expressed by Burrhus.[5] As we know, Néron still has a long and cruel future ahead of him.[6] Therefore, the seductive power of cruelty, which we experience upon watching another cry and taking pleasure in it, can be explained firstly by the horror with which we witness it, but also by its technique, its cold mechanism and its irresistible

cruelty denied, repressed, appears outside text as unspeakable violence

dynamic. What interests the spectator and reader even more, is to observe the way in which cruelty is vainly denied, and also, because it is repressed, the way in which it appears outside the text as an unspeakable violence. Because it is concealed, shut out and repressed,

---

5 Agrippine: Mais Burrhus, allons voir jusqu'où vont ses transports.
                Voyons quel changement produiront ses remords,
                S'il voudra désormais suivre d'autres maximes.
   Burrhus: Plût aux Dieux que ce fût le dernier de ses crimes!
                                    (*Britannicus*, Act V. 9, ll. 1785–8).
6 Which makes reading Tacitus all the more pleasurable . . .

this cruelty is all the more audible, visible and present. Racine shows that cruelty does not and need not find expression in overstated performance, and that when it is tempered, mediated or silenced, an even greater cruelty is obtained, an absolute cruelty established by a subtextual, and therefore all the more perverse, mechanism. In Racine, cruelty, like God and Evil, is hidden and inexpressible. It is obvious then that without cruelty through tears, which is an evil, we would have little pleasure in governing, living, writing and reading, and very little enjoyment in pushing open the theatre's doors. I feel this point cannot be overlooked especially as, in *Britannicus*, it occurs as a representation of the fact, a *mise en scène* of this very pleasure, which enables spectators to see, over Néron's shoulder, an innocent female character in tears as well as an actress acting out the most perfect distress. In spite of all its prohibitions, and the ethical and therapeutic aspirations of tears, could it not be said that the theatre is the *place where Evil takes place* for the greater pleasure of the spectator, a pleasure which involves the feelings of fear, pity, compassion, and also *Schadenfreude*?

The Tears of Bérénice

Although it is obvious from the very beginning of the tragedy, the decision to dismiss Bérénice is taken in the play's final scenes. These scenes are dominated by women, tears, politics, emotional outpouring, sorrow and disappearance, and end with the famous 'hélas!', the 'grand mot' of the up-dated sublime. At the risk of paraphrasing, I should like to revisit these concluding scenes of the play, and illustrate from a dramaturgical, political and emotional point of view the manner in which that final decision is taken, in order to elucidate the role played by tears in the play's ending. The question raised by these final scenes is how can the stage be emptied of its characters without any of them dying? How can the danger of suicide be transcended by a movement towards emptiness, or towards the aesthetic abstraction that must mark the play's finale? Flight, the nullification of signs, and the disappearance of the theatrical space all combine to represent only the memory of suffering, which is forever re-enacted, night after night and forever called on to go away.

Between the fourth and fifth scenes of Act V Antiochus speaks these words:

Qu'ai-je donc fait, grands Dieux! Quel cours infortuné
À ma funeste vie aviez-vous destiné?
Tous mes moments ne sont qu'un éternel passage
De la crainte à l'espoir, de l'espoir à la rage.
Et je respire encore? Bérénice! Titus!
Dieux cruels! de mes pleurs vous ne vous rirez plus
                                                    (Act V. 4, ll. 1309–14).

After this address to the gods and to the two other characters the
stage empties, as Forestier states in his edition, without even *liaison de
fuite* or *liaison de vue*.[7] Tension, therefore, is marked clearly and spatially
by a divergence with theatrical convention, and the spectator, faced
with this minor aesthetic transgression, is able to fear for Antiochus
who, threatening to render his tears efficient, is in other words capable
of suicide: the rage to hope would give way to a rage of despair, to the
point that the tears of despair would force the doomed hero to end his
days. But there is another consequence of this transgression. Spectators,
who throughout the play have been aware of the strict adherence to
the principles of *liaison des scènes* and *liaison des actes*, as well as the
tragedy's continuity in time and in a single space that has never been
empty, now have no solution other than to wait until someone enters the
empty space, exactly as at the beginning of a tragedy. Paradoxically,
what does fill the space is, precisely, emptiness. This void functions,
therefore, both as a sign and as a prolepsis: it announces the *dénouement*
and characterizes the entire tragedy.

This conclusion, based on a misunderstanding, can only be partial
because nothing is yet resolved with regard to the main plot. The
empty stage of Antiochus corresponds to the empty stage of the two
lovers, and all that remains is to mix the two systems so that the stage
is entirely empty once Antiochus, Bérénice and Titus are gone. It is,
therefore, primarily a dramaturgical, even scenographic problem that
Racine poses here: how does he achieve an entirely empty stage? As we
know from the preface, in order to accomplish this the dramatist decides
against violent means, and chooses the dramatic efficiency of tears.

The fifth scene begins with a word often used by Racine at the
beginning of his tragedies, a 'non' spoken by Bérénice (Act V. 4, l.
1315), which expresses a refusal of the situation in which the character
is trapped, and the will to decide in spite of the situation, which could
also be referred to as cruel fate except that, in this case fate is
explained by purely human and legal circumstances. The previous
action is therefore played over again, and the stage continues to

7 Forestier, *Œuvres*, p. 1481; n. 1, p. 502.

empty, but this time with Bérénice as the central figure instead of Antiochus. There are no words possible, no prolonging or arranging of time, no employable space, nothing, save for the exit of all the characters from the *cabinet* in which the tragedy takes place. It is as if everything which has been endlessly distended for five acts (speech, time and the occupation of a space whose only meaning lies in the past) has reached its limit; as though the mechanism of postponement, based on hardening recollections and therefore a sense of loss for words, places and past time, once faced with the emergence of the present political urgency could no longer be prolonged. The foreign queen no longer hears Titus's words, and only hears the angry crowd, while she herself sobs: 'Tandis que dans les pleurs moi seule je me noie' (Act V. 5, l. 1328). Earlier she claims, 'Il n'est plus temps' (l. 1319). In the end, the tragedy's very space has lost all meaning to the point that the queen, most unusually for a tragedy, is prompted to comment on the setting which, never before so clearly, no longer resembles a conventional stage set:

> Je ne vois rien ici dont je ne sois blessée.
> Tout cet Appartement préparé par vos soins,
> Ces lieux, de mon amour si longtemps les témoins,
> Qui semblaient pour jamais me répondre du vôtre,
> Ces chiffres,[8] où nos noms enlacés l'un dans l'autre,
> À mes tristes regards viennent partout s'offrir,
> Sont autant d'imposteurs que je ne puis souffrir
> (Act V. 5, ll. 1332–8).

What this means from a scenographic and dramaturgical viewpoint is that the space of the *cabinet*, where the prince and the foreign queen met and where the tragedy occurred, can no longer exist. All that remains are traces and monograms of Titus and Bérénice, in other words the letters T and B intertwined, noble graffiti which no longer have any reason to exist and are only the cause of regrets because they refer to another time ('cinq années' as Titus indicates precisely in l. 1351), when a father reigned as sovereign and the prince was responsible only for himself. Following the sovereign's death and the prince's accession to power through hereditary rights, the décor-as-witness of the lovers' meeting place must yield to the outside world. In Titus's case this means Rome (the 'sénat auguste'), and for Bérénice an unknown elsewhere. From *tragédie galante*, we have come to *tragédie élégiaque* via the political question. During the tragedy, space has been eviscerated

8 The word *chiffres* becomes *festons* in the 1697 edition.

in tears, in a great elegiac process of discursive postponement. Now the verse, which commented on the interlacing love of T and B, must also empty itself. Because it no longer has any purpose, except nostalgia, it must disappear in tears and in exclamations of 'hélas!'

The play's finale marks not only the end of the dramaturgical experiment of valedictory postponement and the emptying of space, but also the end of discourse, as the rest of the text and the history of the variants indicate. In order for the elegy to continue indefinitely, Titus would have to take pleasure in watching Bérénice cry, and also cry himself ('Quoi, dans mon désespoir trouvez-vous tant de charmes ? / Craignez-vous que mes yeux versent trop peu de larmes?', Act V. 5, ll. 1359–60). This is dramaturgically impossible, so the play must end. The most canonically acceptable ending would require either Bérénice or Titus, or both, to die, and indeed that seems exactly what is indicated in the letter that the queen gives him, if we are to believe what is said in Villars's *La Critique de Bérénice*.[9] However, the violent spilling of blood is not acceptable in Racine's system, because everything must disappear, not in a simple and convenient action, but in a thinning-out which goes beyond elegy: it is the disappearance of places, times and words, more than that of the 'life' of the characters, which must take place. This may explain why, after the second performance, the letter was no longer read aloud; spectators no longer have any access to the expression of the will to die. They can no longer enter into Bérénice's words over Titus's shoulder, and the reading of her letter can only be replaced by a moment's silence. Suppressing the expression of the will to commit suicide without suppressing the idea (the audience knows that Bérénice wants to end her days once Titus, having read the letter, says so) amounts, once again, to the creation of a moment of expectancy and tension for the spectator who listens to the silence, or, rather, the silent reading. Furthermore, this dramaturgical device allows death to be suggested but not entirely expressed, as though something else must be imagined, stronger than blood, stronger than tender or valedictory tears: a total disappearance of the play and all its dramatic components, i.e. characters, time, space, speech.

9 'Cependant l'amoureux Titus estime [la] vertu [de Bérénice], et se laisse tellement aveugler par l'amour qu'il a pour cette belle Surannée, que voyant dans le Madrigal Testamentaire qu'elle lui baille à lire, le dessein qu'elle a fait de mourir, il se détermine aussi à se tuer' [But the amorous Titus respects [the] moral quality of [Bérénice] and allows himself to be so blinded by love for this lovely Lady of the Past that, recognizing in the Testamentary Madrigal that she offers him to read, her intention to take her life, he resolves also to kill himself' (Forestier, *Œuvres*, p. 513. See also p. 1482, n. 2, p. 504).

If death is forbidden, then only silence or the indefinite prolonging of elegy and of Titus's hesitation remains. The spectator, therefore, watches an exceptional *jeu de scène*, rare in this kind of tragedy and thus very important for its interpretation. According to the stage directions, 'Bérénice se laisse tomber sur un siège' (end of V. 5), and does not speak again until the next scene, 105 lines later, if we exclude an 'hélas!', to which I shall return. What is happening? Firstly, a queen seats herself, an action which is in keeping with her role because, in tragedy, the act of seating oneself is a sign of mastery. However, this queen is also a lover under constraint (on Titus's orders, she cannot leave), and who 'se laisse tomber sur un siège', defeated and silent. This explains why her muteness, combined with her posture, produces a double effect. Firstly, her tears (as represented by her 'hélas!') provoke the tears of the spectator. On the other hand, through the physical and symbolic mastery of this posture and the emotion she is supposed to show, Bérénice is in a position to take the only possible decision open to her. She is herself emotionally moved, similarly moving others, falls silent, makes up her mind, and finally speaks. While Titus repeatedly replays the plot and threatens either to abandon his responsibility (which is expressly forbidden if he wishes to be virtuous) or to attempt suicide, thereby pleasantly mixing *galant* tenderness and elegiac distress, Bérénice remains silent and bears the signs of suffering as she sits in the centre of the stage. There is an identifiable link between tears and conversion, we have also seen that it is time for the play to end, that the space is disappearing, that the characters are fading or wish to die, and that discourse exists only between a silent character and a fairly stereotypical lover. A decision must be made, both for the characters and for the author; a conclusion must be envisaged and can be none other than a conversion to another world: political in the case of Titus, if not already accomplished, and an undefined world of suffering and tears for Bérénice.

But, prior to this, Racine imagines another dramaturgical challenge which proves the extent to which he sought to avoid a reversal or a 'coup de théâtre': Antiochus enters, declares himself a rival both in love and in *générosité* and, like Titus, leaves the decision to the silent, seated character who dominates the entire stage. Once tender love has failed, as have pity, blackmail, passion and threats, once the emotional outpouring has taken place and reason has only led to a series of hesitations, another noteworthy *jeu de scène* is presented: the distressed queen rises to her feet. Before this, as she listened to the princes, Bérénice, quite literally, sat in judgement. Vanquished and seated, she played the role of the weeping lover. Read by Titus, she saw herself denied a blood sacrifice; now she, in turn, can deny sacrificial death to the other characters.

Everything then seems to have failed: political reason firstly, because it has been moved into a private space which it cannot accept, which it can resist only by suppressing; so too has failed the *galant* and *mondain* plot, characterized by modish tears and by an a-historical vision of the classical Roman world, to such an extent that, even after crying, the happiness of escaping to a distant elsewhere with one's beloved remains inconceivable. Redemption through tears has also failed since sensitive tears resolve nothing, and only end in an elegy incapable of resolving the story which has been related. If the characters share a compassion for each other, and the spectator for all three of them, this compassion only leads to a splitting of judgements which favours all three roles. As it is impossible to decide which character has suffered most or who is most guilty, the plot cannot be resolved. Finally, the aesthetic establishment of the plot itself fails because the text once again finds itself at an impasse and is necessarily compelled to repeat the same passionate impulses in a flood of tears. In this great dramatic ceremony, the spectators and the characters are on the brink of sharing similar conclusions and of feeling together the same effects of their emotions through their collective crying. How then can the process be interrupted or ended? To what extent can it be preserved? Can the actors be expected to express such emotion indefinitely, and thereby provoke the risk of spectator fatigue?

In consequence, after the anger of Bérénice comes her written decision (not read aloud) to kill herself; after reasoning, Bérénice (seated as queen) has simultaneously examined both the situation and her feelings, has hesitated (defeated as lover) between blood and tears, before finally taking the decision to remove herself. Bérénice is a foreign queen, who, in spite of Racine, has difficulty hiding her past errors; indeed, Villars claimed that her exploits and incest were well known, to the point that he calls her the 'Surannée'.[10] She cannot fight against the fundamental laws of the kingdom or the Empire (the laws of succession, the right of primogeniture, and the inalienability of the royal domain); she can only resist as a private individual against the State, the Senate and Roman virtue. As she has no legitimate status in Rome, she considers, therefore, that after her tears of departure, she must accede to the determination to want nothing other than the complete effacement of her private state, expecting nothing more than the memory and example of a tragedy without bloodshed.

10 See n. 9 above.

Suffering and suffering alone replaces all the other arguments of decision, and it is indeed this female character, foreign to Rome and to the State, who ensures the continued existence of this very State. In one move, Bérénice suppresses the opposition between the private place of the past and the public place of the present, between a happy a-historical time and the time of History, between *galant* discourse and royal discourse. It is thus seated that this female character decided to end the elegy and the play: *Bérénice*, the play, will be 'un exemple de vertu inimitable'/'an example of inimitable virtue', as we read in *La Princesse de Clèves*,[11] which echoes Bérénice's own brief summary of the tragedy. Bérénice, female character and foreign queen, external to Roman politics and outside History, knew how to end this tragedy by indicating through her tears that the difficult question to resolve is that of the soul and not politics, which, in itself, can be easily resolved (Roman law must triumph, as we know, from the beginning if we remain within the political domain). Bérénice transcends the plot by transcending her suffering, but in order to do so she must remove herself from the play and suppress place, time, and the political and romantic action, and, like Junie, go to a place where no one will follow her.

The question of the soul does not belong to tragedy, even if tragedy raises it, and it is by bringing this question into her private a-historical existence that Bérénice begins an inimitable journey after having been at the centre of a story of suffering. It is as if she had to trace an uncertain and distant path of salvation, which was unattainable in performance.

Uncertain Salvation and the Pleasure of Sin

In Racine, women's tears are not solely *galant* or *mondain*, nor are they based on a simple or single emotion. Tears can be dangerous, or they can become a sign of perversity, of dark pleasure. Women's tears can give pleasure to those who cause them to flow or to those who see them flow: Néron enjoys Junie's tears before being defeated by their double power (they resist his enjoyment because they fight him and allow her to flee him), Bérénice accuses Titus of being charmed by her tears, and even the spectators themselves cannot limit themselves to pure and Christian compassion because they can *also* place themselves behind Néron. Because of the ambiguity of the feelings they signal (and of which they are the sign), tears are the anthropological witness

11 [The reference is to the last line of Mme de Lafayette's *La Princesse de Clèves* (1678).]

to a way of showing feelings and, for Racine, a way to deepen meaning in his characters and to gain mastery of the spectators' response. Through tears, Racine shows that salvation may be possible, or rather that an inevitably troubled and uncertain way towards salvation is possible. As a therapy for passions, tears alone can contain emotional overflow, if sometimes only momentarily. Faced with Néron's political *libido dominandi* (the passion for dominating others), with his *libido sentiendi* (sensual passion), and with his amorous *libido*, Junie's only weapon are her tears, but initially she fails and reinforces the power of the passions. The power of faith remains, which, expressed in tears, allows one to glimpse the possibility of escape from the vanity of passions. But nothing says that the way is sure and that there again the efficacy of tears will not fail. However, even if Salvation cannot be known, tears are the only possible way to approach it or even to think of approaching it, if God decides it is possible. Even on stage, tears can change the heart and mind of the spectators, via compassion. It is then possible to attribute to them a moral, even religious efficiency. Given his religious position and Jansenist past, Racine must assume this if he wishes to avoid condemnation from Saint Augustine, Nicole and Port-Royal, so denying him and the theatre any right to, or possibility of, moral utility.

Racine must show that the ceremony of tears gives a chance to approach salvation or at least to indicate the way, because crying for Bérénice and with her, we do not cry for ourselves or for a lost love but for our own finitude.[12] By showing Junie going to the Vestals to weep with God, and Bérénice in tears capable of taking a decision in the place of Titus and Antiochus, Racine moves the spectator and explains, or represents the fact, that emotion can lead those who cry, especially women, to a possible albeit uncertain representation of conversion and redemption. The audience, caught in the same tearful emotion, led by Junie as by Bérénice, can also take the same path, marked by the desire, intention and hope of salvation. After the despair and rationality, there is then a place for pure, useful emotion, for all parts of the theatre. But here again, the aesthetic mechanism, more apt, after a shared emotion, to incite reflection and distance, evokes again in the spectator uncertainty and judgement rather than an intimate communion with the characters.

It is as the hypothetical spectator, not being Bérénice, that 'I' cry for her, that I think about my own finitude, and that 'I' legitimately weep.

12 Here Racine disagrees with Saint Augustine, *Confessions*, 1, 13. See Biet, *Racine ou La passion des larmes*, pp. 129–30. (See *Saint Augustine: Confessions*, trans. by Henry Chadwick (Oxford: Oxford University Press, 1991), pp. 15–16.

It is because 'I' am not Junie, because 'I' cannot follow her to the Vestal convent, that 'I' realize my own failure. It is also because I take pleasure in seeing Néron enjoy Junie cry that I cannot reasonably envisage being holy or saved. These are the disappointing, even deceptive limits that Racine traces at the frontiers of his tragedies.

Tears, because they are emotional, are contradictory. They can be diabolical or show signs of holiness. Even if he realizes, and demonstrates, that they can be perverse, Racine must also show that they can mark a movement towards morality and salvation. As Saint Augustine said, 'les larmes montent de l'abîme mystérieux de l'âme' / 'tears rise from the mysterious depths of the soul', and the whole century knew that they can be a sign, sometimes false sometimes true, of conversion. They can also represent an invitation to a possible conversion for the audience and, through theatre, represent a step leading to something other than theatrical pleasure: meditation and contrition after the curtain has fallen. Through Bérénice and Junie, the spectator can think and meditate, leaving behind *galant* tears and ephemeral *mondain* pleasures, to convert their tears into moral and religious tears. It is important to understand here that Racine uses a technique of sacred rhetoric which Bossuet (who hated theatre) recommended, and which Bernard Lamy recommended to those who wish to stir in their audience a desire for conversion:

> Les hommes ne peuvent pas remarquer que nous sommes touchez, s'ils n'apperçoivent dans nos paroles les marques des émotions de nôtre âme. Jamais on ne concevra des sentiments de compassion pour une personne dont le visage est riant : il faut avoir les yeux abattus ou baignez de larmes pour causer ce sentiment.
>
> [People cannot notice that we are moved, if they do not perceive in our words traces of the emotions of our soul. Never would one feel compassion for someone with a happy countenance. A lowered countenance, and eyes bathed in tears are essential to evoke this emotion.][13]

Through the dangerous and decried discipline of theatre, Racine demonstrates that his opponents are right to use tears; but, like them, he uses the same rhetoric and the same artifice, and for the right reason. If, as Saint Augustine says, tears are the 'blood of the soul',[14] they are also the only way to find God. Obviously the problem is that Racine writes for theatre, a dangerous art that does not allow a single

13 *L'Art de parler* (Paris: A. Palard, 1675), p. 66. See also Sheila Bayne's article, 'Le rôle des larmes dans le discours de la conversion', in *La Conversion au XVII siècle, actes du colloque du CMR 17* (Marseilles: CMR 17, 1982).
14 *Sermo*, 351, n. 7.

function for tears nor a single effect to ensue. Even if he thinks that it may be possible to separate himself from a sensibility which is solely human and *galant* in order to imprint on the soul, *via* tears, the necessity of morality and interest in virtue, Racine must also *interest* his audience, by showing on stage women crying, and must let his actresses seduce their captive audience with their feigned tears.

This is why Junie and Bérénice, representing female characters perhaps more sensitive than men, but above all conceived as external to the political intrigue (Junie is a political stake but has no political action of her own, and Bérénice is a foreign queen fighting against Roman law), can give a meaning to tears: a meaning at once private and apt to lead the spectator towards a reflection on the soul. If there is nothing to say that their sole status as women makes them more effective for this, we can infer, nonetheless, that it is because they are female characters that we can better observe the journey of their souls. Thus, more clearly than the other characters, they represent the status of all mankind.

Because they are different from Agrippine, for example, the roles of Junie and Bérénice are better suited to be at one and the same time objects for other characters and suffering souls who must decide their own way. It is impossible for Racine to glimpse the road to salvation without the necessary punctuation of tears, which is even more important than that of bloody sacrifice. Junie and Bérénice are not martyrs to be sacrificed but suffering souls, whose salvation is uncertain, and who nonetheless show that by refusing blood and taking the path of tears, it is possible to attain hope.

By observing this choice, the spectators can reflect on their own journey, can find themselves caught in their own enjoyment without escaping the pleasure but, by examining these examples, they can also convert their aesthetic tears into moral or religious tears, without knowing for all that if, by so doing, they will be saved.

4

Gender, Power and Authority in Alexandre le Grand *and* Athalie

DERVAL CONROY

Attitudes towards women in power and women in authority permeate all forms of seventeenth-century discourse. While the debate concerning female sovereignty and female regency was at its most heated in the latter half of the sixteenth century, the reality of women in public government was kept very alive throughout the *grand siècle* both by the regencies of Marie de Médicis (1610–31) and Anne d'Autriche (1643–61),[1] and by the reign of the neighbouring Christine de Suède (1632–54). Furthermore the issue of female governance was continually fuelled by the ongoing *querelle des femmes*, in which writers reflected on female 'nature' and capabilities, in order to support the idea of the superiority or inferiority of women, or the equality of the sexes. Parallel to this debate regarding women in authority, and their capacity to rule, a second discourse, separate from the first, although linked, concerned the exercise of power by women, or *le pouvoir au féminin*.[2] Clearly many noblewomen played an extremely important role in court politics, either overtly as for example in the case of the *frondeuses*, or more covertly through their much-maligned intrigues and influence.[3] In the figure of the queen (or in the case of contemporary France, the

---

[1] While Anne d'Autriche's regency ended officially on 7 September 1651 at the declaration of the majority of Louis XIV, she nonetheless continued to run the country with Mazarin until the latter's death in 1661.

[2] For a wide-ranging appreciation of the forms these powers took, see Danielle Haase Dubosc and Éliane Viennot (eds), *Femmes et pouvoirs sous l'ancien régime* (Paris: Rivages, 1991); Kathleen Wilson-Chevalier and Éliane Viennot (eds), *Royaume de fémynie. Pouvoirs, contraintes, espaces de liberté des femmes de la Renaissance à la Fronde* (Paris: Champion, 1999), and *XVIIᵉ siècle*, 144 (1984).

[3] See Ch. 10, 'Women in Political and Civic Life' in Wendy Gibson, *Women in Seventeenth-Century France* (London: Macmillan, 1989), pp. 141–67.

queen regent) became embodied overtones of both power and authority, nonetheless considerable for having been obscured from history.

Much seventeenth-century drama reflects the conflict in opinion on these issues; while many dramatists uphold the patriarchy to portray women as incapable of stable government, dangerous when in power, whose rightful place is one of subservience, other texts implicitly question male hegemony, overthrow seemingly fixed hierarchies, and present alternative realities, within which women either successfully and competently rule, imbued with an authority which is legitimately theirs, or within which their exercise of power is portrayed as a positive influence. Among the most obvious examples of strong, authoritative and powerful female sovereigns are probably those which feature in Corneille's work, a fact which has not escaped critics before now. However, despite the ubiquitous presence of the queen-figure in the Racinian corpus, a corpus in which moreover the theme of sovereignty is so often an important concern, the representation of female sovereignty or women in government has not, to the best of my knowledge, received adequate attention.[4] The aim of this chapter then is to examine the dynamic between gender, power and (sovereign) authority in two plays where, to different degrees and in different ways, it is of considerable pertinence, namely in *Alexandre le Grand* and *Athalie*.

Any examination of this kind of dynamic requires definition of the terms concerned. The notion of gender then, as a conceptual category of analysis, hinges on an appreciation of the dynamics of sociocultural conditioning in defining what is appropriate behaviour for, and hence in constructing attitudes towards, both sexes. The concept of power, within the context of this chapter is used in two ways: firstly I use the concept in the precise sense as defined by Weber, in his classic distinction between power and authority. Power, for Weber, 'is the probability that one actor within a social relationship will be in a position to carry out his own will despite resistance, regardless of the basis on which this probability rests'. Authority on the other hand hinges on concepts of legitimacy, i.e. when a person has the legitimate 'right' to carry out his/her will.[5] This then is what is meant by power and authority

[margin notes: texts = on both sides of ? — ♀ = incapable/ dangerous vs. ♀ = competent, positive influence / extensively studied in Corneille, not so in Racine / here: examine dynamic between gender, power + sovereign authority / defn's: gender / power I (vs authority)]

---

4 One notable exception is Anne M. Menke's article 'The Widow Who Would Be Queen: The Subversion of Patriarchal Monarchy in *Rodogune* and *Andromaque*', *Cahiers du dix-septième*, 7. 1 (1997), 205–14. On the dynamic between power and authority, see Simone Ackerman, 'Roxane et Pulchérie: Autorité réelle et pouvoir illusoire', *Cahiers du dix-septième*, 2. 2 (1988), 49–64. On sovereignty, see for example Timothy J. Reiss's 'Banditry, Madness and Sovereign Authority: *Alexandre le Grand*', in Sylvie Romanowski and Monique Bilezikian (eds), *Homage to Paul Bénichou* (Birmingham, AL: Summa, 1994), pp. 113–42.
5 Max Weber, *The Theory of Social and Economic Organization*, trans. and ed. Talcott Parsons (London: Collier–Macmillan, 1968), p. 152.

within the context of the plays themselves. However on a broader scale, I also draw on the Foucauldian definition of power as a network of relations which informs discourse.[6] Since literature plays a role in the maintenance of hierarchical discursive relations, it is interesting to examine to what extent these two plays of Racine's can be seen to uphold or question the epistemological paradigms of the dominant discourses of the time.

power 2

Finally, the issue of power and authority necessarily evokes the theme of politics. Much ink has been spilt, as Pierre Ronzeaud's recent synthesis indicates, concerning the conflicting viewpoints of the importance of politics in Racine's *œuvre*.[7] It is not the aim of this chapter, however, to enter into this debate, nor to analyse what Racine may have thought himself about female sovereignty. While clearly anxious not to reduce these plays to mere political statement, nor to see them naïvely as a transparent reflection of contemporary ideas, the following analysis aims to examine what role Racine attributes to Axiane and Athalie, and how their power or authority is represented.

all → politics, but here, not reducing plays to political statement

?: what role does R attribute to Axiane + Athalie, sovereigns

Before analysing the representation of these two Racinian female sovereigns, Axiane and Athalie, it is necessary however to outline briefly the conflicting attitudes, alluded to above, which permeate seventeenth-century writings concerning women's power or their ability to rule, and which inform the backdrop of any seventeenth-century drama which discusses these issues. At the risk of simplification, what follows gives an idea of the two most extreme (but very widespread) viewpoints. As is well known, a falsification of the Salic law which excluded women from the French throne had been ratified as the first fundamental law of the state by the Paris *parlement* in 1593. This exclusion was justified throughout much political and legal discourse of the seventeenth century by a repetitive argumentation, marked by the same recurrent topoi. According to Cardin Le Bret, in a text which became the handbook of many theorists, Salic law was perfectly justifiable, since women were physically and intellectually weak and imperfect by nature, while men were endowed with courage, strength and judgement.[8] Some years later, in his *Testament politique*, Richelieu elaborates the same idea and is clearly of the same opinion:

∃ 2 extreme positions in 17c.

1) salic law – 1593 – excluded ♀ from throne, since ♀ = weak, imperfect

(Le Bret, Richelieu)

> Le Gouvernement des Royaumes requiert une vertu mâle et une fermeté inébranlable. [. . .] Les femmes, paresseuses et peu secrètes de

---

6 See for example Michel Foucault, *Power/Knowledge: Selected Interviews and Other Writings 1972–1977*, ed. Colin Gordon (Brighton: Harvester, 1980), p. 198.
7 Pierre Ronzeaud, 'Racine et la politique: la perplexité de la critique', *Œuvres et Critiques*, 24. 1 (1999), *Présences de Racine* (Tübingen: Gunter Narr), pp. 136–58.
8 Cardin Le Bret, *De la Souveraineté du Roy* (Paris: Jacques Quesnel, 1632), p. 31.

leur nature, sont si peu propres au gouvernement que, si on considère encore qu'elles sont fort sujettes à leurs passions et, par conséquent, peu susceptibles de raison et de justice, ce seul principe les exclut de toute administration publique.

[The government of kingdoms requires masculine virtue and unwavering strength. [. . .] Women, lazy and indiscreet by nature, are so little suited to government that, when one also considers that they are strongly subject to their passions, and consequently, little prone to reason and justice, this principle alone excludes them from all public administration.][9]

While Le Bret and Richelieu may be the two best-known examples, they are certainly not the only ones: earlier Louis Turquet de Mayenne had also maintained that gynecocracy (i.e. female rule) can never be stable, since women are delicate and weak, subject to the sways of passion, and, unlike the male sex, bereft of royal virtues such as *fermeté*, *prudence*, and *magnanimité*,[10] while in 1661 Jean François Senault takes another tack and highlights the opinion of 'un grand nombre de Politiques' regarding the pernicious consequences of the qualities which women *do* possess: according to Senault it is commonly held by these 'Politiques' that when women are admitted to, or called upon to assume, sovereign authority, they are ambitious and cruel, 'fatales à leur Empire et funestes à leurs sujets' [disastrous for their empire and fatal for their subjects].[11] These few quotations, of which there are many other examples, illustrate the weight of what can be termed the exclusionist discourse. What becomes evident then is that the exclusion of women from the throne is justified and defended firstly through gender constructions based on an accumulation of essentialisms concerning women's 'nature' – women, for example, are allegedly inconstant, fragile, malicious, false, rash, lascivious, ambitious – which constitutes the social and cultural construction labelled as Woman. It is furthermore justified through the mapping of a so-called natural order as patriarchal and paternalistic, and finally through the construction of sovereignty itself as exclusively male. The definition of the prerequisites for sovereignty in exclusively male terms results in the construction of sovereignty itself as exclusively male, and automatically excludes women. Essentialisms, and consistent use of binary opposites, combine to construct a reality whereby women are prevented from

9 Richelieu, *Testament politique ou Les Maximes d'Etat de Monsieur le Cardinal de Richelieu* (Paris: Complexe, 1990), pp. 31–2. (This text was probably written between 1630 and 1638 and, although unpublished at the time, would have circulated in manuscript).
10 Louis Turquet de Mayenne, *La monarchie aristodemocratique, ou le gouvernement composé et meslé des trois formes de legitimes Republiques* (Paris: J. Berjon, 1611), pp. 59, 62.
11 Jean François Senault, *Le monarque ou les devoirs du souverain* (Paris: Pierre le Petit, 1661), pp. 43–4.

playing a public role by their inherent 'natural' flaws, and by their lack of 'male' virtues. In sum, the dynamics of what excludes them hinges on a fluctuating continuum between what women 'are' and what they 'are not'.

There is of course the other side of the coin, which can be found in the writings of feminists such as Du Bosc, Le Moyne, Saint Gabriel, and Poullain de la Barre, all of whom maintain that women *can* rule. According to Le Moyne,

> Les Estats ne se gouvernent pas avec la barbe, ny par l'austerité du visage: Ils se gouvernent par la force de l'Esprit et avec la vigueur et l'adresse de la Raison: et l'Esprit peut bien estre aussi fort, et la Raison aussi vigoureuse et aussi adroite, dans la teste d'une Femme que celle d'un Homme.

> [States are not governed by a beard or by an austere facial expression. They are governed by strength of mind and by the vigour and skill of Reason; and a mind can be as strong, and Reason as vigorous and skilful, in a woman's head as in a man's.][12]

Theories of intellectual and moral equality between the sexes are consistently toyed with, and are certainly not negligible in their attempt to redefine gender relations. They do, however, have to be treated with a certain caution, as one would treat a double-edged sword: while on the one hand these writings go a considerable way towards questioning the androcentric bias of society, on the other hand some (although not all) of their underlying principles can be seen to be as much of a disenablement as the exclusionist discourse, either once again founded on essentialisms such as *douceur*, *délicatesse*, portraying women as doubly strong and praiseworthy because 'naturally' weak, or relegating women to the sphere of the physical, the status of desired object, maintaining she rules by her beauty or physical traits.

As regards the ubiquitous discourse concerning the exercise of power by women, once again opinions are divided, although as with women in government the overriding attitude is negative. While on the one hand Louis himself warns his son against their pernicious influence,[13]

12 Pierre Le Moyne, *Gallerie des femmes fortes* (Paris: A. de Sommaville, 1647), p. 10. On the debate regarding gender and reason, particularly the idea that reason in women could prevent societal decay, since anti-violent and anti-militarist, see Timothy Reiss, 'Corneille and Cornelia: reason, violence and the cultural status of the feminine; or how a dominant discourse recuperated and subverted the advance of women', *Renaissance Drama*, 18 (1987), 3–41.

13 'Dès lors que vous donnez la liberté à une femme de vous parler des choses importantes, il est impossible qu'elles ne vous fassent faillir. La tendresse que nous avons pour elles, nous faisant goûter leurs plus mauvaises raisons, nous fait tomber insensiblement du côté où elles penchent, et la faiblesse qu'elles ont naturellement leur

on the other hand feminists such as Gerzan are laudatory of the role they play, maintaining that promotion of men or of families often depends on the power-broking of their womenfolk.[14]

Against this backdrop, where, if anywhere, does Racine fit in? Examination of the representation of Axiane and Athalie may throw some light on the different 'discursive elements' concerning gender relations which surface, consciously or unconsciously, in Racine's work.[15]

And Racine?

It is a commonplace by now to say that traces of Corneille can be seen in Racine's early plays. However, while this Cornelian heritage in often perceived in terms of language or the portrayal of heroism, one of the most striking links is in the representation of women. What Harriet Allentuch has said of Corneille's women could equally be applied to many of Racine's early female characters. Allentuch maintains that 'they pursue the characteristic Cornelian dream of complete self-mastery and strive like his heroes to shape their own destinies by the exercise of their will. [. . .] They assert, in play after play, [. . .] a desire to be judged by the same standards as men.'[16] As the following analysis shall indicate, it is precisely in this fashion that Racine portrays Axiane, a figure doubly interesting since entirely invented by the dramatist, although one which seems to have largely escaped critical attention.[17]

Early chars = Cornelian —

self-mastery, will

ALEX LE GRAND

eg. Axane

One of the ways in which both dramatists accord their female characters greater autonomy is by refusing to restrict them to a 'female' ethic. Racine, as Corneille had done before him, transcends the dis-

≠ no 'female' ethic

13 *cont.* fait presque toujours prendre le mauvais parti' [Whenever you give a woman the opportunity to talk to you about important matters, it is inevitable that you will be misadvised. The tenderness we feel for them inclines us to accept their worst reasoning, making us adopt their own point of view, and their natural weakness always makes them follow the wrong course of action]. *Mémoires* pour l'année 1667, cited in Marie-Odile Sweetser, 'Les femmes et le pouvoir dans le théâtre cornélien', in *Pierre Corneille* (Paris: PUF, 1985), pp. 605–14 (p. 606, n. 4).

14 François Du Soucy, sieur de Gerzan, *Le Triomphe des Dames* (Paris: chez l'autheur, 1646), pp. 143–5. See Carolyn Lougee, *Le Paradis des Femmes: Women, Salons and Social Stratification in Seventeenth-Century France* (Princeton: Princeton University Press, 1976), pp. 48–9.

15 I use the idea of discursive elements as defined by Foucault in his conception of discourse: 'We must conceive discourse as a series of discontinuous segments whose tactical function is neither uniform nor stable. To be more precise, we must not imagine a world of discourse divided between accepted discourse and excluded discourse, or between the dominant discourse and the dominated one; but as a multiplicity of discursive elements that can come into play in various strategies. It is this distribution that we must reconstruct'. Michel Foucault, *The History of Sexuality: An Introduction*, Vol. 1, trans. by Robert Hurley (New York: Pantheon, 1978), p. 100.

16 Harriet Allentuch, 'Reflections on Women in the Theater of Corneille', *Kentucky Romance Quarterly*, 21 (1974), 97–111 (p. 97).

17 For a critical bibliography of the play, see Jean Racine, *Alexandre le Grand*, ed. Michael Hawcroft and Valerie Worth (Exeter: University of Exeter Press, 1990), pp. xlvi–l.

course of what according to the *bienséance* is allowed for men and women; what are regarded as masculine and feminine universes may exist but they are not inhabited exclusively by the respective sexes. Male and female roles are reversed; the character most associated with *douceur*, usually perceived as a stereotypically female attribute, is Alexandre.[18] Similarly, from the outset of the play it appears that far from embodying any allegedly feminine ethic, Axiane is on the contrary more easily aligned with a masculine military ethic. It is she who incites others to war. This becomes apparent from the very first reference to her, when Taxile describes her reactions to Alexandre's arrival (*Alexandre le Grand*, Act I. 1, ll. 71–6).[19] Although his comments are marked by the neo-Platonist idea that women wield power through their beauty, an idea highlighted here by the language of *galanterie* used by her admirer, nonetheless her role is clear: 'elle met tout en armes'. Porus later reiterates the same idea, reminiscing on how her beauty inspired neighbouring kings to battle.[20] Interestingly, when it is given to Axiane herself to highlight her role, the emphasis on her beauty is dropped: although she is aware of the power she exerts over her two lovers, Racine nonetheless gives it to her to eschew the language which constructs her as an object of male desire, and which excludes her from the domain of real power. In her own speech, her emphasis is solely on her *gloire*. As she comments to Taxile:

> Il faut, s'il est vrai que l'on m'aime,
> Aimer la Gloire, autant que je l'aime moi-même . . .
> Il faut marcher sans crainte au milieu des alarmes;
> Il faut combattre, vaincre, ou périr sous les armes
> (*Alexandre le Grand*, Act IV. 3, ll. 1197–8, ll. 1201–2).[21]

The role she plays is clear, as she encourages Porus in his decision to fight (Act II. 5), announces her intention to try one last time to incite Taxile's men to battle (l. 667), and later tries to prompt Taxile himself to action (Act IV. 3, ll. 1225–8).

18 See for example ll. 185, 803, 1030, 1125. This association is of course further underpinned by a general contemporary move away from a military ethic towards one of pacifism, or away from heroism towards *tendresse* and *galanterie*.
19 Les beaux yeux d'Axiane, ennemis de la Paix,
  Contre votre Alexandre arment tous leurs attraits.
  Reine de tous les cœurs, elle met tout en armes,
  Pour cette liberté que détruisent ses charmes,
  Elle rougit des fers qu'on apporte en ces lieux,
  Et n'y saurait souffrir de tyrans que ses yeux. (*Alexandre le Grand*, Act I. 1, ll. 71–6).
20 C'est vous, je m'en souviens, dont les puissants appas,
  Excitaient tous nos Rois, les traînaient aux combats.
                (*Alexandre le Grand*, Act II. 5, ll. 651–2).
21 See also Act IV. 3, ll. 1225–8.

yet Ax ≠ warrior?
(R's novelty)

    Despite this alignment with a military ethic, Axiane certainly does not fit into the often-eroticized myth of the warrior woman found in some contemporary representations of Zénobie and Sémiramis. However, it is precisely the fact that she is not a *guerrière* which makes her most interesting. Racine subverts the idea that the association of women with military values is only possible in portrayals of the *guerrière*; instead he constructs the dramatic reality of a woman whose sense of heroism and *gloire* is inextricably linked to a military ethic, but who does not actively participate in battle.[22]

vs. Cléofile –
pacifist

    Axiane's character is thrown into relief by its stark contrast with that of Cléofile, whose value system is a direct antithesis to that of the Indian queen, and who represents the embodiment of sovereign Reason.[23] (Cléofile, as is well known, tries throughout the play to convince her brother Taxile not to fight Alexandre, with whom she is in love). Nowhere is this antithesis more apparent than in Act III. 1 which sees a confrontation between the two women. Resonances of enclosure, of control, and of the association of women with the interior, or private sphere, are evident from the opening lines of this central act when Axiane, furious, discovers that she has been confined within Taxile's camp:

> Quoi, Madame, en ces lieux on me tient enfermée?
> Je ne puis au combat voir marcher mon Armée?
>   (*Alexandre le Grand*, Act III. 1, ll. 685–6).

their confrontations

    The enormous divide between the two women is clear as Cléofile's argument that Taxile is only worried about Axiane's safety (implying that the battlefield clearly is no place for a woman), and that she can be tranquil and safe within the camp, evidently only further infuriates Axiane.[24] The confrontation with Cléofile can be read also as the

---

22 This is not to say of course that Racine necessarily applauds a military, or violent, ethic. On the contrary, as Timothy Reiss has shown, throughout *Alexandre le Grand*, Racine continually highlights the devastation and destruction inherent in any such ethic. See Reiss, 'Banditry, Madness and Sovereign Authority', passim.

23 *Ibid.*, p. 123.

24   Et c'est cette tranquillité
  Dont je ne puis souffrir l'indigne sûreté.
  Quoi lorsque mes sujets, mourant dans une plaine,
  Sur les pas de Porus combattent pour leur Reine,
  Qu'au prix de tout leur sang ils signalent leur foi,
  Que le cri des mourants vient presque jusqu'à moi,
  On me parle de Paix, et le Camp de Taxile
  Garde dans ce désordre une assiette tranquille.
      (*Alexandre le Grand*, Act III. 1, 703–10).
She later adds, 'Ah de ce camp, Madame, ouvrez-moi la barrière . . . ' (738).

confrontation of two ethics, one militarist, one pacifist, both represented here by a woman – further evidence of Racine's subversion of concepts of gendered universes; while there may be two opposing ethics, they are not gender-specific.

Axiane is also clearly an antithesis to Taxile, whom she openly castigates and even mocks throughout the play. Her sense of heroism is implicitly contrasted with his in III. 2 and in IV. 3 when she is evidently disgusted by his hesitancy to act (ll. 781–4 and 1229–32). She is aligned in the play only with Porus. This notion of an equality between them, an equal sense of *gloire* (misguided though it may be),[25] is highlighted in her monologue in Act IV. 2 where, believing Porus to be dead, she maintains that she too will seek death; as she says of Alexandre, in an apostrophe to Porus:

> Il me verra, toujours digne de toi,
> Mourir en reine, ainsi que tu mourus en roi
> (*Alexandre le Grand*, Act IV. 1, ll. 1031–2).

For Axiane, to die as a queen is the same as to die as a king, i.e. with one's *gloire* intact. She perceives her refusal to accept Alexandre's peace and her quest for immediate death as of an equal stature to Porus's death on the battlefield, since she perceives their *gloire* as of equal proportions.

Axiane's sense of heroism clearly influences her attitudes towards her throne and her sovereignty, attitudes which subvert the received idea of women's ambition and thirst for power. Axiane is furious when Taxile implies that her throne would become a gift from her enemies, and that her reign would hinge on an obligation to Alexandre: it becomes clear that she would rather not reign at all, than reign under those conditions (ll. 807–10, ll. 815–16). Interestingly, both Cléofile and Alexandre misjudge Axiane; both believe that Axiane, when offered what Cléofile calls 'l'empire' (l. 834) and what Alexandre refers to as 'trois diadèmes' (l. 870), will accept Taxile as a husband. Neither fully understands the importance to her of her *gloire*, and how she perceives it. Further light is thrown on the issue when she distinguishes between her own ambition and that of Alexandre, juxtaposing the fact that she and Porus were satisfied with their own states, with his policy of conquest, which, echoing Porus (ll. 529 ff.), she criticizes (ll. 110 2 ff.). This comparison is important since it further illuminates Axiane's motivations and makes her more sympathetic a character. Racine ensures that we do not accept unequivocally the portrait of the proud,

25 See Reiss, 'Banditry, Madness and Sovereign Authority', pp. 125–8 on the idea of false glory within the play.

hard, inflexible queen which the others paint of her, and points to the ambiguities within her character. Not only does her tirade to Alexandre implicitly support the idea that her militarism is associated more with a defence ideal, a defence of her states and her subjects,[26] but in addition her reference to Porus, and their mutual feelings ('charmés l'un de l'autre') indicates to what extent Axiane embodies not only a military ethic, but also an affective ethic. Furthermore, while her character for the most part hinges on the dynamic between the two, it seems at times, certainly in her monologue in IV. 1, that her love for Porus is more important to her than her *gloire*:

> J'expliquais mes soupirs en faveur de la Gloire,
> Je croyais n'aimer qu'elle. Ah pardonne, grand Roi,
> Je sens bien aujourd'hui que je n'aimais que toi
> (*Alexandre le Grand*, Act IV. 1, ll. 1010–12).

Through the alleged loss of Porus, Axiane then reaches a greater self-awareness.[27]

What ultimately defines Axiane, however, lies not in her militarism, nor in her love for Porus, but in her sense of self. In Alexandre's invitation to her to continue reigning (ll. 1166–9) and to reassure her states by choosing a husband (i.e. Taxile), Racine reminds us of the very common topos that an unmarried queen cannot reign on her own but must marry.[28] However, the dramatist imbues Axiane with a self-determination which overrides even her interest in her throne, and which is most clearly revealed in her resistance to the patriarchal order, her refusal to conform. While she never insists on her right to reign alone, she does, nevertheless, refuse to marry a man she does not

26 See also Act IV. 3, ll. 1226–7, where she incites Taxile to avenge their freedom and to defend their respective thrones.

27 It has often been remarked upon that there are no *confidentes* in *Alexandre le Grand*, and that it can be therefore more difficult than usual for spectators to pinpoint the characters' motivations or feelings (see for example Hawcroft and Worth (eds), *Alexandre le Grand*, pp. xxvi–xxvii). Racine then seems to attach a certain importance to Axiane by according her the only lengthy monologue in the play (48 lines), which does allow us to a certain extent to understand her character better. (The only other monologue in the play is Taxile's brief eight lines in Act IV. 5, which likewise nuances his character, since it is the first time we see him stirred to action.)

28 This recurrent theme in exclusionist discourse was adhered to among others by Bossuet: 'le peuple de Dieu n'admettoit pas à la succession le sexe qui est né pour obéir; et la dignité des maisons régnantes ne paraissoit pas assez soutenue en la personne d'une femme, qui après tout était obligée de se faire un maître en se mariant' [Christian people did not admit to rights of succession members of the sex which is born to obey; and the dignity of ruling houses did not appear to be adequately maintained in the person of a woman, who, in the last analysis, had to recognize a master when she married], Jacques-Bénigne Bossuet, *Politique tirée des propres paroles de l'Ecriture sainte*, ed. Jacques Le Brun (Geneva: Droz, 1967), p. 58.

love. Even when Taxile is finally provoked by her insults to reply with a vague threat, that her fate and indeed states, are essentially in his hands (ll. 1237–40), it falls on deaf ears; she continues her defiance until the very end – clearly preferring death to subjugation (ll. 1251–2), still railing against her confinement in the camp (l. 1397), challenging Alexandre (ll. 1448–50, ll. 1461–4), and refusing to be used as an object of barter or exchange.[29] Even after Taxile's death, Axiane is prepared to die, proclaiming her love for Porus (ll. 1543–6). Her autonomy as a person transcends even her role as sovereign, and as a young unmarried woman she can be read here, in the same fashion as Anne M. Menke has read the seventeenth-century widow, namely as 'a site of resistance to the political and sexual economies'.[30]

What makes this refusal even more remarkable is that it affects everyone. One of the criticisms aimed at Racine when this play appeared, and indeed to which the dramatist replied in his preface, was the idea that Alexandre was depicted as of lesser heroic stature than Porus.[31] The central character of the play has usually been seen to be one of these two or, more unusually, Cléofile.[32] However, it is arguable that much of the power is in fact in the hands of Axiane. Not only does she exert a large influence over Taxile and Porus and their respective fates, but most interestingly Cléofile and Alexandre are also implicated in her actions: Axiane's decision concerning Taxile indirectly affects the possibility of Alexandre's marriage to Cléofile. As Alexandre comments, regarding Taxile:

> Et puisque mon repos doit dépendre du sien
> Achevons son bonheur pour établir le mien
> (*Alexandre le Grand*, Act III. 6, ll. 983–4).

Since Cléofile's marriage requires Taxile's consent (l. 957), Alexandre's happiness depends on Taxile's, which in turn depends on Axiane. If Alexandre can persuade (or force) Axiane to marry Taxile, the latter would be more likely to favour the union between Alexandre and his sister. Cléofile, who initially persuaded Taxile not to fight Alexandre, and

29 See ll. 1429–70; while this passage (omitted in later editions) is somewhat ambivalent, her seeming acceptance (l. 1447) is undermined by the threats and challenges with which it is followed; furthermore since it becomes clear that she does not save Porus, it would seem that she adheres to her refusal.
30 Menke, 'The Widow Who Would Be Queen', p. 205.
31 According to Saint-Évremond for example, 'Il paraît qu'il a voulu donner une plus grande idée de Porus que d'Alexandre.' (Saint-Évremond, *Dissertation sur le grand Alexandre*, in Forestier, *Œuvres*, pp. 183–9 (p. 183)). For Racine's reply, see Forestier, *Œuvres*, p. 126.
32 For Cléofile's role, see Philippe Lacroix, 'Le langage de l'amour dans *Alexandre le Grand* de Racine', *XVIIᵉ siècle*, 146 (1985), 57–67 (p. 61), and Reiss, 'Banditry, Madness and Sovereign Authority'.

feels responsible on this account for the fact that her brother incurred
Axiane's scorn, is equally aware of the potential consequences of Axiane's
refusal on her own fate. As she comments regarding her brother:

> Tant que Porus vivra, que faut-il qu'il devienne?
> Sa perte est infaillible, et peut-être la mienne.
> Oui, oui, si son amour ne peut rien obtenir
> Il m'en rendra coupable, et m'en voudra punir
> *(Alexandre le Grand*, Act V. i, ll. 1333–6).

Twice Alexandre appears to grant Taxile power over Axiane (l. 869
and ll. 1418–20), but it becomes clear that it is an empty power (just as
Alexandre's own power is consistently thwarted by Axiane since he
insists in channelling it through Taxile); potentially bereft of her states,
a virtual prisoner, Axiane is nonetheless empowered by her refusal. It
is she who, at the centre of this chain reaction, is the controlling
mechanism. It is in fact only Taxile's death – the elimination of the
element which Axiane refused to accept – which finally restores
Alexandre's power to him in the final scene. The dynamics of power
then shift, as Alexandre decides the fate of Axiane and Porus. What is
particularly interesting about this fictional universe, is that while
Axiane's power throughout the play could have been portrayed as a
negative force, leading ultimately to her own death if Alexandre had
not spared Porus (since she was determined to die with him), and
allowing her self-determination and triumph only in death, Racine
on the contrary allows this young rebellious queen to triumph alive.
That this triumph is a necessary corollary of Racine's insistence that
the real subject matter of the play is the *générosité* of Alexandre,[33]
cannot entirely deprive it of significance. We are nonetheless presented
with a portrait of this central figure as a defiant and independent
queen, an agent of her own destiny and to a large extent that of others,
who insists on her autonomy as an individual as any male hero would.
While her capacity to rule is not explicitly discussed, this entirely
invented *souveraine* is depicted as successful and capable, interested in
the defence of her states; she is a character who exemplifies none of the
qualities common in exclusionist argumentation, who does not rule
solely through *douceur*, and whose representation subverts both gender
constructions of woman, and the concept of sovereignty as male. In a
century in which women are clearly excluded from the throne, it
seems to me that Racine manages to create a dramatic universe which
presents an alternative reality to that which predominates in the

---

33 Forestier, *Œuvres*, p. 26.

political, legal and even feminist discourses, without creating an exceptional or 'male' heroine.

If gender is implicitly an issue in *Alexandre le Grand*, it is clearly explicitly so in the powerful representation of the eponymous Athalie. While Axiane seems to have been much neglected by critics, Athalie's characterization, and moreover Athalie's depiction as sovereign, has certainly not escaped recent critical attention. What is most remarkable about the characterization of Athalie is the vast discrepancy between the reported discourse concerning her, and the impressions we receive of her both through her own speeches and through her actions on stage. It becomes clear in fact that Athalie's character can be analysed as a triptych of clearly demarcated (although interlocking) portraits: firstly the queen as she is represented by her enemies, secondly as she represents herself, and finally as she appears on stage – a triptych therefore which, broadly speaking, focuses on Athalie as monster, as sovereign and as woman. It is along these three lines that this analysis shall proceed.

The images of the queen which predominate in the first act (which are all reported since of course Athalie is entirely absent throughout the act) are those of a bloodthirsty, vengeful figure. In describing the massacre of the princes, Josabet comments:

> Un poignard à la main l'implacable Athalie
> Au carnage animait ses barbares Soldats,
> Et poursuivait le cours de ses assassinats
> > (*Athalie*, Act I. 2, ll. 244–6).

Racine reminds us of this role of hers by reiterating the same gory image later, referring to her preparations to attack the temple with her troops (l. 1537). References to her rage, her cruelty and her fury pepper the text, as do allusions to her as *impie, insolente* and *injuste*. The monstrosity of her actions is highlighted since the princes were her own descendants: Athalie is not only a murderer but an infanticide – 'une mère en fureur' (l. 1295). She has (in the past at least) smothered all maternal instinct, and has acted against 'Nature'. Her own maternal lineage is frequently evoked pejoratively by her opponents, who refer to her as 'de Jézabel la fille sanguinaire' (l. 59), 'cette autre Jézabel' (l. 761) and 'de Jézabel la Fille meurtrière' (l. 1329). This portrait of Athalie, hardly surprisingly one propagated by her enemies, contrasts hugely with the Athalie whom we initially see in the play; this contrast is itself highlighted by the differences between her reported entrance into the temple in Act II. 1, and her actual entrance in Act II. 2 and account of the same incident. In Zacharie's account, her violation of convention is highlighted:

Une Femme . . . Peut-on la nommer sans blasphème?
Une Femme . . . C'était Athalie elle-même.
[. . .]
Dans un des parvis aux hommes réservé
Cette Femme superbe entre le front levé,
Et se préparait même à passer les limites
De l'enceinte sacrée ouverte aux seuls Lévites
                    (*Athalie*, Act II. 3, ll. 395–6, 397–400).

The idea of spatial, religious and gender transgression (the latter empha-
sized by Racine's use of anaphora) are highlighted by Joad's immediate
outburst,[34] which apparently she greets with an 'œil farouche.'

All this contrasts radically with her actual arrival on stage, clearly a
distracted and anxious figure. Her opening words are of *trouble, faiblesse*,
and impotence ('je ne puis'); she appears dependent on her male
advisers (sending for Mathan immediately, and later insisting that
Abner stay), and in constant pursuit of peace which clearly escapes her
(ll. 435–8). It also contrasts with her account of her visit to the temple,
in which it becomes clear that she was motivated by 'la frayeur', and
by instinct, anxious not to blaspheme (as Zacharie (l. 408) had earlier
presumed), but to pacify the god of the Jews by offering him gifts
(ll. 526–9). What is reported then as her defiant transgression in one
account becomes the efforts of an anxious woman to ward off danger
in her own account (not that the two are necessarily mutually
exclusive). While flashes of Athalie's authority and pride continue to
appear throughout this first appearance of hers (II. 3–II. 7), nonetheless the overriding image is one of confusion and anxiety. To what
extent this second portrait is essentially one of Athalie as stereotypical
Woman is a point to which I shall return below. Suffice to say here
that by continually reminding his spectators that the images of Athalie
as monster are belied by the anxious, troubled character with which
we are presented for the most part, Racine highlights the ambiguities
in Athalie's character, and manages to evoke considerable sympathy
for his heroine.[35]

---

34 Reine, sors, a-t-il dit, de ce lieu redoutable,
      D'où te bannit ton sexe et ton impiété.
                    (*Athalie*, Act III. 3, ll. 404–5).
35 Bruneau concurs with this idea when she indicates how Racine undermines the
biblical version of the story by allowing Athalie to give her own account, and by
representing her opposing clan as 'méchant, injuste, fanatique et contradictoire'. See
Marie-Florine Bruneau, *Racine, le jansénisme et la modernité* (Paris: Corti, 1986), pp. 125–7.
See also Zimmermann (*La Liberté et le Destin*, pp. 137–9), who highlights the unease
within the play, and the similarities between the orders which Joad and Athalie
represent.

The third aspect of Athalie's characterization, the queen as sovereign, plays a vital role in her self-definition and representation. As Grégoire indicates in a stimulating article concerning the patriarchal law in *Esther* and *Athalie*, the monarchical maxim of 'une foi, une loi, un roi,' to which Racine adhered is unwittingly undermined by another reality throughout these two plays which could be summed up as 'des fois, des lois, des reines'.[36] In this respect, her key speech of II. 5 is particularly revelatory, and merits lengthy quotation:

> Je ne veux point ici rappeler le passé
> Ni vous rendre raison du sang que j'ai versé.
> Ce que j'ai fait, Abner, j'ai cru le devoir faire.
> Je ne prends point pour juge un peuple téméraire;
> Quoi que son insolence ait osé publier,
> Le Ciel même a pris soin de me justifier.
> Sur d'éclatants succès ma puissance établie
> A fait jusqu'aux deux Mers respecter Athalie.
> Par moi Jérusalem goûte un calme profond
> Le Jourdain ne voit plus d'Arabe vagabond
> Ni l'altier Philistin, par d'éternels ravages,
> Comme au temps de vos Rois, désoler ses rivages;
> Le Syrien me traite et de Reine et de Sœur.
> Enfin de ma Maison le perfide Oppresseur,
> Qui devait jusqu'à moi pousser sa barbarie,
> Jéhu, le fier Jéhu, tremble dans Samarie;
> De toutes parts pressé par un puissant Voisin,
> Que j'ai su soulever contre cet Assassin,
> Il me laisse en ces lieux souveraine maîtresse.
> Je jouissais en paix du fruit de ma sagesse.
>   (*Athalie*, Act II. 5, ll. 465–84).

In her version of past events, there is no elaborate justification of her past actions, but rather a brief indication that she was motivated by a notion (misguided or other) of duty (l. 467). Elaborating some scenes later, she justifies her actions in terms of vengeance – an eye for an eye, a tooth for a tooth – and self-defence:

> Oui, ma juste fureur, et j'en fais vanité,
> A vengé mes Parents sur ma postérité. [. . .]
> Où serais-je aujourd'hui, si domptant ma faiblesse
> Je n'eusse d'une Mère étouffé la tendresse,
> Si de mon propre sang ma main versant des flots
> N'eût par ce coup hardi réprimé vos complots?
>   (*Athalie*, Act II. 7, ll. 709–10, ll. 723–6).

36 Vincent Grégoire, 'La femme et la loi dans la perspective des pièces bibliques raciniennes représentées à Saint-Cyr', *XVIIᵉ siècle*, 179 (1993), 323–36 (p. 323).

As Bruneau comments, '[elle] n'a fait que obéir à la loi juive du talion'.[37]

Secondly, what also becomes apparent in II. 5 is that contrary to Joad's perception (l. 73), Athalie clearly perceives herself not as the usurper but rather the legitimate ruler, an idea with which seventeenth-century political thought would have concurred. In the many seventeenth-century political treatises which broached the questions of tyranny, usurpation and political legitimacy, it was commonly upheld, as is well known, that a usurper whose reign was successful became in time legitimate.[38] Racine ensures that what emerges from Athalie's speech is precisely the image of a successful recent reign, which she in turn interprets as divine justification of her actions, and hence proof of her legitimacy.[39] References to the success, power, respect, calm, peace, wisdom of the queen are juxtaposed with the mention of the ravages of previous kings, a juxtaposition underlined by the subversion of the *roi/père* topos of patriarchal thought to *reine/sœur*. It is of further interest to note that this success is depicted as founded on political skill and ability: Athalie has created a situation politically, through the creation of a powerful alliance, which Jéhu cannot change, and which protects her and her subjects from him. The authority of this *souveraine maîtresse,* and the association of her reign with peace and calm, clearly do not spring from any male-constructed so-called female *douceur* but rather from her political skill. Certainly, no description of any reign could be more opposed to the common topos of female government as being synonymous with chaos and disarray, *le monde à l'envers*. Later in the scene a certain political astuteness is once again hinted at, as she outlines what appears to be politically expedient tolerance in her treatment of the Jewish priests:

> Vos Prêtres, je veux bien, Abner, vous l'avouer,
> Des bontés d'Athalie ont lieu de se louer.
> Je sais sur ma conduite et contre ma puissance
> Jusqu'où de leurs discours ils portent licence.
> Ils vivent cependant, et leur Temple est debout.
>
> (*Athalie,* Act II. 7, ll. 593–7).

---

37 Bruneau *Racine, le jansénisme et la modernité*, p. 130.

38 As Bossuet comments, '[Des] empires quoique violents, injustes et tyranniques d'abord, par la suite des temps et par le consentement des peuples peuvent devenir légitimes.' [Empires which are violent, unjust and tyrannical initially, can in time and with the consent of the people become legitimate] (*Politique tirée des propres paroles,* p. 50).

39 The situation is of course made more complex by the sacred context of the play. On legitimacy, see Zimmermann, *La Liberté et le Destin,* pp. 40–1.

Aware of the priests' criticisms of her and her power, she turns a blind eye, prepared to allow different creeds within her kingdom in order to maintain stability. However, Athalie is not prepared to do so any more if pushed to the limit, and is unafraid to exercise her authority and to ensure she is obeyed; as she comments to Abner, 'Je puis, quand je voudrai, parler en Souveraine' (l. 592).[40]

Be that as it may, apart from rare flashes of authority such as this, it is clear that for the most part, Athalie's political skill is portrayed as an attribute of the past, to be implicitly contrasted with her political errors of the present.[41] Her considered and swift judgement is now replaced by fatal indecision, a metamorphosis due less to her dream than to her encounter with Joas. While clearly disturbed by her dream (which explains the inhabitual behaviour to which Abner (ll. 51–2) referred to), she is also aware of the dangers, and orders Mathan to round up her Tyrian mercenaries (ll. 615–16). However, it is following her encounter with Joas that she most hesitates, giving rise to Nabal's and Mathan's comments regarding 'ses voeux irrésolus' (l. 869) and 'son courroux chancelant, incertain' (l. 885) – an indecision all the more surprising since she is aware that Joad knows more about Joas's origins than he pretends (ll. 909–10). It is the physical presence of Joas apparently that has altered Athalie. It is left to Mathan to sum up this change:

> Ami, depuis deux jours je ne la connais plus.
> Ce n'est plus cette reine éclairée, intrépide,
> Elevée au-dessus de son sexe timide,
> Qui d'abord accablait ses ennemis surpris
> Et d'un instant perdu connaissait tout le prix.
> La peur d'un vain remords trouble cette grande âme.
> Elle flotte, elle hésite, en un mot: elle est femme.
>
> (*Athalie*, Act III. 3, ll. 870–6).

Athalie was then, in the past, beyond her sex (here constructed by Racine as the weaker); according to her adviser (and, it would seem, to Racine), her fearlessness, political awareness and astuteness are qualities that are essentially beyond women, just as success as a sovereign is not a female prerogative. Athalie is exceptional to her sex, in a way Axiane

---

40 For a similar analysis of Athalie as monarch see Bruneau (*Racine, le jansénisme et la modernité*, pp. 127–31) and Jean-Marie Apostolidès *Le Prince sacrifié* (Paris: Minuit, 1985), p. 128. It is also noteworthy that the idea of Athalie as a successful sovereign has no foundation in the Bible and is an invention of Racine's.
41 This is, of course, on one level, part of the divine order since Joad has prayed to God that she become confused and imprudent (ll. 290–4).

never was. Where Athalie was in the past beyond her sex, she is now stereotypical Woman, identifiable by her hesitancy and fear.

This idea of her being beyond her sex is constructed within the play along two (related) axes. Firstly she is perceived as exceptional and can rule solely because she plays a male role; secondly it is precisely in smothering all so-called female instinct that she succeeded as she did. As we have seen, she herself has earlier referred to her necessity to smother all maternal instinct; it is the interview with Joas which awakens it:

> Quel prodige nouveau me trouble et m'embarrasse?
> La douceur de sa voix, son enfance, sa grâce,
> Font insensiblement à mon inimitié
> Succèder . . . Je serais sensible à la pitié?
> (*Athalie*, Act II. 7, ll. 651–4).

Nonetheless, lest spectators become too sympathetic towards his anti-heroine, Racine incorporates elements of her own greed and vanity into her downfall. To my mind, however, it is debatable what importance should be attached to her greed (which prior to Act V merits one brief mention (l. 48)) in her entrance into the temple;[42] it seems on the contrary that Racine, having built up considerable sympathy for Athalie, not least by his (unwitting?) portrayal of the so-called original legitimate order as represented by Joad as intolerant and fanatical, needs now to justify her death, and so once again emphasizes her pride and greed.

Ultimately, what defines Athalie is not her depiction as monster, or as sovereign, or as woman, but a complex interplay of all three. On one level, it is arguable that she dies because she is no longer a 'monster', because she allows her smothered so-called emotional feminine qualities to resurface and decide her actions. According to Grégoire, as a 'man' Athalie could rule; however 'redevenue femme', and therefore caught up by her emotions, she can no longer enforce the royal law.[43] This return to her so-called femininity is signalled not only by her maternal reaction to Joas, and her *trouble*, but also by her loss of political astuteness which Racine reflects in her lack of wariness regarding what all seventeenth-century theorists warned consistently against: the perfidious, flattering adviser.[44]

---

42 For a more negative reading of Athalie's arrival in the temple, see Dubu's chapter 'La Venue au Temple' in Jean Dubu, *Racine aux miroirs* (Paris: SEDES, 1992), pp. 199–406.
43 Grégoire, 'La femme et la loi', p. 333. See also Zimmermann, *La Liberté et le Destin*, p. 143.
44 Racine often reminds us of Mathan's role in Athalie's downfall. Referred to as 'plus méchant qu'Athalie' (l. 36), it is he who has put it into her head in the first place that

On another more profound level though, it can be argued that Athalie dies not because of her return to what essentially is a gender construction of Woman, but rather because she is, in reality, a woman in power, a threat to the patriarchy which must be removed. As Bruneau indicates:

or because she is a ♀ in power + must be removed?

> si Athalie est exclue par les Juifs, c'est bien sûr parce qu'elle sert d'autres dieux que le leur, mais d'une autre façon bien plus rédhibitoire, parce qu'elle est femme et qu'elle échappe à la domestication patriarcale et à la symbolisation monothéiste.

> [if Athalie is excluded by the Jews, it is of course because she serves other gods than theirs, but in another more damning way, because she is a woman and because she escapes patriarchal domestication and monotheist symbolization.][45]

Furthermore, in sacrificing her to the patriarchy, Racine paradoxically questions its tenets. According to Grégoire, Racine weakens both the prestige of the patriarchal order and its law, and paradoxically invites reflection on the nature of power, and those who exercise it.[46] Despite Athalie's sometime power, she finishes stripped of both her sovereign authority and power, and is subverted back into the patriarchy by the *dénouement* of the play: it is through the *dénouement* then that Racine ultimately upholds the patriarchy.

In sacrificing Ath to patriarchy, R. ?s its tenets, then reaffirms it...

Now while the purpose of this chapter is certainly not to compare these two radically different plays, it does seem justifiable to say that what was possible to dramatize as a reality in 1665 no longer was the case in 1691. Nonetheless, I cannot agree with Jean Dubu, who maintains that *Athalie* clearly indicates that women are unable to exercise political power.[47] While that is ultimately what the *dénouement* implies, we cannot neglect the constant references to the past success of this *souveraine*. In fact, one of the ambiguities of the play is that Racine has in fact demonstrated that women *can* rule. What he seems to imply, however, is that they *should not*. Theory and practice unwittingly collide.

nb in Ath R does insist that ♀ can rule

...but should not!

To conclude very briefly, it seems to me that the exclusionist discourse examined at the beginning is, to varying extents and in different ways, undermined by these two plays of Racine's. In this respect Racine joins a host of other playwrights who, consciously or unconsciously, question the epistemological paradigms of the dominant discourses

17th c. so; exclusionist discourse = undermined

there is a treasure (ll. 49–50), whose plotting it is feared by Joad (l. 1097), whose lies to the queen incite her to take action (ll. 888–94).

45 Bruneau, *Racine, le jansénisme et la modernité*, p. 135.

46 Grégoire, 'La femme et la loi', p. 336.

47 Jean Dubu, *Racine aux miroirs*, p. 388.

of their own society. The 'known fact' that women cannot rule is challenged, the fact that women are 'by nature' excluded from power is therefore challenged, and alternative possibilities are presented.

5

Constructions of Identity: Mirrors of the 'Other' in Racine's Theatre

JANE CONROY

Julian Huxley has provided us with a negative formulation of the relationship between the Other and the creation of collective self-identity: 'A nation is a society united by a common error as to its origin and a common aversion to its neighbours.' However, in considering Racine's plays as cultural narratives, I should prefer to adopt two more positive lines of thought from Paul Ricœur which are not, of course, exclusively his. Firstly, the notion of narrative identity: the belief that we create a sense of self through our narratives of our own life experience, that this is a shifting 'récit' which perforce requires another to be the hearer. And, of course, that on the macro level this shifting narrative is part of the process of definition of collective identity.[1] One can view the characters in tragedy as performing in front of us this act of narrative identity construction. This is particularly true in Racine's tragedies with their well-known primacy of *Logos* over *Praxis*, or where in fact *Logos* is *Praxis*. Secondly, the idea that the past, as narrated by one or many, is not a burden on the present, but requires us to acknowledge it: what Ricœur calls the 'debt to the dead'.[2] And he emphasizes its role in determining a future. Through dramatizations of historical consciousness Racine, like others, rehearses answers to the questions: 'who are we?' and 'what may we become?' To quote Louis van Delft:

<figure>
[Handwritten marginal notes:]
Other + creation of collective self-identity

∃ narrative ident. ⊆ collective id.

esp in Racine. Logos = Praxis

∃ need to recog past + its role in determining future
</figure>

My thanks go to Tom Duddy and Colm Luibhéid for, respectively, discussion of matters philosophical and classical. Any misinterpretations are entirely my own work.
1 See particularly: Paul Ricœur, *Temps et récit. III. Le temps raconté* (Paris: Editions du Seuil, 1985), pp. 355–9, 371–4; and *Soi-même comme un autre* (Paris: Editions du Seuil, 1990), 5th and 6th 'études'.
2 Ricœur, *Temps et récit. III*, Ch. 3 'La réalité du passé historique', Ch. 5, 'L'entrecroisement de l'histoire et de la fiction'.

À l'instar du navigateur, tout individu, pour survivre, a besoin de se repérer: il lui faut avant tout se situer lui-même, situer autrui, se situer par rapport à autrui.[. . .] Or, l'aventure existentielle se ramène, pour l'essentiel, à des rapports à autrui, à une constellation de rapports psychologiques.

[Like the navigator, for survival all individuals need to be able to locate themselves: they need above all to situate themselves, others, and themselves in relation to others . . . As it happens, the existential adventure comes down in essence to a question of relations with others, and to a myriad of different psychological connections][3]

One aspect of Racine's enterprise, and the legacy of his tragedies, is to provide a terrain for this exploration, along with a series of route-maps. In particular the figure of the stranger, in a variety of forms, places within the plays a device for heightening the sense of self and other. I shall deal briefly with collective ethnic groups, then individual 'strangers', before considering the specific case of *Bajazet* as an extended instance of 'rapprochement' through 'mise à distance', and in conclusion I shall look at its relationship with *Mithridate*.

The use of the collective 'Other' as a foil for the collective 'Us' was not a new enterprise. Self-definition through tragedy has a long history. Of the one thousand Greek tragedies estimated to have been composed in the fifth century BC, some three hundred have left traces. Nearly half of these portrayed barbarian characters, or were set in a non-Greek land, or both. Even those with an all-Greek cast display 'a pervasive rhetorical polarization between Greeks and Barbarians'. They forged a discourse of the 'other', built on a 'complex system of signifiers denoting the ethically, politically and psychologically "other"' with lasting consequences, especially in their 'portrait of the Asiatic peoples as effeminate, despotic and cruel'.[4] When it comes to their approach to pitting the 'then-and-there' of the foreigner against the 'here-and-now' of the audience, the most salient difference between the Greek dramatists and Racine is that Racine does not bring his own nation on stage. On the level of collective identity the comparisons between French and foreigner remain implicit.

A glance at Charles Bernet's vocabulary analysis[5] confirms the textual existence of a wide range of ancient and more modern peoples

3 *Littérature et anthropologie* (Paris: PUF, 1993), pp. 88–9. Of particular interest here is the section on the 'caractères des nations' where the moral profiling of nations is envisaged as a cartography of human nature: the character of a particular race, in its particular geographical place, becomes a 'lieu' [topos] in the rhetorical sense.
4 Edith Hall, *Inventing the Barbarian. Greek Self-definition through Tragedy* (Oxford: Clarendon, 1989), p. 2.
5 *Le vocabulaire des tragédies de Jean Racine* (Genève–Paris: Slatkine–Champion, 1983). See pp. 307–14.

in the plays: Romans, Greeks, Jews, Trojans (naturally), but how many other races, tribes, 'nations' are pulled from their relative obscurity, their distant fastnesses, or the oblivion which befalls the conquered: Chaldeans, Dacians, Indians, Parthians, Pannonians, Phrygians, Sarmatians, Scythians, Syrians, Thebans, Tyrians, and so on? Often, it is true, just a passing nod to local colour. Some are barely named, without so much as a qualifying adjective, for example in Mithridate's tirade where the Dacians and Pannonians are one-dimensional participants in the imaginary coalition which will include the Spanish, and 'surtout' the Gaulois, who have already been hammering at the gates of Rome (*Mithridate*, Act III. 1, ll. 790–862). It is flattering that the great Mithridate should count the Gaulois among the forces to reckon with in 63 BC, alongside 'la fière Germanie'.[6] Their textual presence serves to enhance the sense of an impending *Götterdämmerung*: Rome's later downfall is already written, pre-presented in an enumeration of potentially insurgent provinces and kingdoms. An allusion which functions as the most succinct form of 'prolepse externe', anticipating the culmination of a strand of the plot, a culmination which lies beyond the boundary of the narrative proper.[7]

Aside from the exoticism of any non-Roman, non-Hellenic, non-Jewish, and hence 'uncivilized' peoples of Antiquity, and aside from the contemporary Ottoman Empire, other non-ethnic figures flit around the edges of Racine's stage. In the spread of identities running from the totally aberrational to the highly civilized, monsters, giants and brigands compose a sub-group representative of the moral outer limits. Louis van Delft,[8] followed by Maurice Delcroix,[9] among others, has shown how Racine makes use of monsters from *La Thébaïde* through to *Athalie*. To the disturbing question 'How would we be if we were not what we are?' the ancient study of teratology used to provide a ready answer: we would be monsters. History intimated we would be

6 Racine's audience would probably have been familiar with the arguments which established the French as ancestors of the Germans (rather than the reverse, as was thought 'outre-Rhin'). Here the less active role is that attributed to the latter, who await a leader, whereas the Gaulois have already breached the walls of Rome.

7 It is an instance of what one might call *prememoration*, where historical tragedy embraces the known 'future'. In Jacques Truchet's words, 'il n'est de tragédie que prophétique' [all tragedy is prophetic], and in its temporal sweep history meets future and, beyond human time, eternity. For this particularly French view of tragedy, see Jacques Truchet, *La Tragédie classique en France* (Paris: PUF, 1975, 1989, 1997), p. 28.

8 In *Racine. Mythes et Réalités*, Actes du Colloque de la Société d'étude du XVIIᵉ siècle and University of Western Ontario, 1974, special no., *XVIIᵉ siècle* (1976), 11–24.

9 Maurice Delcroix, 'La poétique du monstre dans le théâtre de Racine', in Christine M. Hill (ed.), *Théâtre et Poésie*. Actes du 3ᵉ colloque Vinaver (Leeds: Francis Cairns, 1991), pp. 175–90.

barbarians. Psychiatry would later suggest we would be psychopaths.[10]
Racine's monsters, chillingly internalized, lie somewhere between history
and psychiatry. As for his brigands, so famously slain by Thésée, leaving
none for Hippolyte, despite their rather unimpressive numbers,[11] they
deserve mention because as early 'hors-la-loi', they represent another
extreme figure of a-social barbarity.[12]

If we turn to the micro level, to those individual 'étrangers' who
actually appear on Racine's stage, their position is variable. What
follows here is not an exhaustive list, merely a survey of the most
revealing 'cas de figure'. Each of his 'strangers' provides a new 'foyer',
a particularly clear conflicting focus within the play. Each is a vocal
incarnation of that 'contrapuntalism' advocated by Edward Said.[13]
Whether they are right or wrong, good or evil, they embody another
civilization and speak with distinctive opposing voices. Racine, through
them, heightens the effect of 'heteroglossia', to use Bakhtin's term.[14]
They may be hated figures, the most recent product of an evil race –
Athalie, Aman – or the sad figure of a virtuous displaced person, a
captive, an exile. Each of them, as called upon by the conventions of
tragedy, and the need for exposition, recounts their story, each constructing, as do other major characters, their own 'identité narrative'.
An extreme case is, of course, Andromaque, whose ineradicable
recollection determines present and future.

Among these 'étrangers', the dominant figure of foreignness is,
unsurprisingly, female. Unsurprisingly, given the patrilocal practices

10 This paraphrases Maurice Daumas's answer to the same question (*La tendresse
amoureuse, XVIe–XVIIIe siècles* (Paris: Perrin, 1996), p. 202). It was not until the nineteenth
century that scientists finally concluded that there was no such species as *homo monstruosus*.
11 Apart from being twice mentioned in *Phèdre*, they are referred to only once, when
Mithridate recalls the Romans' willingness to follow Spartacus: 'S'ils suivent au
combat des Brigands qui les vengent, / De quelle noble ardeur pensez-vous qu'ils se
rangent / Sous les drapeaux d'un Roi longtemps victorieux, / Qui voit jusqu'à Cyrus
remonter ses Aïeux?' (*Mithridate*, Act III. 1, ll. 823–6).
12 They also provide me with a tenuous if not very flattering Irish link: Ménage
derives the word from the 'Brigantes, peuples d'Hybernie, qui sous l'Empire Romain
passerent en Angleterre où ils ravagerent toute la partie Septentrionale' [Brigantes, a
people of Hibernia, who at the time of the Roman Empire moved to England, where
they destroyed the entire North (*Les Origines de la langue françoise*, 1650, article 'Brigands').
He was aware of the rival etymologies proposed by Nicot and by Fauchet (*Traité de la
Milice*). Modern scholarship has absolved the Hibernians and given the etymology, and
the blame, to mediaeval Italy, the currently accepted etymology being *brigante*, irregular
soldier. My wish to bring this in here is an illustration of how we, like Racine's
audiences, scrutinize his texts for every scintilla of reference to ourselves, with which
to build our identities.
13 See his *Culture and Imperialism* (New York: A. A. Knopf, 1993).
14 For Bakhtin on dialogism, see 'Discourse in the Novel' in Michael Holquist (ed.),
The Dialogic Imagination: Four Essays by M. M. Bakhtin, trans. by Caryl Emerson and
Michael Holquist (Austin: University of Texas Press, 1981), pp. 259–422.

of the civilizations evoked by Racine, and which the married women in his audience could readily understand: Bérénice, Monime, Phèdre, Esther, Athalie, possibly Roxane, are where they are because of marriage, or plans to marry. Some are captives. The captive is not always foreign (Aricie), the foreigner is not always captive (obviously), but when the foreigner *is* captive, as in the case of Andromaque, Racine can mine the rich paradoxes inherent in her political vulnerability yet erotic or sentimental hold over her captor:

> Étrangère . . . Que dis-je ? Esclave dans l'Épire,
> Je lui donne son Fils, mon Âme, mon Empire
> *(Andromaque*, Act II. 5, ll. 689–90).

Andromaque herself is an early instance of a motif which was to flourish in later literature, especially 'littérature fantastique', a piece of deadly exotica brought home, a 'souvenir de la Guerre de Troie', a psychological Trojan horse, which destroys the peace and life of its acquirer.

Among the exiles, the greatest pathos attaches to Bérénice whose exile is self-imposed, or imposed by love, but whose foreignness is an insuperable bar to integration. Roman xenophobia, as explained by Paulin, forever excludes her:

> Rome par une Loi, qui ne se peut changer,
> N'admet avec son sang aucun sang étranger
> *(Bérénice*, Act II. 2, ll. 377–8).

It is a law which by another neat paradox turns Titus into an alien in the Imperial City: 'Gémissant dans ma Cour, et plus exilé qu'elle' (Act III. 1, l. 752). But the pathos is largely concentrated on the isolated Queen of Palestine, producing that 'pitié née de l'affliction' of which Christian Biet speaks in his contribution to this volume:

> Étrangère dans Rome, inconnue à la Cour,
> Elle passe ses jours, Paulin, sans rien prétendre
> Que quelque heure à me voir, et le reste à m'attendre
> *(Bérénice*, Act II. 2, ll. 534–6).

The resonances of these lines were no doubt particularly strong for the foreign princesses at Versailles, as was the situation of that other exile, Esther, and of the equally exiled daughters of Sion, with which, like many a foreign-born queen, she has surrounded herself:

> Jeunes et tendres fleurs, par le sort agitées,
> Sous un ciel étranger comme moi transplantées
> *(Esther*, Act I. 1, ll. 103–4).

It is identity, or rather the concealment of identity, of 'sa race et son pays' which provides the mainspring of the plot, and which of course inspired Voltaire's caustic comment on 'un roi insensé qui a passé six mois avec sa femme, sans savoir, sans s'informer même qui elle est'.[15]

Monime, as an Ephesian, descended from 'ou Rois, Seigneur, ou Héros, qu'autrefois / Leur vertu chez les Grecs mit au-dessus des Rois' (*Mithridate*, I. 3, ll. 249–50), considers herself to be an 'esclave couronnée' (I. 3, l. 255) among the less thoroughly hellenized followers of Mithridate. Her situation, and struggle for autonomy, is a *mise en abyme* of one of the projects of tragedy: the recognition and definition of a personal, and collective, identity, in the midst of a world which for her is filled with foreignness.

It is only in *Esther* that the term 'race' is used to mean 'nation', or ethnic group. Elsewhere it means 'house' or 'blood-line'. The determinism associated with that needs no further commentary, except (since we are dealing with 'alterité') to note the horror of mixed blood, or fear of miscegenation, expressed, for example, through Joas and Phèdre. In the mixed race, it is the worse blood which triumphs. One explanation for the future degeneration of Joas may well be the rôle of flatterers, and the corrupting effect of absolute power, which as Joad warns, 'ont des rois égaré le plus sage' (*Athalie*, Act IV. 3, ll. 1387–1402). The other, and more disturbing, explanation is the one suggested by Athalie. Joas, indeed, one day will be as she hopes 'fidèle au sang d'Achab' (*Athalie*, Act V. 6, l. 1786). Her dying wish presages the later evils committed by the now polluted blood of David. Similarly Phèdre is dominated by Pasiphaë's legacy: 'Phèdre est d'un sang, Seigneur, vous le savez trop bien . . .' (*Phèdre*, Act IV. 2, l. 1151).[16]

The quest for identity is expressed in anxiety about origins, most obviously in Ériphile, the 'fille sans patrie', the serially rejected outcast of *Iphigénie*, who nonetheless contrives to find sources of unhappiness more profound even than her status as 'étrangère, inconnue et captive'. The case of Éliacin-Joas is quite different: however crucial the revelation of his identity is to others, he personally experiences no anguish at being without knowledge of his genealogy or homeland since he has found adoptive parents, and sanctuary – 'Ce Temple est mon pays; je n'en connais point d'autre' (*Athalie*, Act II. 7, l. 640). Almost as bad as having the wrong origins, of being, say, of the 'race de Laïus' (*La Thébaïde*, Act I. 1, l. 28), or 'fils d'Atrée' (*Iphigénie*, Act V. 4, l. 1686),

15 *Le Siècle de Louis XIV* (Paris: Garnier–Flammarion, 1966), i, p. 358.
16 In a more socially conscious way, one reason for Bajazet to refuse Roxane is his horror at the thought of allying his Ottoman blood with an 'Esclave attachée à ses seuls intérêts' (Act II. 5, l. 719).

or 'de Jézabel la fille' (*Athalie*, Act I.1, l. 59), is having the obscurest sort. Of Roxane, it is almost impossible to say what her origins are, from where she has 'arrived': 'Esclave barbare' (*Bajazet*, Act V. 8, l. 1658) – the epithet is Atalide's – her status as former slave makes her as much an alien as Athalie. A double maxim in Corneille's *Cinna* summarizes the irremediable nature of such exclusion:

> Jamais un Affranchi n'est qu'un esclave infâme;
> Bien qu'il change d'état, il ne change point d'âme
> (*Cinna*, Act IV. 6, ll. 1409–10).

There is, finally, Athalie, usurper and idolator, 'impie étrangère'. The figure of the stranger is here the means of expression of a radical separation from even the closest kin:

> David m'est en horreur, et les fils de ce Roi
> Quoique nés de mon sang, sont étrangers pour moi
> (*Athalie*, Act II. 7, ll. 729–30).

It is an alienation which enables her to 'veng[er] [s]es Parents sur [s]a postérité' (Act II. 7, l. 710). But it is, as we know, 'la fille d'Achab' who is the true stranger. Stranger to the Jews, and estranged from herself. Controlled by the 'impitoyable Dieu' of the Jews, and 'vingt fois en un jour à [s]oi-même opposée' (Act V. 6, ll. 1774, 1776).

It is, ultimately, this internalization of the sense of alien otherness which dominates Racine's exploitation of the connotations of words such as 'étranger', 'barbare', 'monstre', and the struggles of a 'moi-même à moi-même opposée'. He constructs, through the *dramatis personae*, and the 'para-personnages', a continuum extending from *soi-même/nous autres* to the extremes of alien otherness. This sliding scale measures difference on both the collective and the individual level. It implicitly positions the subjects of Louis XIV at the opposite pole to, let us say, the Scythians who, proverbially, lie beyond the limits of civilization, or those seemingly civilized monsters who flourished in Rome itself: 'Caligula, Néron / Monstres . . . / . . . qui ne conservant que la figure d'Homme . . .' (*Bérénice*, Act II. 2, ll. 397–9). But also the 'Other' is the other-who-oppresses-me. Perhaps an-other. Or perhaps oneself. Through a characteristically Racinian process of inter-nalization, the Scythian, or the monster, or the barbarian, lurks within the individual consciousness.[17] The continuum is in the heart and mind of man, the barbarian has invaded the citadel. The history

---

17 This is, of course, another way of expressing those conflicts of the two-sided character which Georges Forestier's chapter in this volume addresses.

and diversity of human civilization are potentially present in each human microcosm.[18]

margin note: quintessential Other = Oriental

For early modern Europe, however, the quintessential 'Other' was the Oriental. What was Racine undertaking when he decided to compose a modern 'Turkish' play? When he wrote *Bajazet*, instead of recolonizing an old myth to explore current identity, he was developing a new one, by drawing together new and old elements. And he was abandoning the culturally close Graeco-Roman world for a wholly foreign one. *Bajazet* is, in that sense, a myth of transition. Pierre Ronzeaud, in a valuable recent survey of virtually everything which has ever been written about the political aspects of Racine,[19] underlines the contradictions and perplexity displayed by critics in this area. He warns against the tendancy to see Racine's plays as allegories, or a series of coded commentaries on contemporary events – a tendancy typified by René Jasinski and, to a lesser extent, Jean Orcibal. However, he is more indulgent towards readings which incline towards the contextual, rather than the allegorical, and that is the direction I shall briefly explore in looking at the image of the dark empire of Islam projected by Racine in *Bajazet*.

margin note: ms Bajazet + dark empire of Islam

margin note: Compagnie du Levant ⇒ oriental texts → Paris, 1645-1682

It was in 1670 that the *Compagnie du Levant* was created. The importance of the Levant within Louis XIV's overseas strategy is well known. One of its cultural signs was the marked upturn in the inward flow to Paris of oriental texts. Between 1645 and 1682 the number of oriental manuscripts in the Bibliothèque du Roy had tripled.[20] Their presence, and the competition which existed for their acquisition, a

---

18 Self as barbarian is an image linked to conduct of affairs of the heart, ranging from the preciosity of Alexandre's 'Vous croyez donc qu'à moi-même barbare / J'abandonne en ces lieux une beauté si rare?' (*Alexandre le Grand*, Act III. 6, ll. 925–6), through Titus's 'Non, je suis un barbare. / Moi-même je me hais. Néron, tant détesté, / N'a point à cet excès poussé sa cruauté' (*Bérénice*, Act IV. 6, ll. 1212–14) and Bajazet's 'Je me trouvais barbare, injuste, criminel' (*Bajazet*, Act III. 4, l. 995). The image of self as monster is rarer, with Phèdre, of course, providing the clearest case. It must be an intentional irony that of all Racine's characters the one most often qualified as 'barbare' is the very Greek Agamemnon (ten times).

19 'Racine et la politique: la perplexité de la critique', *Œuvres et Critiques*, 24. 1 (1999), *Présences de Racine* (Tübingen: Gunter Narr), pp. 136–58.

20 This figure is reached if one compares Jacques et Pierre Dupuy's catalogue, at the start of the reign, to the inventory prepared by Nicolas Clément and others in 1682, where the manuscripts are methodically organized into linguistic categories. The Royal Library benefited from transfers from Fouquet's library and the Collège Mazarin, as well as from the acquisitions made by Colbert's envoyés (e.g. Jean-Michel Vansleb deputed in 1671 to track down valuable works throughout the Middle East). Some, of course, ended up in the 'Colbertine'. See Marie-Rose Séguy, 'L'Orient – Attrait de l'Exotisme', in Roseline Bacou, Marie-Rose Séguy and Hélène Adhémar (eds), *Collections de Louis XIV: dessins, albums, manuscrits. Orangerie des Tuileries, 7 octobre 1977–9 janvier 1978* (Paris: Éditions des Musées nationaux, 1977), pp. 198–200.

competition led by the King, is a clear statement of an opening out of the reign towards the East. However little might have been understood of their contents, such visible testimony of a sophisticated Other World could hardly fail to induce some relativist thoughts.[21] Certainly they represent an impressive degree of cultural activity on the part of French orientalists, and the second half of the century saw Paris become an important market for the dispersal of oriental books and manuscripts, as London had in the previous half century. When we consider Racine's sense of things Eastern, a significant aspect of this upsurge of interest in oriental civilization is the involvement with Port-Royal of the noted orientalists, Eusèbe Renaudot and Antoine Galland (1646–1715, translator of the *Mille et Une Nuits*).[22] The marquis de Nointel, another fervent Jansenist, was sent in 1670 as ambassador to the Sublime Porte, and with Antoine Galland, at the behest of Louis XIV, obtained 'attestations' from the Patriarchs of the Eastern churches regarding their eucharistic beliefs.[23] The engagement with the East was not merely political, economic and aesthetic, but also philosophical and theological.

Apart from the well-known sources used by Racine (Segrais's *Floridon* (1656), the verbal account given by M. de Cézy, and, more distantly, *Théagène et Chariclée*) there are three types of discourse which provide a general intertextual background: firstly, accounts of the Levant provided by missionaries and travellers, secondly, discourse on French imperial claims, with their highly motivated scrutiny of French origins, and finally the growing output from French orientalists. At the ontological outset there is the crucial fact that Racine's knowledge of Greece and Rome comes from Greek and Roman texts, his knowledge of the Orient, like that of his audience, comes from sources which are not oriental. While Alain Grosrichard is correct in saying that the growing number of travel accounts of the Levant familiarized French audiences with some of the details of its history,[24] its geography and

---

21 Just as the Jesuits' accounts of the history of China had led Isaac de La Peyrère to develop his theory of the Pre-Adamites, thereby construing the Bible as merely the history of the Jews, rather than of mankind, as testified by his *Systema theologicum ex Preadamitarum hypothesi*, 1655.

22 Their knowledge of Greek and Oriental languages was to prove useful in the preparation of studies and works of controversy.

23 These were of interest not merely to Port-Royal but to Louis XIV, who wished to have proof of the Greek and Eastern Church views on transubstantiation. These superbly illuminated 'attestations' were deposited in the Royal Library.

24 Alain Grosrichard, *Structure du sérail. La fiction du despotisme asiatique dans l'Orient classique* (Paris: Editions du Seuil, 1979), pp. 26–7. Quoted by Marie-Odile Sweetser, 'Visions de l'autre dans la tragédie classique: le Romain et l'Oriental', *French Literature Series*, 23 (1996), p. 63.

what passed for its beliefs and *mores*, these accounts remained heavily stereotyped, while the works of the more erudite orientalists who examined Persian and Turkish texts in the original were of much lesser influence.[25]

If we accept the hypothesis of a Racine conscious of Louis as one ideal 'destinataire' of Racine's tragedies from *Alexandre* on, we can suppose that *Bajazet*, to some extent, is intended to fit with the king's attitude to discourses offered elsewhere on his prospect of one day ruling the world, or a larger part of it. The view that this may come to pass is not merely expressed in encomiastic literature, as a hyperbolic expression of Louis's present powers, personal merit and moral authority, it is still in the post-Fronde period a serious topic of politico–juridical debate, and indeed the object of prophecies.[26] If Louis, or 'Mars Christianissimus' as Leibniz was to call him in 1684,[27] required justification for his ambitions, *Bajazet* certainly could be read as just what was needed. By showing a competing Empire, that of the Ottomans, in the worst possible light it enhances the image of a 'roi juste et bon'. In other words, if the *imperium romanum* provided the ideologues of Early Modern Europe with the language and political models they required to construct new empires, the Ottoman empire, reign of darkness, in Racine's version and in the travel literature of the time, could provide a black or inverse image of the government of Louis.

25 For example André Du Ryer's translation of the Coran (*L'Alcoran de Mahomet, translaté d'arabe en françois*, Paris: A. de Sommaville, 1647) was virtually ignored in France, where preference was given to modern editions of Pierre Le Venerable's twelfth-century Latin version, and subsequently to Maracci's 1698 translation, itself based on the medieval one, and where each *sourate* was accompanied by its refutation. Du Ryer's work was, in fact, better known in England, where in 1649 it was 'Englished' for the benefit of 'all that desire to look into the Turkish vanities', as the title proclaims. For details concerning the diffusion and reception of the Coran in France see Dominique Carnoy, *Représentations de l'Islam dans la France du XVIIe siècle. La ville des tentations* (Paris: L'Harmattan, 1998).

26 Alexandre Yali Haran in 'Les droits de la couronne de France sur l'Empire au XVIIe siècle' (*Revue historique*, 299. 1 (1999), 71–91) provides an account of the arguments in favour of French imperial claims, and the survival into the seventeenth century of a current of Messianic prophecy regarding French universal dominion. See also: Gaston Zeller, 'Les Rois de France candidats à l'Empire: Essai sur l'idéologie impériale en France', *Revue historique*, 173 (1934), 273–311; Klaus Malettke, 'Le Saint Empire Romain Germanique et sa constitution vus par des juristes et historiens français au XVIIe siècle', in Wolfgang Leiner (ed.), *Horizons européens de la littérature française*. Dix-septième colloque du Centre méridional de rencontres sur le XVIIe siècle (Tübingen: Gunter Narr, 1988), pp. 185–95. On the general decline in enthusiasm and respect for the notion of the Holy Roman Empire in seventeenth-century France, see Anthony Pagden, *Lords of All the World. Ideologies of Empire in Spain, Britain and France, c. 1500–1800* (New Haven, CT: Yale University Press, 1995).

27 *Mars Christianissimus autore Germano Gallo Graeco ou Apologie des Armes du Roy Très-chrestien contre les Chrestiens* (Cologne: David Lebon, 1684).

It may even be possible to see in *Bajazet* a consciousness of French claims to the vacant throne of the *basileus*. Constantine was allegedly originally from Gaul (according to Raulin and Charron) and French polemicists frequently laid claim to the throne of the Eastern Empire, without an incumbent since the fall of Constantinople (1453).[28]

Bajazet thus belongs to the category of works which 'sought to define the character of European culture by ideological opposition with the oriental order',[29] as opposed to those orientalist texts which offered displaced critiques of European culture. When Montaigne, through praise of the 'cannibales', implies criticism of his own society, he does so by absolving them of the vices of the inhabitants and institutions of Europe. In this he follows a rhetorical topos, evocations of the Golden Age being traditionally expressed in terms of the absence of defects, precisely because they are conceived as the reverse of a description of the 'here-and-now' of the author.[30] In a symmetrically opposite manner *Bajazet*, through its negative projection of Ottoman society, implies that Louis XIV's France is enjoying, if not a Golden Age, at least a lesser set of evils.

On the purely political level such a message has several uses: to induce a feel-good factor at home; to disparage a dangerous rival power, albeit an ally; and implicitly to justify France's activities in the New World. The idea of French colonialism as 'mission civilisatrice' had already taken root. We can take two contemporary examples among many. Charles de Rochefort, in 1665, in his *Histoire naturelle et morale des Iles Antilles de l'Amérique*, claims that the sole object of the first French colonies had been 'the edification and instruction of the poor barbarians'.[31] Panegyrics such as Balthazar de Riez's two-volume disquisition on *L'incomparable piété des très-chrétiens rois de France*, dedicated to Louis XIV, in 1672 linked claims to the Imperial crown with wider

28 Antoine Aubéry: 'nos roys . . . sont les vrays successeurs des anciens Empereurs, tant de Rome que de Constantinople' [our Kings are the true successors of the former Emperors, both of Rome and Constantinople], *De la prééminence de nos Roys et de leur préséance sur l'Empereur et le Roy d'Espagne* (Paris: chez Michel Soly, 1649), p. 182). Earlier French kings (Charles VIII in 1494, and François Ier) had obtained the title, an empty one unless the Ottoman empire were destroyed.

29 Bashir El-Beshti, 'Signifying Texts and Displaced Contexts: Orientalism and the Ideological Foundations of the Early Modern State', in David Lee Rubin (ed.), *EMF, Studies in Early Modern France*, 3 (Charlottesville: Rookwood Press, 1997), pp. 80–93; see p. 84.

30 Tzvetan Todorov, *Nous et les autres. La réflexion française sur la diversité humaine* (Paris: Editions du Seuil, 1989), pp. 356–7. The paradox of exoticism, he states, is its wish to be an *elogium* without genuine knowledge of the culture in question.

31 Charles de Rochefort, *Histoire naturelle et morale des Iles Antilles de l'Amerique*, p. 283. Quoted in Pagden, *Lords of All the World*, p. 35.

world domination, and, in part, justified them by the missionary activity promoted by Louis XIV, so zealous for 'la conversion des peuples Infideles qui sont dans le Canada, dans la nouvelle France, dans l'Empire du Turc & du Persan'.[32] It is thus possible at one level to read *Bajazet* as a cultural *aition* of expansion. Redrawing geopolitical boundaries requires the support of all kinds of fictions. Racine's projection of the Orient parallels a process engaged in the *Iliad*, whose poets at a non-literal level produced 'a discourse which tamed and subordinated in the Greek imagination the land mass which came to be known as Asia, by creating Troy'. As Greek cities expanded all over the Mediterranean and the Black Sea, 'Asia was [. . .] familiarized and defused by assimilation into hexameter poetry'.[33] A similar dynamic informed the literature of the discovery of America and such heavily mediated colonialist discourse as, for example, *The Tempest*.

How successful is Racine's projection of another contemporary civilization? Audience reaction was mixed. On the one hand, *Bajazet*'s ending appeared too arbitrarily brutal to Mme de Sévigné. Its justification eluded her: 'on n'entre point dans les raisons de cette grande tuerie' (16 March, 1672). Robinet on the other hand levelled the same type of reproach against *Bajazet* as had earlier been made against Pyrrhus, and as Dryden would later make against Hippolyte: the hero is not *sufficiently* brutal. Racine has created a 'Turc aussi doux qu'un François', a 'Musulman des plus courtois', which for Robinet is evidently an oxymoron. Donneau de Visé, tongue in cheek, agrees that Racine is right to invent 'des caractères d'honnêtes gens et de femmes tendres et galantes' rather than create 'barbares' who would be less pleasing to the ladies.[34] Critics have at times tended to see *Bajazet* as another 'turquerie' in a superficial sense, simply exhibiting some of the symbols and trappings of the Ottoman world. Today one can only agree with Louis van Delft in doubting whether Racine's statement in the preface to *Bajazet* that he has aimed to preserve the 'coutumes et mœurs de la nation', and that he has underlined the 'férocité de la nation turque' constitute sufficient grounds for thinking that he is involved in a 'caractérologie des nations'.[35] But in a more creative, poetical manner Racine converts the essential features of Islam (as they were perceived

---

32 *L'incomparable piété des très-chrétiens rois de France, et les admirables prérogatives qu'elle a méritées à Leurs Majestés, tant pour leur royaume en général, que pour leurs personnes sacrées en particulier*, par le R. P. Balthazar de Riez, 2 vols (Livre I: Paris, G. Alliot, 1672; Livre II: Aix, imp. de C. David, 1674). See 'Épitre', third page (unpaginated).

33 Hall, *Inventing the Barbarian*, p. 48.

34 Rohou, *Théâtre*, p. 995.

35 van Delft, *Littérature et anthropologie*, pp. 97–8.

in his day) into the very conditions which tragically destroy individual freedom. Whether 'tuerie' or 'turquerie', the play provides a specular image of French society, both in itself and in the comments it provokes.

Racine, in locating *Bajazet* in Byzance-Constantinople (Istanbul), is using a 'lieu de mémoire' almost as potent as Jerusalem, or Rome. The poignant, yet ambivalent, image of Byzantium, like that of Jerusalem, carries the sense of a fall from grace (through its schismatic defiance of Roman papacy) and, like Rome, the suggestion of deca-dence. Although it was a place where the remaining Christians were tolerated, their numbers decreased, and the impression given would have been of a slow asphyxiation. Accounts of the Levant dwell on the harem. The 'sérail' in *Bajazet*, of which much has been written (should we see there the shared fantasy of literary critics?), is indeed an 'antre tragique: lieu exemplaire du désir et du pouvoir',[36] an 'ensemble clos et labyrinthique',[37] accentuating the frenetic and futile nature of the characters' ever more urgent twisting and turning. It offers Racine a location in which to develop 'à sa condensation maximale l'unité de lieu',[38] which is his trademark, and where, as Christian Delmas remarks, the enclosed space of the action contrasts with the vast distance separating Byzantium from Babylon, where the real power lies, where the 'Grand Seigneur' as military commander deals with those other Orientals, the Persians. The contrasting concentration and distension of space accentuate the sense of 'sans appel'. But the 'sérail', or the harem, and the 'volcanic temperament' of Eastern women, are already obsessions of travellers, not to mention missionaries, of the period. There is a significant intertext at work, which is mentioned in Racine's second preface. Against the accusation that his 'Héroïnes étaient trop savantes en amour et trop délicates pour des Femmes nées parmi des Peuples qui passent ici pour barbares' [His heroines were too know-ledgeable in love and too refined for women born among peoples who are considered here to be barbarians], he instances all the 'Relations des Voyageurs' which bear him out. As for the 'sérail', the contrast with local French and European courts is marked by a rhetorical question: 'Y a-t-il une Cour au monde où la jalousie et l'amour doivent être si bien connues que dans un lieu où tant de Rivales sont enfermées ensemble, et où toutes ces Femmes n'ont point d'autre étude dans une éternelle oisiveté, que d'apprendre à plaire et à se faire aimer?' [Is

---

36 Rohou, *Théâtre*, 'Notice de *Bajazet*', p. 979.

37 Georges Forestier, 'Introduction', in *Bajazet* (Paris: Livre de Poche, 1992), p. 27. Also *Œuvres*, p. 1504.

38 Christian Delmas, 'Préface', in *Bajazet*, coll. Folio Théâtre (Paris: Gallimard, 1995), p. 11.

there a Court in the world where jealousy and love can be more rampant than in a place where so many rival women are locked up, and where all these women have nothing else to do in their endless idleness than to learn how to please and be loved?].[39] The Court of Lubricity is undoubtedly the Court of Evil, when judged from the moral standpoint of Racine's contemporaries. Even Versailles can appear virtuous in such company.

The 'sérail' is also presented in travel accounts as the place where the contrast between the outside and the inside, appearance and reality, is particularly marked: beyond the severity of the blank walls, the armed guards and the locked doors, there is a world of unbridled sensuality, or so the the travellers' stories go. *Bajazet* takes the audience into that inaccessible world. The 'sérail' becomes, in Racine's play, the habitus of duplicity, in a play dominated by artifice, pretence and concealment, and desperate efforts at reaching the truth. A further contrast (and another fantasy) underlies the Western construction of the 'sérail'. From the 'possédées de Loudun', whose possession is ascribed to the effect of 'la fureur utérine',[40] through to Diderot and beyond, communities of women, particularly convents, exercise the minds of men. The 'sérail' as the reverse of the convent, is an avatar of the inverted Satanic world; Racine's later description of Port-Royal provides its antithesis, from which all hint of sensuality is banished and where the interior is in perfect harmony with the exterior.[41]

39 2nd Preface (1676), in Forestier, *Œuvres*, p. 626.

40 'On appelle en Medecine fureur uterine une maladie de la vulve ou matrice qui jette des fumées au cerveau qui causent de grands emportements & deshonnestes aux femmes qui ont une passion d'amour indomptable. La plus-part des Religieuses qu'on croit possedées, ne sont que des malades de fureur uterine' [The disease of the vulva, or the womb, is called in Medecine the uterine rash, which causes vapours to the brain, and great excesses and unreliability among women provoked to insatiable amorous passion. Most of those Nuns who were believed to be possessed were only sick with uterine rash] (Furetière, *Dictionnaire universel*, 1690, article 'uterin'; cf. Thomas Corneille, *Dictionnaire des Arts et des Sciences*, 1695). The blame, as we can see, has shifted most rationally from the devil to the physiological composition of women.

41 Port-Royal, as it appears in the *Abrégé* provides the opposite pole to the harem, where industry and holiness reign both within and without the walls: 'Tout ce qu'on en voyoit au dehors inspiroit de la piété. [. . .] Mais combien les personnes qui connoissoient l'intérieur de ce monastère y trouvoient-elles de nouveaux sujets d'édification! Quelle paix! Quel silence! Quelle charité! Quel amour pour la pauvreté et pour la mortification! Un travail sans relâche, une prière continuelle, point d'ambition que pour les emplois les plus vils et les plus humiliants, aucune impatience dans les sœurs, nulle bizarrerie dans les mères, l'obéissance toujours prompte, et le commandement toujours raisonnable' [Everything that could be seen from without inspired Christian devotion [. . .], but what new sources of edification were revealed to those who knew the life within the walls! What peace! What silence! What charity! What love of poverty and self-denial! A ceaseless labour, unremitting prayer, only ambition for the most menial and humiliating tasks prevailed, no impatience amongst the Sisters,

The 'sérail' is then both 'gynécée' and prison. It would not be a *tragic* prison if there were some hope of escape, something like a tiny grid high in the dungeon wall, through which the sky is visible. Or the discreet window in the seraglio from which the ladies of the harem could look out, but not be seen. Bajazet, like Hippolyte, dreams of a wider world, of earning a name, asserting an identity. But these hopes are futile. In *Bajazet*, doors open only to close, as Jean Dubu has shown in his semiotic reading of the 'portes du palais' and the Sublime Porte,[42] which emphasize the claustration of the 'sérail'. Turned in upon itself it becomes a self-sustaining 'microcosme infernal'.[43] With its 'Esclaves obscurs, / Nourris loin de la guerre, à l'ombre de ses murs' (*Bajazet*, Act IV. 7, ll. 1419–1420) it is a dark enclosure, reminiscent surely of the prisons in which Christian slaves languished, those into which Guez de Balzac imagined he saw the rays of Louis XIII's benevolence penetrating,[44] those prisons which are so prominent in missionary and polemical accounts of the Orient and Barbary Coast, as, for example, in René de Lucinge's *Histoire de l'origine, progrez, & declin, de l'Empire des Turcs* (1614),[45] or in le Père Pierre Dan's *Histoire de la Barbarie & de ses corsaires* (1637).[46] In the mind of the audience aware of the Turkish slave trade, the 'foule [. . .] d'Esclaves' (*Bajazet*, II. 1, l. 435) may be partly composed of Christians. The same audience might well have been less aware of another irony: the fact that slaves were regularly bought from the Turks for the galleys of Louis XIV's Navy, among them Eastern Rite Christians from Greece and Central Europe.

no moodiness in the Mother Superiors, always prompt obedience and moderate instructions], *Abrégé de l'histoire de Port-Royal*, in *Œuvres complètes*, ed. Luc Estang (Paris: Editions du Seuil, 1962), p. 323.

42 '*Bajazet*: "serrail" et transgression', in *Racine aux miroirs* (Paris: SEDES, 1992), pp. 137–48.

43 Eléonore M. Zimmermann, *La Liberté et le destin dans le théâtre de Jean Racine, suivi de deux essais sur le théâtre de Jean Racine* (Geneva: Slatkine Reprints, 1999), p. 14 (orig. Saratoga, 1982).

44 'Quelle apparence, que je ne me réveille point à ce grand bruit, qui se levant icy, se fait entendre aux extremitez de la terre, et que je ne reçoive aucune impression d'une lumiere si proche et si éclatante, qui s'épand desja au delà de la mer, et jette ses rayons jusques dans les cachots de Barbarie?' [What an idea, that I should never wake up to this great din which arising here can be heard in the far extremities of the Earth, and that I should not receive any impression of a light so close and brilliant, spreading already beyond the sea, and casting its rays even into the cells of Barbary?], *Le Prince* (Paris: La Table Ronde, 1996), p. 45. This passage follows his encounter with a Flemish gentleman who had been captured at sea and sold as a slave in Algiers.

45 The full title is: *Histoire de l'origine, progrez, & declin, de l'Empire des Turcs. Où sont declarees les causes de l'agrandissement & conservation de leurs Estats. Et comme on les pourroit destruire & ruiner. Avec une Complainte d'un Esclave Chrestien, adressee aux Princes Chrestiens* (Paris: chez Pierre Chevalier, 1614).

46 Paris: P. Rocolet, 1637; 2nd edition in 1649.

The King personally gave instructions regarding the acquisition of slaves 'aux meilleures conditions'.[47]

Another sharp contrast with French practice is seen in Roxane, 'un des personnages les plus noirs de Racine' [one of the darkest characters of Racine],[48] who embodies the perversion of power, although she possesses only the illusion of power. The ignominy of her origins is exceptional in a protagonist (Narcisse, Ériphile, Œnone, Aman are all secondary characters). Her position of authority symbolizes the reign of unreason, is yet another form of inversion, in this play of inverted values. Narcisse, in *Britannicus*, had offered a similar but less developed exploration of the slave mentality. As Eléonore Zimmermann remarks, Roxane as a slave can see only the exterior aspects of freedom, while Bajazet has an interiorized concept.[49] With Orcan and Zatime we descend the degrees of humanity: Orcan, of the 'visage odieux', 'né sous le ciel brûlant des plus noirs Africains' adds blackness to his slavish status: black slave of a black sun (Amurat is the anti-Sun-King, whose realm is darkness), while Zatime is 'd'une esclave barbare esclave impitoyable'. The 'muets' [mutes] are the ultimate victims of despotism, for to be deprived of speech, in Racine's world, is the final extinction of identity.

Against these forces the individual's struggle for autonomy appears hopeless. *Bajazet* presents, in a sense, an inversion of genre. It is, as Georges Forestier has pointed out, a black pastoral, with a 'trame' [plot] borrowed from that genre, and set in the least pastoral of locations, the closed and glittering world of the Ottoman court. Bajazet, a 'berger en rupture de paradis' [a pastoral shepherd bereft of paradise],[50] provides the most acute instance of disparity between the aspirations of a hero and the choices open to him. The world and the individual are locked in deadly combat. In the words of Alain Viala, 'autour du Sérail, l'Empire bouge, l'armée au loin triomphe, et leurs forces énormes noient dans l'inutile les soubresauts des amants qui se débattent sur scène' [around the Harem, the Empire stirs, far afield the

---

47 Quoted by André Zysberg, *Les galériens, vies et destins de 60 000 forçats sur les galères de France 1680–1748* (Paris: Editions du Seuil, 1987), p. 67. The market in humans was conducted in a number of ports of the Christian Mediterranean (Leghorn, Venice, Malta, Alicante, Majorca, Cagliari). To the galley slaves provided by the Turks were added, experimentally, Iroquois, and black Guineans who were to be 'acclimatés' – in the latter case the experiment was as short-lived as the slaves themselves who proved unable to survive the conditions. After October 1685, of course, Huguenots, the 'galériens pour la foi' [galley slaves of religion], helped to make up the numbers.
48 Forestier, 'Introduction' in *Bajazet* (Livre de Poche, 1992), p. 32.
49 Zimmermann, *La Liberté et le destin dans le théâtre de Jean Racine*, pp. 17–18.
50 Forestier, *Bajazet* (Livre de Poche), p. 44.

Army triumphs, and their enormous forces swamp in futility the antics of the lovers who tumble about on stage].[51]

Ancestry, lineage, especially of royal or imperial families, may be a source of legitimacy and stability. However, in the world of *Bajazet*, reverential reference to the Ottoman blood has an ironic ring. It is not the defiant attachment to a notoriously impure bloodline displayed by 'la fille de Jézabel'.[52] Bajazet's nostalgia for the 'grands noms de [sa] race' (Act II. 5, l. 738) is heard rather as the error of a hero whose points of reference, unbeknownst to him, are dubious.[53] The effect here, as in his rememoration of specific ancestors, an earlier Bajazet, or Soliman, or Osman, is pathos. Similarly when Atalide swears by le 'Ciel', and 'Par ces grands Ottomans, dont [elle est] descendue' (*Bajazet*, Act V. 5, ll. 1597–8), there is tragic irony in her emprisonment in a belief system which is doubly erroneous: her 'ciel' [heaven] is a Mahometan one, and the ruling dynasty is *not* hallowed. It is logical that she should similarly and tragically remain a prisoner of her passions. The genealogical impulse, here as elsewhere, corresponds to an attempt 'to reinscribe the time of the narrative within the time of the universe'.[54]

The notion of a legitimate *translatio imperii*, a central argument in French commentary on French rights to the empire, is perverted in *Bajazet*. In the Ottoman empire, the transfer of power as described by Acomat is illegitimate: the route to the throne is over the dead body of one or several brothers. If Bajazet kills Amurat he will merely be perpetuating a tradition of violence:

> L'exemple en est commun. Et parmi les Sultans,
> Ce chemin à l'Empire a conduit de tout temps
>
> (*Bajazet*, Act II. 1, ll. 443–4).

Racine presents here the violent alternative, in a dynastic system, to a strict adherence to the law of primogeniture, the unquestioned inheritance by the eldest brother. The inevitable enmity between brothers,

51 Racine. *La stratégie du caméléon* (Paris: Seghers, 1990), p. 151.
52 Cf. *Athalie*, Act II. 7, ll. 709–30 and V. 6, ll. 1768–90. [This study was completed before the publication of Volker Schröder's *La Tragédie du sang d'Auguste. Politique et intertextualité dans* Britannicus, coll. Biblio 17, no. 119 (Tübingen: Gunter Narr, 1999).]
53 In this he is a little like Junie who only sees among her ancestors the virtuous Augustus. This point is made by Eléonore M. Zimmermann: 'De même que Junie ne voit chez ses ancêtres qu'un Auguste vertueux, Bajazet puise sa force dans un passé mythique' [Just as Junie identifies among her ancestors only a virtuous Augustus, so Bajazet derives his strength from a mythical past], *La Liberté et le destin dans le théâtre de Jean Racine*, p. 17.
54 Ricœur emphasizes the role of genealogical references as a form of symbolical and biological inscribing of the self in time (*Temps et récit. III*, Ch. 3).

while it is, of course, a feature of Racine's tragedies, must here be seen as regressive, archaic, even primitive, in the context of one of the seventeenth century's great powers. The recent history of France had contained examples of tension between royal brothers but Louis XIV's reign saw, on the contrary, public displays of royal fraternal harmony, and a proliferation of paintings and medals celebrating that solidarity – for example, Louis conferring the Order of the Saint-Esprit on Monsieur, or the series of medals and portraits showing the extended royal family. In this way *Bajazet* provides a gauge of French progress. The seizure of power by Bajazet, although he is 'of the blood' and morally superior to Amurat, would then be little more than a *coup militaire* supported by the Janissaries, a regression to the practices of the dark days of a decadent Roman Empire, and the violent antithesis of the sacred rites associated with the conferring by the Pope of the *imperium* on Charlemagne, or the transmission of royal power at the *sacre*. The equivalent ceremony in this play, should Bajazet decide to oust his brother, would hardly appear adequately solemn: Roxane would display the Divine Prophet's dread banner to the terrified people, and Acomat would proclaim Bajazet emperor (ll. 847–52). So *Bajazet* enhances Bourbon legitimacy. The people are 'épouvanté' (l. 847), 'alarmé' (l. 244), 'rempli d'une juste terreur' (l. 851), 'craintives' (l. 1669), and 'effrayés' (l. 1670). Of course, a docile population is generally seen as a desirable quantity in seventeenth-century political discourse, including tragedy. But here it is a blind obedience, a characteristic stressed by contemporary French commentaries on Islam. It is a sign of servility, of a mercenary system, of the consequences of despotism. So Roxane can boast that the 'people' of the 'sérail' [harem] are her creatures, bought and paid for, over whom she has unlimited rights:

> . . . [ces] âmes asservies
> M'ont vendu dès longtemps leur silence et leurs vies
> (*Bajazet*, Act II. 1, ll. 437–8).

This power is eloquently attested in Act V, scene 8, by Zatime's obstinate silence: 'Il y va de ma vie, et je ne puis rien dire' (l. 1654).

The absence of Amurat (only emissaries penetrate the 'sérail', slaves with deadly instructions) symbolically expresses a perception of the 'vide' which runs through the orthodox exegesis of oriental life and beliefs. And rather as the absence of the Moors from the actual stage of *Le Cid* can be seen as their concealment and absorption within the dominant discourse,[55] the absence of Amurat is also a form of denial of the power

---

55 This view of Corneille's decision to relegate Spain's enemies to the 'coulisses' is developed by Michèle Longino in 'Politique et théâtre au XVIIᵉ siècle: Les Français

of the sultan-emperor. In European portrayals of Ottoman rule the very absence of sedition is interpreted as a sign of despotism. What might otherwise pass for civic order is construed as alien, almost idolatrous. Orcan, for example, anticipates that the sight of the Sultan's written order will produce instant submission, a form of adoration, on the part of Osmin:

'Adorez, a-t-il dit, l'ordre de votre Maître'
(*Bajazet*, Act V. 11, l. 1683).[56]

The foundation of the Turkish Empire is the concentration of power in the person of the Sultan. As Rycaut, one of Racine's sources, puts it: 'la puissance sans bornes de l'Empereur, est le *principe* de l'Empire des Turcs' [the limitless power of the Emperor is the *principle* of power among the Turks],[57] and he cites as a further 'maxime de la politique des Turcs' that 'le Prince soit servi par des personnes, qu'il puisse élever sans envie, & ruiner sans danger' [the Prince should be served by persons whom he can elevate without envy and destroy without risk].[58] This policy to European eyes seemed to abolish any proper hierarchy of power, leaving a void where the aristocracy should be.

The only power other than that of the Sultan, and the precarious Vizir, lies with the dangerously volatile Janissaries (who previously murdered Osman, on the pretext that he had married against their wishes), a military force but not an aristocracy. If the Sultan were to suffer a defeat at Babylon, the Janissaries, 'à la haine joignant l'audace' (*Bajazet*, Act I. 1, l. 66) would interpret it as 'un arrêt du ciel qui réprouve Amurat' (Act I. 1, l. 68); this was obviously not the type of superstitious judgement to which any military leader, for example Louis XIV, would wish to be exposed. But should he succeed they will display 'une aveugle et basse obéissance' (*Bajazet*, l. 62). The fidelity of the 'braves janissaires' (l. 29) to Amurat is, then, as suspect as that commanded by any despot, and as suspect as Bajazet's 'foi'. Their heart is a difficult text to read: 'Dans le secret des cœurs, Osmin, n'as-tu rien lu / Amurat jouit-il d'un pouvoir absolu?' (ll. 31–2). His 'pouvoir absolu' has the usual limitation. The fate predicted for Néron[59]

---

en Orient et l'exotisme du *Cid*, in Dominique de Courcelles (ed.), *Littérature et exotisme, XVIᵉ–XVIIᵉ siècle* (Paris: École des Chartes, 1997), pp. 35–59.

56 In the original edition, 'adorez' is replaced by 'connaissez'.

57 Paul Rycaut, *Histoire de l'État présent de l'Empire des Ottomans contenant les maximes politiques des Turcs, traduit de l'anglois […] par M. Briot* (Amsterdam: Wolfgank, 1670), title of Ch. II. My emphasis.

58 *Ibid.*, title of Ch. V.

59 'Craint de tout l'univers, il vous faudra tout craindre' (*Britannicus*, Act IV. 3, l. 1452).

is experienced by Amurat. He is feared by the Janissaries and his position is thus insecure:

> Moi-même j'ai souvent entendu leurs discours,
> Comme il les craint sans cesse, ils le craignent toujours
> (*Bajazet*, Act I. 1, ll. 43–4).

[margin note: his position = insecure (Js fear him)]

The spiritual predicament is as grave as the political. Mahometanism was, in Christian eyes, an empty display, and a distortion of Christian truth: 'Il n'y a personne qui ne sçache que la Religion des Turcs est un composé extravagant de celle des Chrétiens & de celle des Juifs' [Everybody knows that the religion of the Turks is an excessive mixture of the Christian and Jewish faiths].[60] The benighted subjects of the Sultan are as credulous in religious matters as their religious leaders are corrupt. By her 'brigues secrètes' Roxane has won over the 'sacrés interprètes' of the Muslim Faith. Her order, 'rentre dans le néant dont je t'ai fait sortir', is, as Eléonore Zimmermann has pointed out,[61] tantamount to arrogating the rôle of God to herself. *Bajazet*'s world is one which is 'atrocement humain', more or less deprived of divine law. In such a world, without the 'true' faith, the characters are exposed to destructive doubt, and obsessively pursue elusive reassurance. The word 'foi' is used 24 times in the play, 'fidèle' and 'infidèle' 14 times. It is a world where promises, as Acomat states, are never binding on the ruler. Moral values are so inverted that to keep a promise is, for Acomat, to act like a slave: 'Le sang des Ottomans / Ne doit point en Esclave obéir aux serments' (ll. 643–4), and the throne, which is supposedly 'si saint' has as foundation 'la foi promise et rarement gardée' (l. 650).

[margin note: no divine law; promises do not bind rulers]

In the context of the confusion which was commonly believed to reign in the minds of the followers of Mahomet, there is peculiar significance in Racine's use of the word 'nœud'. Racine in *Bajazet* uses it in a way which is properly poetic, if we adopt the definition proposed

60 Rycaut, *Histoire de l'État*, p. 249. The religion of Islam is presented as both a confused mixture of truth and error, and, in some of its manifestations, as a direct opposite of Christianity. For example, when describing the Order of 'Kalendivis', Rycaut states that 'Ceux qui font profession de cét Ordre, méritent mieux d'estre appelez Epicuriens, que personnes retirées du monde pour mortifier leurs passions, comme font tous les autres Religieux Turcs. Cependant ces phanatiques prétendent par une voie toute opposée à celle des autres, estre de bons religieux en s'abandonnant au libertinage & au relâchement . . .' [Those who belong to this Order deserve to be called Epicureans rather than people who retire from the world to mortify their passions, as do all other Turkish religious communities. However, these fanatics claim by a completely opposite path to the rest, to be good holy people in surrendering to a life of laxity and libertinage], *ibid.*, p. 264.

61 Zimmermann, *La Liberté et le destin dans le théâtre de Jean Racine*, p. 72.

by Maurice Delcroix, speaking of the 'monstre': 'il spécule sur la plurisémie du mot'.[62] The word 'nœud' is indeed remarkably polysemic. Most commonly in tragedies it elegantly expresses the union, variously perceived as 'funeste', 'saint' etc., between man and wife, or the bonds of kinship or friendship. It thus holds society together. But the 'nœud' is also a difficulty, or problem — the Gordian knot, the heart of a litigation. Hence its dramaturgical meaning of 'l'endroit de la pièce où la principale intrigue se forme, où les affaires commencent à s'embarasser' [the part of the play where the main plot begins to form, and the situation becomes complex].[63] As he had done in *Britannicus* with the notion of 'poison', and would later with 'monstre' in *Phèdre*, Racine adopts an emblematic term, stretching it between its figurative (rather overworked) meaning and the first-level or primary meaning. Thus the 'nœuds par le sang commencés', which formed in childhood between Atalide and Bajazet, are distinct from the conjugal 'nœud sacré' which Roxane demands, the marriage 'en bonne et due forme' which will bind Bajazet to her, that demeaning bond to be the paradoxical price of his freedom. As the *dénouement* approaches, the real 'nœud' – the noose – shows itself and achieves concrete form in the 'nœuds infortunés' with which Roxane threatens to have Bajazet strangled. The sadistic ambiguity of her promise to Atalide exploits the multiple meanings of 'nœud':

> Loin de vous séparer, je prétends aujourd'hui
> Par des nœuds éternels vous unir avec lui
> *(Bajazet*, Act V. 6, ll. 1631–2).

A further meaning surfaces in Atalide's final use of the word, rightly berating herself for having woven the web of deceit in which Bajazet is snared:

> Moi seule j'ai *tissu* le *lien* malheureux,
> Dont tu viens d'éprouver les détestables *nœuds*
> *(Bajazet*, Act V. 12, ll. 1739–40) (my emphasis).

The association is made between the multiple twists in the plot and the complexity and artifice which had become synonymous with Byzantium and oriental sophistication, as well as the horrific manner of Bajazet's death. To an aristocratic French mind, this is a particularly ghastly end. The tragic hero – and indeed any *noble d'épée* – would prefer to perish by the sword. Execution by strangulation is both

---

62 Delcroix, 'La poétique du monstre', p. 179.
63 *Dictionnaire de l'Académie Françoise* (1694), article 'nœud'.

ignominious and one of the cultural differences which caracterize, in French eyes, the 'barbarity' of the Ottomans.[64]

In his Preface to *Bajazet*, Racine invites us to consider the Ottoman Empire as a throwback: 'les Personnages Turcs, quelque modernes qu'ils soient ont de la dignité sur notre Théâtre. *On les regarde de bonne heure comme Anciens*. Ce sont des mœurs et des coutumes toutes différentes. Nous avons si peu de commerce avec les Princes et les autres Personnes qui vivent dans le Sérail, que *nous les considérons, pour ainsi dire, comme des gens qui vivent dans un autre siècle que le nôtre*' (my emphasis) [Turkish characters, however modern they are, have a certain dignity on our stage. They can easily be viewed as Ancients. They have customs and usages which are very different from ours. We have so few dealings with the Princes and other persons who live in the harem, that we consider them, so to speak, as a people who live in another time].[65] He revealingly draws the parallel between Athenian dramatists' treatment of Persians, notably Æschylus's treatment of Xerxes's mother, and his own approach to the seventeenth-century Levant. The Preface displays the tendency common in 'récits de voyage' to identify the unfamiliar societies encountered in long-distance travel with one's early ancestors; exoticism merges with a primitivism which is also chronological.[66] Bakhtin's concept of the chronotope is also useful here, in conveniently summarizing the way in which the literary imagination represents time as a malleable, unevenly paced and unevenly distributed phenomenon.[67] The Byzantium ruled over by Amurat is outside the highroad of progress. Or, in Christian Biet's words, speaking of *Mithridate*, the Occident is the world of History, the Orient is infra-history.[68]

As a corollary of this, comparison with former selves is for Racine's audience a way to measure progress. According to Christian Delmas, Racine, like Delacroix 'present [. . .] que l'Orient n'est que l'Antiquité vivante' [feels that the Orient is simply Antiquity brought to life].[69] The cultural distance, as much as the geographical, produces the gap in which 'l'élaboration poétique de la matière tragique' may take place.

64 The association is so strong that it surfaces in unexpected places: Richelet, defining 'lacs', informs us that 'Les muets du serrail estranglent des Princes, des Visirs, avec des lacs de soye' (*Dictionnaire*, 1694).
65 Forestier, *Œuvres*, p. 625.
66 Todorov, *Nous et les autres*, p. 358.
67 'Forms of time and of the chronotope in the novel', in Holquist (ed.), *The Dialogic Imagination*.
68 '*Mithridate*, ou l'exercice de l'ambiguïté', in Claire Carlin (ed.), *La Rochefoucauld, Mithridate, Frères et Sœurs, Les Muses sœurs*, coll. Biblio 17, no. 111 (Tübingen: Gunter Narr, 1998), pp. 83–98 (p. 89).
69 Delmas, 'Préface', in *Bajazet*, p. 26.

This is the crossover of the distances (space/time) applied in his Greek and Roman tragedies: the Greeks are culturally closer, temporally further off. In a study of the play's debt to *Othon*, Jacques Morel remarks on this same sense of non-progress: the Turkish 'férocité' claimed by Racine in the Preface seems equally applicable to Rome in the aftermath of Nero.[70] Perhaps, like Hegel, Racine viewed Asian cultures as a prelude to European civilization. It is nonetheless true that in *Bajazet* his refiguration of time is a new departure in his continuing exploration of the 'entrecroisement entre l'histoire et la fiction'.[71]

Bajazet is not a propaganda piece. It does, however, project an image of a dark empire, a parallel realm to the luminous, legitimate world of Louis XIV. Its inhabitants are lost in the toils of deceit and false appearance, in a world of Error, with its secular and its religious connotations. It is, too, a displacement onto the Orient of the darker fears of the individual confronted with the reality of absolutism. The characters' autonomy, their liberty, the relative liberty of Roxane and of Acomat, is never more than an illusion. These are 'marionnettes dérisoires en attente d'exécution' [absurd puppets awaiting execution].[72] Virtue here presents itself like an astonishing, paradoxical aberration: in *Bajazet* the real strangers are Bajazet and, to a lesser extent, Atalide.

Racine produces in his plays his own 'histoire universelle', one which is much more readable than Bossuet's. Where Bossuet is moralistic, I would claim that Racine is ethical, in Ricoeur's sense of 'the search for self and communal identity [as strengthening] the ethical dimension of history.'[73] When we view his plays as cultural

---

70 'Racine lecteur d'*Othon*', in *Agréables mensonges. Essais sur le théâtre français du XVIIᵉ siècle* (Paris: Klincksieck, 1991), pp. 237–8. The original text appeared in the 'Preface' to *Corneille: Othon*, ed. J. Sanchez (Mont-de-Marsan: José Feijoo, 1989).

71 See Ricœur for this relationship: '… l'*entrecroisement* entre l'histoire et la fiction dans la refiguration du temps repose, en dernière analyse, sur cet empiètement réciproque, le moment quasi historique de la fiction changeant de place avec le moment quasi fictif de l'histoire. De cet entrecroisment, de cet empiètement réciproque, de cet échange de places, procède ce qu'il est convenu d'appeler *le temps humain*, où se conjuguent la représentation du passé par l'histoire et les variations imaginatives de la fiction, sur l'arrière-plan des apories de la phénoménologie du temps' [. . . the *interweaving* of history and fiction in the refiguration of time rests finally upon this reciprocal trespassing, on the quasi-historical moment of fiction changing places with the quasi-fictive moment of history. From this interweaving, from this reciprocal trespassing, comes what is commonly called *human time*, where history's representing of the past and the imaginative variants produced by fiction come together, against the background of the phenomenology of time and its aporias], *Temps et récit. III*, p. 279.

72 Rohou, 'Notice de *Bajazet*', p. 988.

73 Edi Pucci, 'History and the Question of Identity: Kant, Arendt, Ricœur', in R. Kearney (ed.), *Paul Ricœur. The Hermeneutics of Action* (London: Sage, 1996), pp. 125–36 (p. 134). For this aspect of Ricœur's view of the past see in particular *Soi-même comme un autre*, 'Le soi et la visée ethique', pp. 199–236.

play = cultural narrative, attempt to locate Fr. identity

narratives, and as an attempt to locate French identity in the vast sweep of human civilization, the links between them are worth attention. They cast an often ironic light on history: *Iphigénie* prequel to *Andromaque*, *Athalie* prequel to *Esther*, *Mithridate* prequel to *Bajazet*. On the relationship between these two 'oriental' plays, Paul Mesnard in 1865, while recognizing that Roman accounts of Mithridate's domestic arrangements suggest parallels with the *mores* of the Sultans, rejected any intention of reduplication on Racine's part.[74] His commentary betrays the difficulty he, and others of his time, had in reconciling 'grandeur' with 'barbare': Mithridate, he says, has a 'grandeur' which is 'toute romaine'. Clearly he would have been happy to erase the memory of the oriental half of Mithridate's ambiguous identity, another 'indigne moitié d'une si belle histoire'. However, despite their very different dramatic structure, there

Mithridate = B's precursor

are enough similarities between these two oriental plays for the connection to be valuable: there is common ground in the series of illusions experienced by the characters of both plays, and in the cruelty and tyranny of Mithridate, precursor of Amurat and yet his superior.

There is a meaning to be derived from the relationship between *Mithridate* and *Bajazet*. According to the general verdict, *Mithridate* passes for one of Racine's more cheerful plays, 'an optimistic interlude',[75] or an almost operatic 'tragédie lyrique',[76] where, for the first time the young couple are not separated at the end. Yet it carries a dark message about civilization. Certainly about the impermanence of empires. For not only does Mithridate's empire crumble around him, it has itself possessed lands which once had held sway over its own heartland. Monime is, in a sense, a piece of Greek booty,[77] albeit acquired in less violent circumstances than Andromaque. Thus we have within the play, in the person of the reluctant fiancée, the image of Greece, and a hellenized Asia Minor, succumbing to Mithridate. If Mithridate represents active resistance, Monime is emblematic of the colonized. Her body may go to the altar with Mithridate's, her mind and heart, to use the metaphor of the time, will resist. Her point of

---

74 'Notice' for *Mithridate*, in G.E.F., *Œuvres*, 3 (Paris: Hachette, 1865), p. 3.

75 William J. Cloonan, *Racine's Theatre: The Politics of Love* (University, Miss.: Romance Monographs, 1977), title of chapter on *Mithridate*.

76 Alain Niderst, '*Mithridate*, opéra?', in Carlin (ed.), *La Rochefoucauld*, pp. 125–36.

77 Plutarch, Racine's main source for Monime, underlines this theme of exile among savage men: 'She [. . .] often bewailed her beauty, that had procured her a keeper, instead of a husband, and a watch of barbarians, instead of the home and attendance of a wife; and, removed far from Greece, she enjoyed the pleasure which she proposed to herself only in a dream, being in the meantime robbed of that which is real' (Plutarch on Pompey, trans. by John Dryden in *Plutarch. Lives, translated [. . .] by several hands* (London, 1716).

revolt is Pharnace: Pharnace would be a conqueror too many.[78] Her parents' submission to Mithridate's will summarizes the submergence of Greek civilization by the 'Eastern threat', with all the resonances that situation might have for a seventeenth-century audience, accustomed to hearing that 'les Turcs sont aux portes de Vienne'.[79] But Mithridate represents a nation which is seen at the point where the Roman Empire overwhelms it. Within the play the fall of Rome is itself predicted. Racine's layering of these time-frames, when taken in conjunction with the image of the Ottoman empire in *Bajazet*, conveys not merely the mutability of political power, but the painful possibility of a teleological reading of history which leads downwards, and away from progress. Seventeen centuries, the 'benefits' of Roman civilization, the reign of Constantine, Christianity, the rise and the fall of Byzantium, modern 'progress', contacts with Europe have changed nothing. An implication of this may, of course, be that a political saviour is ready and available, to lead seventeenth-century Europe away from any such catastrophe: 'Mars Christianissimus' is waiting in the wings.

Leibniz, in 1671–2, drew Louis XIV's attention to the desirability of a new crusade against the Turks – the irony here is that his real purpose is to divert France's attention from Europe, by providing a new 'theatre' for Louis's war-games.[80] The Turkish threat has become a way to divert the French threat. What could more aptly illustrate the complexity of the relations between the nations of Europe and the Ottoman Empire? And the fact that Amurat might not lie so far from Louis.

Finally, Racine was perhaps not a relativist, in Todorov's sense. But he was supremely aware that 'civilization', whether individual or collective, and in whatever land it is found, is a fragile thing.

78 Her situation, as representative of a subjugated people, is close to that of Esther. In both instances the dominated but, as the seventeenth-century scale of values would have it, the more civilized race and weaker sex has acquired unusual power over the (quasi) barbarian: '. . . le Persan superbe est aux pieds d'une Juive' (*Esther*, Act I. 1, l. 28). Cf. Andromaque, whose status as supposedly less civilized Trojan vis-à-vis supposedly more civilized Greek creates a different but equally ironic configuration.

79 Since Suleiman the Magnificent's siege of Vienna (1529), this expression had become a topos, as Laura Alcoba has pointed out ('La question du pouvoir au miroir Ottoman: Le *Viaje de Turquía*', in de Courcelles (ed.), *Littérature et exotisme*, pp. 17–33 (p. 23)). To the longstanding threat posed in the Mediterranean by Turkish naval strength was henceforth added the menace of a major land force. The fear of encirclement is a fear of asphyxiation. Western European anxieties about this slow strangulation are projected in Bajazet's wish for expansion beyond the prison of the 'sérail', and in the whole emphasis on death by garotting.

80 As well as extolling the spiritual and material advantages to be gained from attacking Egypt, he explicitly attempts to persuade Louis that 'une guerre européenne serait inconsidérée' [a European war would be foolhardy], *Projet d'expédition d'Égypte présenté à Louis XIV*, in *Œuvres de Leibniz publiées pour la première fois d'après les manuscrits originaux*, ed. A. Foucher de Careil (Paris: Firmin Didot, 1864), p. 5.

6

Racine's 'Jacobite' Plays:
The Politics of the Bible

EDRIC CALDICOTT

Racine's last two plays, *Esther* (1689) and *Athalie* (1691), are in many respects his most innovative. They differ from all his other theatrical works in three fundamental respects: (1) they were derived from the Bible; (2) choruses were written for them; (3) music was composed to accompany the choruses, *en l'occurrence* by Jean-Baptiste Moreau. Despite this significant new departure, the critical reception of the plays has been dominated by reference to political allegory and historical events of the time. On the basis of Racine's known admiration for his co-religionist of Port-Royal, Antoine Arnauld ('le grand Arnauld', 1612–94), and at the cost of properly literary considerations (including the information on the title page of the first edition of both plays that they were 'tirées de l'Ecriture Sainte' [derived from Holy Scripture]), the distinguished historian of Port-Royal, Jean Orcibal, propounded a thesis supporting an interpretation of *Esther* and *Athalie* as political allegories for the plight of the Jansenists and the Jacobites respectively,[1] to be resoundingly supported by René Jasinski thirty-five years later.[2] The temptation of Jansenist interpretations of Racine's work is enduring and omnipresent, while Jacobite allegory can be traced back to Michelet ('Louvois et St-Cyr', *Revue des Deux Mondes*, 1 June 1861), G. Charlier ('*Athalie* et la Révolution d'Angleterre', *Mercure de France*, 1 July 1931), and Raymond Lebègue (*Nouvelles Littéraires*, 13 February 1932). Orcibal and Jasinski leave no stone unturned to prove the existence of Jacobite allegory in *Athalie*, but they do not make the same claims for *Esther*, even though its committed anti-Williamite prologue, performed at its

---

1 Jean Orcibal, *La Genèse d'*Esther *et d'*Athalie (Paris: Librairie philosophique J. Vrin, 1950).
2 René Jasinski, *Autour de l'*Esther *racinienne* (Paris: Nizet, 1985).

première in the presence of James II himself, may have prompted comment of this kind among Racine's contemporaries. Such is the weight of Orcibal's influence as an historian that the received historical view has been that *Esther* is Jansenist inspired and *Athalie* a Jacobite play; without ever seeking to refute this view, admirers of Racine's last two plays have simply tended to ignore it, in order to seek interpretations elsewhere. It seems appropriate that this view should be re-examined in a work published in Ireland, the first point of resistance of the Jacobites. Accordingly, the purpose of this study will be to test the historical evidence which has been used as a basis for the interpretation of *Esther* and *Athalie*, and then to explore other perspectives, including rhetorical processes and biblical interpretation as well as the function of music in tragedy.

In a heavily documented historical account, Orcibal argues that the key for *Esther* is Arnauld's tract of 1687 entitled *L'Innocence Opprimée par la Calomnie, ou l'histoire de la Congrégation des Filles de l'Enfance de N.S.J.C.* The arbitrary closure by royal decree of the convent in Toulouse in 1686, and Arnauld's condemnation of that decision, were taken to be the secret trigger for Racine's play. As a consequence of this, we are implicitly invited to construe Mme de Maintenon's commission of a work for performance by the orphaned daughters of Saint-Louis at Saint-Cyr as a mere cover-up for the true analogy which lay, supposedly, between the destitute young sisters of the Jansenist-inclined convent in Toulouse and the 'nombreux essaim d'innocentes beautés' (*Esther*, Act I. 2, l. 122) in the chorus of 'jeunes lévites'. This is justified in an extraordinary demonstration of circular reasoning, used as a justification for the process of looking for hidden keys, in which Orcibal writes: 'on ne peut pas voir dans *Esther* une œuvre de circonstance sans en faire en même temps une pièce à clés' [you can't construe *Esther* as a punctual commission without showing it to be a work with an historical key].[3] It is also Arnauld who is credited by Orcibal with the inspiration of the Jacobite allegory of *Athalie*, this time with his anti-Williamite tract of February 1689, *Le Véritable Portrait de Guillaume Henri de Nassau, nouvel Absalon, nouvel Hérode, nouveau Cromwell, nouveau Néron*. Published in exile at the time that *Esther* was being performed for its exclusive audiences at Saint-Cyr, Arnauld's tract defended so stoutly the God-given rights of Kings that Louis XIV himself approved of it. The seventeenth-century taste for antonomasia is evident enough in Arnauld's titles, grounds perhaps for believing that it was a taste that Racine shared, but Orcibal's twentieth-century obsession with it goes

3 Jean Orcibal, *La Genèse d'Esther et d'Athalie*, p. 20.

as far as accounting for every character, seeing Sancroft, Archbishop of
Canterbury, as Joad, and John Churchill, future Duke of Marlborough,
as Abner. The central allegory hinges on the acceptance that Athalie
represents illegal incursion and that Joas(h) stands for Stuart legitimacy, whether in the person of James II or his son the future James
III. Unfortunately, no reference is made to the tragic irony of the
subsequent moral degradation of Joas(h) in his career as King. The
arguments and the evidence of Orcibal were taken up thirty-five years
later by Jasinski, and greeted with reverential approval by journals
such as *XVII* siècle*.[4]

Esther was performed six times between 26 January 1689 and 19
February, and only for an exclusive selection of courtiers. Newly
arrived in France after his escape from captivity in England (Madame
de Sévigné's correspondence suggests that the first formal meeting of
Louis XIV and his first cousin James II took place on the Fête de Rois,
Epiphany, 6 January[5]), James II attended two of these performances
prior to his departure for Ireland in March 1689. The story of a
people fulfilling its own prophecies by salvation from exile, punctuated
by the music composed by Moreau for the uplifting choruses in praise
of resolute kingship, was certainly an appropriate send-off for the
King of England setting out to reconquer his kingdom. His part in the
plot (Racine's plot) could be given even more weight by the bonds of
affection which almost certainly existed between him and his royal
cousin Louis XIV. Grandchildren of Henri IV, both monarchs had met
forty years earlier at the start of the first Stuart exile, when the
brothers Charles and James had followed their mother Henriette de
France and their sister Henriette d'Angleterre to refuge in France
from the English Civil War. In the course of that first exile which
lasted eleven years, James, then Duke of York, danced in the *Ballet
Royal de la Nuit* with Louis XIV in 1653, and fought at the battle of the
Dunes under Condé in 1658; six years older than Louis XIV, he
would certainly have given an example of courtly accomplishment.
Seven years after James II found refuge in France, La Bruyère's final
revision of *Les Caractères* (1696) confirmed the heroic anti-Orangist
interpretation of Louis XIV's behaviour at the time, 'un seul toujours
bon et magnanime ouvre ses bras à une famille malheureuse, tous les

---

4 See the review of Jasinski's *Autour de l'Esther racinienne* by Nicole Ferrier-Caverivière,
XVII siècle*, 150 (1986), 99–102.
5 See her letter to her daughter of 10 January, 1689, and notes by Roger Duchêne in
his Pléiade edition of *Correspondance*, 3 vols (Paris: Gallimard, 1978), 3, p. 466 (notes on
p. 1379).

autres se liguent comme pour se venger de lui'.[6] Had Racine begun *Esther* later than he did, it might have been possible to accept that the intimate affinity of royal cousins contributed to the theme of salvation in the play, but Dangeau's *Journal* tells us as early as 18 August 1688, four months before James II sought refuge in France, that Racine had chosen the topic of a new play from the book of *Esther*. Whether *Esther* was or was not a 'Jacobite' play is a question which contributes little to a refutation of Orcibal's interpretation which, it will be recalled, focused on Arnauld's condemnation of the closure of the convent of Notre Seigneur Jésus-Christ at Toulouse, but the train of related contemporary events does indicate that the dramatist would have had other, more topical, issues on his mind, more flattering for his monarch and less invidious for himself than the closure three years earlier of a Jansenist-inclined convent. This is made abundantly clear by the later composition of the prologue to *Esther*.

There was, of course, a political context to *Esther*; the shadows cast by the threatening League of Augsburg, the Grand Alliance which now threatened Louis XIV as none ever before, called for tough political realism. If contemporary political allegory is not evident in any explicit form in the text of the play proper, the prologue to *Esther* is unmistakably explicit. Exploiting the political isolation of France in order to extol the king's heroism, the 'historiographe du roi' composed the *Prologue* in the voice of Piety presenting Louis XIV to God:

> Lui seul invariable, et fondé sur la foi,
> Ne cherche, ne regarde, et n'écoute que toi
> (*Prologue*, ll. 37–8).

The identification of the war against William of Orange as a crusade for the one true church was of course a French view, and certainly not recognized by the Pope (who was neutral enough for later commentators to imagine that he was on the side of William of Orange). The political bias of the *Prologue* takes the opportunity to create a heroic role for the King in the darkening political situation in those early years of the League of Augsburg, so distant now from the triumphant treaty of Nijmegen (1678–9), and still so far from the shelter of Ryswick (1697). Its sombre, realistic tone is highlighted by comparison with the unfocused optimism of the prologue written by Molière for *Le Malade Imaginaire*, after the deceptively easy victories in Holland and the 'passage du Rhin' of 1672:

---

6 *Les Caractères* (1696), ed. Louis van Delft, 'Des Jugements', 118 (Paris: Imprimerie Nationale, 1998), p. 407.

Vos vœux sont exaucés, Louis est de retour,
Il ramène en ces lieux les plaisirs de l'amour,
[. . .]
Par ses vastes exploits son bras voit tout soumis:
Il quitte les armes,
Faute d'ennemis
    (*Le Malade Imaginaire*, 'Le Prologue' [1673]).[7]

'Faute d'ennemis' in 1689, Louis XIV certainly was not. More explicit than the text of *Esther*, the prologue of the play was a later composition – as all contemporary scholarship shows;[8] a separate piece of work, facilitating a punctual compliment to the King, it is not to be confused with the main text of the play. No convincing case has yet been made to prove the validity of political allegory, whether Jansenist or Jacobite, in the play *Esther*; even the implicit homage to Madame de Maintenon must be treated as coincidental, for fear of taking the analogy Louis XIV–Assuérus too far. The Prologue, however, is a different matter; it appears to espouse the Jacobite cause, but in presenting Louis XIV as the champion of Christendom, it goes, in fact, much further. The play itself diverged very little from the biblical original – 'ce qui serait, à mon avis', wrote Racine in his preface, 'une sorte de sacrilège, je pourrais remplir toute mon action avec les seules scènes que Dieu lui-même, pour ainsi dire, a préparées' [it would be, in my opinion, a kind of sacrilege, given that I could fill the whole of my action with the scenes the God himself, so to speak, prepared]. Taken with the approval of the play recorded by Arnauld, and the attendance of the redoubtable bishop of Meaux, Bossuet himself, at one of the command performances at Saint-Cyr,[9] these words of Racine's preface ring true, leaving little room for hidden agendas. It is in this context that the homage offered in the Prologue to Louis XIV fulfilling his role as 'Sa très Chrétienne Majesté' can be matched with the concern for scriptural fidelity in the play itself. It will be seen that these are preoccupations which transcend conjunctural issues such as the closure of a Jansenist convent or the temporary absence from home of James II.

It is, of course, to *Athalie* that the Jacobite allegory has been most persistently applied, due in no small part to the prestige of its best-known

---

7 Couton, *Molière*, 2, pp. 1094–5.
8 See, for example, the editorial comment of Raymond Picard, in Picard, *Œuvres*, notes sur *Esther*, p. 1156; and Forestier, *Œuvres*, p. 1690.
9 For Arnauld's judgement, see *Mémoires* of Louis Racine, quoted by Forestier, *Œuvres*, p. 1181; for Jansenist approval of *Esther*, see also Raymond Picard, *Nouveau corpus racinianum* (Paris: CNRS, 1976), pp. 238–48. For attendance of Bossuet, see Dangeau's *Journal*, 26 January 1689, quoted by Forestier, *Œuvres*, p. 1678.

promoters, Michelet and Orcibal. Unfortunately, they made little use in their work of seventeenth-century diplomatic archives, therefore no clear definition of the term 'Jacobite' emerges from it. Because the first two and a half years of the Jacobite wars were fought on Irish soil by a Franco–Irish alliance, the subject has drawn the interest of Irish historians. In the work done on this subject in Ireland, there are five important volumes of French diplomatic and military correspondence, these are: *Negociations de M. le Comte d'Avaux en Irlande 1689–90*, vols 1 and 2, and *Franco-Irish Correspondence December 1688–February 1692*, 3 vols.[10] Compiled from material available in French archives at Vincennes and the quai d'Orsay, this correspondence confirms that, far from being a quixotic attempt to achieve the impossible by putting the incompetent James II back on his throne, the Irish campaign of the French army (one of the longest it ever fought overseas) was an extended front, designed with great realism in face of a pan-European alliance against France in order to divert as many British troops as possible, and as far away as possible, from mainland French territory. In this respect it was a highly successful operation, part of a grand Ludovician design in which the Jacobite crusade was used as an image and a lever to mobilize otherwise motiveless local levies on the far periphery of Europe. As the work of James Hogan and Sheila Mulloy shows, French opinion of James II and his Irish auxiliaries was too low for us to imagine that their interests could ever constitute a priority for French military strategy. This can be illustrated with examples from the Irish compilations of French archival material; the evidence reveals how uncharacteristically inept it would have been for Racine, a consummate courtier and 'historiographe du roi', to graft the picaresque adventures of James II on a biblical story designed for the personal and private entertainment of Louis XIV.

First of all, the circumstances of James's escape from England to France in January 1689 were seen in Paris as far from heroic. The popular view was that William of Orange had so little to fear from him that he actually organized his father-in-law's escape. In a letter to her daughter of 10 January 1689, Madame de Sévigné wrote with some disapproval, 'Pour la fuite du roi, il paraît que le prince d'Orange l'a bien voulue' [As for the King's escape, it seems that it was what the Prince of Orange wanted].[11] For William of Orange, at least, the future in London looked perfectly secure, but just as revealing (and

10 James Hogan (ed.), *Négociations de M. le Comte d'Avaux en Irlande 1689–90*, 2 vols (Dublin, Irish Manuscripts Commission, 1934); Sheila Mulloy (ed.), *Franco-Irish correspondence, December 1688–February 1692*, 3 vols (Dublin: Irish Manuscripts Commission, 1983).
11 Duchêne, *Correspondance*, 3, p. 466.

damning) is the correspondence of the comte d'Avaux. One of the most successful French diplomats of his day, Jean-Antoine II de Mesmes (1640–1709), le comte d'Avaux, had been one of the French negotiators at Nijmegen and subsequently ambassador to Holland (where Racine's son Jean-Baptiste also served on the staff) before being given the onerous charge of 'ambassadeur extraordinaire du roi d'Angleterre' for the Irish mission. The delicacy of his responsibilities becomes abundantly clear in the high-level correspondence maintained from Ireland with Louvois (secrétaire d'Etat de la Guerre), Colbert-Croissy (secrétaire d'Etat aux Affaires étrangères, one of the nego-tiators at Nijmegen with d'Avaux, and younger brother of the 'great' Colbert), Colbert-Seignelay (a protector of Jean Racine, son of 'le grand Nord', and secrétaire d'Etat de la Marine, who had commissioned *L'Idylle de la Paix* from Racine for performance at his residence at Sceaux), and Louis XIV himself. The first despatch of d'Avaux was sent to Louis XIV from Kinsale on his arrival in Ireland on 23 March 1689, after a week at sea with James II. With astonishing bluntness he wrote, 'la seule chose, Sire, qui pourra nous faire de la peine est l'irresolution du Roy d'Angleterre, qui change souvent d'avis, et ne se détermine pas toujours au meilleur' [the only thing, Sire, which could trouble us is the indecisiveness of the King of England, who often changes his opinion, and does not always decide for the better].[12] Writing to Louvois seven months later from the camp at Ardee, north of Dublin, he is even more damning: 'Je ne puis m'empescher de vous dire qu'il [le roi d'Angleterre] n'agit pas avec la noblesse de cœur qu'on devrait attendre non pas d'un Roy, mais d'un simple gentilhomme' [I am obliged to inform you that he – the King of England – does not act with the nobility of heart to be expected not only of a King, but of an ordinary gentleman].[13] There are many more comments of this kind about the deficiencies of the king, but just as interesting is French realism on the matter of Irish troops and equipment.

Within a month of landing, the state of the Irish regiments appeared so deplorable to d'Avaux that he was driven to propose a scheme for troop exchanges The Irish troops would go to France to be properly drilled and equipped; in exchange, trained, battle-hardened French soldiers would be sent from France to bolster what feeble resistance James II could offer. The deal is proposed to Louvois in quite a hard-headed way in a despatch from Dublin dated 6 May 1689: 'Je puis bien vous asseurer que pour 4,000 hommes qui soient envoyez ici, vous en pourriez tirer six et mesme huit mille de ce pays' [I can

12 Hogan, I, p. 23.
13 *Ibid.*, p. 517.

certainly assure you that for the 4,000 men you send here, you could get six or even eight thousand men from here].[14] Unless planned as a totally cynical scheme to drain the English king's cause to reinforce Louis XIV on the mainland, this was a realistic adjustment to the crisis that d'Avaux saw looming ahead, and precisely the kind of initiative for which a man of his distinction had been appointed. That the scheme was not finally implemented until a year later, when d'Avaux was due to depart, was due to the resistance of James's Scottish commanders, notably John Drummond, Earl of Melfort, who realized, of course, that the substitution of troops was final confirmation that Stuart dynastic priorities had been superseded by the political and military objectives of France. Never would James II be able to march on London at the head of French troops. D'Avaux was timetabled to sail back to France with the Irish troops in March 1690 on the return journey of the French fleet which brought out the new French regiments to Ireland under their commander Lauzun, but on 15 March he sent a despairing despatch to Louvois summarizing the situation. Of the four Irish regiments designated to return with him, he wrote:

1. For the regiment of Lord Mountcashel, 'on peut compter au moins douze cents bons hommes' [you can count on twelve hundred good men, at least].[15]

2. 'Pour ce qui est du régiment d'OBryan, fils de Mylord Claire [sic], nous n'avons trouvé dans les treize vieilles compagnies de son regiment et dans les trois nouvelles, que sept cens quarante-huit hommes, encore y en a-t-il quelques-uns à rejeter. Mylord Claire a si peu dessein de mettre ce regiment en état d'aller en France, qu'il n'a pas averti aucun capitaine de mettre sa compagnie à cent hommes; d'ailleurs il n'y a que trois capitaines dans ce regiment qui ayent des commissions du Roy' [As for the regiment of O'Bryan, son of Lord Claire (sic), we were only able to muster in the the thirteen original companies of his regiment, and in the three new ones, seven hundred and forty-eight men, and some of those need to be retired. Lord Claire has so little intention of putting his regiment in a state of preparedness for travel to France, that he has not even instructed any of his captains to bring their company strength up to one hundred men; besides which, there are only three captains in the regiment who have the King's commission].

14 *Ibid.*, p. 120.
15 *Ibid.*, p. 689.

3. For the regiment of Fielding, he wrote: 'Filding [*sic*] travaille avec tout le zèle et toute l'application possible, mais comme il est Anglais il a de la peine à faire ses levées, quoyqu'il ait espousé une femme de la première qualité de ce pays cy' [Filding (*sic*) is working with all the energy possible, but because he is English, he has trouble raising his levies, although he is married to a high-bred lady of this country].

4. 'Pour ce qui est du regiment de Dillon, on me le promet tousjours mais je n'ai aucune nouvelle: je ne say où il est. Mylord Douvre dit qu'il n'en sait rien non plus' [As for the regiment of Dillon, I'm constantly being promised it, but I have no news: I don't know where it is. Mylord Douvre [Henry Jermyn, Lord Dover, a member of James II's general staff] says that he doesn't know either].

The judgements of d'Avaux show the same dispassionate attention to detail and efficiency in his assessment of the officers remaining in Ireland, whether English or Irish. Of the officer commanding 'le regiment du grand Prieur', that is the grand Prieur himself, Lord FitzJames teenage son of James II, he wrote to Louis XIV from Dublin on 11 February 1690: 'C'est un jeune homme fort débauché, qui se crève tous les jours d'eau de vie, et qui a esté tout cet été par ses débauches hors d'état de monter à cheval' [he is a very debauched young man, who swills himself full with brandy every day, and has been all summer so incapacitated by his excesses that he cannot even get on a horse].[16] Conversely, he is warm in praise of men who can contribute to the effectiveness of the military operation for which he was responsible: of Patrick Sarsfield, for example, who became a legendary hero in Ireland (and who subsequently died in the service of Louis XIV at the battle of Neerwinden in 1693), he wrote to Louvois as early as October 1689, 'il a de la valeur, mais surtout de l'honneur, et la probité à toute épreuve, et c'est un homme sur qui le Roy [Louis XIV] pourroit compter . . .' [he has quality, but above all a sense of honour, and integrity enough for all occasion, and is a man on whom the King can count].[17] In return, the despatches from Paris could leave him in no doubt that, pressed on all fronts, the king relied on total realism. In a communication from Versailles signed by Croissy and Louis XIV and dated 11 August 1689, he reads: 'Vous serez

16 *Ibid.*, p. 645.
17 *Ibid.*, p. 519.

informé de ce qui se passe à Mayence et à Bonn [. . ..], et pourveu que les affaires du Roy d'Angleterre se soutiennent en Irlande j'ai lieu d'espérer que mes ennemis ne remporteront aucun avantage' [You will be kept informed of events at Mainz and Bonn [. . .], and as long as the fortunes of the King of England can be maintained in Ireland, I have reason to believe that my enemies will gain no advantage].[18]

In summary, it is clear that, exploited at a local level as a rallying call, the Jacobite cause was an instrument skilfully wielded as a military and political diversion in a strategy which spanned all of western Europe. By December 1689, when Louis XIV was literally melting down the silver furnishings of Versailles, and when the incompetence of James II was a by-word, there could have been no illusions about restoring the Stuart dynasty in England. In the words of Sheila Mulloy's summary of the contents of her edition of Franco–Irish correspondence from 1688–92: '[France] would help them [James II and his Irish supporters] as long as they could be of use to her and a nuisance to William, but neither James's desire to recover his crown nor the national aspirations of the Irish seriously concerned her [France]'.[19] Given this evidence, never tapped by Orcibal or Jasinski, it is simply not possible to believe that as accomplished a courtier as Racine, 'historiographe du roi' and an intimate of Seignelay, could remain so out of touch with the situation as to plead the case of James II by means of political allegory in his theatre. In these circumstances, the attempt to argue the case for the Jansenists would have been even more tactless.

What then, are we left with if we evacuate assumptions of Jansenist and Jacobite allegory from Racine's last two plays? In the first place, obviously, Racine moves from 'l'antiquité païennne' to 'l'antiquité chrétienne'. And what would have been the literary implications of moving from one 'antiquité' to the other? It has already been seen that Racine's preface to *Esther* confirmed the obligation to remain faithful to the biblical text. But this is a scruple about content. What about dramatic means? As Roger Zuber has pointed out in an important study of Guez de Balzac's perception of the 'deux antiquités', it had been possible earlier in the century to assert that ' "les plus sévères chrétiens peuvent sans scrupule estre eloquens" ' [the most austere Christians may without qualms indulge in fine language] (Guez de Balzac, 2, 372). As Zuber adds, 'jamais contredite, cette phrase de l'auteur jeune trouve partout son application' [never contradicted, this expression of

---

18 *Ibid.*, pp. 482–3.
19 Mulloy (ed.), *Franco-Irish correspondence*, 1, Introduction, p. xiii.

the young author can be seen to be valid everywhere].[20] From this it can be inferred that the devices and figures from the pagan sources of rhetoric could still be employed in Christian apologia. In particular, there remains in Racine's biblical plays a sense of conjunctural topicality; it is used to enhance the universality of a given theme through a process of echoing layers of associated meanings. This is, of course, associated with the rhetorical process of innutrition. Following work by Basil Munteano and Gilles Declercq,[21] innutrition has been described most recently within the French tradition by Emmanuel Bury as 'la pratique du dramaturge qui aime à enrichir la donnée initiale par tout un réseau de réminiscences puisées à d'autres textes' [the craft of the dramatist who wants to enhance his basic material with reminiscences drawn from other texts].[22] Within the English literary tradition, a similar train of reflexion (not about Racine but about creative work in general) has been inspired by the work of Frances Yates, in particular her book *The Art of Memory* (Chicago, 1966), translated into French in 1975. In the wider application proposed by Yates, the 'réseau de réminiscences puisées *à d'autres textes*' [my italic] can be extended to include momentous events of the present (i.e. Racine's present). Racine's son Louis offers us an interesting example from his father's life. As 'historiographe du roi', instrumental in the creation of the Académie des Inscriptions (once called 'l'Académie des Médailles'), Racine became responsible for the inscriptions to be added to commemorative medals, therefore professionally obliged to pay attention to momentous contemporary events. One particular case is described thus in the memoirs of his son, Louis Racine:

> Mon père a donné dans quelques occasions des devises, qui, dans leur simplicité ont été trouvées fort heureuses, comme celle dont le corps était une orangerie, et l'âme, *conjuratos ridet aquilones*. Elle fut approuvée parce qu'elle avait également rapport à l'orangerie de Versailles bâtie depuis peu, et à la ligue qui se formait contre la France.

> [My father created on several occasions mottoes and blasons which, because of their simplicity, were deemed to be very good, like the one with the design of an orangery and the message, *conjuratos ridet aquilones* (he / it scorns the conspiring north winds). It was approved of because

20 Roger Zuber, 'Guez de Balzac et les deux Antiquités', *XVIIᵉ siècle*, 131, no. spécial 'Antiquité chrétienne antiquité païenne dans la culture française du XVIIᵉ siècle'(1981), 135–48 (p. 145).
21 Basil Munteano, 'Sur le jeune Racine: culture et découverte de soi', *XVIIᵉ siècle*, 134 (1982), 3–18; Gilles Declercq, 'Le lieu commun dans les tragédies de Racine: topique, poétique et mémoire à l'âge classique', *XVIIᵉ siècle*, 150 (1986), 43–60.
22 Emmanuel Bury, 'Les Antiquités de Racine', *Œuvres et Critiques*, 24. 1 (1999), *Présences de Racine* (Tübingen: Gunter Narr), p. 30.

it applied equally well to the recently built orangery of Versailles (the second Orangery at Versailles, by Mansart, was completed in 1688), and also to the league which was being formed against France (the League of Augsburg)].[23]

The truth value of a given literary text appears to be enhanced by the multiplication of references that can be identified in it, and these references fell into two categories: (1) mutations of classical sources, as Declercq has shown, for example, in the creation of a second Troy in *Andromaque* (see note 9 above); (2) incorporation of contemporary persons or events disguised by the processes of antonomasia or prosopopeia, as Georges Couton has illustrated.[24] With Racine's career as 'historiographe du roi' (as a reader, therefore, of events and a creator of emblems), intervening between his dramatic exploitation of 'l'antiquité païenne' and 'l'antiquité chrétienne', it is entirely to be expected that the process of innutrition should remain constant even if the nature of the sources changes; as Bury put it in the article quoted above, the practice 'demeure présente même dans le domaine de la tragédie sacrée, ce qui dénote bien un type de lecture identique des textes anciens, fussent-ils sacrés ou profanes [is also present in the domain of sacred tragedy, which indicates a common mode of reading old texts, whether religious or not']. As if in corroboration of this, in his description of the reception of *Esther* (a biblical play, after all), Louis Racine wrote that in current opinion of the time, 'l'Auteur avait suivi l'exemple des Anciens, dont les Tragédies ont souvent rapport aux événements de leur temps' [the Author had followed the example of the Ancients, whose tragedies are often linked to contemporary events of their time].[25] Between the composition and the reception of the work there is ample room for mis-attribution, but the polysemic process of innutrition appears to be accepted and understood by the author and his public, both in work derived from classical sources and that derived from biblical ones. In terms of seventeenth-century rhetoric it could serve either the *inventio* or the *dispositio* of a theatrical work, as a familiar setting or organic part of action, or both. In the case of biblical texts, it appears less likely to reach (for Racine, at least) the point of confiscation of the original topic as a vehicle for contemporary allegory. The aim was presumably to enhance the message of biblical truth by illustrating its continuing relevance in the contemporary world. It was all a question of degree. And there was the music of Moreau.

23 Forestier, *Œuvres*, p. 1156.
24 See the article by Georges Couton, 'Langages de l'allégorie au XVIIᵉ siècle', *CAIEF*, 28 (1976), 81–101.
25 Forestier, *Œuvres*, p. 1176.

Paradoxically, and in reverse of the tendency in opera, the shift in the 'deux antiquités' sees the theme of love going out of Racine's repertoire as music came in. The revival of interest in the music of Jean-Baptiste Moreau allows us to understand much better several aspects of the last two plays of Racine. The music of Moreau is used, not as in opera to emphasize human emotion, but to underscore a deeper sense of spirituality. This is particularly the case in *Esther* where, like an oratorio, the chorus sweeps beyond individual motivation and conflict to reach a triumphant, transcendent truth. The study of Moreau's music by Warnecke and Hartwig (see pp. 188–208) has pointed out the musical significance of the last phrases of *Esther*, the final word, 'L'Eternité', ringing out like a triumphant 'Amen', is vested with the same status of thematic summation as the 'pureté' of *Phèdre*. But the music of Moreau enhances this impact to situate 'l'éternité' beyond time, beyond the scale of human conflict.[26] The two scales of time are also implicit in the conclusion of *Athalie*: the ultimate, post-performance fall from grace of Joas(h), who as king was to murder Zacharie, permits Racine to expose the ephemeral, illusory meaning of the tragedy played out before us. It means that there is another interpretation and another future to be found beyond the immediate events. The hidden God is inscrutable, but faith in his constancy must be absolute. Henry Phillips has suggested that 'Racine's plays are very often plays of broken vows',[27] but in *Athalie*, as Joad assures Abner, God will demonstrate 'que sa parole est stable, et ne trompe jamais' (*Athalie*, Act I.i, l. 158). This is a recurrent theme of the Psalms, and Forestier's edition points out that this specific formulation is almost identical in Psalms 109 and 110. Presented in the *Prologue* to *Esther* as 'seul invariable, et fondé sur la Foi' (l. 37), Louis XIV is no different from God in this respect.

The dominant themes in the passages which are highlighted by the accompaniment of Moreau's music are those of kingship and the law of God, echoing in *Esther* the Psalms, and in *Athalie* the books of the prophets and Deuteronomy. The form and imagery of all the choruses of both plays are inspired by the Psalms, which are, after all, the one part of the Bible originally designed to be accompanied by music; often published in seventeenth-century France under the title *Les Psaumes de David*, they also exalt the theme of kingship through homage to David, the royal musician and the original creator of the Psalms. The theme of kingship appears to remain constant in both the pagan and biblical

---

26 For discussion of the meaning of 'l'éternité', see Henry Phillips, *Racine, Language and Theatre* (Durham: Durham University Press, 1994), notes to Ch. 4, p. 152.
27 *Ibid.*, p. 110.

cycles of Racine's theatre, but it is in fact elevated in the biblical plays to a unique relationship with God. This may also be seen as part of a wider tendency, as Alexandre Aran suggests in his article 'L'idée de *translatio electionis* des Juifs aux Français au XVIIe siècle', 'la France est ainsi investie au même rôle messianique que le peuple de la Bible' [France is thus invested with the same messianic role as the people of the Bible].[28] Particularly marked in the symbolism of the monarchy, with the chrism of royal anointment, and not only the lily of Sharon (taken from the *Song of Songs* and the Book of Esdras, 4) but the pillars of the Temple used as royal emblems, this tendency can also be seen as a manifestation of the 'gigantisme' that Nicole Ferrier-Caverivière observed in the inflation of the royal image at the end of the reign of Louis XIV.[29]

[margin: France as Messiah]

[margin: y. inflated image of LXIV, full of Bib. borrowings]

Going beyond the image of the monarch in the earlier pagan emulation of Rome, Racine's biblical plays exalt more than ever the status of the king. The cycle of Psalms which evoke Sion and the central impregnable refuge of the Temple have been identified by modern scholarship as sharing 'le motif de la lutte contre le chaos' [sharing the motif of struggle against chaos];[30] Psalm 48 provides an even more significant insight by identifying Sion as the 'cité du grand roi', and it is 'quoted' almost directly in the chorus of Athalie, Act II. 9.[31] As Jane Conroy's thoughtful analysis of the 'Other' in Racine's work suggests, the 'other' point of reference is Louis XIV himself (see pp. 75–99): in the case of 'l'antiquité païenne' this is an opposite, but in the case of 'l'antiquité chrétienne', it is a cultural extension. France as a Christian citadel, 'la fille aînée de l'Eglise', is governed by a defender of the faith ('Un Roi qui me protège, un Roi victorieux',

[margin: Esther + Athalie exalt status of King]

---

28 *XVIIe siècle*, 194, no. spécial 'La Bible au 17e siècle' (1997), 105–27 (p. 107).

29 Nicole Ferrier-Caverivière, *L'Image de Louis XIV dans la littérature française* (Paris: PUF, 1981).

30 See L. Pirot, A. Robert, Henri Cazelles and André Feuillet (eds), *Dictionnaire de la Bible* (Paris: Letouzay & Ané, 1928–85), vol. x, 'Psaumes', more particularly 'les cantiques de Sion', pp. 23–6.

31 See also Pirot *et. al.* (eds), *Dictionnaire de la Bible*, vol. x, 'La Royaute', by E. Lipiński, pp. 392–414. With regard to the numbers of the Psalms, the reader should remember that different versions of the Bible reflect different editorial or theological positions; for this reason the numbers of the Psalms may vary, as does the text, from one version of the Bible to another. The text of the Bible was in a dynamic state of change in Racine's time, and the version that he knew particularly well was a contemporary translation (to which he may himself have contributed) by Louis-Isaac Lemaître de Sacy; it is available in a modern edition prepared by Philippe Sellier, *La Bible, traduite du grec et du latin par Louis-Isaac le Maître de Sacy*, coll. Bouquins (Paris: Laffont, 1998). The version used for the present study was *La Bible de Jérusalem* (Paris: Editions du Cerf, 1973). See also the notes on biblical references in chapters by Viala, and Hartwig and Warnecke (pp. 200 and 231).

Prologue, l. 9) ensconced in a modern-day Sion. Strongly dependent upon this cycle of Psalms, the choruses of *Esther* and *Athalie* extol a peculiarly royal theme in the conflation of the divinity of kingship and the majesty of God. As Ernst Kantorowicz pointed out in his book, *The King's Two Bodies. A Study in Mediæval Political Theology* (Princeton, 1957), it is a theme which plays an indispensable part in early modern concepts of kingship; it therefore found a prolonged resonance in works of art. He suggests that the miniature of the Gospel Book of Aachen, representing the symbiosis of earthly and heavenly kingship, was inspired by the glosses of St Augustine's *Enarrationes in Psalmos*; in more recent times, Shakespeare explored its dramatic interest in *Richard II*. As a constant theme in the Psalms, the theme of harmonious union of the King on earth and God in heaven would necessarily be absorbed and reproduced in later adaptations of them, but Racine's exploitation of it, reinforced by his collaboration with Moreau, has nothing accidental about it (see also the study of *Esther* by Hartwig and Warnecke). His biblical adaptations are both intensely lyrical, and quite deliberate in their use of sources

In the study of Racine's exploitation of biblical themes, and particularly the Psalms, it is his erudition and literary skill which hold our interest. His spiritual devotion in later life appears to be beyond doubt, explaining how he was so steeped in the Psalms, but his successful reworking of them is an undeniable literary achievement, exploiting biblical sources even more artfully than he did the texts of 'l'antiquité païenne', from Euripides to Ovid and Tacitus. Steeped in the liturgy, as his *Hymnes du Bréviaire Romain* show, he was also close to Lemaître de Sacy's translation of the Psalms.[32] Following the example of Mauriac's *Vie de Racine* (Paris, 1928), it was argued by the English scholar Geoffrey Brereton, and then by Clarac in the *Intégrale* edition of the *Œuvres Complètes*, that it was Racine who wrote the *Ode tirée du Psaume XVII*, composing it as solace in the dark moments of the 'affaire

32 In his article 'Notes sur les origines des chœurs d'*Esther*', *Revue d'Histoire Littéraire de la France*, 26. 5 (1909), 110–30, Joseph Vianey argued for a close identity between Racine's rendering of the Psalms and that of the translation from Latin by Antoine Godeau, bishop of Grasse. Vianey restricts himself to the comparison of specific passages, but the model offered by Godeau's career deserves more attention. Familiar with the 'beau monde' as an habitué of Madame de Rambouillet's salon, yet reputedly sensitive to Jansenist doctrine, Godeau would have been an interesting figure for Racine: his 'paraphrases' of passages from Holy Scripture, including the Psalms, were published as *Œuvres chrétiennes* in 1633, accompanied by his *Discours* on biblical translation, to be followed in 1648 by his collection of 'paraphrases' of the Psalms which, according to Jean-Pierre Chauveau, 'Godeau, Antoine' (*Dictionnaire du Grand Siècle* (Paris: Fayard, 1990), 'connut un succès durable, au point de solliciter le talent des musiciens', p. 662, col. 1.

des poisons'.[33] He is also reported in his son's memoirs to have read the Psalms to great effect to his ailing protector Seignelay on his sickbed.[34] It is thus not surprising that the recurring themes and the complex sonorities of the Psalms should ultimately find expression in his dramatic work. In *Esther*, with the all the lyric expression of the Psalms, he captures the same range of emotion, from lamentation for a lost opportunity and a distant haven ('Déplorable Sion', *Esther*, Act I. 2, l. 132), innocent and occasionally fearful trust, to the celebration of God's will and salvation ('Que son nom soit béni. Que son nom soit chanté', *Esther*, Act III. 9, l. 1283). The range of the chorus in *Athalie* is less extensive, but although remaining focused in one way or another upon the 'divine et charmante loi' (*Athalie*, ll. 347, 360, 371), it retains a central interest in the responsibilities of the King (or indeed Queen, as the case may be).

[margin: captures wide range of emotion]

As if in confirmation of this, and in one of his most remarkable innovations, Racine openly and systematically acknowledges his inspiration by making explicit reference in the choruses to their principal, original source – the Psalms. In *Esther*, the chorus responds at its first appearance (Act I. 2) to the specific request of Esther herself:

> Mes filles, chantez-nous quelqu'un de ces cantiques
> Où vos voix si souvent se mêlant à mes pleurs
> De la triste Sion célèbrent les malheurs.
> *Esther*, ll. 128–31).

This is a process which can be called dramatic actualization. Taking the original circumstances of the Psalms into account, with their forms, themes, and the people who inhabit them, Racine composed a stage version which not only reproduced all these details, but announced in his text at regular intervals that this was what he was doing. The Psalms are brought to life at the French Court, and as Psalms their musical accompaniment is of prime importance; Racine's pen and Moreau's baton are the replacements for David's harp. As if the original circumstances of composition of the Psalms were being enacted on stage, Racine gives added dramatic weight to his chorus by signalling the assimilation. He frequently resorts to an evocation in the chorus of the original political functions of the Psalms; this, again, is an organic part of the action, impacting therefore on the immediate present:

[margin: R. even announces in text that he is invoking Psalms]

[margin: and their original political fun]

33 Geoffrey Brereton, *Jean Racine: A Critical Biography* (London: Cassels, 1951), p. 253; it is a view dismissed by both Picard and Forestier.
34 See Forestier, *Œuvres*, p. 1170.

Chantons, on nous l'ordonne; et que puissent nos chants
Du cœur d'Assuérus adoucir la rudesse
Comme autrefois David, par ses accords touchants,
Calmait d'un roi jaloux la sauvage tristesse!

                (*Esther*, Act II. 3, ll. 996–9).

It was originally David who struck a chord which was pleasing to
the Lord, but Racine here reveals his ambition to accomplish, in
collaboration with Moreau, something similar with Louis XIV. A
further example of dramatic actualization can be observed in the
chorus of *Athalie*, where one of the soloists refers to the sanctity of the
original themes of the Psalms in order to stress their present scenic
state of defilement:

Au lieu des cantiques charmants,
Où David t'exprimait ses saints ravissements,
Et bénissait son Dieu, son Seigneur, et son Père;
Sion, chère Sion, que dis-tu quand tu vois
Louer le Dieu de l'impie Etrangère
Et blasphémer le nom qu'ont adoré tes Rois?

                (*Athalie*, Act II. 9, ll. 804–9).

By this means, adapting the music and the principal themes of the
Psalms with great artistry to the taste of their patrons and to the
demands of dramatic action, Racine and Moreau manage at the same
time to call attention to the authority of their sources. All the sequences
of the Psalms identified by modern literary exegesis can be found in
the choruses of *Esther* and *Athalie* (i. Hymns of Praise; ii. Thanksgiving,
iii. Individual and Community Laments, and iv. Trust Songs), but
pride of place goes to the Royal Psalms of the King (Psalms 2, 18, 20,
21, 45, 72, 78, 89, 101, 110, 132, 144), and the Royal Psalms of Yahweh
as King (29, 47, 48, 93, 95–9). Dominant, however, in Racine's time
would have been the original classification of so many Psalms as the
Psalms of David, of royal origin. As in the sequence of 'royal Psalms',
the common bond in power of God and the earthly King is the
principal theme of *Esther* and *Athalie*. In *Esther*, from Act II. 8 and the
veneration of God, 'Plus heureux le peuple innocent, / Qui dans le
Dieu du Ciel a mis sa confiance' (ll. 792–3), the chorus of Act III. 3
turns to specific praise of the strong King, 'J'admire un Roi victorieux,
Que sa valeur conduit triomphant en tous lieux.' (ll. 889–900). In
Athalie, the chorus of Act II. 9 not only refers to the young Joas(h) in
the symbolic language of seventeenth-century France as a 'jeune lys'
(l. 781), but invokes David as an example for him.

The musical accompaniment is, of course, an integral part of the message, indeed in *Athalie* it is used literally to introduce the voice of God himself (Act III. 7). In *Esther*, the chorus is actively involved in seven scenes, and is a silent onlooker in no less than thirteen additional ones, with a musical passage linking Acts II and III. The relationship of the music with the text in *Esther* is thus more complex than in *Athalie* which simply has five choral scenes, most of which are introduced, or closed, in an arbitrary way ('Mes filles, c'est assez, suspendez vos cantiques', commands Josabet at the start of Act II). In an important study of the biblical dramas staged at Saint-Cyr under the direction of Madame de Maintenon (of which the first was *Esther*, followed by *Athalie*, *Jephté* [l'abbé Boyer, published 1691], *Judith* [anonymous], and *Jonathas* [Duché de Vancy, published 1700]), Anne Piéjus has demonstrated that *Esther* was by far the most ambitious, with almost 30 per cent of its 1286 verses being sung – and the fact of being sung gave those verses a far greater preponderance in the overall production than their simple mathematical third. With over 1800 verses, *Athalie* was in appearance a longer play, but only seven per cent of them were sung; the following productions of Saint-Cyr maintained this tendency towards increasing simplicity.[35] A remarkable literary homage to the influence of the Psalms, the choruses in *Esther*, accompanied by strings and harpsichord, using varying line length and anaphora to create recurring rhyme and a melodic strophic structure, are above all a truly unique dramatic evocation of the lyric outpourings of the unknown psalmists. Even in *Athalie*, with its reduced scale of the chorus designed to be accompanied only by harpsichord, the language of the Psalms is brought to life in the last words of Joas(h):

> Dieu, qui voyez mon trouble et mon affliction,
> Détournez loin de moi sa malédiction . . .
> *(Athalie*, Act V. 7, ll. 1797–8).[36]

The last speech of *Athalie* belongs, of course, to Joad, whose message remains that earthly kings ignore the will of God at their peril. The realistic contemporary corollary to that was that those earthly kings who do act in the name of God can claim greater privilege: like Louis XIV, they are uniquely entitled, for example, to wage just wars. Entirely at one with Louis XIV's posture as defender

---

35 Anne Piéjus, 'Esther, un modèle paradoxal de théâtre musical pour Saint-Cyr', *PFSCL*, 24. 47 (1997), 395–420.
36 Since the provenance of the *Ode tirée du Psaume XVII* remains in dispute, attributed to Racine by Pierre Clarac (Edition Intégrale) but not by Picard (Pléiade), we shall refrain from comparing this passage with the message of that poem.

of the faith, Racine's biblical plays articulate the monarchical doctrine of his time, bringing the issues of kingship much nearer the real world than they were in the work derived from classical antiquity. Indeed, providing the only possible vehicle for sentiments of nationalism under the ancien régime, the royal theme became a nationalist one. The *Mémoires* of the duc de Luynes inform us that, after a production of *Esther* at court in January 1756, Louis XV felt so engaged by the royal theme of the play that he himself wrote additional verses for it:

> Dieu qui consacrez notre enfance
> A prier pour nos souverains
> Recevez l'encens de nos mains
> Versez vos dons les plus chers sur la France.[37]

For all these reasons, Racine's shift to 'l'antiquité chrétienne' may perhaps have stemmed as much from the worldly concerns of a courtier as from his own deepening spirituality; the argument presented here is that his sensitive reproduction of the themes and rhythmic patterns of the Psalms in courtly performance reveals not only intimacy with his biblical sources but a determination to propagate them as an act of homage to Louis XIV. As always with Racine, we find an allusive, elusive 'effet du caméléon'.[38] If biblical themes were an expression of personal faith, they undeniably served other purposes, most notably as a vehicle for royal propaganda. As we have seen, some critics have confused the part with the whole by claiming the plight of the Jansenists as the key for *Esther*, and the Jacobite cause as the sole inspiration of *Athalie*. These are interpretations which take no account whatsoever of the specific and consistent themes presented here. And what about the music? Why did Racine decide to introduce music into *Esther*? Surely not because of the Jansenists. Was it because Madame de Maintenon wanted an appropriate exercise for the young girls of Saint-Cyr, or because the taste for opera required it? Was it on account of his own spiritual exaltation, or was it a tactically expedient acknowledgement of the oratorio *Esther*, written by Giulio Rospiglioso, the future Pope Clement IX, for the court of the Barberini in 1632?[39] Why *Esther*? Because the Bishop of Langres had preached a retreat to Henriette de France (another Stuart exile, and mother of the dedicatee

37 Related in the *Mémoires* of the duc de Luynes (Paris: Firmin Didot, 1864), vol. XIV, pp. 384 ff., the incident (and the verses) are quoted in the unpublished doctoral thesis of Carol Oncley Irwin, 'An investigation of Moreau's incidental music for Racine's play *Esther*', University of Rochester, NY, 1983.

38 See Alain Viala's book, *Racine. La stratégie du caméléon* (Paris: Seghers, 1990).

39 Margaret Murata, *Opera for the Papal Court (1631-68)* (Ann Arbor: UMI Research Press, 1981), p. 20.

of *Andromaque*), on that theme?[40] Or because Bossuet had used the Book of Esther as illustration for his *Discours sur l'histoire universelle*? All these reasons are possible, but none of them are individually satisfying. In the topicality of them all we find an illustration of the rhetorical process of innutrition, absorbing contemporary references to highlight the universality of the central theme.

It is at this juncture that consideration of matters rhetorical runs into those of dramaturgy and textual genetics, both of which Georges Forestier has investigated in his introduction to his Pléiade edition of Racine and in these pages (see pp. 14–26). The question to be put here is the same as the one asked of the rhetorical process: to what extent does the exploitation of biblical material entail a different process from the exploitation of classical sources? The analysis offered by Forestier is convincing, arguing that Corneille's formula of 'des violences au sein des alliances' is adapted by Racine to an internalized conflict between 'convenance' and 'ressemblance', to a point where Saint-Evremond could complain that 'les caractères l'emportent sur les sujets' [the characters win out over subject matter]. Can this be also true of the biblical plays, after the introduction of music and Holy Scripture? The answer appears to be mixed, because *Esther* has been reproached for its subservience of character to a pre-ordained script whereas *Athalie* has sometimes been taxed with making the daughter of Jezabel too attractive. In one sense, the Cornelian formula of violence between close partners returns in the biblical plays, with the suspenseful confrontation of Esther and her husband Assuérus on the one hand, and that of Athalie and her descendant Joas on the other. But the sources impose a greater change: with an omniscient and inscrutable God in control, the conflict and the reversal are more sudden and absolute in the biblical plays than in Racine's earlier ones. The recompense unwittingly decreed for Mardochée by Aman (*Esther*, Act II. 5), and Esther's final denunciation of Aman (*Esther*, Act III. 4) brook no answers; they are as complete and one-sided as Athalie's disintegration in her final confrontation with Joas. In any other circumstances, the uncompromising zealotry of Joad would pass as fanaticism. In all cases, the confrontations and their outcome are anticipated and celebrated by Racine's unique adaptations of the Psalms sung by the chorus. By reducing the blurred edges of historical causality and human morality, the introduction of the Divine Will makes the plays more one-sided, and the irony more extreme.

40 Jean Dubu, 'Racine prophète? A propos d'une récente reprise d'*Esther*', *PFSCL*, 15. 29 (1988), 446.

shift:
tragedy →
drama of
kingship

There is, therefore, a shift in the dramaturgical balance of the plays adapted from 'l'antiquité chrétienne', and this is because their focus has shifted from the universal legacy of tragedy to the specific drama of kingship. The intimacy of the circle before which the plays were performed at court only serves to emphasize the weight of royal majesty which they celebrate. The message was both a biblical one and a contemporary political one, but how could it have been a tragic one? How do we avoid the paradox presented by Steiner with the incompatibility of Christianity and tragedy? It is Steiner himself who provides the answer: 'In *Esther* and *Athalie*, he writes, the tension between fable and rational form, which is the mainspring of energy in Racine's previous plays, is resolved. Deriving from Scripture, the truth of the dramatic action is no longer conventional or figurative. It is actual'.[41] In other words, adds Steiner, the dramatist 'regarded sacred history as materially true'. In these stark and simple terms, the drama-

of Steiner:
not traditional
sense of tragedy —

but mystery, power,
liturgy of kingship

tization of God's word played before His chosen monarch brings us a strangely compelling spectacle, situating the audience between their Maker and their Monarch. It may not be tragedy in the strict sense of the word, but all the mystery and power of a unique confrontation are there in a liturgy of kingship.[42] In such an ambitious enterprise as this, offering the *credo* and the *gloria* of Bourbon monarchy, it was inevitable that James II and his entourage should have caught some of the reflected rays of the Sun − even if dispossessed and in exile, they were, after all, royal cousins, distantly touched by the sacred droplets of the Sainte-Ampoule used in the ritual of French coronations. But even at that, they were, in political terms, no more than inconvenient satellites in a higher order of things.

41 George Steiner, *The Death of Tragedy* (London: Faber & Faber), p. 97.
42 The wider aspects of this interpretation were explored in subsequent discussion with Dr Angela Ryan of University College Cork. I am grateful to her for pointing out the analogy with the enduring perception of the King's two bodies, as traced in its artistic and social development by Kantorowicz's *The King's Two Bodies: A Study of Medieval Political Theology* (Princeton NJ: Princeton University Press, 1957), translated into French by Jean-Philippe and Nicole Genet, *Les Deux Corps du Roi: essai sur la théologie politique du Moyen Âge*, coll. Bibliothèque des Histoires (Paris: Gallimard, 1989). This perspective underlines the orthodoxy of Racine's homage to the King not only in his temporal power and physical presence, but also in his spiritual dimensions as 'Sa très Chrétienne Majesté'.

7

Les frères ennemis: Racine, Molière and 'la querelle du théâtre'

ROBERT MCBRIDE

Racine and Molière were both writing plays during the years 1660–70, a period described by a recent critic as 'the moment of crisis' during the seventeenth century's 'querelle du théâtre'.[1] The years which produced some of the greatest plays in the history of the French theatre also witnessed the most determined attack on its right to exist. How convenient it would have been for the historian of the theatre to record that Racine and Molière mounted a united front against their mutual enemies! Goethe and Schiller, Mendelssohn and Schumann have left examples of their joint productions,[2] but nothing could be further from the truth concerning Racine and Molière.

1660-1670- Reign of querelle du théâtre

As far as we are able to ascertain, the French playwrights remained in a state of enmity towards each other throughout the controversy surrounding the theatre, during which they mounted separate and very different defences of their art. According to Grimarest, the first biographer of Molière, it was the latter who by a supreme irony provided the title for Racine's first tragedy, *Les Frères ennemis* (June, 1664), which was followed by *Alexandre Le Grand* (December, 1665), both performed by Molière's troupe of actors at the Palais-Royal. The definitive separation occurred following Racine's dissatisfaction with the acting style of Molière's troupe, and their animosity continued during the 'querelle du théâtre' itself. At the end of the preface to his sole

Racine vs. Molière - enmity

break after Alex

---

1 Pierre Nicole, *Traité de la comédie: et autres pièces d'un procès du théâtre*, ed. L. Thirouin (Paris: Champion, 1998), p. 7.
2 The former created the periodical *Die Horen* (1795–97), and the latter the state academy for music, in Leipzig (1843). In spite of the fact that both partnerships were of relatively brief duration, the point to underline is the readiness of those involved to co-operate with fellow artists of genius.

comedy, *Les Plaideurs* (1668), Racine congratulates himself on his avoid-
ance of 'ces sales équivoques' [these unsavoury innuendos] and 'ces
malhonnêtes plaisanteries, qui coûtent maintenant si peu à la plupart
de nos Écrivains; et qui font retomber le Théâtre dans la turpitude,
d'où quelques auteurs plus modestes l'avaient tiré' [these scabrous
jokes which are effortlessly recycled by most writers and bring the
theatre into that state of disrepute from which it had been rescued by
dramatists with a greater sense of propriety]. This shaft was destined
for his erstwhile collaborator and benefactor, who was warding off
attacks against the supposed immorality of his *Dom Juan* (1665), not to
mention *Tartuffe* (still proscribed by the authorities), or *Amphitryon* (1668)
with its concluding praise of cuckoldry. There would seem to be many
reasons for their state of antipathy. Racine, some seventeen years
younger than Molière, must have considered the latter as an oppressive
and eminent presence in the theatre. La Grange describes the older
playwright as being polite but somewhat taciturn in nature, his
manner concealing a great depth of humanity.[3] It is more than likely
that the youthful Racine was altogether too impetuous and ambitious
to appreciate the qualities of the more mature playwright. It must be
added that Molière's troupe does not seem to have performed serious
plays well, which explains at least Racine's desire to have his second
tragedy *Alexandre Le Grand* (1665) put on elsewhere, if not his decision to
have it played by the royal actors at the Hôtel de Bourgogne at the
same time as it was being produced by Molière. A third factor underlying their incompatibility is to be found in the contrasting influences
which to a large extent shape their views of life. Racine was educated
at Port-Royal by the Jansenists, Molière at the Collège de Clermont,
by the Jesuits.[4] The very different influences encountered by each go
a long way towards explaining their divergent stances during the
polemics about the theatre, even if at that particular time both seemed
to be independent of religious influences. In this chapter, I wish
to examine their respective approaches to the controversy, and to
assess how effective these were. More particularly in the case of
Racine, I shall consider how his approach reflected his experiences of
Port-Royal.

In Molière's case, there is an immense difference between the way
in which he initially defends his theatre before the sole performance
of *L'Imposteur* in 1667 and thereafter, with the subsequent intervention

---

3 Preface of the edition of 1682, Couton, *Molière*, 1, p. 999.
4 See the well-researched article by E. Dubois, 'L'Education de Molière au collège de
Clermont', *Le Nouveau Moliériste*, 2 (1995), 21–33.

of La Mothe Le Vayer which brought a new dimension into the polemics.[5] In his *Premier Placet* to the king of 1664 on *Tartuffe*, Molière stresses three points which in his view ought to persuade the king to allow the performance of his play. The former pupil of the Jesuits skilfully deploys his argument, setting out premise, deduction and conclusion: (*a*) 'Le devoir de la comédie étant de corriger les hommes en les divertissant, j'ai cru que, dans l'emploi où je me trouve, je n'avais rien de mieux à faire que d'attaquer par les peintures ridicules les vices de mon siècle' [since the duty of comedy is to correct people by amusing them, I thought that there could be nothing better for a dramatist to do than to attack abuses of society];[6] (*b*) 'j'avais eu, Sire, la pensée que je ne rendrais pas un petit service à tous les honnêtes gens de votre royaume, si je faisais une comédie qui décriât les hypo-crites' [I imagined that I was performing a small service to all civilized people in France by holding up to ridicule those who make a living out of hypocrisy];[7] (*c*) he concludes that 'Les tartuffes, sous main, ont eu l'adresse de trouver grâce auprès de votre Majesté; et les originaux enfin ont fait supprimé la copie' [the hypocrites have deviously managed to find favour with Your Majesty, the very people who recognized themselves in the play have had it suppressed for no other good reason].[8] Then the hapless Molière detailed the care with which he distinguished true religion from hypocrisy, and he repeated this in 1667 and 1669.[9] During the period 1664–67 his defence was at times indignant or naïve, but always transparently honest. It collapsed, however, when confronted with the devastating charge put to him by the Premier Président, Lamoignon, whom he visited with Boileau in August 1667 in order to have the ban on *L'Imposteur* revoked: 'je ne saurais vous permettre de jouer votre comédie. Je suis persuadé qu'elle est fort belle et fort instructive, mais il ne convient pas à des comédiens d'instruire les hommes sur les matières de la morale chrétienne et de la religion; ce n'est pas au théâtre de se mêler de prêcher l'Evangile' [I cannot conceivably allow your comedy to be performed. I am persuaded that it is well written and instructive, but it does not behove actors to teach people about issues pertaining to Christian doctrine and religion; it is not the function of the theatre to involve itself in

---

5 See my editions of Le Vayer, *Lettre sur la comédie de l'Imposteur* (Durham: DMLS, 1994), and of the reconstruction of *L'Imposteur* (Durham: DMLS, 1999).
6 Couton, *Molière*, 1, p. 889.
7 *Ibid.*
8 *Ibid.*, p. 890.
9 *Placet*, 1664, second paragraph; *Placet*, 1667, second paragraph; *Préface*, 1669, third paragraph, all in Couton, *Molière*, 1, pp. 884–93.

preaching the Gospel].[10] By denying Molière's premise, Lamoignon cut the ground from under his feet.

From Molière's point of view, his comedy *Tartuffe* had been ready for a long time, and his very livelihood depended on him overcoming the hostility of his enemies, but the circumstances giving rise to Racine's entrance into the controversy could not be more different. It results from a set of circumstances, apparently fortuitous but probably inevitable, involving the clash of a certain kind of temperament with the clearest expression of that religious dogma in which he had been brought up. The tactics employed by both dramatists could not differ more, with the former pupil of the Jesuits underlying the moral duty of the theatre, and the erstwhile pupil of the Jansenists emphasizing its function as a source of amusement. Molière's argument, unfortunately for him, only served to strengthen his opponents' case, since the Church has always jealously guarded its exclusive right to teach on moral issues. Racine, very astutely, situated the discussion in an area which he knew to be highly dangerous for intractable moralists to enter. Molière made every attempt to avoid offence to those who, in good faith, disagreed with his play.[11] Racine, on the other hand, made no pretence

10 Brossette's note of 9 November 1702, in *Correspondance Boileau-Brossette* quoted by G. Mongrédien, *Recueil des textes et des documents relatifs à Molière* (Paris; CNRS, 1973), 1, p. 291: 'Molière, qui ne s'attendait pas à ce discours, demeura entièrement déconcerté, de sorte qu'il lui fut impossible de répondre à M. le premier Président. Il essaya pourtant de prouver à ce magistrat que sa comédie était très innocente, et qu'il l'avait traitée avec toutes les précautions que demandait la délicatesse de la matière du sujet; mais, quelques efforts que pût faire Molière, il ne fit que bégayer et ne put point calmer le trouble où l'avait jeté M. le Premier Président' [whereupon Molière,who was not at all expecting this argument, was nonplussed and found himself unable to reply to the Premier Président. However, he attempted to convince him that his intentions in the play were blameless, that he had treated its sensitive subject with the greatest care: but try as he might he was unconvincing and was unable to recover his poise]. Molière was obviously floundering here, and it was thanks to his friend Le Vayer that he was able to regain the initiative. See my reconstruction of *L'Imposteur* of 1667 note 5 above. Lamoignon, himself a member of the Company of the Blessed Sacrament, could well have found his cogent objection in the works of another member, Antoine Godeau, Bishop of Grasse and afterwards of Vence, whose poem about the theatre states that while it may reform unbalanced minds, Christians have the Church, not the theatre at their disposal to effect moral change and guide their reasoning; see Thirouin in Nicole, *Traité de la comédie*, p. 124.

11 '. . . pour mieux conserver l'estime et le respect qu'on doit aux vrais dévots . . .', 'Je ne doute point, Sire, que les gens que je peins dans ma comédie ne remuent bien des ressorts auprès de Votre Majesté, et ne jettent dans leur parti, comme ils l'ont déjà fait, de véritables gens de bien, qui sont d'autant plus prompts à se laisser tromper qu'ils jugent d'autrui par eux-mêmes' [in order to retain the esteem and respect of truly religious people . . . I have no doubt,Your Majesty, that the kind of people I describe in my comedy are trying to influence your judgement by any means, and that they have succeeded in winning over to their position those who are well intentioned,

whatever of placating or assuaging the Jansenists in the two letters which he wrote against their position on the theatre.[12] He simply began an 'argumentum ad hominem' or, to be more precise, 'ad causam jansenicam', trying to inflict as much damage as he could on his adversaries, in whose thinking he was extremely well versed. Whereas serious argument and moral duty are to the fore in Molière's defence, Racine sets out to amuse both himself and the public at the expense of the Jansenists.[13] Having considered the general principles behind his intervention, we now look in more detail at the tactics he deployed.

From the outset of the controversy about the theatre, it is clear that Racine enjoyed a singular advantage over Molière, that of knowing precisely the mind of his adversary. All Molière's pleas fall on deaf ears for one reason: he believes that in order to demonstrate his sincerity to those truly devout people who are opposed to his play, it is sufficient to confront them with reasonable and logical argument.

who are always easier to deceive since they judge others by their own standards], *Premier Placet, Second Placet*, Couton, *Molière*, 1, pp. 890, 892.

12 This controversial exchange is analysed in Picard, *Œuvres*, 2, pp. 13–31. These letters were written in the period 1666–7 in reply to the sequence of eighteen *Lettres sur l'hérésie imaginaire* of Racine's former teacher at Port-Royal, Nicole, who added eight others, subtitled *Les Visionnaires* (1664–66). In summary, the object of Nicole's criticism was Desmarets de Saint-Sorlin, author of the comedy *Les Visionnaires* (1637), who was a keen critic of the Jansenists. The première of Racine's *Alexandre Le Grand* took place on 14 December, 1665, at Molière's theatre, Palais-Royal, two weeks in advance of the first of the *Visionnaires* by Nicole, in which he described every novelist and dramatist as 'un empoisonneur public, non des corps, mais des âmes des fidèles, qui se doit regarder comme coupable d'une infinité d'homicides spirituels, ou qu'il a causés en effet ou qu'il a pu causer par ses écrits pernicieux' [a poisoner of people, not of their bodies, but of the souls of the faithful, and thus guilty of innumerable spiritual deaths, which have been caused directly by them or their pernicious writings], Picard, *Œuvres*, 2, p. 13 (see also G.E.F., 4, p. 258). According to Racine's son, Jean-Baptiste, 'mon père prit cela pour lui; il écouta un peu trop sa vivacité naturelle; il prit la plume; et sans rien dire à personne, il fit et répandit dans le public une lettre sans nom d'auteur, où il turlupinoit ces Messieurs de la manière la plus sanglante et la plus amère' [my father interpreted Nicole's comments personally: took up his pen, and without a word to anyone, wrote and published an anonymous letter in which he satirized these gentlemen in the most vicious way possible], G.E.F., 4, p. 259. Racine's first letter is entitled 'Lettre à l'auteur des *Hérésies Imaginaires* et des deux *Visionnaires*'; after two writers took up the cudgels on Nicole's behalf in 1666, Racine wrote a second letter in reply, entitled 'Lettre aux deux apologistes de l'auteur des *Hérésies Imaginaires*', which he simply read to his friends (the ms. was subsequently found in his papers and published posthumously). On publication of a second edition of the *Imaginaires*, in 1667, in which Nicole wrote about ' un jeune poète [qui] l'attaqua par une lettre où il contait des histoires faites à plaisir . . . Tout était faux dans cette lettre, et contre le bon sens' [a young poet who attacked him in a letter containing all sorts of fabrications from beginning to end], G.E.F., 4, p. 260, Racine had to be dissuaded by his friends from publishing both his letters with an accompanying preface, G.E.F., 4, p. 264.

13 Thirouin sums up Racine's arguments as a 'leçon d'éristique' [a model lesson in the art of polemics], in Nicole, *Traité de la comédie*, p. 217.

What he perceives as the distinction between true and false piety in his play should be equally as obvious to other well-intentioned people, if only he is allowed to explain his position to them. By so doing, he betrays his ignorance of the thinking of rigidly devout people, in whose minds there exists an unbridgeable gulf between the world and God. To this kind of fundamentalist cast of mind in the seventeenth century, it is the function of comedy to amuse just as it is the duty of religious teaching so to edify its adherents that they are kept safe from the temptations of the world, the flesh and the devil. In short, Molière may well have an excellent case to argue, but it is virtually meaningless because he lacks credibility in the eyes of spiritual leaders and their flocks.

In contradistinction, Racine is so familar with this kind of thinking that he short-circuits the argument for the defence of the theatre to concentrate on the kind of view which chooses radical separation from the world and the theatre. His arguments aim to enclose such people in their chosen retreat and to leave them there as easy targets for his ridicule. On a superficial level his missives represent the act of revenge of a youthful and liberated mind over a fundamentalist doctrine which limits the horizons of its followers. On a deeper level, they symbolize the refusal of the moral superiority assumed by a tightly knitted community, who dismiss all views perceived as being outside their own rigid system of belief. From beginning to end, Racine questions the right assumed by Nicole to sit in judgement on the theatre's freedom to entertain people. The weapon he chooses is that of satire, which he wields with more venom in response to his former teacher Nicole than to the latter's two stalwart defenders.[14] It is to them that the second letter, entitled 'Lettre aux deux apologistes de l'auteur des *Hérésies Imaginaires*', is addressed, and in it Racine visibly makes little effort to exert his intellectual prowess, contenting himself with ironic allusions to the differing style of each writer: 'le mélancolique me fait rire, et [. . .] le plaisant m'a fait pitié' [the lugubrious nature of the first makes me laugh, and the jocular tone of the second fills me with pity].[15] As we shall see, the second letter sustains in minor key the substance of the first one to Nicole, 'Lettre à l'auteur des *Hérésies Imaginaires* et des deux *Visionnaires*'.

The example of the *Provinciales* looms large in Racine's letters. Like the identity Pascal created for their fictitious author, Louis de Montalte, Racine assumes the pose of naïve observer at the beginning.

14 The first of the two letters has been attributed to Goibaud du Bois, the second to Barbier d'Aucour. Their authors were to become Racine's fellow academicians in the Académie Française (G.E.F., 4, pp. 290–322).
15 Picard, *Œuvres*, 2, p. 25.

He reveals how perfectly he has assimilated the master's polemical techniques. His pose serves as a shield, from behind which he attacks his enemy as he pleases, able to enjoy the effect of surprise. In his first letter, he affects total indifference towards the subject of Nicole's attack: 'Je vous déclare que je ne prends point de parti entre M. Desmarets et vous. Je laisse au monde de juger quel est le visonnaire de vous deux' [Let me inform you that I take no sides between M. Desmarets and yourself. I leave it to others to judge which of you is the real visionary].[16] Having pretexted his disinterest in the actual argument, he claims that he is merely curious about the manner in which the letters are written. This excellent subterfuge allows him to gain two immediate advantages over his opponent: it opens the way for a sustained comparison with Pascal, whose satirical verve cannot but contrast sharply with Nicole's more laboured style, and it enables Racine to deflect the reader's attention from what matters most to Nicole – the moral cogency of his argument. The result is that the most formidable proponent of Port-Royal is made to appear as a very pale imitation of Pascal. He is reduced to the ranks of the mediocre by his former pupil, but not before he is reminded of a very unpalatable truth: 'Je remarquais que vous prétendiez prendre la place de l'auteur des *Petites Lettres*; mais je remarquais en même temps que vous étiez beaucoup au-dessous de lui' [I noted that you were attempting to take over the mantle of the author of the *Petites Lettres* (the name by which Pascal's *Provinciales* were known to contemporaries); and I also happened to notice that you fell far short of his standards].[17]

Pascal is thus present right from the beginning, representing the first of the two leitmotifs which Racine's rapier-like satire uses with bewildering rapidity. He stands as the supreme standard of spiritual, intellectual and stylistic excellence, acknowledged as such both by Racine and Port-Royal. The second leitmotif is the Jansenists' obsession with their perennial enemies, the Jesuits, used to symbolize the pettiness which haunts blinkered minds. Racine takes over one of Pascal's favourite devices to deride in his opponents 'une disproportion surprenante entre ce qu'on attend et ce qu'on voit' [that glaring disparity between what one expects from someone and what he actually does].[18] No one was better qualified than Racine to lampoon the discrepancies of the Jansenists, especially whenever they began to write about worldly activities from which they chose to separate themselves. As regards reading novels and attending plays, he asks

16 *Ibid.*, p. 18.
17 *Ibid.*
18 Blaise Pascal, *11ᵉ Provinciale*, ed. Louis Lafuma (Paris: Editions du Seuil, 1963), p. 420.

disingenuously, 'Et qu'est-ce que les romans et les comédies peuvent avoir de commun avec le jansénisme?' [What possible connection could there be between such activities and the Jansenists?].[19] Behind the facetious question lies Racine's refusal of the fundamentalist attitude and the short shrift it gives to discrimination and perspective on such matters. It was such an attitude which led Nicole and the Jansenists to begin by condemning Desmarets, only to end by condemning all novels and plays. It is reflected in the kind of language in which writers are portrayed, namely as public poisoners of souls, and spiritual homicides.[20] At this point Pascal enters on cue, with Racine's not-so-discreet reminder to Nicole that the author of the *Provinciales* took great care to avoid such extremist generalizations, and even went out of his way to praise eminent authors.[21]

It is the same lack of proportion which impels the Jansenists to go beyond the practice of their own austere moral code and to impose it on others. Racine's response is to accept that they do not honour secular writers, and then to deny their right to legislate for the taste of others: 'Hé! Monsieur, contentez-vous de donner les rangs dans l'autre monde: ne réglez point les récompenses de celui-ci. Vous l'avez quitté il y a longtemps: laissez-le juger des choses qui lui appartiennent' [Sir, if you please, be content to regulate degrees of esteem in the next world: don't attempt to adjust them in this world. You have decided to forsake the world: let it then bestow its own judgements in its own domain].[22] He does warn them that they are involving themselves in an unequal struggle, since the works of the classical authors have withstood the test of time. The guiding principle commanding the fierce attack on Nicole is the contemptuous rejection of an absolutism which prevents the Jansenists from perceiving what is or is not an appropriate criterion of judgement within a specific setting. Having established this, the former pupil of the Jansenists now proceeds to lay bare in ruthless fashion the motives underlying Nicole's criticism of secular authors.

Racine chose his target with care. Of all the Jansenist moralists, none devoted more time and effort to describe, analyse and repudiate the virulent effects of the passions, and especially that of self-love, than

19 Picard, *Œuvres*, 2, p. 19.
20 Nicole's two defenders use the same terminology, G.E.F., 4, pp. 291–2 (p. 311).
21 Pascal, *11ᵉ Provinciale*. In a letter at the end of the second *Provinciale* its author praises 'un des Messieurs de l'Académie, des plus illustres entre les hommes tous illustres' [an academician who is one of the most distinguished writers among the élite], p. 379.
22 Picard, *Œuvres*, 2, pp. 19–20. For the Jansenists' criticism of worldly honour, see the two letters in reply to Racine, G.E.F., 4, p. 296, p. 312.

Nicole, in his *Essais de morale* (1671–78) and his *Traité de la comédie* (1667). These 'puissances trompeuses' [the powers which subvert all our channels of perception], to use Pascal's graphic phrase, remain our deadly enemies as long as we live,[23] and the theatre is the culture in which they flourish.[24] And it is precisely the existence of these same passions in those who go to great lengths to detect them in others that Racine takes particular pleasure in demonstrating. For Nicole's criticisms of classical and contemporary writers are inspired visibly by the same passions which incite him to be more zealous in attacking the Jesuits than in praising the great writers.[25] Once again, Racine reminds us caustically of the petty and parochial nature of the Jansenist objectives, rendering them purblind to enduring greatness: 'On peut arriver à la gloire par plus d'une voie' [We all achieve distinction by different means].[26]

One may admire the studied insolence with which the former Jansenist detects the lust for glory in the austere moralist who, at the close of his *Traité de la comédie* warns the faithful of the seductive vanity of the world, with its innumerable follies 'dont la comédie est comme l'abrégé' [of which the theatre is the compendium].[27] As a shrewd tactician, however, and unlike Molière, Racine refuses to let himself be drawn into theological disputes about the theatre. He is well aware of the strength of his opponent in that area. To retain his tactical advantage, he claims not to be 'un théologien comme vous' [a theologian

23 Blaise Pascal, *Pensées*, ed. Louis Lafuma (Paris: Editions du Seuil), 1963), fragment 45.
24 See Ch. 3 of Nicole's *Traité*: 'Il est inutile de dire, pour justifier les Comédies et les Romans, qu'on n'y représente que des passions légitimes; car encore que le mariage fasse un bon usage de la concupiscence, elle est néanmoins en soi toujours mauvaise et déréglée; et il n'est pas permis de l'exciter en soi ni dans les autres. On doit toujours la regarder comme le honteux effet du péché, comme une source de poison capable de nous infecter à tous moments, si Dieu n'en arrêtait les mauvaises suites' [It is beside the point to claim in justification that plays and novels merely portray harmless passions; for although marriage serves to legitimize sexual desire, it still remains in itself wrong and uncontrollable: it is not permissible either to arouse it in oneself or in others. We must always consider it as being the shameful result of original sin, as a source of poison able to contaminate us at any moment, unless God puts a stop to its evil effects], p. 40. In all the attempts to make the theatre morally respectable 'on tâche donc de faire en sorte que la conscience s'accommode avec la passion, et ne la vienne point inquiéter par ses importuns remords' [its defenders endeavour to reconcile conscience with passion, with the result that the former does not trouble the latter], *ibid.*, Préface, p. 32. For Nicole, 'Dieu ne veut point d'un cœur partagé' [God does not tolerate a divided heart], *ibid.*, p. 54. Likewise in the *Traité de la comédie et des spectacles* (1666), Molière's former patron, the Prince de Conti, wrote 'la vie de l'homme sur la terre est un combat continuel' [life is an unwearying struggle], against the passions, in Thirouin (ed.), p. 208.
25 Picard, *Œuvres*, 2, p. 20. Racine alludes here to the controversies of 1654 involving Lemaître de Sacy, and of 1665 concerning Nicole, see G.E.F., 4, p. 280, n. 1.
26 *Ibid.*
27 Nicole, *Traité de la comédie*, p. 108.

like you].[28] He limits himself modestly to pointing out that the Church Fathers made much use of the theatre, and that the Church's position on the morality of the theatre is far from absolutist.[29] In his second letter, Racine alludes simply to several examples of the Church Fathers looking favourably on the theatre, before appending the mocking remark: 'Pour les Pères, c'est à vous de nous les citer; c'est à vous, ou à vos amis, de nous convaincre, par une foule de passages, que l'Église nous interdit absolument la comédie, en l'état qu'elle est' [As for the Church Fathers, it's up to you to find the apposite passages. You and your colleagues will now have to convince us from official doctrine that the Church expressly forbids us to go to the theatre as we now find it].[30]

Racine then leaves such general points to devote his attention to a lengthy and bitter examination of the countless discrepancies between Jansenist doctrine and their manner of life. He points out their flagrant contradiction in having translated into French the comedies of Terence. The Jansenists argue of course that they are engaged in 'clothing the passions in decorous modesty', but to do that is to render them all the more insidious by Nicole's definition and to cast themselves in the role of the public poisoners he has apportioned to them.[31]

28 Picard, Œuvres, 2, p. 20.

29 Ibid. On this point he is correct, since the condemnation of the theatre in the seventeenth-century is based less on absolute pronouncements by the Church than on interpretations of canonical texts for polemical purposes, as Jean Dubu has demonstrated in Les Eglises chrétiennes et le théâtre (Grenoble: Presses Universitaires de Grenoble, 1997).

30 Picard, Œuvres, 2, p. 29. The two other letters merely repeat Nicole's absolute condemnation of the theatre, see G.E.F., 4, p. 291, pp. 295–6, p. 311, p. 320.

31 Picard, Œuvres, 2, 21. D'Aucour and Du Bois take care to explain that the purpose of translating non-Christian authors (such as Terence) is purely pedagogical, which allows Racine to advise them to choose more edifying works to translate in future ('mais pourquoi choisir Térence?', Picard, Œuvres, 2, p. 30). In his Traité de la comédie, Nicole states that 'quelque honnêteté qu'on se puisse imaginer dans l'amour d'une créature mortelle, cet amour est toujours vicieux et illégitime, lorsqu'il ne naît pas de l'amour de Dieu; et il n'en peut naître lorsque c'est un amour de passion et d'attache, qui nous fait trouver notre joie et notre plaisir dans cette créature' [however modest love may appear to be in a mortal creature, it is still sinful and unlawful whenever it does not originate from love of God; and this cannot happen so long as it remains a carnal and contingent passion which makes us find joy and pleasure in a creature], pp. 54–6. Molière responded thus to Nicole in his Préface to Tartuffe (1669): 'Je sais qu'il y a des esprits dont la délicatesse ne peut souffrir aucune comédie, qui disent que les plus honnêtes sont les plus dangereuses; que les passions que l'on y dépeint sont d'autant plus touchantes qu'elles sont pleines de vertu, et que les âmes sont attendries par ces sortes de représentations. Je ne vois pas quel grand crime c'est que de s'attendrir à la vue d'une passion honnête; et c'est un haut étage de vertu que cette pleine insensibilité où ils veulent faire monter notre âme' [I know that there are those who are so prone to take offence that they cannot tolerate comedies in any shape or form, who tell us that the more refined they seem, the more dangerous they are, that the

Here we touch on one of Racine's principal grievances against the members of Port-Royal, the fact that they are no more immune from the temptations of self-love than the rest of humanity. Racine, educated at the Petites Écoles, is perfectly aware of the way in which the Jansenists trace the motivation for each human act back to ubiquitous self-love. Nicole himself ruthlessly lays bare the ugly reality lurking behind apparently virtuous actions in his *Essais de morale*. No one could have been more attentive to the foibles and failings of his teachers than the young Racine. No master is a hero to his servant, and few teachers to their pupils. He thus takes a malicious delight in retailing two stories as proof of the subtle ways in which the Jansenists invariably seek to gain advantage from any event however small. The first centres on the arrival at Port-Royal of two Capuchin monks who are greeted with traditional hospitality. At table, the wine which has been served is suddenly removed and replaced by water and cider, on the orders of Mère Angélique, who has just discovered that one of them is trying to obtain a papal bull against the doctrine of Jansenius. The following day, hearing that the suspect is on the contrary very sympathetic to the monastery, the two find themselves feted royally.[32] The second anecdote recounts how Molière had been invited to read his banned play *Tartuffe* at the home of a friend of the Jansenists because the latter were convinced that he was satirizing their enemies the Jesuits.[33]

It is this self-interested motivation which Racine had claimed to detect in Nicole's attitude towards Desmarets. His verdict could not be more damning: 'Voilà, Monsieur, comme vous avez traité Desmarets et comme vous avez toujours traité tout le monde' [You, Monsieur, have treated Desmarets in precisely this fashion, as you have always done with everyone else].[34] In summary, Racine's comments run as follows: you make a practice of using weights and measures which

passions they depict are more likely to affect us if they appear virtuous, and that our minds are moved by such performances. I really do not understand how being moved by the expression of authentic passion should be sinful; to be insensitive to such feelings is to aspire to a lofty degree of virtue indeed], Couton, 1, *Molière*, p. 888. Cf. Conti's *Traité de la comédie et des spectacles*: 'le but de la Comédie est d'émouvoir les passions, [. . .] et au contraire, tout le but de la religion chrétienne est de les calmer, de les abattre et de les détruire autant qu'on le peut en cette vie' [. . . the goal of the theatre is to excite passions, . . . whilst the Christian religion aims chiefly to calm, subdue and destroy them as far as is possible in this life], Thirouin (ed.), p. 208.

32 Picard, *Œuvres*, 2, p. 22. In the second letter, Racine makes the suggestion to the two Jansenist sympathisers that they include a chapter in Mère Angélique's biography entitled 'De l'esprit de discernement que Dieu avait donné à la sainte Mère' [How the divine gift of prophecy came to the holy mother], Picard, *Œuvres*, 2, p. 31.

33 *Lettre aux deux apologistes*, Picard, *Œuvres*, 2, p. 28. It is probable that the friend in question was Mme de Sablé, see G.E.F., 4, p. 332, n. 2.

34 Picard, *Œuvres*, 2, p. 22.

vary according to the advantage which you think may accrue to you from a given situation. You curry favour with people who are liable to be of use, and persecute those who do not agree with you. You do not protest at the flattering description of Port-Royal contained in Mlle de Scudéry's novel *Clélie*.[35] If condemnation falls heavily on the head of Desmarets, whose youthful excesses are cast in his teeth, the past misdeeds of the former lawyer Antoine Le Maître, now one of the saints of Port-Royal, are conveniently overlooked (the latter had had the privilege of being able to excise from the productions of his youth anything offensive to Jansenist doctrine).[36] Nicole's apologists protest about such an unjust comparison, to which Racine rejoins that they should accord the same right to Desmarets as to their own hero of the faith.[37] With the Jansenists, as with everyone else, prejudices are transformed into truth, the sole difference consisting in the dogmatic vein in which Jansenist doctrine is proclaimed to be universally binding.

It is curious to note that Racine does not develop overmuch his response to Nicole, any more than to his two other adversaries. The reason seems to me to lie in the fact that he knows full well in advance what their arguments against the theatre will be, and that his own defence will be summarily rejected by them. Why then take the trouble replying to them? Doubtless the human if uncharitable urge to let those very people who had enjoined him to renounce his writing for ever know what he thought of them was present.[38] The principal reason, however, may be found in his determination to define himself as a writer, to protect the integrity of his art form in the face of those who claim to legislate for artistic taste and right of choice. Hence the leading question at the end which underlies all his arguments: if you

[margin note: R. does not reply directly to their arguments (which he foresees)]

[margin note: R's need to define self as a writer]

---

35 *Ibid.*, p. 21. Mlle de Scudéry starts her description with the words 'Ce n'est pas sans sujet que vous avez la curiosité de savoir quelle est la forme de vie de ces illustres solitaires [de Port-Royal]' [you would like to know, with good reason, more about the manner of life of those distinguished people who have withdrawn from the world to Port-Royal], G.E.F., 4, p. 283, n. 2.

36 Picard, *Œuvres*, 2, p. 23.

37 See their letters, G.E.F., 4, pp. 299–300 (p. 301), pp. 315–16 (p. 318): 'je crois bien que si Desmarets avait revu ses romans depuis sa conversion, comme on dit que M. Le Maître a revu ses plaidoyers, il y aurait peut-être mis de la spiritualité; mais il a cru qu'un pénitent devait oublier tout ce qu'il a fait pour le monde' [I believe firmly, wrote Racine, that if Desmarets had revised his novels after his conversion, as M. Le Maître is said to have done with his speeches in court, he would have improved their spiritual tone; instead he is of the opinion that a truly penitent person ought to forget about his past worldly achievements], Picard, *Œuvres*, 2, p. 30.

38 His aunt Agnès calls him 'malheureux pour n'avoir pas rompu un commerce qui vous déshonore devant Dieu et devant les hommes' [wretched because you have not put a stop to an activity which is dishonouring to you both before God and man], see R. Picard, *La Carrière de Jean Racine* (Paris: Gallimard, 1956), p. 80.

forbid the reading of novels and attendance at the theatre, which forms of reading and recreation can you recommend? One must be able to relax the mind in harmless activity. Racine is, needless to say, very familiar with Nicole's answer to his rhetorical question: 'le besoin que les hommes ont de se divertir n'est pas de beaucoup si grand que l'on croit, et il consiste plus en l'imagination, ou en l'accoutumance, qu'en une nécessité réelle.' [The need for recreation is not nearly as great as is commonly believed, being more a product of imagination or habit than an actual necessity].[39] Racine nevertheless poses the question for the pleasure of being able to provide his testy rejoinder: we cannot spend our lives reading books written by Jansenists, firstly because they are all out of date, and secondly for the excellent reason that they merely replicate each other in such otiose vein.[40] We note that this vitriolic barb is aimed at the would-be successor to Pascal.

His second letter may be seen as a homage to Pascal, as (expanding somewhat on the need for amusement) its facetious tone momentarily gives way to an attempt to answer the question, 'Is the theatre capable of transforming human nature?': 'je dirai que non, mais je vous dirai en même temps qu'il y a des choses qui ne sont pas saintes, et qui sont pourtant innocentes' [I would say no, but hasten to add that there are activities by no means holy but yet perfectly innocent in their nature], and among such activities is to be counted the pleasure of laughter, in which the Jansenists indulge themselves at the expense of the Jesuits in the *Provinciales*![41] Here at last we have a point of agreement with Molière who, in his 1669 preface to *Tartuffe*, wrote in reply to Nicole:

> J'avoue qu'il y a des lieux qu'il vaut mieux fréquenter que le théâtre; et, si l'on veut blâmer toutes les choses qui ne regardent pas directement Dieu et notre salut, il est certain que la comédie en doit être, et je ne trouve point mauvais qu'elle soit condamnée avec le reste. Mais, supposé, comme il est vrai, que les exercices de la piété souffrent des intervalles et que les hommes aient besoin de divertissement, je soutiens qu'on ne leur en peut trouver un qui soit plus innocent que le théâtre.

> [I must admit that there are better places to attend than the theatre; and, if we are to reject everything which is not directly bound up with God and our salvation, there is no good reason why comedy should be afforded favourable treatment. But accepting that we engage in activities other than strictly religious ones, and that human beings need a change in routine, I would maintain that it is impossible to find a more innocent form of recreation than that offered by comedy][42]

39 Nicole, *Traité de la comédie*, p. 86.
40 Picard, *Œuvres*, 2, pp. 23–4.
41 *Ibid.*, p. 29.
42 Couton, *Molière*, 1, p. 888.

Racine, like Molière, maintains that we need to laugh,[43] a feature which does not figure much in the Jansenist outlook on life. A specific allusion to Pascal and the comedy of the *Provinciales* serves again to point up the unremitting didacticism of Nicole, 'mais cet enjouement n'est point du tout votre caractère: vous retombez dans les froides plaisanteries . . .' [but this gaiety is not part of your character; you lapse into faded witticism . . .][44] In the second letter, he writes of Nicole as being 'un homme qui ne prend rien en raillerie, et qui trouve partout des sujets de se fâcher' [a man who takes nothing in jocular fashion, and who finds something to be angry about wherever he goes].[45] Likewise, the defenders of the Jansenist theologian are indefatigable in their gravity, an attitude very appropriate to doctrinal disputation but not at all to a discussion on forms of recreation, about which they have no knowledge.[46] Nicole and Port-Royal were by no means impervious to such sharp blows. We find Nicole writing of the enormous interest aroused by the missive unleashed against him by Racine and of 'la satisfaction qu'il avait de son ouvrage' [the great sense of satisfaction which the author derived from it].[47] There is no greater source of irritation for the members of a closed community than that occasioned by a former member who is well informed about their innermost secrets and decides to make them public. This is exacerbated for them when the writer's pen happens to be so steeped in vitriol.

Racine's first ten (secular) plays could only have been written as a result of him emerging (if only provisionally) from the long shadow of Jansenism. In their very existence we may well find sufficient and good reason to overlook the acerbic and hurtful tone of his letters. We may also conclude that both tone and content find their justification in the fundamentalist, dogmatic, if doubtless sincere, arguments in Nicole's attempt to override the free judgement of others in matters of aesthetic taste.

43 For Molière, to be human is to be inherently comic, because there is an inbuilt comic dimension in each individual as well as in humanity at large, as may be glimpsed from the comment of Dorante in *La Critique de L'École des femmes* (sc. 6): 'il n'est pas incompatible qu'une personne soit ridicule en de certaines choses et honnête homme en d'autres' [. . . there is no contradiction whatever in someone being ridiculous in some things and perfectly sensible in others], Couton, *Molière*, 1, p. 666.
44 Picard, *Œuvres*, 2, p. 24.
45 *Ibid.*, Second letter, p. 28.
46 *Ibid.*, p. 31.
47 Picard, *La Carrière de Jean Racine*, p. 124. See also the anonymous *Lettre à l'auteur de la réponse aux hérésies imaginaires et aux deux visionnaires* of 30 April 1666, in support of Racine, informing us that 'jamais pièce anonyme ne causa un empressement plus général d'en découvrir l'auteur que la vôtre [. . .] il est bon que vous sachiez la consternation dans laquelle vous avez mis les jansénistes' [no anonymous letter ever aroused such feverish attempts to uncover the author than this one [. . .] you ought to know of the total disarray into which it plunged the Jansenists], G.E.F., 4, pp. 323–4.

8

Voltaire, Women and Reception: Racine in the Eighteenth Century

MARC SERGE RIVIÈRE

Voltaire's pronouncements on Racine's theatre

There is little doubt that the seventeenth century was Voltaire's preferred epoque aesthetically, and that within the *grand siècle* it was Racine who was his preferred dramatist. Even if he acknowledged the notion of the relativity of taste[1] and cultural values in his *Lettres philosophiques* of 1733,[2] he could never overcome his own *parti pris* for the previous century, and its aesthetic rules and conventions. Letters XVIII–XXIV of the *Lettres philosophiques* expressed his strong support for English writers, such as Addison, who came close to the great writers who had graced the age of Louis XIV. Shakespeare posed the thorny problem of how to assess genius, but although Voltaire was fully aware of the fact that taste could be accompanied by mediocre talent, he objected publicly to Shakespeare's infringements of classical rules, especially that of propriety. Throughout his career, his objections continued to be voiced as strongly as they were in Letter XVIII of the *Lettres philosophiques* (*LP*, p. 104). Voltaire's ideal was genius tamed by taste, a blend of English vitality and French elegance.

Such a happy mixture he saw embodied, to a large extent, in Jean Racine, who is celebrated in *Le Temple du goût*, a work contemporary with the *Lettres philosophiques* and first published without a privilege by Jore in Rouen in March 1733. According to David Williams, this work contains 'one of the most explicit expositions of the inner mechanics of

---

1 For Voltaire's views on taste, see David Williams, *Voltaire Literary Critic: Studies on Voltaire and the Eighteenth Century*, 48 (1966) and Raymond Naves, *Le Goût de Voltaire* (Geneva: Slatkine, 1967).
2 *Lettres philosophiques, ou, Lettres anglaises*, ed. Raymond Naves (Paris: Garnier, 1964), p. 128 (henceforth *LP*).

Voltaire's literary taste in its role as a practical critical weapon'.[3] In the inner sanctuary of the deity Taste are to be found eight seventeenth-century writers who have reached the summit of their respective craft: Bossuet, Fénelon, Corneille, La Fontaine, Boileau, Quinault, Molière and Racine, about whom Voltaire waxes lyrical:

> Plus pur, plus élégant, plus tendre,
> Et parlant au cœur de plus près,
> Nous attachant sans nous surprendre,
> Et ne se démentant jamais,
> Racine observe les portraits
> De Bajazet, de Xipharès,
> De Britannicus, d'Hippolyte.
> A peine il distingue leurs traits;
> Ils ont tous le même mérite,
> Tendres, galants, doux et discrets;
> Et l'Amour, qui marche à leur suite,
> Les croit des courtisans français.[4]

As an intermediary between taste and art, 'la Critique, à l'œil sévère et juste' [Criticism, with a severe and fair eye] (p. 141), the custodian of the castle, admits only those artists who abide strictly by the rules prescribed by the taste of 'honnêtes gens'. Undoubtedly, *Le Temple du goût* and letters XVIII–XXIV of the *Lettres philosophiques* display fully Voltaire's *parti pris* as a literary critic and confirm those qualities and principles which the dramatist valued most in classical theatre, and that of Racine in particular. These are identified by Raymond Naves as 'le naturel: [la] simplicité et [la] justesse'; 'la pureté: [la] correction et [la] propriété'.[5]

In one of the two chapters on the arts, in *Le Siècle de Louis XIV*,[6] which in the original plan of 1735 were intended to mark the apex of Louis XIV's age and close the work, Voltaire pays high homage to Racine: 'Sa réputation s'est accrue de jour en jour, et celle des ouvrages de Corneille a un peu diminué. La raison en est que Racine, dans tous ses ouvrages, depuis son *Alexandre*, est toujours élégant, toujours correct, toujours vrai; qu'il parle au cœur; et que l'autre manque trop souvent à tous ces devoirs' [His reputation grew daily, while that of Corneille's works diminished somewhat. The reason for this is that Racine, in

---

3 Williams, *Voltaire Literary Critic*, p. 163.
4 Voltaire, *Mélanges*, ed. Jacques van den Heuvel, Bibliothèque de la Pléiade (Paris: Gallimard, 1961), p. 153.
5 Naves, *Le Goût de Voltaire*, pp. 206, 216.
6 *Le Siècle de Louis XIV*, in *Voltaire: Œuvres historiques*, ed. René Pomeau, Bibliothèque de la Pléiade (Paris: Gallimard, 1957). All references henceforth will be inserted in the text and indicated by *OH*.

all his works from *Alexandre* onwards, is always elegant, always correct, always true, that he speaks to the heart; and that [Corneille] too often fails in all these duties] (*OH*, p. 1011). *Athalie* is deemed to be 'le chef-d'œuvre de la scène' [the masterpiece of the stage] (*ibid.*), while in the *Catalogue de la plupart des écrivains qui ont paru dans le siècle de Louis XIV* [. . .], Voltaire denounces St Evremond's lack of judgement in putting Corneille's *Sophonisbe* in the same class as *Andromaque* (*OH*, p. 1196). Surprisingly, Voltaire produced no single literary study of Racine's theatre with the scope and depth of the *Commentaires sur Corneille*,[7] of which David Williams has produced a masterly scholarly edition.[8] Instead, his comments are scattered here and there in his vast corpus.

In his introduction to the *Commentaires*, Williams sums up the place occupied by Racine in Voltaire's literary canon as follows: 'With Racine's work the French classical theatre was of course seen by Voltaire in its most favourable light. Racine was for Voltaire the more sophisticated artist, who came as close as possible to his ideal of aesthetic perfection' (*CW*, 53, p. 310). In his *Commentaires sur Corneille*, misled by Louis Racine and labouring under the misapprehension that Henrietta of England had set the same task to both dramatists, Voltaire inserted an unexpected comparison between Corneille's *Tite et Bérénice* and Racine's *Bérénice*, in order to introduce a relativistic and comparative approach. This enabled him in 1764 to argue strongly for Racine's supremacy in French seventeenth-century theatre. Such views were repeatedly put forward in his correspondence in the years immediately preceding the first edition of the *Commentaires*; thus in February 1763, he had written to Claude Henri de Fuzée de Voisenon: 'C'est Racine qui est véritablement grand, et d'autant plus grand qu'il ne paraît jamais chercher à l'être. C'est l'auteur d'*Athalie* qui est l'homme parfait. Je vous confie qu'en commentant Corneille, je deviens idolâtre de Racine' [It is Racine who is truly great, all the more great since he never seems to seek to be so. It is *Athalie*'s author who is the exemplary figure. I must confess to you that in commenting on Corneille, I am beginning to idolize Racine].[9] Voltaire gave clear instructions to Cramer to print the section on *Bérénice* before the analysis of Corneille's *Tite et*

---

7 See A. Ages, 'Voltaire on Racine', *Zeitschrift für französische Sprache und Litteratur* 87 (1968), 289–301; and R. Lowenstein, *Voltaire as an Historian of Seventeenth-Century French Drama* (New York: Johnson Reprint Co., 1973).
8 *Commentaires sur Corneille*, ed. David Williams, *The Complete Works of Voltaire*, vols 53–5 (Oxford: Voltaire Foundation, 1974–5). All references henceforth will be inserted in the text and indicated by *CW*, followed by the volume number.
9 Voltaire, *Correspondance*, ed. Théodore Besterman, *The Complete Works of Voltaire* (Geneva and Oxford, 1968–77) Best. D11041. Further references will be inserted in the text and indicated by Best. D.

Bérénice (*CW*, 53, p. 309), to leave no doubt as to Racine's pre-eminence. All along, Voltaire had been more than willing to give Corneille his due, but only as a praiseworthy pioneer. It was Racine who had taken tragedy to its highest aesthetic point; to the d'Argentals in 1763, Voltaire expressed his growing irritation with Corneille's supporters who were seemingly blind to his limitations (Best. D11021).

However, Voltaire was impartial enough to realize that Racine had weaknesses; he relied excessively on love as a subject matter. According both to Aristotle's *Poetics* and, significantly too, Corneille's *Discours de l'utilité et des parties du poème dramatique* of 1660, love in itself was not a suitably tragic subject.[10] In his own *Discours sur la tragédie* which accompanied *Brutus* (1728), Voltaire had echoed Corneille's views: 'Vouloir de l'amour dans toutes les tragédies me paraît un goût efféminé,' [To want love in all tragedy seems to me to be effeminate in taste] but he added: 'L'en proscrire toujours est une mauvaise humeur bien déraisonnable' [To banish it entirely is unreasonable bad humour].[11] Such reservations about love as a suitable subject for tragedy were voiced even more strongly in Voltaire's private comments, as in the following statement in his notebooks: 'Si l'autheur d'Athalie avoit traitté Electre, Iphig. en Tauride, Œdipe, point d'amour. Il rougissoit sur la fin de sa vie d'avoir amolli la scène' [If the author of *Athalie* had treated Electre, Iphig. en Tauride, Œdipe, no love. He blushed at the end of his life for having softened up the stage].[12] However, in public Voltaire expressed his dissatisfaction with the content of Racine's plays much more tamely as the years wore on, and he visibly changed course on this issue, arguing in the *Commentaires sur Corneille* that, although love was a less than satisfactory subject, once the theme was chosen as in *Bérénice*, what ultimately mattered was the manner in which it was treated. Voltaire also believed firmly that, had it not been for the elegance of Racine's style in *Bérénice*, the expression of love would have been 'languissant' [listless] (*CW*, 55, p. 943).

Thus it was that in the 1760s, the literary critic preferred to turn the spotlight more on style, language and grammatical usage, than on content and characterization. This growing preoccupation with correctness and poetic creativity in tragedy is borne out by Voltaire's frequent allusions to Racine's purity and elegance, and by way of contrast on Corneille's gross stylistic lapses, in his correspondence prior to the

10 Corneille, *Discours de l'utilité et des parties du poème dramatique*, in Couton, *Corneille*, 3, pp. 117–41.
11 *Théâtre de Voltaire* (Paris: Firmin Didot, 1851), p. 70.
12 Voltaire, *Notebooks*, ed. Théodore Besterman, *The Complete Works of Voltaire*, vol. 82, p. 455.

publication of the *Commentaires* in 1764 and again before the second edition of 1774. To Augustin Marie, marquis de Ximénès, he avowed on 18 March 1767 that he was prepared to forgive Racine for the weakness of his plots: 'Je sais bien que Racine est rarement assez tragique; mais il est si intéressant, si adroit, si pur, si élégant, si harmonieux, il a tant adouci et embelli notre langue rendue barbare par Corneille, que notre passion pour lui est bien excusable' [I know that Racine is rarely tragic enough; but he is so interesting, so skilful, so elegant, so harmonious, he has so softened and embellished our language which Corneille had made barbarous, that our passion for him is very excusable] (Best. D14054). Corneille's 'minéral brut' [raw mineral] is compared unfavourably in the same letter to 'l'or pur de Racine' [Racine's pure gold]. Even excessive reliance on love in French seventeenth-century theatre was publicly ascribed by Voltaire in the 1760s not to Racine, but to Corneille.

Although Voltaire applauded many sublime scenes in Corneille, he consistently held up Racine's plays as models of poetic style, to be imitated by future generations of dramatists. Racine may have had his defects, but all this could be overlooked because of 'la magie enchanteresse de ce style qui n'a été donné qu'à lui' [the enchanting magic of this style which has only been given to him] (*CW*, 55, p. 940). Voltaire's increasingly balanced and rationalistic appraisal of Racine's theatre is best summed up in a letter to d'Olivet of 20 August 1761:

> Dans le siècle passé, il n'y eut que le seul Racine qui écrivit des tragédies avec une pureté et une élégance presque continue; le charme de cette élégance a été si puissant que les gens de lettres et de goût lui ont pardonné la monotonie de ses déclarations d'amour, et la faiblesse de quelques caractères, en faveur de sa diction enchanteresse. (Best. D9959)

> In the last century, only Racine wrote tragedies with an almost continuous purity and elegance; the charm of this elegance was so powerful that literary people and people with taste forgave him the monotony of his declarations of love, and the weakness of some characters, on account of his enchanting diction.

Voltaire's reactions to two female contemporaries' views of Racine: Mme de Sévigné and Mme de Caylus

From tolerating Corneille's pioneering work early on in his career as a literary critic, Voltaire became progressively more committed to a public campaign for Racine's pre-eminence against the encroaching corruption of the English stage. T. W. Russell, for one, has noted this marked shift from an early acceptance of Corneille's sublimity towards a greater focus on stylistic and linguistic yardsticks to confirm Racine's supremacy.[13] Two years before his death, Voltaire's *Lettre à l'Académie Française*, inserted as the preface to *Irène*, was read to the audience on 25 August 1776; in it Voltaire upheld once more the values of purity, correctness and elegance, allied to that of naturalness which he admired in Racine's theatre:

> Racine, celui de nos poètes qui approcha le plus de la perfection, ne donna jamais au public aucun ouvrage sans avoir écouté les conseils de Boileau et de Patru; aussi c'est ce véritablement grand homme qui nous enseigne par son exemple l'art difficile de s'exprimer toujours naturellement [. . .] Il mit dans sa poésie dramatique cette élégance, cette harmonie continue qui nous manquait absolument, ce charme secret et inexprimable, égal à celui du quatrième livre de Virgile, cette douceur enchanteresse qui fait que, quand vous lisez au hasard dix ou douze vers d'une de ses pièces, un attrait irrésistible vous force de lire tout le reste.

> [Racine, our poet who came nearest to perfection, never produced a text for the public without listening to the advice of Boileau and Patru. Thus, it is this truly great man who teaches us by his example the difficult art of expressing himself naturally. [. . .] He put in his dramatic poetry an elegance, a continuous harmony which were entirely lacking, a secret and inexpressible charm, equal to that in Virgil's fourth book, this enchanting magic which means that, when you read ten or twelve lines at random of one of his plays, an irresistible appeal forces you to read all the rest.][14]

Significantly, many of the qualities identified here by Voltaire are precisely those which female spectators and readers found most appealing in his own works in general, and in his plays in particular. Voltaire described Racine as the poet of women 'par excellence'; in a rather patronizing note on *Bérénice*, he argued that not only did its author know the human heart best, but he was able to convey with great sensitivity the full range of emotions experienced by women better than Corneille: 'Presque toutes les héroïnes de Racine étalent ces sentiments de tendresse, de jalousie, de colère, de fureur; tantôt soumises, tantôt désespérées. C'est avec raison qu'on a nommé Racine le poète des femmes' [Almost all Racine's heroines display sentiments of tenderness, jealousy, anger, fury, sometimes submissive, sometimes despairing. Racine is rightly called the poet of women] (*CW*, 55, p. 950–1). An interesting parallel can be drawn here with Voltaire's own appeal to female audiences in the eighteenth century. In their

---

13 T. W. Russell, *Voltaire, Dryden and Heroic Tragedy* (New York: AMS Press, 1966), p. 123.
14 *Œuvres complètes de Voltaire*, ed. Louis Moland, 52 vols (Paris: Garnier, 1877–85), 6, p. 326. Further references will be inserted in the text and indicated by *OC*.

private correspondence with Voltaire, his female acquaintances often stress their appreciation of the pathos of his plays, and they underline the fact that, like Racine, he had considerable insight into women's hearts; in August 1758, the margravine of Baden-Durlach, who had entertained Voltaire at her residence, wrote to him: 'Come vous avés si bien sçu dévelloper [*sic*] le cœur de Zaïre, pourquoi ignoreriés-vous le mien?' [Since you were so well able to develop Zaïre's heart, why do you not know mine?] (Best. D7827). In the light of the above, one may well ask what Voltaire himself made of the responses of Racine's female contemporaries to his theatre? Did he share their views of the great dramatist's qualities and weaknesses? Could he accept these views for what they were, or did he use them to fight his own polemical battles, be these literary or critical? Was he promoting his own works by playing the role of Racine's champion?

To answer such questions, one must turn first to Voltaire's handling of the verdict of two of Racine's contemporaries on performances at Saint-Cyr and Versailles of *Esther* and *Athalie*, that of Mme de Sévigné and Mme de Caylus. Voltaire's reporting of Mme de Sévigné's comments on Racine and his edition of the *Souvenirs* of Mme de Caylus demonstrate clearly that he was inclined to pay little attention to the point of view of others, and women in particular, as he set about exploiting the borrowed material to his own ends. An analysis of Voltaire's responses to women's writings on Racine sheds light on his short-sightedness and egocentric approach, as much as on the androcentric values typical of the interpretative community of his day. Moreover, Voltaire was insensitive to the opinion voiced by women whose letters and memoirs he used for his own historical writings, as demonstrated in a recent article.[15] Although he could bring himself to admire the artistic achievements of a selected few female artists, and he readily acknowledged that women had had a civilizing influence on French society in the seventeenth and eighteenth centuries, Voltaire the historian praised women artists chiefly for their 'esprit', 'naïveté', 'charme' and 'grâce', rather than for making a substantial contribution to philosophical thought or serious literary genres. Above all, he selected from their memoirs what suited his personal aims at the time of writing, and his own subjective assessment, however unfair, determined his treatment of the borrowed material. In brief, female memorialists' values, vision and point of view took second place to Voltaire's own polemical and philosophical aims. Such are the

15 Marc Serge Rivière, 'Voltaire, Reader of Women's Memoirs: "The Difference of Value"', *Studies on Voltaire and the Eighteenth Century*, 371 (1999), 23–52.

conclusions one can also draw from his treatment of Mme de Sevigné's comments on Racine's plays *Esther* and *Athalie*.

(i) MME DE SEVIGNÉ

V. praised Sévigné

Voltaire's attitude towards Mme de Sevigné's letters is at once typical of his treatment of women's writings in general, and much more perplexing and paradoxical. While he deemed Mme de Sévigné worthy of taking her seat among the best-loved authors of the classical period (in for example *Le Temple du goût*, she is clearly preferred to Balzac, Voiture and Benserade)[16] and apparently appreciated her 'naturel', 'grâce' and 'esprit,' [naturalness, grace and wit] – all leitmotivs in his assessment of women's writings (see *OH*, p. 1209) – he was ready at the same time to denounce the apparent lack of substance in her letters and her excessive preoccupation with 'bagatelles' [trivialities] (*OH*, p. 1011).

yet claimed her work had ? substance

Above all, in spite of the high regard which he professed for her epistolary style, Voltaire was exasperated, so he tells us in the *Siècle*, by Mme de Sévigné's lack of judgement: '[Elle] croit toujours que Racine *n'ira pas loin*. Elle en jugeait comme du café, dont elle dit *qu'on se désabusera bientôt*. Il faut du temps pour que les réputations mûrissent' [(She) always thinks that Racine *won't go far*. She speaks about him as one would coffee, which *people will soon tire of*. It takes a long time for reputations to mature] (*OH*, pp. 1011–12).[17]

In his wish to become the premier public advocate of Racine's genius and achievements, Voltaire is grossly unfair to Mme de Sévigné. Worse still, because he is over-eager to ride his hobby-horse of pleading for Racine's superiority over Corneille, Voltaire purposely misquotes the original passage to drive home the alleged machinations of the anti-Racine 'cabale'. R. Lowenstein therefore hits the nail right on the head when he concludes: 'The troublesome quotation (XIV, 544) from Mme de Sévigné was, to my mind, less the result of careless recollection, than the desire to paint a woefully black picture.'[18] Mme de Sévigné had, in fact, written to Mme de Grignan on 16 March [1672], after a performance of *Bajazet*, not '*Racine n'ira pas loin*', but:

V. selects quotes from Sév. + alters them to suit his purpose

> Le dénouement n'est point bien préparé; on n'entre point dans les raisons de cette grande tuerie. Il y a pourtant des choses agréables; et rien de parfaitement beau, rien qui enlève, point de ces tirades de

16 Voltaire, *Le Temple du goût*, in *Mélanges*, p. 148.

17 This charge is repeated in the *Catalogue* of the *Siècle*, where Voltaire deplores, in even stronger terms, Mme de Sévigné's lack of taste and her failure to recognize Racine's obvious talent. (See *OH*, p. 1209).

18 Lowenstein, *Voltaire as an Historian*, p. 158.

Corneille qui font frissonner. Ma fille, gardons-nous bien de lui comparer Racine; sentons-en la différence. Il y a des endroits froids et faibles, et jamais il n'ira plus loin qu'*Alexandre* et qu'*Andromaque*. *Bajazet* est au-dessous, au sentiment de bien des gens, et au mien si j'ose me citer.[19]

[The *dénouement* is not well prepared; there are no reasons given for this great slaughter. There are, however, some pleasant things; and nothing perfectly beautiful, nothing which carries you away, none of Corneille's tirades which make you shiver. My daughter, we must be wary of comparing Racine to him; let us feel the difference. There are cold and weak parts, and he will never go further than *Alexandre* and *Andromaque*. *Bajazet* is inferior, in the eyes of many people, and in my own, if I dare to take myself as an example.]

Such a deplorable practice of transforming a quotation, or selecting from a source or a text that best suits his polemical purpose at the time of writing, is fairly typical of Voltaire the historian and emerges from a close analysis of his utilization of sources for *Le Siècle de Louis XIV*.[20]

Moreover, to accuse Mme de Sévigné of having misjudged Racine's talent, and of having attempted to lead a public campaign against him is a misrepresentation of the facts. Even in her private letters to her daughter, she is keen to applaud Racine's success and genius. Voltaire purposely ignores her positive comments, as on 15 January 1672, two months before the letter which he selects, when she pronounces *Bajazet* to be a fine play, though inferior to *Andromaque*:

La comédie de Racine m'a paru belle, nous y avons été. [. . .] *Bajazet* est beau; j'y trouve quelque embarras sur la fin. Il y a bien de la passion, et de la passion moins folle que celle de *Bérénice*. Je trouve cependant, selon mon goût, qu'elle ne surpasse pas *Andromaque*, et pour ce qui est des belles comédies de Corneille, elles sont autant au-dessus, que celles de Racine sont au-dessus de toutes les autres.[21]

[I thought Racine's was a fine play, we were at it. [. . .] *Bajazet* is fine; I think there is some confusion at the end. There is a lot of passion, passion which is less wild than in *Bérénice*. I think, however, that for my taste, it doesn't outdo *Andromaque*, and as regards Corneille's fine plays, they are as superior [to Racine's] as Racine's are superior to all the others.]

19 *Mme de Sévigné. Correspondance*, ed. R. Duchêne, 3 vols, Bibliothèque de la Pléiade (Paris: Gallimard, 1972–8), 1, p. 459.
20 See Marc Serge Rivière, 'Voltaire's concept of dramatic history in *Le Siècle de Louis XIV*', *Studies on Voltaire and the Eighteenth Century*, 284 (1991), 179–98; 'Voltaire's use of eyewitness reports in *Le Siècle de Louis XIV*, with special reference to the *Mémoires de Torcy*', *New Zealand Journal of French Studies*, 9. 2 (1988), 5–26.
21 *Mme de Sévigné. Correspondance*, 1, p. 417.

Few would disagree that Mme de Sévigné is here giving a positive assessment of Racine's three plays. That Voltaire distorts her statement and charges her with bias and injustice towards Racine, is all the more surprising in view of the fact that he is quite capable of reading closely and reporting accurately, when he so wishes. Thus, he draws on Mme de Sévigné's account of a performance of *Esther* at Saint-Cyr, for a detail regarding the presence of Jesuits and inserts it into *Le Siècle* (*OH*, p. 941); Mme de Sévigné had written on 31 January [1689]: 'Le Roi et toute la cour sont charmés de la tragédie d'*Esther*. Mme de Miramion et huit jésuites, dont le P. Gaillard était, ont honoré de leur présence la dernière représentation' [The King and all the court are charmed by the tragedy *Esther*. Mme de Miramion and eight Jesuits, including Father Gaillard, honoured the last performance with their presence] (3, p. 491). But what Voltaire fails to report in his eagerness to place Mme de Sévigné firmly in the anti-Racine lobby, is her warm tribute to *Esther*'s qualities and success. Thus, she adds in the same letter of 31 January in a tongue-in-cheek manner: 'Enfin c'est un chef-d'œuvre de Racine. Si j'étais dévote, j'aspirerais à la voir' [It is a masterpiece from Racine. If I were devout, I would long to see it] (3, p. 491). Two months later, in a statement which resembles the one misquoted by Voltaire – 'jamais Racine n'ira plus loin qu'*Alexandre*' – Mme de Sévigné expresses her high regard for *Esther*, even before she has attended a performance: 'Racine aura peine à faire jamais quelque chose d'aussi agréable, car il n'y a plus d'histoire comme celle-là' [Racine will have difficulty ever doing anything so pleasant, because there is no other story like this one] (3, p. 549). Having at last been invited to attend a performance at Saint-Cyr, she reported on 21 February 1689 to Mme de Grignan and waxed lyrical about the harmony and poetic quality of *Esther*:

> Je ne puis vous dire l'excès de l'agrément de cette pièce. C'est une chose qui n'est pas aisée à représenter, et qui ne sera jamais imitée; c'est un rapport de la musique, des vers, des chants, des personnes, si parfait et si complet qu'on n'y souhaite rien [. . .] Tout y est simple, tout y est innocent, tout y est sublime et touchant.[22]

> [I cannot tell you the exceeding pleasantness of this play. It is something which is not easy to perform, and which will never be imitated. There is a rapport between the music, the lines, the songs, the characters which is so perfect and so complete that one could wish for nothing more. [. . .] Everything in it is simple, everything is innocent, everything is sublime and moving.]

22 *Mme de Sévigné. Correspondance*, 3, p. 508.

Those are hardly the words of someone, who, in Voltaire's scheme of things, 'se piqua toujours de ne pas rendre justice à Racine' [always prided herself on not being fair to Racine] (*OH*, p. 1011). While it is true that Mme de Sévigné was a devotee of Corneille's theatre all her life, many similar statements testify to her scrupulous fairness and to her openness towards the innovations of Racine's theatre. Voltaire's tendentious interpretation of events and his portrayal of courtiers in Louis XIV's day often rested on using anecdotes and quotations out of context and, worse still, on transforming statements and embroidering on the borrowed material. The end result bears his indelible stamp as he seeks to present his own original, yet at times overtly biased, version of events. In the process, the memorialist's − in this case Mme de Sévigné's − values and opinions are sadly lost sight of.

[handwritten margin note: She was fair + open-minded toward R.]

(ii) THE *SOUVENIRS DE MADAME DE CAYLUS*

It was seemingly Voltaire's attempt to revamp the *Siècle* and his urgent search for relevant additional material, which led him in 1768 to edit the little-known diary of Marthe-Marguerite Le Valois de Villette-Mursay, marquise de Caylus (1663–1729). The first edition of the *Souvenirs* was published in Amsterdam by Jean Robert and contained a preface and thirty anonymous notes by Voltaire.[23] Voltaire's annotated edition of the *Souvenirs*[24] served a dual polemical purpose: first to renew interest in Louis XIV's reign and to provide ammunition against his critics, and secondly to refute further 'toutes ces impostures imprimées, et surtout les prétendus *Mémoires de madame de Maintenon*' (*OC*, 28, p. 287).[25] Mme de Caylus had been brought to the court by Mme de Maintenon, her relative, in 1680. As a result of intrigues, she was forced to leave the court in 1694 but returned in 1707 following her husband's death. She had, however, kept a careful diary of events and comings and goings in the inner sanctum of Versailles and was

[handwritten margin note: V's edition of mémoires of Mme de Caylus]

23 See *Les Souvenirs de madame de Caylus*, ed. B. Noël (Paris: Mercure de France, 1986), pp. 16 ff. A second edition soon followed without the preface, but with additional notes, from the printing press of Marc-Michel Rey in 1770; and a third edition was later published in Maestricht in 1778, with a full array of Voltaire's notes, but without the preface.
24 See Marc Serge Rivière, 'Voltaire Editor of Dangeau', *Studies on Voltaire and the Eighteenth Century*, 311 (1993), pp. 15–38, (pp. 20–2 and 37–8).
25 In the preface, Voltaire launches a devastating attack on Laurent Angliviel de La Beaumelle, his adversary of old, who in 1753 had published an annotated edition of *Le Siècle de Louis XIV*, as well as the *Mémoires pour servir à l'histoire de madame de Maintenon* (Amsterdam, 1755–6) and her letters (1752), which are deemed nowadays to be largely apocryphal. For a discussion of these memoirs, see Claude Lauriol, *La Beaumelle: Un protestant cévenol entre Montesquieu et Voltaire* (Geneva: Droz, 1978).

highly intelligent, witty and observant (Noël, pp. 13–14). Voltaire's edition of the diary of Mme de Caylus is more sober, scholarly and generous than his edition of the *Journal de la cour de Louis XIV* [. . .], an annotated selection of entries from the manuscript memoirs of the marquis de Dangeau.[26] For all that, Voltaire is preoccupied with his own agenda and his polemical aims, as shown by the inevitable jibes at members of the clergy and several comments on the fact that Mme de Caylus is far too preoccupied with salacious *galanteries* and courtly intrigues.[27] One may therefore conclude that Voltaire had no wish to convey the spirit of the original text, nor was he concerned with the values and vision of the author. Instead, he selected and presented what he deemed important and failed to remain in the background. In other words, his notes and his selection tell us much more about Voltaire himself than about Mme de Caylus.

It is in this context that one must read what is without doubt the most informative and serious section of Voltaire's extracts of the *Souvenirs de madame de Caylus*, which deals with performances of Racine's plays at Saint-Cyr and Versailles, *Esther, Andromaque* and *Athalie* (*OC*, 28, pp. 300–3). Mme de Caylus was herself a fine actress, as Saint-Simon and Choisy remarked.[28] Mme de Caylus's account of performances at Saint-Cyr struck Voltaire, not just because of the authentic details observed at first hand – such as the reasons for *Andromaque* being shelved, which are given in Mme de Maintenon's letter to Racine: 'Nos petites filles viennent de jouer *Andromaque*, et l'ont si bien jouée qu'elles ne la joueront plus, ni aucune de vos pièces' [Our little girls have just performed *Andromaque*, and they performed it so well that they will never perform it again, nor any other of your plays] (*OC*, 28, p. 300) — but also because such little-known material served his polemical purposes well and added to his campaign to promote Racine's theatre, and theatre in general against the Jansenists' opposition.

Racine's success with *Esther*, the unlikeliest of subjects, in a highly acclaimed performance by the unlikeliest actors, the *demoiselles de Saint-Cyr*, is confirmed by Caylus' comment: 'Elle eut un si grand succès que le souvenir n'en est pas encore effacé' [It enjoyed such great success that the memory of it is not yet erased] (*OC*, 28, p. 301). Moreover, this gives Voltaire *dramaturge* a chance to return to the charge against the anti-theatre lobby, by underlining the intrinsic moral and pedagogic value of the theatre. Thus, he gleefully chooses to reproduce

26 See Rivière, 'Voltaire Editor of Dangeau', p. 37.
27 On this aspect, see Rivière, 'Voltaire, Reader of Women's Memoirs', pp. 48–9.
28 *Mme de Sévigné: Correspondance*, 3, p. 1390, n. 3.

Mme de Caylus's assertion that even in a convent, young women can develop intellectually and emotionally, through performance: 'Cependant, [. . .] elle était persuadée que ces sortes d'amusements sont bons à la jeunesse, qu'ils donnent de la grâce, apprennent à mieux prononcer, et cultivent la mémoire' [However, [. . .] she was convinced that these types of pastime were good for the young, that they give [the girls] grace, teach them how to articulate better, and develop their memories] (*OC*, 28, p. 300). Voltaire's notes betray once more the presence of the advocate of Racine's superiority over Corneille: 'Il n'est pas étonnant que de jeunes filles de qualité, élevées si près de la cour, aient mieux joué *Andromaque*, où il y a quatre personnages amoureux, que *Cinna* dans lequel l'amour n'est pas traité fort naturellement, et n'étale guère que des sentiments exagérés et des expressions un peu ampoulées' [It is not surprising that young girls of good stock, brought up so near to the court, performed *Andromaque* better, where there are four people in love, than *Cinna* where love is not treated very naturally, and which is scattered with only exaggerated feelings and pompous expressions] (*OC*, 28, p. 300). In another footnote, Voltaire the dramatist puts in a plea for harmony in tragedy, while he cannot overcome his *parti pris* when he declares religious subjects to be unsuitable for tragedy, without justifying such an assertion (*OC*, 28, p. 301, n. 2). The propagandist, too, is keen to underline Mme de Caylus's allusion to the senseless opposition to *Athalie* by the 'canaille dévote', the Jansenists: 'Mme de Maintenon reçut de tous côtés tant d'avis et tant de représentations des dévots, qui agissaient en cela de bonne foi, et de la part des poëtes jaloux de la gloire de Racine [. . .] qu'ils empêchèrent *Athalie* d'être représentée sur le théâtre' [Mme de Maintenon received from all sides so many opinions and so many representations from the *dévots*, who were acting in good faith, and from poets who were jealous of Racine's glory [. . .] that they prevented *Athalie* from being performed in the theatre] (*OC*, 28, p. 302).

It is clear, therefore, that far from allowing an interesting text to speak for itself, Voltaire selects what he personally deems useful and valuable from it, before proceeding to impose his own highly subjective interpretation on the material. What is more, when he comes across a statement from Mme de Caylus, which he strongly disagrees with because of his own preconceptions, he does not mince words. Voltaire attended the first public performance in Paris of *Athalie* in March 1716;[29] Mme de Caylus firmly believed that the play had

29 See R. Pomeau, *Voltaire en son temps*, 2 vols (Oxford and Paris: Voltaire Foundation and Fayard, 1995), I, p. 90.

made a greater impact when performed in ordinary dress in Mme de Maintenon's private quarters at Versailles (*OC*, 28, p. 302). Voltaire was aware of these facts, but because his main aim was to decry the allegedly unfair treatment meted out to Racine by the French court and opposition to his theatre towards the end of his life – a myth which was spread by Louis Racine – he went out of his way to paint a more sombre tableau, almost as if obstacles to *Athalie* were a repeat of the anti-*Phèdre cabale*: 'Cela n'est pas vrai: elle fut très dénigrée, les cabales la firent tomber. Racine était trop grand, on l'écrasa' [That is not true. It was highly disparaged, the *cabales* brought it down. Racine was too great, they crushed him] (*OC*, 28, p. 302, n. 2). It is true that Mme de Caylus had very good reasons to overstate the relative success of the performance in camera. The lack of state support for artists in France became a leitmotiv in Voltaire's writings after his stay in the Bastille in 1718 and following his exile in England in 1725; there he saw for himself the public honours conferred on such writers as Addison, Swift, and Congreve. In his edition of Mme de Caylus, as is so often the case, the propagandist had the better of the literary critic, as objectivity lost out to personal bias. The editor decided to put the author firmly in her place, by stressing Racine's fall from grace in the autumn of his career. Thus, paradoxically, Voltaire who, as a historian, frequently sought to authenticate his narrative of events by quoting eye-witness reports, undermined on this occasion the candid observations of a rare witness. Mme de Caylus was in the privileged position of being able to compare the reception accorded at Versailles to the play and the Paris production of 1716. While he went out of his way to praise highly the integrity of Mme de Caylus in his preface, Voltaire was keen in his editorial notes, and in his more private statements about the *Souvenirs*, to demonstrate his own superior bookish knowledge over that of other historians of the age of Louis XIV; to Richelieu, for example, he wrote somewhat maliciously on 3 December, 1769: 'C'est dommage que Mad^e De Caylus ait eu si peu de mémoire' [It is a pity that Mme de Caylus had such poor memory] (Best. D16019). Yet, true to form, he was not reluctant to cash in on this little-known diary.

Voltaire and Racine, perceived by women as the
'poète[s] des femmes'

Although Voltaire's Roman and epic tragedies had much in common
with Corneille's concept of heroic tragedy, it became relatively easy for
his supporters and for him to draw a parallel between Racine's theatre
and his, all the more since his plays were frequently performed at the
Théâtre-Français alongside those of his illustrious predecessor. By
insisting on sensibility, pathos, harmony, elegance of language and
purity of diction in the classical tradition, Voltaire could hold Racine
up as his model. The latter had been *historiographe du Roi*, although it is
doubtful whether he had achieved as much in that role as his colleague Pellisson and Voltaire who was named in 1745. For very good
reasons, Voltaire was eager to remind Louis XV on numerous occasions
of the patronage extended to Racine by Louis XIV at the apex of his
career. In much the same way, the *Siècle de Louis XIV* was meant to
convey a clear message to the ruling monarch about the importance of
royal protection for literary artists. In a letter to d'Argental of 14
August, 1749, Voltaire recalled that Racine's success was due in no
small measure to Madame – a myth spread by Louis Racine – and he
intimated that he would not fail to draw Mme de Pompadour's
attention to this fact (Best. D3977). There is no doubt that Voltaire's
reputation as a dramatist, and with it that of Racine, was greatly
enhanced by the activities of his large European network of female
correspondents and patronesses. Mme de Pompadour and her troupe
of amateurs successfully staged *Alzire* at Versailles in 1749 in the small
theatre; she also managed to secure funds from Louis XV for the
rather lavish decor, and Voltaire proudly attended the second performance.[30] The king's influential mistress was not averse to drawing a
parallel between Voltaire and Racine; thus, she wrote to the former
when he became the target of much public criticism in 1749:
'Rappellés vous ce qui est arrivé aux Corneils, Racine &^{ca}, et vous
verrés que vous n'estes pas plus maltraité qu'eux' [Remember what
happened to the Corneilles, Racine etc., and you will see that you
are no more ill-treated than they] (Best. D4012).

At that time and until his death in 1778, there is little doubt that
Voltaire's plays were seen by female European contemporaries as
clearly in the Racinian tradition. In several private correspondences,
Voltaire emerges, like Racine, as 'le poète des femmes', not just because
several of his plays bore the names of female protagonists, for example
Zaïre, Alzire, Eriphile, Mérope, to name but a few, but also because the

30 J. Sareil, *Voltaire et les grands* (Geneva: Droz, 1978), p. 117.

chief devotees of his theatre were women, who actively supported and promoted public and private performances of his and Racine's plays across Europe.[31] A brief glance at the correspondence of Mme de Graffigny illustrates the point that Racine's and Voltaire's plays often coincided, both on the bills of the Théâtre-Français, and in the minds of female audiences. Françoise Paule d'Issembourg d'Happoncourt Higuet de Graffigny (who died in December 1758) is remembered nowadays chiefly as the author of the *Lettres d'une Péruvienne* (1747) and a few plays. Although her relationship with Voltaire changed radically after her eventful stay in Cirey, when she was accused by the *philosophe* of having taken and circulated an incomplete manuscript of *La Pucelle* in December 1738, she remained a regular spectator at performances of his plays until her death in 1758.[32]

One recurrent theme in Mme de Graffigny's twenty-three-year correspondence, accordingly, is the theatre, and in particular, references to performances of Racine's and Voltaire's plays. As she recounts her daily activities to François-Antoine Devaux, dit Panpan, not only does she comment frankly on Voltaire's plays, but she also discusses at length public performances of Racine's which she has attended. Such performances were staged in the first half of the eighteenth century, not just at public theatres but also, at private ones, such as the residence of Frederick, then Prince of Prussia, in 1736 at Rheinsberg, where Voltaire's *Œdipe* and Racine's tragedies formed part of the regular repertoire.[33] Mme de Graffigny's increasing passion for Racine strikes the reader of her correspondence as greater than her diminishing respect for Voltaire the dramatist; she repeatedly hailed *Athalie* to be one of the finest examples of dramatic innovation (1, p. 421); she saw *Phèdre* performed at the Théâtre-Français in February 1739 and was rapturous in her applause (1, p. 322). She witnessed Mademoiselle Clairon's first performance in the role of Phèdre at the same theatre on 19 September 1743, and commented: 'Elle a un son de voix charmant et cent mille inflections, mais la plus ignoble figure qui ait jamais été: grosse, courte, une maussaderie répandue dans toute sa personne qui

31 Significantly, Voltaire *dramaturge* was far more appreciated than the *philosophe* by female readers in his day. In the only *Eloge de Voltaire* entered by a woman for the Prix de l'Académie Française in 1778 after Voltaire's death, and published by J. Vercruysse as part of his excellent series *Les Voltairiens* (Nendeln: K.T.O. Press, 1978, II, no. 7), Mademoiselle de Gaudin saw the dramatist's achievements as the high point of a most productive artistic career.

32 See *Correspondance de madame de Graffigny*, ed. E. Showalter *et al.*, 5 vols (Oxford: Voltaire Foundation 1985–97), 1, p. xx. All the following references are to this edition. Spelling has been modernized.

33 Pomeau, *Voltaire en son temps*, 1, p. 324.

répugne' [The sound of her voice is charming, and has a hundred thousand modulations, but she has the most vile figure that ever was: fat, short with a revolting glumness spread throughout her body] (4, p. 381). She appeared to have known *Andromaque* almost by heart and frequently quoted lines which she enjoyed adapting to her own ends (e.g. 2, p. 93; 3, p. 442), and she never relented in proclaiming the unique qualities of Racine's language (2, p. 314).

Yet she was impartial enough to share Voltaire's views that *Athalie* was not a tragedy in the true sense of the word: 'C'est un beau poème, bien conduit, bien versifié, mais ce n'est pas une tragédie' [It is a fine poem, well organized, well versified, but it is not a tragedy] (2, p. 314). On one occasion, although she later admitted to having joined in the mirth, she expressed her outrage to Devaux that the parterre had behaved disgracefully during a performance of *Athalie* at the Théâtre-Français on 16 December 1739: 'Ce chien de parterre a pourtant ri à bien des endr[oits] au sujet de la pièce' [The cursed parterre nonetheless laughed in many places at the subject of the play] (2, p. 282). In her numerous reviews of performances of Racine's plays, Mme de Graffigny displays great insight and critical judgement, despite her intense devotion to Racine; for example, a performance of *Iphigénie en Aulide* at the Théâtre-Français on 19 November 1742 failed to move her (3, p. 454). Her most oft-quoted play, interestingly enough, is *Les Plaideurs*, for which she had a special affection. Having attended a free performance of the comedy on 18 June 1744, to celebrate the French victory at Menin, she wrote to Devaux: 'De monde et de cahos, j'en ai la tête tournée' [My head is spinning, from the people and the hubbub] (5, p. 316), skilfully adapting a line from Act III. 3, 'j'ai la tête troublée'.

When dealing with Voltaire's theatre after 1738, Mme de Graffigny adopted a more critical stance and challenged the partisan responses of Devaux to the works of his 'hero', Voltaire. While she was keen to select for his sake those lines from *Mahomet* which she deemed admirable (3, p. 413), she was sufficiently detached to deplore a large number of 'vers pitoyables' and 'mauvais raisonnements', in the first two acts (3, p. 427), and consistently championed the need for critical distance (3, p. 443). She was seemingly a fixture at the Théâtre-Français whenever Voltaire's plays, *Alzire*, *Zaïre* (3, p. 123) and *Mérope* (4, p. 149) were staged. After a performance of this last play at the Théâtre-Français on 20 February, 1743, she expressed her unequivocal admiration to Devaux (4, p. 155). On the other hand, she was more scathing of the lack of success of *La Mort de César* at the Théâtre-Français, where it was billed seven times from September 1743 onwards (4, p. 362). Mme de Graffigny's critical approach is precisely what makes her comments all

for her, R = yardstick
by which to judge ✓

the more valuable and sincere; it is also apparent to the reader of her private correspondence that she uses Racine's theatre as a yardstick by which to measure Voltaire's dramatic productions and that the two dramatists were inseparable in her scheme of things. Thus she had no difficulty in concurring with the parallel, drawn by Devaux, between the fates of *Mahomet* and *Athalie* as follows: 'Je compte que, quand le torrent des préjugés contre Voltaire sera écoulé, cette pièce sauvera sa réputation comme *Athalie*, négligée si longtemps, a consacré celle de Racine' [I think that when the flood of prejudices against Voltaire has abated, this play will save his reputation as *Athalie*, neglected for so long established Racine's] (3, p. 428, n. 2).

Graffigny = typical
of whole generation
of ♀ theater goers

In drawing attention to the similarities between the productions of the two leading dramatists and their reception by French audiences, Mme de Graffigny was typical of a whole generation of female theatre-goers. She was herself a close friend of the Quinaults and of Mademoiselle Gaussin, and her *salon* attracted established actors, producers and dramatists on a daily basis. Her views reflected much debate in her circle and may be said to be generally representative both of those of her fairly well-educated entourage, and of female audiences in Europe. From Paris to Berlin, influential female devotees and patronesses of Voltaire and Racine worked assiduously for the cause of their theatre. H. A. Stavan has argued convincingly that the duchess of Saxe-Gotha was one such tireless worker; at Friedenstein in winter and Friedrichswerth in summer, her francophile court revelled in performances of Racine, Regnard, Marivaux, La Chaussée and Voltaire.[34] To Voltaire himself, the duchess confessed that *Alzire* and *Zaïre* had brought tears to her eyes and in November 1754, she wrote that she found in the *Orphelin de la Chine* 'des tableaux d'une beauté ravissante, d'une force infinie' [scenes of a ravishing beauty, of an infinite strength] (Best. D5992).

German,
Prussian

Other German and Prussian princesses, with varying degrees of insight and education, were constant in their devotion to Racine and Voltaire. When the *philosophe* took refuge in Berlin in 1750 at Frederick's request, he was hailed by the Queen Mother, Frederick's sisters and other ladies of the Prussian court as a worthy successor to Racine and as the supreme living dramatist. *Rome Sauvée* was staged at the residence of Princess Amelia, the king's sister who later became Abbess of Quedlinburg (Best. D4226), so was *Zaïre* (Best. D4302) on 5 January, 1751, while Voltaire himself was invited to take the part of Lusignan at another performance (Best. D4344). Alongside his plays, there was a

34 H.A. Stavan, 'Voltaire et la duchesse de Gotha', *Studies on Voltaire and the Eighteenth Century*, 185 (1980), 31.

full répertoire of Racine's. The residence of the Queen Mother, Sophia Dorothea, at Monbijou, became a favourite meeting place for devotees of Voltaire's and Racine's tragedies,[35] while a number of other margravines and princesses regularly communicated their veneration and passion for his plays to the dramatist. The margravine of Bayreuth wrote that she had been moved to tears by *Mahomet* (Best. D4873), while another sister of Frederick's, Ulrica of Sweden, revealed her special liking for *Sémiramis* (Best. D3953). This support and adulation did much to raise Voltaire's spirits in Berlin in 1752–3, as Frederick became increasingly hostile and neglectful. One may surmise that such private performances evoked for Voltaire those of *Esther* and *Athalie* at Saint-Cyr and in Mme de Maintenon's apartments. As late as 3 September, 1758, long after he had left Frederick's court, Voltaire could recall the tributes lavished on Racine in Prussia which he had personally witnessed, as he wrote to Mme du Bocage from the Délices: 'Notre siècle vit sur le crédit du siècle de Louis XIV. On parle, il est vrai, dans les pays étrangers la langue que les Pascal, les Despréaux, les Bossuet, les Racine, les Molière ont rendue universelle, et c'est dans notre propre langue qu'on dit aujourd'hui dans l'Europe, que les français dégénèrent' [Our century lives on the credit of the century of Louis XIV. It is true that in foreign countries people speak the language which the Pascals, the Despréaux, the Bossuets, the Racines, the Molières made universal, and it is in our language that it is said today in Europe that the French are degenerating] (Best. D7846).

There is ample evidence to suggest that the well-orchestrated campaign on behalf of Racine, sustained by Voltaire over many years, paid ample dividends for him both as a dramatist and as a literary critic. Female readers and audiences played a significant role in spreading the word; they responded warmly to Racine's and Voltaire's reliance on *sensibilité* and approved of the purity, clarity and simplicity of their language. In the last phase of Voltaire's life, the pairing of his name and Racine's remained fresh in the minds of his female supporters. Thus, when a group of devotees of Voltaire's theatre decided to erect a statue to him in April 1770 and commissioned Pigalle to work on it, it was a woman, Suzanne Necker, who was delegated to discuss with him the proposed location of the statue: 'Où la mettrons-nous cette statue? Sera-ce là à la nouvelle sale de la comédie? Là j'irois chaque jour la baigner de mes larmes en sortant de *Zaïre* ou de *Tancrède*, et si quelque jeune auteur avait eu du succez, il poserait une guirlande de fleurs sur la tête du Vieillard' [Where will we put this statue? Will it be in the new theatre? I would go there every day to bathe it with my tears, when I came out of *Zaïre* or *Tancrède*, and if some young author was successful, he would place a garland of flowers on the Old Man's head] (Best. D16485). Voltaire, who, as noted above, had written of *Bérénice* and Racine in the *Commentaires sur Corneille*, 'c'est avec raison qu'on a nommé Racine le poète des femmes' (*CW*, 55, p. 951), owed the supreme accolade given to him as a dramatist to an educated woman. In *Le Siècle*, as we saw earlier, Voltaire summed up Racine's success thus: '[Racine] parle au cœur' (*OH*, p. 1011). Significantly, in her moving, albeit flattering, tribute, Suzanne Necker referred to Voltaire's knowledge of the human heart but arguably went further than many of her female contemporaries in asserting that by his standing and popularity as a dramatist at the time, he outshone Racine: 'Il faut savoir à présent où nous placerons cette statue. Nous pourrions la mettre [. . .] à la comédie françoise où vous faites oublier Corneille et Racine' [We must decide presently where we shall place this statue. We could put it in the Comédie française where you make people forget Corneille and Racine] (Best. D16284). Had the apprentice and disciple finally upstaged his master and mentor? Voltaire himself had no doubt as to the answer.[36] And to the d'Argentals on 9 March 1763, he had proclaimed: 'Mes divins anges, il n'y a que Racine dans le monde' [My divine angels, there is only one Racine in the world' (Best. D11078). In the final analysis, Voltaire, 'homme de passion', as René Pomeau has described him,[37] was empowered as a dramatist by the unrelenting passion of his many female devotees for Racine's theatre and his own. However sincere Voltaire's own passion was for the seventeenth-century ideals exemplified by Racine, the fact remains that by constantly publicising it in European intellectual and female circles, he was promoting his own image as the logical and only heir to the throne of supreme French dramatist. As he once wrote in an *alinéa* on Pope in the *Lettres philosophiques*: 'Il en est des livres comme du feu dans nos foyers: on va prendre ce feu chez son voisin, on l'allume chez soi' [A book is like a fire in the hearth; the light is taken from your neighbour's and is lit at home].[38] By all accounts, Voltaire astutely used Racine's reputation and achievements to 'fire up' further the enthusiasm of his own network of passionate devotees, and this paid ample dividends.

36 See above n. 9.
37 R. Pomeau, *La Religion de Voltaire* (Paris: Nizet, 1956), p. 384.
38 Quoted by H. T. Patterson, in her introduction to Voltaire, *Traité de métaphysique* (Manchester: Manchester University Press, 1937), pp. xii–xiii.

9

Pleasure in Racine

LOUIS VAN DELFT

'Pleasure in Racine' . . . the subject can be approached in several different ways. The first, of course, would simply be to present an inventory of occurrences of the word 'plaisir'. There are many of them, from the question of Jocaste, 'Prennent-ils [les dieux] donc *plaisir* à faire des coupables?' (*La Thébaïde*, Act II. 2, l. 695) to the intimate revelation of Esther, 'Aux pieds de l'Eternel je viens m'humilier, / Et goûter *le plaisir* de me faire oublier (*Esther*, Act I.1, ll. 109–10). The word 'plaisir' recurs forty-nine times in the work of Racine, and the plural 'plaisirs' eleven times. Naturally, one would have a clearer idea of what the word means exactly if the search were extended to other words belonging to the wider semantic field of 'plaisir'. By taking into account the concept as well as the term itself, the exercise would become more convincing; in consequence, it would be noted that the infinitive 'plaire' occurs fifty-three times in Racine's theatre, and reference to Freeman's *Concordance*[1] shows a further forty-one occurrences of morphological variants of the same verb other than the infinitive (Britannicus to Junie: 'Néron, vous *plairait-il?* Vous serais-je odieux?', *Britannicus*, Act II. 6, l. 738); Antiochus: 'Ah! Que *nous nous plaisons* à nous tromper tous deux!', *Bérénice*, Act III. 2, l. 798). But there must be doubts about the validity of such an exercise; all that would emerge from it would be nebulous, a meaningless, accumulating conglomeration of words. It is by no means guaranteed that such a method could produce anything meaningful, whether a philosophy, an ethical overview, or a clear Racinian concept of pleasure. Furthermore, the sense of pleasure has nearly always been so close to the central

1 Bryant C. Freeman and Alan Bateson, *Concordance du Théâtre et des Poésies de Jean Racine* (Ithaca: Cornell University Press, 1968).

concerns of everyone who has ever studied Racine, from the times of his early plays to tercentenary colloquia, that even if these analyses vary considerably from each other it seems unlikely that a genuinely new point of view would emerge on this topic. So this first suggested approach promises nothing new.

R's pleasure in writing

A second possible approach would be to abandon the perspective of the characters to focus on the dramatist himself. As a title, 'Pleasure in Racine' could then refer to the satisfaction that the man, the writer, derived from his creative writing. But here, too, it must be admitted that there are problems of method, even if this approach has been adopted and pursued with great success by Jean-Michel Delacomptée in his *Racine en majesté* (Paris: Flammarion, 1998). It is not only the example of Racine which gives rise to second thoughts about this particular angle of approach. It is universally the case that it is difficult, most often impossible, ever to truly know any other person, whether our contemporaries or those closest to us, or even ourselves. It is simply impossible to truly know another of those specimens of humanity whom Montaigne described as 'de la basse forme'.[2] So how much more difficult it is, then, to know intimately somebody who has been dead for three hundred years, and who was not in any way 'de la

... did it ?

commune sorte'. For these reasons, it seems necessary also to abandon the unverifiable question of the pleasure that Racine himself derived – perhaps (for we cannot assert that he did), from his work.

* audience's pleasure

In the wake of the dramatic characters and the person of the writer, there remains a third party to be reckoned with, and that is obviously the audience: apart from unfortunate schoolchildren, the audience has only ever come to the theatre in search of pleasure, even if in seventeenth-century Paris this included the pedantic pleasure of sitting in critical judgement. Of course, no public is ever homogeneous from one generation to another; indeed, within the one generation of spectators there can be divergent views on the same spectacle (as our own era shows), and 'la demande de plaisir' [the requirements of pleasure] can vary considerably. It is nevertheless the case that Racine himself defined in one of his most famous statements the specific kind of pleasure he set out to offer his public. The definition he proposes is abrupt, and it flirts with the absolute in claiming to circumscribe a 'totality' in the form of a maxim. In complete accordance with the spirit of the time which, anthropologically and æsthetically, aspired to enduring, universal values, Racine's formula leads us to believe that, for him, there are only a limited number of 'plaisirs' offered in tragic

2 Montaigne, *Essais*, ed. Villey–Saulnier (Paris: PUF, 1965), 3, 9, p. 988.

theatre. The famous expression used in the preface to *Bérénice* has already been identified by many readers: 'cette tristesse majestueuse qui fait tout le plaisir de la tragédie'. It is in this pleasure of our third party, the audience, that this investigation will seek its focus. The angle of approach proposed here may perhaps differ slightly from others insofar as the writer is also a theatre critic as well as a university professor, but it has always been the tradition of *Commentaire* to respect Raymond Aron's example of the 'spectateur engagé' [the committed spectator].[3]

The guiding principle and the plan of this study are as follows: there now exist very few authentic, informed stage directors, and there are just as few members of an audience in tune with 'le plaisir de la tragédie' [the pleasure of tragedy], as it was understood to Racine and the public who supported him understood it. The three parts of the argument are: (1) the dumbing-down of Racine; (2) the sense of pleasure, according to Racine and his admirers; (3) losing the plot.

Dumbing-down

It is occasionally essential to act on the advice offered by the maxim of La Rochefoucauld, 'Nul ne mérite d'être loué de bonté, s'il n'a pas la force d'être méchant' [Nobody should be praised for kindness if they don't sometimes have the strength to be cruel][4], but to avoid the opprobrium of being personally cruel or unkind, the academic-cum-theatre critic can communicate an honest view by hiding behind the comments of those few reviewers who still provide reliable analysis (and there are no more than four of five of them left in Paris). Alternatively, it is equally effective sometimes to let the stage directors condemn themselves out of their own mouths, so to speak, by direct quotation from their programme notes or interviews. So, hiding behind the wall of others' comments, let me proceed.

3 Raymond Aron, *Le Spectateur en gage* (Paris: Julliard, 1981); reprinted by Julliard in the series 'Essais–études'.
4 La Rochefoucauld, *Réflexions ou sentences et maximes morales*, ed. D. L. Gilbert, G.E.F. (Paris: Hachette, 1868), maxim 237, 1, p. 127.

Voices off

A SELECTION OF ILLUSTRATIVE COMMENTS ON
RECENT RACINE PRODUCTIONS IN FRANCE[5]

Antoine Vitez, production of Phèdre, *Théâtre des quartiers, Ivry, 1975*
'L'histoire des larmes. Les larmes, pour qu'on les voie, doivent bar-
bouiller le visage. D'où l'idée de la confiture sur le visage, en guise de
maquillage [. . .] Une seule couleur, le rouge. La honte. La confiture –
l'idée de l'enfance, aussi [. . .] Prendre garde à maintenir cet air de
caravansérail que j'aime tant: le baquet de larmes, l'éponge de larmes,
la serviette pour essuyer les larmes (ou le sperme), etc.' (Antoine Vitez,
'Journal de Phèdre', in: *Ecrits sur le théâtre II, La scène, 1954–1975* (Paris:
P.O.L., 1995), pp. 427, 428, 432.

Yannis Kokkos, production of Iphigénie, *Comédie-Française, 1991*
'Clytemnestre est déguisée en Fée Carabosse du Boulevard du
Crime qui pousse des hurlements et jette au ciel ses griffes. Délirant, et
l'actrice n'est pas responsable, elle est dénaturée par sa présentation.
Iphigénie [. . .] est grossie par son costume et 'draculisée' par son
maquillage' (Michel Cournot, *Le Monde*, 26 octobre 1991).

Christian Rist, production of Bérénice, *Théâtre de l'Athénée, 1992*
'Dédoublement de chaque acteur et tenue de gym obligatoire
soumettent Racine à un traitement de choc. [. . .] Les comédiens [. .
.] restent en tenue de sport. "Je demeurai longtemps errant en
Césarée", raconte Antiochus, et nous nous disons que le malheureux,
sous le soleil assassin de cette ville étrangère, se transbahutait, d'un
gymnase à l'autre, en quête de barres parallèles ou de trapèze de son
choix. C'est bien. Tout ce qui peut rajeunir nos bons vieux classiques
est à prendre' (Michel Cournot, *Le Monde*, 25 mars 1992). On the
question of doubling the characters of Bérénice, Titus et Antiochus,
played simultaneously by two actors (or actresses, as the case may be),
the director added: 'Faute de temps pour [faire] travailler tout le monde,
j'ai pensé à scinder un même rôle entre deux personnes' (Christian
Rist, interviewed by Mathilde La Bardonnie, *Libération*, 27 mars 1992).
The interviewing journalist specified 'Ce n'est qu'ensuite que le metteur
en scène l'a [cette expérience] justifiée en se référant aux réflexions de
Claudel sur le théâtre japonais . . .'

5 The editors have left the original texts in French in order to preserve their
particular succulence and flavour; this is neither an act of camouflage/censorship
nor of support for views presented.

Pierre Marcabru, on the role and future of stage directors (Le Figaro,
23 janvier 1994)

'Faut-il tuer les metteurs en scène ? [. . .] Un Vitez, un Lassalle, un
Chéreau, un Benoin, un Braunschweig, un Nordey [. . .] cherchent
d'abord non pas à nous offrir le texte dans son intégrité, dans son
innocence première, celle de la lecture, mais à l'interpréter, à le solliciter, jusqu'à ce qu'il réponde à l'idée qu'ils s'en font [. . .] La glose,
le commentaire, traduits scéniquement par des signes parfois arbitraires,
font écran entre l'auteur et le spectateur, à qui on retire tout libre-
arbitre devant le fait théâtral [. . .] [Les] metteurs en scène, [les]
régisseurs (le mot est plus exact) qui se refusent à aller au-delà de leur
fonction, qui se contentent de mettre en place, sont en général
méprisés et considérés comme des tâcherons'.

Anne Delbée, production of Phèdre, *Comédie-Française, 1995*

'Insensé. A-t-on le droit de rater un spectacle ? Oui, on a le droit. [. . .]
Il y a des échecs féconds [. . .] Rien de tel, hélas, dans ce spectacle,
furieusement disparate, mis en scène par Anne Delbée, dans un décor en
aluminium à la Paco Rabanne, avec des costumes de (à la) Christian
Lacroix. On frise l'imposture la plus funeste (je pèse mes mots). Sans
être un puriste, on a du mal à détecter, sous le faste voulu, le sérieux
de l'intention. Aucun enjeu, hormis l'emphase, la mode et le tradéridéra,
aucune tension qui ne soit forcée et artificielle. Aucune dramaturgie,
même absurde; aucune avancée, même provocante [. . .] Non, on
perd pied, on boit la tasse, sans avoir quitté le bord; on sombre sans
rémission, pris au piège d'une *heroic phantasy*, d'une fantasmagorie
chétive et incohérente. Comme si la tragédie de Racine se transmuait
en conte de sorcières, farci d'allusions pédantes et débiles, en turlupinade
réservée aux fans de Dorothée, enclins à imaginer le jansénisme sous
les oripeaux de *Dragon Ball Z* et la fille de Minos sous les contours
d'une gitane'.

'Dès lors, les Comédiens-Français, braves soldats, tous admirables
de courage et d'abnégation, sont envoyés au casse-pipe sur l'autel où
la pythonisse Anne Delbée brûle de tous ses émois, de toutes ses
fictions [. . .] On est au cirque, à la corrida, chez Barnum plutôt que
chez Saint-Cyran, l'austère abbé de Port-Royal. Très vite, le spectacle
s'abîme dans les grandes largeurs, entre la broutille et le mythe,
l'extase et les simagrées. Plus rien dans la diction [. . .] ne nous
touche, faute d'un travail humble de reconquête' (Frédéric Ferney, *Le
Figaro*, 7 décembre 1995).

Eric Vigner, production of Bajazet, *Comédie-Française, Théâtre du Vieux-Colombier, 1995*

'Eric Vigner. L'un de ces metteurs en scène usurpés, à qui le public n'ose pas crier: 'Otez-vous de là que j'y voie quelque chose, que j'y entende quelque chose! La mise en scène enterre la pièce et empêtre les comédiens [. . .] Les maquillages carnavalesques (de Bernard Floch) sont du plus pur style pilotes-suicides japonais. Au point que les vers en perdent leur sérieux. Mais impossible de rire parce que ces comédiens ont reçu l'ordre d'observer un très long et profond silence toutes les douze syllabes du texte. Résultat: la soirée, sur les fauteuils, se passe à bouillir d'impatience. Ce n'est plus un théâtre, c'est une salle d'attente. [. . .] La grande nouba-chichi parisienne . . .' (Michel Cournot, *Le Monde*, 18 mai 1995).

Daniel Mesguich, production of Mithridate, *Comédie-Française, Théâtre du Vieux-Colombier, 1995, and re-run in 1999*

'Racine s'est emmerdé à écrire tout cela en vers, et nous allons nous efforcer de nous emmerder à le dire en vers' (Véronique Vella, in conversation with Pierre Notte, *La Terrasse*, juin 1999). 'La sauce Mesguich relève le plat' (Pierre Notte, *ibid.*).

'*Mithridate*, c'est Barbe-Bleue en turban. Mieux: prenez Ivan le Terrible, mettez-lui des babouches cousues de fil d'argent, donnez-lui deux fils: Xipharès et Pharnace. Faites-lui dire: 'Quoi ! prince. . . ' ou 'Hé là! Madame . . . ' sans tricher sur l'acrostiche, Racine n'est pas Queneau. Et quand il prononce le nom de Rome, qu'il ait l'air dégoûté, comme si son inconscient – ça compte l'inconscient – disait: 'Serbe' ou 'Croate'. Et quand il prononcera le mot: 'Malheur', qui est un bon mot dans une tragédie, on entendra: 'Ding! Dong!' pour faire fatidique. Vous y êtes?[6] Pourtant, Mesguich le sait bien, fidèle à l'esprit du jansénisme, Racine fait de l'intelligence une duperie. Chez Racine, le jeu intellectuel s'estompe dans l'élan profond, dans l'ardeur de la tendresse, du reproche, de l'abandon, dans la courbe attendrie de la plainte liée à la cruauté. La belle parleuse hautaine s'absorbe dans la

---

6 Ce 'Ding ! Dong!' est une allusion à la sirupeuse et 'hollywoodienne' (S. A. Heed) 'réalisation sonore' (programme du spectacle) d'une Madame Miniature [*sic*], à laquelle D. Mesguich a eu l'esprit de faire appel pour sa mise en scène de *Mithridate*, comme pour celle d'*Andromaque*. On sait assez que la musique racinienne n'est rien par elle-même et doit être constamment soutenue de 'composition acousmatique'. *Commentaire* a rendu compte ailleurs du travail de notre homme sur *La Vie parisienne* d'Offenbach (Jean-Claude Yon, 'Le vandalisme de bon ton. Une mise en scène de Daniel Mesguich', 79 (1997)).

victime secrètement gémissante. Claude Mathieu (Monime) a d'ailleurs de très bons moments, dans ce registre-là, notamment à la fin, quand elle renonce à son fume-cigarettes et à son verre de whisky [. . .]. Résumons. Racine, Jean. Auteur français. Très influencé par Freud et Kafka dans sa jeunesse, il devint un adepte de la littérature fantastique. Daniel Mesguich, parce qu'il identifie le sublime au subliminal, se croit plus savant que lui [. . .] Quand on a une clé, on peut l'essayer sur toutes les portes. On peut aussi ouvrir la porte et poser la clé' (Frédéric Ferney, *Le Figaro*, 9 mars 1996).

Muriel Mayette, Professor at the Conservatoire national d'art dramatique in Paris, presentation of three of her students in Phèdre, *in the annual 'Journées de juin', designed to bring to public attention those who 'nous enchanteront bientôt sur toutes les scènes'*
'C'est un garçon, Joseph Menant, un grand brun au profil droit, qui, bien à son aise dans une robe noire, joue Phèdre, la fille de Minos et de Pasiphaé [. . .] Une Phèdre évidente, d'une solitude entière. Très beau' (Michel Cournot, *Le Monde*, 27 juin 1997).[7]

Luc Bondy, production of Phèdre, *Festival d'automne, Odéon–Théâtre de l'Europe, 1998*
'[Chez Hippolyte], c'est plutôt la diction qui frappe: celle d'un Johnny Hallyday au Palais des Congrès [. . .] Par bonheur, il débite son texte à une allure de TGV pour s'en débarrasser plus vite: les bonnes choses n'ont qu'un temps. Rien à voir avec sa chère Œnone [. . .] On dirait d'elle que son rôle a doublé de volume. Elle a sûrement appris à s'exprimer dans quelque cité des Tarterets à Mantes-la-Jolie, lieux où, par crainte de rester incompris, on renchérit sur ses propos par d'incessants gestes des bras. Vous voyez la marionnette du beur aux Guignols de l'Info? On n'en est pas loin [. . .] Pourquoi Luc Bondy éprouve-t-il le besoin de la [Phèdre] faire pirouetter comme un derviche afin d'exprimer qu'elle a perdu la boule et que le sexe la possède ? [. . .] Une frange du public [se] pâme néanmoins d'émoi: elle est préconquise depuis le très branché Théâtre Vidy de Lausanne, producteur du spectacle, d'où Bondy surfe avec la mode' (Bernard Thomas, *Le canard enchaîné*, 21 octobre 1998).

7 La même année, Muriel Mayette mettait en scène *Clitandre* de Corneille, à la Comédie-Française, sur 'un arrangement symphonique des vieux disques de Pink Floyd. [. . .] Amateurisme subventionné? Via la Comédie-Française, le Conservatoire et le JTN [Jeune Théâtre National], l'idéologie du "vachement sympa" d'Etat triomphe' (Christophe Deshoulières, *Cassandre*, 13 (1997)).

rythmes diffs selon le pers, emaniques

'La diction de Racine selon Bondy est moins "fausse" qu'incohérente, erratique d'un personnage à l'autre. . . . Imaginez les musiciens d'un orchestre de chambre qui joueraient la partition d'un octuor chacun dans son coin, à son propre rythme et avec des ornementations de styles différents! Au nom de l'idée "réaliste" qu'il se fabrique de son personnage, chaque comédien cultive son petit système et tente de l'imposer aux autres, sans jouer sur la moindre évolution, ni sur le moindre échange [. . .] Au nom du "corps contemporain" qui animerait "une Phèdre réaliste", Bondy ne fait qu'emprunter et mélanger des fragments de codes empruntés au drame romantique, à la comédie de boulevard et au cinéma social comme à l'idéologie dominante: le "jeunisme" [. . .] Hippolyte est un vrai jeune d'aujourd'hui, DONC il ne sait pas s'exprimer. Est-il artiste, pédé ou drogué? Et sa nullité devient vachement contemporaine . . . Certes, il est plus facile de faire passer Œnone pour la Yolande de Jérôme Deschamps que de la travestir en mâle matrone de la commedia dell'arte ou du dramma per musica vénitien, ce qui eût été plus pertinent et truculent. De même, que Phèdre partage ses états d'âme avec Marie Tudor et Scarlett O'Hara est plus facile à imposer qu'une recherche vocale et gestuelle sur la rhétorique élégiaque baroque, dont l'étrangeté pourrait être d'une beauté fulgurante . . .' (Christophe Deshoulières, *Cassandre*, 25, octobre–novembre 1998).

trop d'influence anachroniques

Sotha, production of Phèdre, *Café de la gare, Paris, 1999*
'En vérité, quel enfant n'a pas soupiré d'ennui à l'idée de devoir analyser une tirade de *Phèdre*, quel spectateur n'a pas somnolé à l'énumération des exploits mythologiques de Thésée, quel acteur ne s'est pas énervé en essayant de rendre "parlantes" les innombrables inversions grammaticales de certains alexandrins, quel mauvais esprit n'a pas ricané en entendant parler de "ce sacré soleil dont je suis descendue", ou du "reste d'un sang fatal conjuré contre nous", ou surtout des "entrailles qui pour moi se troublent par avance"? [erreur de l'artiste: Thésée se dit, en pensant à son fils: "Je t'aimais. Et je sens que malgré ton offense, / Mes entrailles pour toi se troublent par avance" (Act IV, sc. 3)]. [. . .] [Racine] était un excellent faiseur, pas un artiste. Il y a quelquefois de la paresse dans ses rimes, de la faiblesse dans son vocabulaire, de l'à-peu-près dans ses arguments [. . .] J'ai ravalé *Phèdre* pour que ce soit toujours un chef d'œuvre lumineux, et non un pensum obscur [. . .] J'ai supprimé les nombreuses allusions à des faits historiques ou légendaires oubliés, à des lieux dont les noms n'évoquent plus rien, à des héros dont les exploits n'ont pas été remis en lumière par un dessin animé récent. Merci quand même, Walt

l'ennui (!) de Racine

: le metteur-en-scène supprime bp de refs

Disney. J'ai remplacé les tournures obsolètes qui font pouffer de rire les adolescents, réduit le nombre des mots dont la . . . grandiloquence est devenue déplacée dans la conversation: *fatal, funeste, odieux, infâme, perfide, opprobe* [sic], *profane, criminel,* et même *horrible.* Non que j'aie voulu banaliser les intentions du texte, mais parce que je pense qu'un emploi trop fréquent de ces termes les banalise, justement [. . .] Mon but étant d'être accessible au public le plus attentif et le plus passionné par ce western sentimental et psychologique: les jeunes gens, j'ai voulu que le texte soit le plus proche possible de leur entendement et de celui des acteurs [. . .] Les acteurs sont les meilleurs menteurs qui soient, encore faut-il qu'ils sachent où est la vérité. A chaque fois que je dois expliquer à un acteur la phrase qu'il dit, je pense qu'il faut plutôt changer la phrase' (Sotha, 'Déclaration d'intention', press release and performance programme).

Eugène Green, production of Mithridate, *presented as part of the activities to mark the tercentenary of the death of Racine, Sorbonne chapel, 1999*
'Le spectacle évoque par bien des côtés le "théâtre Nô" [. . .] Le Théâtre de la Sapience [fondé par E. Green] propose une esthétique théâtrale différente, qui peut apparaître aussi lointaine que les traditions du théâtre classique de l'Extrême-Orient, transmis de génération en génération' (Company press release).

'Eugène Green ou la fascination de la radicalité [. . .] En ces temps de facilité médiatique, tout spectacle réclamant un réel effort d'auto-persuasion pour passer la rampe devient "culte". . . Green est-il en passe de rejoindre Marc François et quelques autres metteurs en scène "cultes" qui font croire aux spectateurs que leur ennui profond est une expérience métaphysique ?' (Christophe Deshoulières, *Cassandre,* 13, mars 1997).

'. . . un M. Eugène Green, qui prétend avoir retrouvé la prononciation authentique du français à la Cour et à la ville du XVIIe siècle, et qui fait dire par des comédiens les vers de Racine ou de La Fontaine comme les auraient ânonnés les paysans de Molière' (Marc Fumaroli, *Commentaire,* 88, hiver 1999–2000).

The sense of pleasure

It is now time to leave this scene of desolation. In order to investigate more closely Racine's own æsthetic of pleasure, so sadly traduced in present-day productions, we return to the formula which identifies

return to R's formula *plaisir = tristesse maj.* 'tout le plaisir de la tragédie' [all the pleasure of tragedy] with 'la tristesse majestueuse' [majestic sadness]. This very particular kind of sadness has been subjected to far less scrutiny than the too-familiar terror and pity of catharsis,[8] and because it is not backed by the high authority of Aristotle, it could never be defended with the unanswerable retort 'magister dixit'. Sadness is not a mainspring or lever of action, nor is it an indispensable cornerstone of tragic structure. Even when it's 'majestic', it remains in the domain of affective mood, and is clearly more moderate than terror or compassion. It neither shocks nor shakes us. Nor does it produce an unpredictable élan. It is not so much a disturbance as a suffused emotion, spreading slowly to find its way into the soul and gently to win the heart.

Forestier on tristesse as novel aesthetic concept Let us turn to the observations of a specialist in the matter. For Georges Forestier, Racine's preface to *Bérénice* had recourse to the notion of 'tristesse' only in an accidental, conjunctural way. In the introduction to his edition of Racine's theatre, Forestier develops the view that 'tristesse' as a source, or even the sole source of 'le plaisir de la tragédie', was used by Racine in an entirely modern but exceptional sense: 'Racine se trouva contraint de forger un concept esthétique inédit' [. . .] 'La tristesse majestueuse [est] une émotion tragique imaginaire' [Racine found himself obliged to create a novel æsthetic concept . . . majestic sadness is not an authentic tragic emotion].[9] Racine's discovery of 'tristesse' would have been, therefore, little more than an incident in the course of his unremitting theatrical rivalry with Pierre Corneille, so influential in the maturing growth of Racine's creativity. Far from being one of the principal supports of his dramatic system, it would more likely have been of use as a contigency measure. The sudden appearance of the term in classical dramaturgy, and its brief existence as a theoretical construct, were an accident of *... an accidental, fleeting...* literary controversy. Once over the peculiar and particular hurdle of *Bérénice*, Racine 's'empressera bien vite d'oublier' [will hasten to forget][10] this terminological convenience to which he had recourse at a significant time in his competition with Corneille [who at the same

---

8 Among recent studies, see particularly: Ronald Tobin, 'Le plaisir chez Racine', in Christine M. Hill (ed), *Racine. Théâtre et poésie* (Leeds: F. Cairns, 1991), pp. 49–58; Jean Emelina, 'Le plaisir tragique', in J. Emelina, *Comédie et tragédie* coll. 'Traverses' (Nice: Centre de Recherches Littéraires Pluridisciplinaires de l'Université, 1, 1998), pp. 24–36, first published in *Littératures classiques*, 16 (1992). For an interesting overview, see Patrick Dandrey, 'La rédemption par les lettres dans l'Occident mélancolique (1570–1670). Contribution à une histoire de la jouissance esthétique', in Marc Fumaroli *et al.*, *Le Loisir lettré à l'âge classique* (Geneva: Droz, 1996), pp. 63–91.

9 Forestier, *Œuvres*, pp. xxvi–xxvii.

10 *Ibid.*, p. xxvii.

time had composed his *Tite et Bérénice*, ed.], and for purely strategic reasons. And it must, of course, be remembered that no other treatise and no other preface, by Racine or by any other, would ever again propose 'tristesse' as an essential component of the tragic canon.[11] It would therefore be entirely erroneous, according to Forestier, to see in this eye-catching but misleading formula a key feature of Racine's dramatic system.

All that being said, there are two alternative points to be considered in answer to the views summarized above. In the first place, the term 'tristesse' did not have in Racine's work the same connotation as today. The meaning was closer to the Latin 'tristitia', or affliction. In addition, the *Dictionnaire* of Furetière (1690) suggests that it was a 'passion de l'âme'. In fact, reference to *Les Passions de l'âme* of Descartes reveals that 'tristesse' is not only a 'passion de l'âme' but one of the six 'passions primitives'.[12] These considerations suggest there is a risk of underestimating the meaning that 'tristesse' might have had in Racine's dramaturgy. Naturally, it would be overstretching the point to see in it a stimulus for tragic emotion as important and as effective as terror and pity, or as constantly exploited, but it would also be a mistake not to appreciate to what extent Racine, as a skilful manager and economist of speech (the rhetorical organization of *dispositio* is linked, it should be remembered, to *oikonomia*), believed in what he uttered, practised and invested in it throughout his dramatic work. Between over-emphasis and a lack of consideration for contemporary attitudes, we should try to find a balanced judgement. Apart from this, the example of Ovid, with his lyric vein and elegiac inspiration, are rightly stressed in the new Pléiade edition, bringing an appropriate level of reflexion to the question.[13]

In addition to these considerations, if 'tristesse' represents an entirely 'modern' source for the 'plaisir de la tragédie', it is also specifically French. It is not to be found anywhere in the precepts of tragic writing in English, German, Italian, or Spanish literature. This is probably owing to the fact that it corresponds to the constant search for balanced judgement in the canon of classical æsthetics, and to an ideal of emotional middle ground. The famous lines of Boileau in *L'Art Poétique*, Chant III, urging tearful tragedy to delight him 'pour me tirer des pleurs' [to draw tears from me], clearly help to explain the coexistence of opposites in Racine's æsthetic system, with its subtle mixture and a delicately refined and fragile balance of contrasting elements. The

11 *Ibid.*, p. 1461.
12 René Descartes, *Les Passions de l'âme* (1649), article LXIX.
13 See also Georges May, *D'Ovide à Racine* (Paris: PUF, 1948).

tristesse maj. = oxymoron

expression 'tristesse majestueuse' is like an oxymoron, because the idea of majesty refers to the great and the magnificent, at the elevated and sublime level of rhetoric, whereas 'tristesse', unlike 'la fureur mélancolique' [the fever of melancholy], remains confined to the middle ground in the order of the passions. The 'effet de sourdine' [muting effect] identified by Leo Spitzer,[14] which is so typical of Racine, is not confined to matters of style. One only has to situate Racine in the context of Greek or Roman tragedy, even of baroque or pre-classical French dramatists, to appreciate that constant 'tempérament' [balanced judgement], that same concern to hold 'le plaisir de la tragédie' within *but cf justo milieu, desire for balance* the extreme limits, in a 'juste milieu', a middle way which many authors of the time considered to be part of the character of the French nation. So 'la tristesse majestueuse' corresponds in this way to a complex admixture of strength and gentleness, corresponding to the golden mean of the classical canon of writing in France.

According to Lessing, French literature cannot truly claim to have a tragic repertoire because French tragedy is *flach* [flat] and *kalt* [cold].[15] It is a reflexion which reminds us how little attention is given today by academic specialists or university curricula to these still-*? of perceived char + aesthetic values of a nation* relevant questions of identification of the perceived character and æsthetic values of a given nation, to the links between 'sympathie' and 'antipathie' [liking and disliking], terms used to characterize the apparent imcompatibility of Spanish and French temperaments. At the confluence of literary history and anthropology, this issue would, if properly studied, allow a fuller exploitation of the 'examen des esprits' [scrutiny of minds] to which Juan Huarte was was so committed.[16] In any event, if 'la tristesse majestueuse' does not exactly constitute all of 'le plaisir' for which we are seeking the properties, it remains the principal and most important element (and we should remember that there were some eminent figures of the seventeenth century who remained insensitive to the pleasures of Racine, notably Saint-Evremond and, for some of Racine's works, Madame de Sévigné).

In the search for the properties of Racine's notion of pleasure, a *Poussin: art = délectation* well-known remark comes persistently to mind, like some passage of forgotten music. It is Poussin's 'l'art est délectation' [art is the taking of

14 This analysis was first put forward by Leo Spitzer in 'Die klassische Dämpfung in Racines Stil', *Archivum Romanicum*, 12 (1928), 361–472, and 13 (1929), 398–9; it was then published in French as 'L'Effet de sourdine dans le style classique', *Etudes de style*, ed. Jean Starobinski (Paris: Gallimard, 1970). It is now available in English as 'Racine's Classical Piano', in *Leo Spitzer: Essays on Seventeenth-Century French Literature*, ed. David Bellos (Cambridge: Cambridge University Press, 1983), pp. 3–113.
15 Gotthold Ephraim Lessing, *Hamburgische Dramaturgie*, 80 (5 February 1768).
16 Juan Huarte, *Examen de ingenios para las ciencias* (1575).

pleasure].[17] 'Délectation' is a term that is richer, wider, and deeper ~~délectation=broader~~ *délectation=broader + physiological*
than than 'plaisir', which it subsumes; it refers to pleasure in its most
physiological sense. And so, if 'tristesse', identified as a 'maladie de
l'âme' [a soul sickness] by the Ancients,[18] and still attributed by
Robert Burton to the 'aduste' (i.e. scorched and dried-up) humour of
melancholy,[19] is considered in the French classical era to be a 'passion
de l'âme' [a passion of the soul], these other elements should also be
seen as entering into 'le plaisir de la tragédie'; they are elements which *vs tranquillity of the mind;*
relate more directly to tranquillity of mind, and to a sensuous, even *sensuous/sensual*
sensual, physical satisfaction. But there are also other aspects of 'le *satisfaction*
plaisir' to be examined; these are 'le plaisir de l'esprit' [pleasure of the
mind] and 'le plaisir de l'oreille' [aural pleasure].

Plaisir de l'esprit . . . the public which fêted Racine was, in a sense, on *Plaisir de l'esprit*
the same level as he in the appreciation of tragedy. It would have felt *< audience's ident*
a sense of association and belonging, able to identify with the subjects, *w/R's chars*
heroes, crises, and the vision of the world and man purveyed by
Racinian tragedy. It would have recognized the same gods, passions,
topics of discussion, inflexions of behaviour, and ways of loving. Racine's
public would have recognized these features of his work because they *< tradition,*
belonged to a tradition, to a cultural memory that it had itself studied *cultural memory*
and helped to sustain, and all because they offered, more directly than
to us and despite the literary stylizing of language, an image of contemporary existence. The feeling of belonging rests on the notion of
shared assets and a common heritage, and Racinian tragedy offered a
privileged public the distinctive pleasure of identifying characteristics
which linked it with a wider community, across time. Everywhere
immanent were signposts, markers, references, echoes, allusions, and
even a code, which formed a familiar environment, a *terra cognita*, even
if it were only the mythological references, or the story of ancient
classical literature.[20] There would have have been little of a truly alien *little would have been alien to them*
world, and nothing which would totally disorientate the audience in its
basic vision of the world. In addition to this, and as a consequence, the
pleasure felt by the audiences (of middle-class or noble origins) would

17 'Sa fin est la délectation' [Its goal is the taking of pleasure], says the painter
Nicolas Poussin (letter to M. de Chambray, dated 1 March 1665), in Anthony Blunt
(ed.), *Lettres et propos sur l'art* (Paris: Hermann, 1965), p. 163.
18 See Jackie Pigeaud, *La maladie de l'âme. Etude sur la relation de l'âme et du corps dans la
tradition medico-philosophique antique* (Paris: Les Belles Lettres, 1989), pp. 512–14, 533.
19 Robert Burton, *Anatomy of Melancholy* (1621), Part 1, Section 3, Mem. 1, Subs 3. See also
the three-volume translation into French by Bernard Hœpffner (Paris: José Corti, 2000).
20 What Emmanuel Bury has called the 'antiquités de Racine' [Racine's antiquities]
in *Œuvres et Critiques*, 24. 1 (1999), 29–48, may be also said to apply to his audiences of
the time.

?of identification + recognition > plaisir!

have been heightened by the added flavour of satisfaction and self-respect. It could be said that through identification and recognition lay also the sense of a literature of class, or caste.

The pleasure of tragedy lies in this process of recognition, in the repossession of the certain cultural sites of the time which were part of a common topography, a familiar landscape with horizons extending to Olympus itself and its residents, where everything shared familiar attributes, belonged to the same family. These are the places and the sites where, from the beginning of time, all of humanity has met: these are the common places, the topoi, the humus, and nutrient soil of literature and other arts. From the perspective of literary creativity, it is as if we find there a *commonplace rhapsody* or, in other words, a stitching together, patching, a work of highly skilled needlework[21] on a fabric of ancient but highly respected banalities and repetitions, as Walter Ong showed in a study of Shakespeare which still remains too little known in France.[22] Well-versed observers found a large part of their 'délectation' in the dexterity of the *retractatio*, in the game of commonplaces, their variation and adjustment, and virtuosity in the management of their permutations.

?of commonplaces

+ complicity w/ audience

There was therefore still 'connivence', complicity with the audience, and a process of harmonizing – the recognition of places and commonplaces – in the order of rhetoric,[23] but in this case more in relation to organization, or composition in its most technical sense, rather than to 'invention'. From this point of view, Racine's audiences would not have set out to learn of the misfortune of Queen Bérénice. No, instead of that they would go to the theatre to discover just how Racine, for his part, would represent this already known misfortune, and how his particular version differed from that of his rival Corneille's in *Tite et Bérénice*. One would create too dry an impression by qualifying this pleasure as 'intellectual'. This is still the pleasure of the well-versed observer, of those who know how many 'savants calculs' [artful calculations] and 'ruses pourpensées' [finely contrived devices] there are in the making of a play stamped with the hallmark of a craftsman.[24] The pleasure derived from this recognition consists of

not dry intellectual pleasure

?of craftsmanship

21 Etymologically, the work of the rhapsodist (Greek 'rhapsôdos', one who sings, and 'ôdê', song) can be related to that of the seamster / seamstress.
22 Walter J. Ong, 'Commonplace Rhapsody: Ravisius Textor, Zwinger and Shakespeare', in R. R. Bolgar (ed.), *Classical Influences on European Culture, AD 1500–1700* (Cambridge, New York, Melbourne: Cambridge University Press, 1976), pp. 91–126.
23 See Terence Cave, *Recognition. A Study in Poetics* (Oxford: Clarendon, 1988).
24 'Ceux qui protesteraient contre l'idée de tout calcul en ces domaines prouveraient seulement qu'ils n'entendent rien à l'art théâtral, où il y a toujours beaucoup de calcul, ou, si ce mot choque trop quelques sentimentaux, beaucoup de ruses savantes et

establishing whether the craftsman has all the skill required, that gifted touch required to extricate himself from the most challenging passages, and from all the myriad difficulties put in his path by the considerations of 'vraisemblance' (verisimilitude) and 'bienséance' (the decorum of the rules); it consists of seeing whether the dramatist can raise the level of excitement artfully, by degrees, up to the appropriate fever pitch, avoiding the pitfalls which can be encountered in every scene, speech, or aside, and concocting the volatile mixture of *vis* [life] and *suavitas* [delicacy]. This is the pleasure of the well-versed observer, the connoisseur, attentive to the arrangement of the machinery, of that high-precision mechanism, which all truly *effective* plays are.

Plaisir de l'oreille . . . Nietzsche compared the prose of the French classical moralists to chamber music.[25] How much more appropriate this observation would be if applied to the alexandrine! To make my point more directly, I shall quote from what I have written already about Jean-Marie Villégier's 'mémoire du Grand Siècle' [memory of the Great Century].[26] I have maintained that the most authentic modern understanding of the alexandrine is to be found in the work of Jacques Roubaud or Jean-Marie Villégier.[27] For Villégier every line of Racine is a 'prodigieux tissu d'indications musicales' [an extraordinary texture of musical instructions]. 'Musique surcroît de sens. Musique dans laquelle se construit le personnage, se modulent ses humeurs, le rhythme de ses poumons, la contraction ou la décontraction de ses muscles, la tension ou le dérèglement de son esprit [Music an overflow of meaning. Music through which character is constructed, and its humours adjusted, with the rhythm of the lungs, contraction and expansion of the muscles, and the tension and release of the mind] . . . Musique de *e*, tout à fait muet, ou suprêment éloquent, syllabe volée ou point d'orgue. Musique où adviennent des êtres de théâtre, plus humains, plus divins que nature.' [Music of the vowel *e*, totally mute or supremely eloquent, a furtive syllable or an organ crescendo. Music in which gather theatrical beings, more human and divine than life].[28] The sense of 'délectation' – the enjoying – derived from the alexandrine

pourpensées' [Those who resist the idea of anything calculated in this area simply prove that they understand nothing about dramatic art, in which there is so much calculation or, if this term seems too shocking for sensitive souls, artful, finely contrived devices] Etienne Souriau, *Les deux cent mille situations dramatiques* (Paris: Flammarion, 1950), p. 8.
25 Friedrich Nietzsche, *Jenseits von Gut und Böse*, no. 254.
26 Louis van Delft, 'Mémoire du Grand Siècle. Jean-Marie Villégier ou l'honneur de la mise en scène', a review *in Commentaire*, reprinted in my *Le Théâtre en feu. Le grand jeu du théâtre contemporain* (Tübingen: Gunter Narr, 1997), pp. 103–14.
27 See article above, p. 103 ff.
28 Jean-Marie Villégier, 'Curriculum vitae', *NRF*, 534–5 (1997), 139–51.

*not music < one
instrument,
but < quintet...*

understood in this way, played and heard, is not what one hears from
one single instrument, but from the performance of a quintet, sextet,
octet, or a cantata: the instruments or the distinctive personality of the
voices represent a formation which might justly be assimilated with
chamber music. All the associations between Racinian tragedy and dramatic music must be stressed. There is no better study from this point
of view than that of Jean Mesnard, in which he not only examines the
measure and the tempo of Racine's verse, the intervals, and the
relationship between low and high notes, but also shows the way in

J. Mesnard

which passages of his verse match the recitative and arias of opera.[29]

Losing the plot

*all of these secrets
seem lost to
modern directors*

We have therefore evoked secrets of creation which are now lost. In
consequence, season after season, we have productions which are
either restrictively esoteric or enticingly crowd-pulling, untidy or
ostentatious. It is not just lack of coordination any more, or a sudden
slide in standards, it is the total loss of the plot . . . Certainly, we all
agree that the theatre must evolve, and that stasis and conservatism in
the theatre are infallible harbingers of death, and who could boast a
sure and certain knowledge of the conditions of theatre production
in France at the time of Racine?

But why should things go so badly wrong? There are such obvious
explanations that they can be quickly presented, even if they go back
a long way. If, with a few exceptions, the the days of the connoisseur,
the well-versed observer, are no more, it is because post-1970
audiences do not realize the importance of the 'métier', craftsmanship,

*audience doesn't
recognize importance
of craftsmanship*

a notion which has become foreign to them. For Racine and creative
people of his time and stature, 'c'est un métier de faire un livre' [writing
a book requires craftsmanship], and 'il faut plus que de l'esprit pour
être auteur' [you need more than wit to be a writer].[30] For them it was
a self-evident truth. To contest it, or even not to know it (which, for
want of learning or appreciation of the the real nature of literary
creativity has today become the norm) would be for La Bruyère's
contemporaries to doubt the obvious. A completely mistaken interpretation of Romantic æsthetics has led audiences to believe that

29 Jean Mesnard, 'La musicalité du texte dans la tragédie classique', in Irène
Mamczarz (ed.), *Les premiers opéras en Europe et les formes dramatiques apparentées* (Paris:
Klincksieck, 1992), pp. 117–31.
30 La Bruyère, *Les Caractères*, 'Des Ouvrages de l'esprit', 3. [*Les Caractères* can be
consulted in the edition produced by Louis van Delft, coll. 'La Salamandre' (Paris:
Imprimerie Nationale, 1998].

inspiration is purely the result of a natural gift, of some extraordinary extra-terrestrial favour, or a genetic predisposition, 'in the blood'.

In an era pompously identifying itself as 'postmodern', what was once an absolute and fundamental truth for all creative artists (and still is today for the better ones) is now located beyond the public field of vision. That is to say that artists are first and foremost craftsmen, that they never stop learning their craft, and that a humble and constant reflexion on their art, and the quasi-spiritual search, constantly renewed, for the foundations of beauty remain throughout their lives an equal and essential part of their existence. In this way, the lost treasure, not just of 'savoir-faire' but of true 'savoir' or knowledge ('habileté' [skill] in the language of the seventeenth century, or 'doctrine'), is not only undetected, but not even suspected by a public which remains blind to the amazing 'horlogerie' [clock-work, the term is La Bruyère's.[31] which is entailed by the the construction of a play (as for any other true work of art). Blindness in the audience is often matched by aphasia in the actors, who can nowadays dispense with a proper apprenticeship, and this despite the efforts of the enlightened director of the Conservatoire National d'Art Dramatique, Marcel Bozonnet.[32] The implications of actors' aphasia must be appreciated in the context of that other 'treasure', which is the alexandrine, declaimed with all the effect of a child's rattle and producing what is still called in the language of the professionals 'l'effet machine à coudre' [the sewing machine effect]. And to this we must add the deafness of the public. These comments may appear to be inadmissably dismissive, but they are not mine; they come from two practioners of spoken verse who have already been mentioned, Roubaud and Villégier. In relation to the metric qualities, the phrasing, and the scores of Racine, we are today 'out of tune', as one says of musical instruments. If our ear can no longer hear, capture, or receive these verse texts, the loss of pleasure and fuller enjoyment should not seem so surprising. We can only be surprised by the surprise.

[handwritten margin notes: and, similarly, neither do actors / of declamation of alexandrine / our ears are "out of tune"]

31 *Ibid.*

32 'Les élèves ont toujours tendance à penser que le théâtre s'apparente à quelque chose de spontané, et que les connaissances, la culture, le savoir leur paraissent un peu suspects par rapport à ce qu'on pourrait appeler inspiration [. . .] J'ai élargi le département Histoire du théâtre: il me semble nécessaire qu'il y ait aussi un peu d'enseignement théorique pour élargir le champ culturel de nos élèves' [Students today tend to think that the theatre is linked to something spontaneous, so knowledge, learning, knowledge seem suspect to them in comparison with what one might call inspiration [. . .] I have expanded the History of Theatre section: it seems to me essential that there should be a little more instruction in theory in order to widen the sultural range of our students], interview with Marcel Bozonnet (*Cassandre*, 17, July–August, 1997), p. 9.

It is at this point that the comparison with chamber music assumes its full significance. Beyond that harmonically versatile instrument which is a line of Racine's verse, we find, in *Bérénice*, the pure expression of sadness, and elsewhere in his work a whole world of musical associations. Do we really know what 'out of tune' means? 'In tune. In tune!' would storm César Franck at his young pupil Debussy in the Conservatoire. And he would reply with that impertinence which was already so typical of him, 'But why in tune when I'm already fine in this key?' Present-day stage directors are always trying to get 'in tune', in every possible way, and if Racine were to come back to life he would assuredly tax them as Debussy did his fellow students: 'Foule ahurie! N'êtes-vous pas capable d'écouter des accords sans les rapporter aussitôt à ceux qui sont les plus familiers? D'où viennent-ils? Où vont-ils? Ecoutez. Cela suffit. Si vous ne comprenez pas, courez chez le directeur et dites-lui que je vous abîme les oreilles' [Blockheads! Can't you hear a new chord without trying to match it with ones that you are more familiar with? Where do they come from? What are they for? Listen, that will do! If you don't understand, run off to your supervisor and tell him I'm ruining your hearing!][33] We have become deaf to the 'effet de sourdine', and look instead for the grating notes of Ekfriede Jelinek, Lars Norén, Heiner Müller, Xavier Kroetz, Edward Bond, Steven Berkoff, or Serge Valetti. And so, it is not just a melody which is lost, but a whole cultural memory. There are stage productions now which are not even pitched in the key of the musical score.

There remains a more sensitive issue. Between the era of Racine and the present, the nature of tragedy has changed, rendering all its former mechanisms, of action and emotion, invalid, obsolete. It is certainly the case that the æsthetic ideal of French classicism, close as it came to the ideal of beauty, has now reached the limits of its acceptability. But on the question of tragedy, we have now gone beyond anything the tragic imagination of the seventeenth century could have created. The 'death of God', as examined by Nietzsche, marks a cut-off point, raising consequences which could not have been foreseen, even to those most inclined to 'secouer le préjugé' [dislodging prejudice]. The content and the implications of what is understood by 'tragic' among the representatives of our modernity (Schopenhauer, Nietzsche, Kierkegaard, Unamuno) or in the analyses of Jean-Marie Domenach (*Le Retour du tragique*) and George Steiner (*The Death of Tragedy*) are now only remotely connected to the ideas of Aristotle's *Poetics* and his French followers in the Grand Siècle.

33 Quoted by Jean Barraqué, *Debussy*, coll. 'Solfèges' (Paris: Editions du Seuil, 1962), pp. 45, 49.

In the theatre, the tone is even more brutal and the invective more direct than in *Athalie* ('Impitoyable Dieu, toi seul as tout conduit', Act V. 6, l. 1774). The act of accusation addressed by humanity against the condition that is imposed on us not by God but by History or Society is no longer cluttered by consideration of rhetoric in the register of the sublime, or by stylistic ornament. 'Il n'y a pas de beauté sans voiles' [There is no beauty without veils], said Anatole France.[34] It is precisely the veils that many present-day spectators do not appreciate, as if they can no longer guess what it is that the author has taken such great pains to to wrap up and hide in the hope of awaking the desire and the pleasure of independent discovery. The idea of the tragic has become more complex and more diverse. The ghost of what was once tragic now includes ideological tones (social and political, for the most part), which are different from those of the seventeenth century, and providing contemporary catalysts to 'le plaisir de la tragédie'. The great success of Brecht's theatre is due to this primping-up of the idea of the tragic. By the same token, as marked as the evolution of the tragic may seem to be after Schopenhauer and Nietzsche, it would be contradictory to claim that the public of today is resistant to the well-tried Aristotelian cocktail of a little pity laced with terror. The whole repertoire of modern and contemporary theatre proves that this is not so. Consider the following plays, *Miss Julie* (Strindberg), *Le Roi se meurt* (Ionesco), *En attendant Godot* (Beckett), *Port-Royal* (Montherlant), *Becket ou l'honneur de Dieu* (Anouilh), *Caligula* (Albert Camus), *Huis-Clos* (J.-P. Sartre), *Les Bonnes* (Jean Genet), *Henri IV* (Pirandello), or *Desire under the Elms* (Eugene O'Neill); although none of them is presented as a tragedy, seeking rather the term 'drama' or nothing at all, they all extract a quality of pleasure from the basis of those two powerful instincts of the soul highlighted by Aristotle two thousand years ago. Furthermore, Racine's innovative 'tristesse majestueuse' is itself one of the most reliable agents for success that Racine has known, even today. Of his various works, *Bérénice* has become, after a subdued reception (except at its initial production), one of Racine's most successful plays. It is an appropriate vindication for a writer who was mercilessly reprimanded by the ever-present pedants of his day.

However, despite the enduring success of *Phèdre*, and the more up-and-down fortunes of *Bérénice* and other works, the popularity of Racine among a handful of students and some of their teachers cannot delude us. Various soundings, and the tercentenary conferences, all confirm the same thing: at the turn of the century, the reception of Racine's

34 Anatole France, *Le Jardin d'Epicure*.

work and his popularity are in evident decline. In spite of occasional
successes, and curious or provocative productions, linked often to the
star system or media promotions, interest is on the wane, even in
France.[35] But not all hope is lost: the French TV channel TF1 has
announced its production of *Bérénice*, with a starring role for Gérard
Depardieu as Tite. With a bit of luck the Emperor of Rome will
become as well known as the Count of Monte-Cristo. Where, then, are
the problems? What is the main cause for this loss of direction, and for
the absence of an understanding, of 'elective affinities', between Racine
and what we call the 'wider public'? For spectators in the third
millennium, it is the clothing of tragedy which has changed, not the
body. The circumstances, and the 'dressing' of the subject and the
decor, the surroundings in which the condition of humanity is presented, have changed. Neither these heroes nor their problems affect
us any more – not in a direct manner, anyway, which is the
indispensable condition of pleasure in the theatre. These circumstances
are no longer clearly present in our cultural memory, they no longer
excite or disturb our sensitivity, even if the issues at stake can still
move us. The characters, as the spectator in tune with the times of
today will say, have become strangers to us. These gods and princes no
longer dwell within us, and the exploits of these heroes are sung no
more. How can our dialogue with them be life-bearing? They do not
belong to our family any more. The locations disorientate us, and
their place in time confuses us. Nothing is familiar, nothing identifiable.
No more markers, no more signals.

It is a fact, then, that the places in time and space in which Racine
inscribed his work have now become an obstacle, and so a feeling of
malaise and frustration grows. This lack of immediate, spontaneous
association blocks a sense of communion or attachment, of pleasure.
'Tout le plaisir de la tragédie' is now riddled with the dissatisfaction of
having to admit to amnesia.

* * *

Just over forty years ago, a violent literary controversy broke out; it
lasted for several weeks, and was reported by *Lettres françaises*. The
most extreme position was held by none other than Jean Vilar, who

---

35 See Fritz Nies, '"Le premier poète moderne" ravalé au rang de "farce bigarée"?
Prolégomènes à un Racine allemand', *Œuvres et critiques*, 24. 1 (1999), 264–80; Sven
Åke Heed, 'Jean Racine mis en scène', to be published in proceedings of the Colloque
Jean Racine de l'Ile-de-France (25–30 May, 1999). For an excellent overview, see
Ronald Tobin, *Jean Racine Revisited* (New York: Twayne, 1999).

fired the first salvo: 'Non, Racine n'est pas universel' [No, Racine is not a writer accessible to all]. He went even further: 'A regarder de près les pièces de Racine, on y trouve une sorte d'ultra-finesse telle que la question se pose pour moi de savoir s'il est vraiment un auteur dramatique' [On examining his plays closely, you find a kind of super-sensitivity such that I wonder whether he is a writer for the theatre at all]. This is a point of view which is still found shocking today. It appeared even more shocking in 1956. In a letter to Aragon, Jean-Louis Barrault wrote: 'Pas du théâtre, Racine? Et ces mises à mort constantes, ces fauves aux prises avec les innocents! [*sic*: n'étaient-ce pas, déjà en ce temps-là, des innocents aux prises avec des fauves?] On peut aimer Racine comme on aime la boxe ou les courses de taureaux. Pourquoi alors Racine ne serait-il pas populaire?' [Not theatre? Racine? And what of those endless executions, and innocent victims locked in struggle with wild animals? You can love Racine like you love boxing, or bull-fighting. So why should Racine not be popular?].

In reality, the accusations laid against Vilar were initially quite unjust. His ideas on Racine, the author of plays which were 'admirable-ment conçues, admirablement construites' [admirably conceived and constructed], but also 'l'auteur dramatique français le plus difficile à interpréter' [the most difficult French dramatist to perform], can be explained by his theatrical responsibilities [as director of the Théâtre national Populaire], which he expressed as follows: 'Ayant disons des devoirs vis-à-vis du public populaire, j'ai préféré présenter Corneille pour les leçons qu'il donne, [plutôt] que les œuvres de Racine pour les leçons qu'il s'abstient de donner. Je crois que c'est une raison un peu simpliste, mais valable pour un directeur de théâtre populaire' [Having, shall we say, responsibilities towards the wider public, I preferred to present Corneille, for the lessons he teaches, rather than the work of Racine for the lessons he fails to offer. The reasoning is probably a little simplistic, but valid for the director of a public theatre].[36] To judge from subsequent events, Vilar had measured quite accurately the pulse of his time. 'Le théâtre élitaire pour tous' [An élite theatre for everyone], the motto and rallying call of all servants of the theatre, as committed as the now-lionized Antoine Vitez, remains a superb pro-gramme for action. But the facts show that it was a Utopia, as generous as they all are. At the very least, it becomes a password which opens the way for the undertakers to cheerfully bury French classical theatre.

36 *Lettres françaises*, 509, 1–7 March, 1956. The controversy rumbled on until 618 (3–9 May), stirred by a questionnaire of Vilar, in nine questions (612, 22–28 March).

In summary, the factors for consideration that we have examined are as follows: (1) our blatant ignorance of matters relating to the writer's craft; (2) our situation of incomprehension in relation to what we have called chamber music; (3) our cultural amnesia which renders us as perplexed by a text of Racine as we are by a painting by Poussin. But there is a further cause for the misunderstanding which divides us from 'le parfait classique', and that is our imperturbable, incurable, and very comical 'esprit de sérieux [taste for the serious]. Nothing could be further from the sociability and the ideal of classicism than the mania of our age, of our servants of theatre above all, for serious thought, injecting it into everything they touch, endlessly intellectualizing and cerebralizing. Nothing could be less congenial to them than the spirit of play, a principle of art dating from before the time of *Mithridate* and *Iphigénie*. A great specialist of Molière once asked a highly relevant question 'Molière pense-t-il?' [Does Molière think?]. The very title of his book provided the answer: *Molière, homme de théâtre*.[37] We find the same sort of mishap in the work of Racine. How many boring productions (perhaps we should say reductions) have we seen which go no further than to paste on to the plays of Racine, without the slightest discrimination and in the most pontificating and flat-footed way, all the tragic anachronisms of our own twentieth century.[38]

And now the curtain is about to fall, reminding us of the good Boileau's judgement when he complained that out of a 'divertissement' was made 'une fatigue'.[39]

---

37 René Bray, *Molière homme de théâtre* (Paris: Mercure de France, 1954).

38 Georges Forestier refers justifiably to 'cette vision radicalement désespérée de la condition humaine que nos contemporains attendent de la tragédie et dans laquelle ils croient reconnaître Racine' [that radically desperate vision of the human condition that our contemporaries expect of tragedy, and in which they think they recognize Racine]; he also evokes 'la lecture de nos contemporains qui se sont fait une conception tragique de la tragédie' [the contemporary interpretations which create a tragic conception of tragedy]. *Œuvres*, pp. 1527, 1535.

39 Boileau, *Art poétique*, Chant III, l. 32.

10

The Majesty and the Pleasure of Bérénice Today

JEAN-MICHEL DELACOMPTÉE

Personal enmities, professional rivalry, social jealousy, doctrinal conflict, Racine's reputation among the writers of his time was subject to all these pitfalls. But of all the controversies he was involved in, the best known after that of *Phèdre* was probably the one surrounding *Bérénice*. There was the direct competition declared with Corneille, the success of the play, and *La Critique de Bérénice* published in 1671 by the abbé de Villars,[1] to which Racine replied in his preface. The cruel sarcasm of the abbé de Villars has an added interest today, not only because it reveals the tone of literary criticism of the time, but, most of all, because it highlights the points of contention provoked by the innovative aspects of *Bérénice*.

The obvious starting point for consideration is the first argument developed by Villars, who questions the usefulness of Act I, and the role of Antiochus; these were destined, according to Villars, to compensate for such a thin subject, theoretically restricted to the relationship of Titus and Bérénice, and to the way in which Titus abandoned her, *dimisit invitus invitam*, despite himself, despite herself. A second argument questions the emotional over-sensitivity which dominates the tragedy, this 'tissu galant de madrigaux et d'élégies' [courtly fabric of madrigals and elegies] composed 'pour la commodité des dames, de la jeunesse de la cour, et des faiseurs de recueils et de pièces galantes' [to please the ladies and the youth of the Court, and the compilers of anthologies and genteel extracts].[2] One has to admit to some agreement with Villars on this point, but since Villars's two arguments are linked, the purpose of this study will be to show how the functions of Antiochus

1 *La Critique de Bérénice* has been reproduced in Forestier, *Œuvres*, pp. 511–19.
2 *Ibid.*, p. 516.

confirm the central role of Titus, thus displacing the notion of 'tristesse majestueuse' [which, as Racine's preface says, 'fait tout le plaisir de la Tragédie'] from love to the political arena. This, then, will enable us to establish just how we can enjoy *Bérénice* today.

The Law of the Father, the Law of the Brother

As we know, the abbé de Villars identifies in Antiochus 'un acteur de protase' [a protatic actor], in other words a purely expository role; he is 'un acteur inutile' [an unnecessary protagonist], whose farewells are invented, alleges Villars, pour 'gagner du temps, pour tricher et pour fournir un acte' [to gain time, sidestep the rules, and to provide an extra act].[3] Villars deplores the fact of having to wait until the second act for Titus's appearance, and expresses astonishment at seeing Antiochus emerging in the first act from the door indicated as leading to the apartments of Titus. 'Ne pouvait-il aller chez sa Bérénice, pour lui dire adieu *incognito*, que par le cabinet de Titus?' [Could Antiochus only gain access to his Bérénice to bid her his incognito farewells via the apartment of Titus?],[4] asks Villars.

Villars had a point: the role of Antiochus raises difficulties. Just how essential to the plot is he? He has no influence on the final decision of Titus, therefore appears to have no part in the *dénouement*, and appears to serve only to condition Bérénice for the supreme test of hearing from the mouth of the Emperor himself that he is to abandon her. It is, however, evident that Titus and Antiochus are inseparable. They are a twinned couple, to be assimilated into the theme of the 'double', which runs through the theatre of Racine from from *Les Frères ennemis* to *Phèdre*. The friendship of Titus and Antiochus appears to be so close, in fact, that while talking to Antiochus, Bérénice expresses 'une douceur extrême / D'entretenir Titus dans un autre lui-même' (Act I. 4, ll. 271–2). The same idea is taken up by by Titus when he says to Antiochus 'que ma victoire / Devait à vos exploits la moitié de sa gloire' (Act III. 1, ll. 687–8), adding, 'Vous ne faites qu'un cœur et qu'une âme avec nous' (l. 698). This friendship fused into twinship is the basis of the perfectly balanced triangle formed by the three protagonists, Titus 'l'amant', Bérénice 'l'amante', Antiochus 'l'ami'. The triangle is, however, destroyed when, in the first act, Antiochus declares to Bérénice that he always loved her – at the moment, therefore, when 'l'ami' becoming an 'amant' declares himself to be a rival.

3 *Ibid.*, p. 511.
4 *Ibid.*, p. 512.

The point of breakdown lies not in the fact that Titus must renounce Bérénice, and still less in the love that they share for each other, but in the idea that he is going to marry her – or so thinks Antiochus. It is therefore marriage not love, nor their break-up, which destroys the harmony. Love unites the trio in an affection which is, in fact, extended by the emotional break-up at the end. On the other hand, marriage is shown to be incompatible with the twinned relationship of Titus and Antiochus. This is because marriage here is not between two people; there is a third party involved, bringing in the law of the social group, either that of the father or of the brother.

The law of the brother relates to Agrippa, who had previously promised his sister Bérénice to Antiochus:

> J'aimai; j'obtins l'aveu d'Agrippa votre Frère.
> Il vous parla pour moi. Peut-être sans colère
> Alliez-vous de mon cœur recevoir le tribut:
> Titus, pour mon malheur, vint vous vit, et vous plut
> (Act I. 4, ll. 191–4).

As for the law of the father, it relates to the sacred elevation of Vespasian on the night of his apotheosis, and to the ban imposed by Rome on marriage with a foreign queen. This is the central law. By reason of his pre-eminence, Titus ceases to be a son and becomes himself a father at the moment when Vespasian dies. He is not the father of any particular individual, but the idealized Father of Rome and the World, to whom he will dedicate himself unreservedly:

> Mais à peine le Ciel eut rappelé mon Père,
> Dès que ma triste main eut fermé sa paupière,
> De mon aimable erreur je fus désabusé:
> Je sentis le fardeau qui m'était imposé;
> Je connus que bientôt, loin d'être à ce que j'aime,
> Il fallait, cher Paulin, renoncer à moi-même,
> Et que le choix des Dieux, contraire à mes amours,
> Livrait à l'univers le reste de mes jours
> (Act II. 3, ll. 460–6).

This is also the moment chosen by Antiochus to become a rival, by attempting to replace Titus in the queen's affections. But he does not realize that Titus is no longer the same man, or that the open rivalry which thus ensues has no meaning for the new emperor. In consequence, this one-sided rivalry does not provoke the breakdown of the reflecting unity of the doubles, but, on the contrary, leads to its reinforcement, to the point of making Antiochus a substitute for Titus, who himself becomes the centre of the world and of the tragedy.

Of this trio, Titus is the only one to evolve and change. He is the very symbol of time which snatches us away from ourselves, of change, and of death, which concludes all change.[5] So the life of Titus is divided into three phases. First there is the young Titus, a debauchee at the court of Nero; the second phase began when he met Bérénice, and thought then of nothing more than pleasing her and becoming worthy of her (Act II. 2, ll. 422–45). The third phase opens with Titus emperor, and its beginning coincides with that of the play. Like the play itself, this third period is divided into two parts. In the first, we see the transitional Titus hesitating between options, still unsure about his final decision, until his confidant Paulin, charged to discover what Rome might think of an eventual marriage, informs him that Rome would disapprove:

> Si je t'ai fait parler, si j'ai voulu t'entendre,
> Je voulais que ton zèle achevât en secret
> De confondre un amour qui se tait à regret
> (Act II. 2, ll. 448–50).

Only then does Titus decide to abandon Bérénice. Until that point, he had been bent not on leaving her, but on leaving her were Rome to insist upon it. But he must still declare his position to her. The transitional Titus was the bewildered Titus, silent, speechless in every sense of the term — incapable of announcing to the queen that he is going to leave her, and turning to Antiochus to ask him to be his mouthpiece, 'D'un amant interdit soulagez le tourment' (Act II. 1, l. 741). The second part of this final phase in the career of Titus begins in Act IV. 3, when Titus, now convinced of the opposition of Rome to his marriage, finally tells the queen of his decision. It is only then that he assumes to the full his new status as emperor.

In parallel with this division into three periods, the image of Titus is split into two personalities, his own and that of Antiochus. To the lovelorn Titus of the second phase, terminated by the death of Vespasian, the double in friendship, that 'autre lui-même', the mute and secret lover of the queen ('Je me suis tu cinq ans', Act I. 4), the matching figure is Antiochus. To Titus, emperor of the third phase, the one who begins the play, Antiochus is still the corresponding double, but as an inverted double: the friend reveals himself as a rival, the silent lover declares himself, but the declared lover falls silent. Antiochus assumes the discourse, the role, and even the same itinerary as Titus. But this Titus who is replaced by Antiochus is not the one

---

5 The complexity of the indications of time in *Bérénice* is matched only by that of the linking of scenes (*liaison des scènes*).

who was solemnized on the night of his father's apotheosis; he is the previous Titus, the lover so impatient to marry his queen that he hopes impatiently for the death of his father ('J'ai même souhaité la place de mon père', Act II. 2, l. 431), thereby reinforcing his filial status.[6] That Titus has disappeared, changing not only his status, but his character. The character of Titus crowned is no longer that of a lover, but patriarchal, no longer filial but imperial, and Antiochus is as incapable as Bérénice of recognizing it. The play's forward dynamic thus stems from the complete transformation of Titus, accomplished on the night of his father's apotheosis after the eight days of mourning.[7]

when Titus patriarchal the others don't see it

Antiochus becomes Titus

The interpretation of Antiochus as a substitute for Titus, as another manifestation of his identity, brings us back to the *Critique* of the abbé Villars. Why, asks Villars, does the King of Comagène, pass through the emperor's study on his way to bid his masked farewell to Bérénice? It is indeed a strange choice. This secret study, situated between the apartments of Bérénice and Titus, guaranteed the latter access to Bérénice, 'lorsqu'il vient à la Reine expliquer son amour' (Act I. 1, l. 6).[8] Why did Antiochus have to pass that way too? It is because he, too, is about to declare his love for her. On the psychological level, to take up station in the secret study of Titus appears to make Antiochus disloyal to his friend, but he is not. In another respect, the position is entirely logical: Titus and Antiochus are one person.

Ant passes through T's secret study

he can because they are one

As if by coincidence, it is in this passing-through point that first Antiochus and then Titus ask themselves who they are, and what exactly they are looking for: 'Hé bien, Antiochus, es-tu toujours le même?', asks Antiochus (Act I. 2, l. 19). To which the question of Titus echoes: 'Hé bien! Titus, que viens-tu faire?' (Act IV. 4, l. 987). By following the direction taken habitually by Titus on his way to the queen, Antiochus assumes in the identified domain of love the place of the new emperor, whom the queen has not seen for more than eight days.

6 In two ways: as son of Vespasian, whom he resists, and also of Bérénice, who is the initiator in the Freudian perspective.
7 The precise nature of the metamorphosis can be debated. In his own edition of the play (in the Garnier–Flammarion edition), Marc Escola suggests that we are witnessing the psychological consequences of a transformation which has already occurred. The situation is ambiguous: Titus has no doubt about what he should do, but he still does not know what Rome will insist upon.
8 See also the opening description of the stage décor, 'La Scène est à Rome dans un cabinet qui est entre l'Appartement de Titus et celui de Bérénice', and the accompanying comment by Forestier, *Œuvres*, p. 454, and pp. 1470–1.

With his confession of love he replaces, and compensates for, the admission of a break-up which Titus cannot bring himself to make. He goes even further: he engages the queen with the language of love that she was expecting of her [former] lover. This explains how the anxiety shown by Bérénice at the start of her conversation with Antiochus is subsequently transformed into a reaction of joy, as she assures Phénice that Titus loves her and that they will marry; the night of the apotheosis is interpreted as a cause for hope, not as the obstacle it really is:

> Le temps n'est plus, Phénice, où je pouvais trembler.
> Titus m'aime, il peut tout, il n'a plus qu'à parler
> (Act I. 5, ll. 297–8).

But what is the justification for her confidence? Nothing, other than that the piety of Titus, satisfied by the completion of the religious obligations to his father Vespasian, has now given way, she explains, 'au soin de son amante' (Act I. 4, l. 168). But Titus has yet to speak to her, so how do we know exactly what this 'soin' is? She infers it from the unreliable voices of the emperor's entourage, and from his 'serments redoublés mille fois' (Act I. 4, l. 174). In other words, it is merely conjecture on her part. Far from making her more cautious, Phénice's warning, 'Titus n'a pas encore expliqué sa pensée' (Act I. V, l. 292) seems to stimulate her mood of exultation. The cause of this paradox lies in the declaration of love by Antiochus. Everything unfolds as if his smouldering passion were communicated directly to the queen, as if Titus were declaring his own passion to her through the mouth of Antiochus, his double, as if the Titus of an earlier existence had survived in that voice.

The same mechanism can be observed when Bérénice, worried by the inability of Titus to express his feelings, evokes the declaration that Antiochus had made to her in Act I:

> L'amour d'Antiochus l'a peut-être offensé.
> Il attend, m-a-t-on dit, le roi de Comagène.
> Ne cherchons point ailleurs le sujet de ma peine [. . .].
> Si Titus est jaloux, Titus est amoureux
> (Act 1. 4, ll. 650–66).

Titus is not, of course, jealous, because he holds himself aloof from the domains of love. But the recollection by Bérénice of Antiochus's declaration of love rekindles her hope. Bérénice raises Titus above all social constraints ('Titus m'aime, il peut tout', l. 298), right up to the level of the ultimate source of power, endowed with absolute authority which is enhanced by his charisma. She even identifies him with the principles of love itself, in a surrounding nimbus of natural majesty which owes nothing to worldly honours or titles, and which does not have to comply either with the voice of the people or with the laws of Rome:

> Ce port majestueux, cette douce présence.
> Ciel ! avec quel respect et quelle complaisance
> Tous les cœurs en secret l'assuraient de leur foi!
>
> (Act I. 5, ll. 313–15).

By believing that she can identify the radiance of the lover beneath the imperial mantle from which he has disappeared, Bérénice confuses the laws of love with the laws of State. That is why Antiochus is a past trace, a memory.

A rival instead of a friend, the inverted double of Titus, Antiochus is an incarnation of the previous Titus, Titus-as-lover, the private being, a friend and a brother. As early as the first act, Antiochus reminds the queen that Agrippa her brother had promised her to him, long before Titus appeared on the scene. But it is love in its intimate privacy which overwhelms family, or even tribal, law as expressed by Antiochus; he accepted the superiority of love, to the point of becoming the silent double of Titus. The laws of love reign between those of the brother, whom they ennoble in an equality of love and friendship, and those of the father, in whose shadow they hold sway. Never does Antiochus free himself from this region which lies beyond the bonds of family, an Eden free of responsibility, which Titus shared with him. But the death of Vespasian drove Titus out of this haven. Does he, or does he not, still love Bérénice? The question is futile: Titus has abandoned marriage, not love, because he recognizes the law which commands it. It is no longer to the laws of love, but to the law of the father-become-god, which is also that of Rome, that Titus ties his fate. In contrast, Antiochus has the task of remaining, between the law of the brother and the law of the father, a lover, friend, and rival. Titus remains in love, but as the emblem of Law, he is longer a double in intimate passion, and so ceases to be a lover.

The Majesty of Empire

Dividing the destiny of Titus in three parts and splitting his identity into two characters amounts to focusing the whole play on him. In this respect, Titus is on stage all the time, whether in his role as emperor, or in that of a contrasting double. The title of the play is deceptive. It facilitates an interpretation through the eyes of Bérénice, imparting an elegiac tone and winning favour at Court, but the main character who gives the play its meaning and movement is Titus in the final accomplishment of his metamorphosis, from son and lover to emperor. The status of neither Antiochus nor Bérénice develops, despite their final resignation. They both submit to a law which transcends them and which Titus alone freely assumes. His freedom lies in respect for the law, not in the violation of it. It is an ambiguous freedom, both accepted and imposed, and this finally explains the ambiguity of his behaviour. But this freedom, founded as it is on the godly elevation of his father, imposes upon him limits similar to those that sacred values hold over the basis of political power. For the conclusion we reach is that *Bérénice* is only superficially a play about love, or the unhappiness of broken relationships. Taken in depth, it is a political play, to the point that in the expression 'tristesse majestueuse', the importance of majesty overshadows that of 'tristesse'.

On the one hand, there is the majesty of Titus in person, that of his 'front majestueux', corresponding to his congenital dignity, to his natural authority, his charisma, and the radiance of the hero, stemming only from him, and thereby justifying love outside all considerations of worldly power. On the other hand, there is also the majesty of Empire, as expressed by Paulin against the opinion of Antiochus who urges Titus to go to the queen:

> Quoi? Vous pourriez, Seigneur, par cette indignité,
> De l'Empire à vos pieds fouler la majesté?
> (Act IV. 8, ll. 1245–6).

As the historian Yan Thomas has shown in his analysis of the fifth book of Ovid's *Fastes*,[9] majesty represents the principle by which the scale of unequal values is organized and maintained. Majesty, which is of divine origin, is the coping stone of balance in the political order. *Majestas*, the armed divinity, preserves and magnifies the pyramid of hierarchy with the prestige which renders it inviolable. It is in the name of *Majestas* that the judicial identification of the Individual is organized, conferring a place and function on each of constituent parts of the imperial system.

The majesty of Titus has the same effect as that of Empire: it exerts control over the people, and unites them. One has only to read Bérénice's account of the night of apotheosis to be persuaded of it:

9 'L'institution de la majesté', *Revue de Synthèse*, 3–4 (1991).

> De cette nuit, Phénice, as-tu vu la splendeur?
> Tes yeux ne sont-ils pas tout pleins de sa grandeur?
> Ces Flambeaux, ce Bûcher, cette nuit enflammée,
> Ces Aigles, ces Faisceaux, ce Peuple, cette Armée,
> Cette foule de Rois, ces Consuls, ce Sénat,
> Qui tous de mon Amant empruntaient leur éclat
> > (Act I. 5, ll. 301–6).

In submitting to the law of Rome, Titus turns away from the original founding splendour of his person, which was also the splendour of love. His prestige lies henceforth not in his 'front majestueux', but in the union he forms with the empire. Abandoning his personal and private interests in order to leave 'un Exemple à la Postérité' (Act IV. 5, l. 1169), the imagined body of the emperor becomes as one with the body social. Desire moves from the heart towards power, from Woman to Empire. Eros is converted to a political source: such is the significance of the refusal by Titus to shed blood. In response to the scornful dismissal of the people by Bérénice, 'Voyez-vous les Romains prêts à se soulever' (Act IV. 5, l. 1138), Titus replies:

> Et qui sait de quel oeil ils prendront cette injure?
> S'ils parlent, si les cris succèdent au murmure,
> Faudra-t-il par le sang justifier mon choix?
> > (Act IV. 5, ll. 1139–41).

The people are not resigned to being an anonymous voice with only latent power; they represent an active force, as Arsace explains to Antiochus at the end of the play:

> Le Peuple avec transport l'arrête, et l'environne,
> Applaudissant aux noms que le Sénat lui donne;
> Et ces noms, ces respects, ces applaudissements,
> Deviennent pour Titus autant d'engagements,
> Qui le liant, Seigneur, d'une honorable chaîne,
> Malgré tous ses soupirs et les pleurs de la Reine,
> Fixent dans son devoir ses voeux irrésolus
> > (Act V. 4, ll. 1283–9).

Rome functions like a machine which progressively tightens its hold on Titus, and, like him, advances the action to the point where they are fused in each other. At that point, Bérénice can say, 'Adieu, Seigneur, régnez: je vous verrai plus' (Act V. 7, l. 1506). She accepts her condition as a lasting future example, immutable as majesty itself, while Antiochus, having declared himself a rival, recovers his status as friend, thus restoring the triangular harmony which reigned at the beginning, but is now divested of personal passions.

A symbol of the discourse of the passions, of the private being and intimate emotions, Antiochus is the incarnation of everything that Titus renounces. His farewells say farewell also to passion. Titus is transformed into a monument to love, but an exemplary love, deprived of any passionate ardour. The man of metamorphoses is frozen in the eternity of the State. His splendour will henceforth be that of the Law. What the abbé de Villars failed to grasp was that a fundamental question presented itself to Racine: how could he represent the passionate love of Titus for Bérénice, and at the same time show him freed from the laws of love? By showing him at the same time both within love and outside it, in the non-responsible Eden of an arranged marriage and in the majestic harmony of effective power? It was through recourse to a substitute, Antiochus, that Racine resolved the potential conflict. In this way he was able to stage simultaneously both what was and what was not, celebrating in the same movement the unhappy love of what passes and dies, and the patriarchal majesty of the unchanging order of things.

The question remains: where lies the pleasure that we now derive from Bérénice today? Is it at all certain that the play offers us pleasure? Are we still moved at all by that mood of tenderness and *galanterie* that the abbé de Villars condemned, when even then it provoked amusement or even open laughter?[10] The answer depends, of course, upon each reader and spectator of the play. It is nonetheless the case that the spectacle of an emperor torn between duty and tears does not come across easily. Short of adopting the readers' pact proposed by Thierry Maulnier in his *Racine*, contemporary taste would find it difficult to take seriously lines such as:

> Ah Rome! Ah, Bérénice! Ah, prince malheureux!
> Pourquoi suis-je empereur? Pourquoi suis-je amoureux?
> (Act IV. 6, ll. 1221–2).

Voltaire remarked of them in his *Remarques sur Bérénice* that they 'appartiennent plus à la haute comédie qu'à la tragédie' [belong more to high comedy than to tragedy]. Similarly, these lines:

> Moi-même je me hais. Néron, tant détesté,
> N'a point à cet excès poussé sa cruauté
> (Act IV. 6, ll. 1209–10).

What makes it difficult to accept today the tragic dimension of the play is the fact that Titus is at the same time emperor and lover; the

---

10 See the last sentence of Villars's *Critique*: 'C'est assez, Monsieur, je suis las de rire; l'envie m'en prendra peut-être quelqu'autre fois'. Forestier, *Œuvres*, p. 519.

emotional and the political mingle as if the two spheres were equal, with equal seriousness attaching to them. History in general, and that of the twentieth century in particular, does not allow us to believe in that kind of parity. What could possibly be the significance of a love story as opposed to the weight of the State, and the immense drama of history? How can one feel moved by the exaggerated style of the lamentations of Titus, he whose authority, we are told, eclipsed all Roman virtue (Act IV. 5)? There is here a form of innocence that the contemporary spectator cannot easily accept. This is why *Bérénice* is better considered from the political perspective, as a study of the fusion of power between man and the state, rather than as the separation of a man and a woman. To renew the setting of the play is another way of reflecting on the decisions we must take in order to present the work of Racine in the way his genius demands.

II

Esther: *Prototype of an Oratorio?*
The Collaboration of Racine
and Jean-Baptiste Moreau

SUSANNE HARTWIG AND BERTHOLD WARNECKE

> Mais il faudrait que les paroles de la musique fussent des réflexions sur ce qu'on aurait vu, et comme l'expression de l'esprit de chaque acte' [But the words of the music should be a reflexion on what we have seen, and the expression of mood in each act], Saint-Evremond[1]

In his dedicatory letter of 1689, Jean-Baptiste Moreau wrote that 'selon toutes les apparences', he owed the success of *Esther* 'à la beauté du sujet et à la magnificence des paroles [. . .] plûtost qu'à la délicatesse de [s]es Chants' [in all probability', the success of Esther was due to the beauty of the subject rather than to the delicacy of its music].[2] The music of *Esther* thus appears to be primarily just a means of highlighting the text of the great tragic dramatist and, from a more practical point of view, of ensuring a sufficient number of parts for the young pupils of Saint-Cyr. However, it can be shown that with its distinctive musical characteristics, Moreau's score goes beyond a mere musical setting for a theatrical text. If, in fact, Moreau's music underlines the quality of Racine's text, it does so by creating a musical work of art which is unique. In his description of the music of *Esther*, Jean Rohou lays particular emphasis on the work of close collaboration between the composer and the dramatist:

> Partout prédominent largement les lignes mélodiques conjointes. A partir de cette sobriété, Moreau fait preuve d'ingéniosité au service du

The authors and editors would like to record their gratitude to Anne Sophie Meine and Douglas Smith for their assistance in the work of translation from German, and to Gráinne Gormley for advice on the language of music.

1 Letter of 4 February, 1676, quoted by Rohou, *Théâtre*, p. 1094.

2 See *Œuvres*, G.E.F., 9, *Musique des Chœurs d'Esther et d'Athalie et des cantiques spirituels, nouvelle éd., revue sur les plus anciennes impressions et les autographes*, p. 1.

texte, respectant les combinaisons métriques les plus diverses, soulignant les termes affectivement ou sémantiquement importants par des accents de hauteur, de durée, d'intensité, ou par d'autres ornements. Les parties instrumentales (ritournelles, préludes, ouverture à la française, entracte, marche) qui ponctuent l'intrigue reprennent en écho figuratif le thème des vers qui précèdent: des chromatismes illustrent les moments de tension, des successions de croches appellent à la mobilisation, des rythmes pointés évoquent la triomphale majesté de Dieu. Tout cela suppose une étroite collaboration entre le musicien et le poète.

[Converging melodic lines dominate throughout. With this essential sobriety as his basis, Moreau serves [Racine's] text in a skilful, original way, respecting the most varied prosodic options, highlighting forms of expression which are affectively or semantically important with high-pitched, long, or intense musical phrasing, or with other variations of musical ornament. The instrumental sequences (whether ritornellos, preludes, overtures 'à la française', interludes, or marches) which punctuate the story are used to provide a figurative echo to the poetic lines they follow: moments of tension are illustrated by chromatic passages; sequences of quavers, or half-crotchets, correspond to more intense activity; accentuated rhythms evoke the triumphant majesty of God. All of which implies a close collaboration between the poet and the musician.][3]

Until recently, however, the compositions of Jean-Baptiste Moreau have enjoyed the critical attention of but a few musicologists, and that in studies dating only from the turn of the century.[4] As for information on Moreau's career, such as commentaries on the music of *Esther*, little is in print. If one tries to find an explanation for the lack of interest, whether real or apparent, in the music of *Esther*, one central answer immediately presents itself, and that is the problem of generic definition. Moreau's techniques of composition were shaped by the limited scope of the performing space available at Saint-Cyr, and also he had to allow for the expectations of an audience which was more readily responsive to spoken theatre.[5] For these reasons, the nature

[handwritten margin note: paucity of critical attn pd M's text]

[handwritten margin note: work shaped by limitations of perf. space, expectations of audience]

3 Rohou, *Théâtre*, p. 1095. Similarly, Rohou speaks of 'une discrète harmonie au service du sens' [a discreet harmony which serves the meaning], p. 1095.
4 On *Esther*, see, for example: Julien Tiersot, 'Les Chœurs d'*Esther* de Moreau', *Revue Musicale* (January, 1903), 35–40 (p. 39); on *Esther* and *Athalie*: Charles Bordes, 'Les Chœurs d'*Esther* et d'*Athalie* par J. B. Moreau', *Tribune de St.-Gervais* 11/Paris (1905), 68–77 (p. 75). The paucity of earlier material underlines the interest of a new study by Anne Piéjus, '*Esther*, un modèle paradoxal de théâtre musical pour Saint-Cyr', *PFSCL*, 24. 47 (1997), 395–420.
5 Manuel Couvreur, *Jean-Baptiste Lully. Musique et dramaturgie au service du Prince* (Brussels: Vollar, 1992), p. 145: '*Esther* et *Athalie* répondent à l'attente d'un certain public qui accepte que les endroits passionnés soient chantés, mais qui pense que le reste de la piece qui n'est pas naturellement susceptible des ornemens de la Musique, doit estre simplement recité par de bons Comediens.' [*Esther* and *Athalie* answer the expectations

of the composition was determined by the need for easily memorized melodies, simple polyphonic forms, clear harmonic structures, and by quite short musical units clearly distinguishable one from another. The orchestral forces accompanying the choir were thus 'colla voce',[6] meaning that the instruments supported the melody and harmony of what was sung by choristers who, for the most part, were not trained as musicians.[7]

The purpose of this study will therefore be to show how closely text and music are linked and, in the words of Racine's preface to *Esther*, that this 'espèce de Poème, où le chant [est] mêlé avec le récit' [this kind of poem in which the singing is linked to the story] constitutes a coherent whole in which the music is an integral part. As Rohou puts it, 'plutôt qu'une tragédie entremêlée de chœurs, *Esther* est bien un poème pieux partiellement déclamé et partiellement chanté à une ou plusieurs voix' [rather than a tragedy punctuated by choral interventions, *Esther* is a devotional poem which is partially sung, either by one or several voices].[8] In its conclusion, our study will then pose the question of genre: although reminding us of the dramatic dialogues in Latin which were so popular in Jesuit colleges, *Esther* also prefigures the form of the oratorio perfected by George Frederick Handel (1685–1759) in the following century. Handel's own *Esther* (1732) was first performed privately in 1720 as a masque (therefore with action and costumes) entitled *Haman and Mordecai*.[9] In order to

5. *cont.* of a certain public which, while accepting that the more emotional passages should be sung, believed that the remaining parts of the text not normally requiring musical ornament should simply be recited by good actors].

6 For the distribution of orchestral and choral parts, see Bordes, 'Les Chœurs d'*Esther* et d'*Athalie*', p. 75; Tiersot confidently asserts that the basso continuo was maintained orchestrally ('Les Chœurs d'*Esther* de Moreau', p. 39), but this interpretation of the musical score seems to us unsustainable, both musically and philologically.

7 See, for example, Achille Taphanel, *Le théâtre de Saint-Cyr (1689–1792) d'après des documents inédits* (Paris: Cerf, 1882), p. 78. Also Tiersot, 'Les Chœurs d'*Esther* de Moreau', p. 37, 'Les mélodies claires et bien dessinées abondent. La plupart, d'une gracieuse tonalité majeure, sont d'un caractère doux qui est bien celui des vers, et qui convient à des chants destinés à une récréation de jeunes filles.' [Clear and well-defined melodies abound. Most of them, set elegantly in a major key, have the softer quality which stems from poetic verse, and which is therefore appropriate to choral parts designed for the entertainment of young girls].

8 Rohou, *Théâtre*, p. 1089. In a letter of 21 February 1689, Madame de Sévigné had already confirmed that she found 'tous les chants convenables aux paroles, qui sont tirées des Psaumes ou de la Sagesse' [all the music is adapted to the words, which are taken from the Psalms or the Book of Wisdom].

9 See also the introduction to *Esther* by Jacques Morel: 'Au-delà de l'opéra à l'italienne, c'est à l'oratorio que l'œuvre de Racine doit peut-être l'essentiel de son inspiration.' [Beyond the italianate opera, it was essentially to the oratorio that this

proceed with this analysis, we shall begin with a systematic study of each of the three acts in turn.

The structure of the play follows a simple and direct line of progression: the first act indicates the danger, the second emphasizes it, and the third act eliminates it. This structure is already anticipated in the first act when the distress of the chorus of young Israelite girls gradually changes to a total confidence in God; this progression confers on the first act a quality of implicit unity, reflecting as it does the movement of the play in its entirety. By means of its interspersed laments, the chorus first underlines the terror felt by Esther then offers in the concluding passages its praise of God.[10] It is above all in the pathos of its finale, sung by everyone on stage, that the first act assumes its real importance: the central conflict of its last scene, and the struggle between the true faith and heresy, will be revealed as the main issue of the tragedy.[11]

How did Moreau set to music the action of the first act? After the prologue of la Piété and an overture (whose musical structure is repeated at the end of the act), it is in the second scene that the chorus performs for the first time. Two Israelites announce the arrival of Queen Esther; after a question from an Israelite and a reply from another soloist, the two voices join to form a duo, followed by the other girls. The passages sung by two voices are characterized by movements in thirds, sixths, and tenths. In the seven lines thus delivered, Moreau is already putting into effect all the different expressive forms which will subsequently characterize the musical form of the choruses. A highly appreciated stylistic device, borrowed from French opera of the time, is to be found in the repetition of verses contained within a refrain, such as 'La Reine nous appelle, / Allons, rangeons-nous auprès d'elle' (ll. 118 ff., 120 ff.). In the song beginning 'O rives de Jourdain' (l. 141),[12] Moreau uses for the first time the entire ensemble of voices

work of Racine owed its inspiration], *Racine. Théâtre complet*, ed. Jacques Morel and Alain Viala (Paris: Garnier, 1980), p. 637.

10 For example, Esther: 'Mes filles chantez-nous quelqu'un de ces cantiques, / Où vos voix si souvent se mêlant à mes pleurs, / De la triste Sion célèbrent les malheurs.' (ll. 129-31).

11 This gives rise to a sense of repetitiveness arising from the highly simplified structure of the play, as pointed out by Rohou in the following terms: 'Ces passages [du chœur] ont l'inconvénient de passer un peu trop systématiquement d'un premier moment de frayeur à une heureuse assurance.' [These passages (of the chorus) have the disadvantage of progressing a little too mechanically from the initial moment of terror to a hopeful confidence], Rohou, *Théâtre*, p. 1094 ff.

12 Tiersot ('Les Chœurs d'*Esther* de Moreau', p. 37) underlines the resemblance of this passage with 'Pleure, ô patrie, ô Thessalie' from l'*Alceste* (1767) by Christoph Willibald Gluck (1714-87).

and instruments: two violins with basso continuo, and a three-part vocal ensemble.[13]

The close link between text and music is demonstrated in an exemplary manner in the fifth scene of Act I in which the musical gradation at the end of the act matches the dramatic gradation, so illustrating the virtuosity of Moreau, 'musicien dramatique'.[14] The stylistic range of this scene includes a number of ornaments and modes of expression in what is known as 'la rhétorique musicale' of the baroque era.[15] Moreau underlines the initial despair of the girls with a concentrated three part composition, whose expressive harmony has a quality which is entirely new within the choral range of Esther. The most striking feature in this scene is the 'passus duriusculus' in the basso continuo (see example 1, p. 207). In the terminology of the time, this 'pas un peu dur' marks the chromatic fall of four steps which symbolize distress and death. According to Christoph Bernhard (1628–92), a German composer and theorist of the seventeenth century, this stylistic device does not belong to the inventory of decoration in the 'common style'.[16] In noting how this exceptional use of the 'passus duriusculus' underlines the depressing mood of the scene, we can appreciate how Moreau creates the musical equivalent of the tragic text itself. There are other musical features in the score which are used to translate the terror of the Israelites. Moreau uses the tritone, an augmented fourth, known as a 'diabolus in musica' (see example 2, p. 207). Since the Renaissance, this interval was used not only to symbolize suffering and death, but also treachery and sin ('O mortelles alarmes', ll. 297, 301, 305, 308). Similarly, the complexity of the counterpoint developing into a very concentrated three-part imitative structure ('Pleurez mes tristes yeux', l. 298, see example 3, p. 207) skilfully matches the tension of the situation. In this way, it can be seen that the dramatic mood of the text is reinforced in a subtle way by three musical devices: a melodic motif, the 'passus duriusculus'; a characteristic interval, the tritone; and complex polyphonic writing (see example 4, p. 208).

13 Although the second voice (identified as 'contre-partie') has no text, it is quite clear that the score anticipates the use of three different voices. It is also the case that by occasionally using horizontal bars and jumping octaves, the score indicates an instrumental 'contre-partie'.

14 See Madeleine Garros, 'Moreau', in Die Musik in Geschichte und Gegenwart, 9 (Kassel/Stuttgart: Bärenreiter / Metzler, 1961), col. 570.

15 This term causes some difficulty, especially in the areas of French and Italian music, see Arno Forchert, 'Musik und Rhetorik im Barock', in Schütz-jahrbuch, 7/8 (1986), 8.

16 See Christoph Bernhard, 'Tractatus compositionis augmentatus', in Joseph Müller-Blattau (ed.), Die Kompositionslehre Heinrich Schützens in der Fassung seines Schülers Christoph Bernhard (Kassel/Stuttgart: Bärenreiter / Metzler, 1999), pp. 77 ff.

Moreau managed to integrate the different musical parts into a coherent whole, and because of his composition the fifth scene assumes a character of finality. The link between the textual divisions is maintained by instrumental interludes: ritornellos, a symphony, and a prelude. The regular shifting between recitative and a variety of airs, so characteristic of earlier passages, is replaced by a series of short movements. A gradation of formal and stylistic divisions can be observed at the end of the act until the final triumphant chorus; in other words, each of the three voices reveals a musical quality that is distinctive to it.

In terms of music alone, the last scene of Act I can be divided into nine formal units which are clearly differentiated from each other but, by means of recurring motifs, these successive units are also linked. Moreau gives, for example, two variations of a single motif, the first delivered by a single Israelite, then to be taken up by the whole chorus ('Arrachons, déchirons', ll. 309, 314), the totality of which forms a musical unit of ten bars. Larger units arise out of the ritornello structure which can be detected at a number of points, as for example in the song 'Le Dieu que nos servons (l. 336) whose different parts are arranged in a perfectly symmetrical manner (see Table 1).

Table 1.

Ritornello	Instrumental	9 bars
Chorus	'Le Dieu que nous servons' (ll. 336–8)	9 bars
Recitative/Air	'Hé quoi . . .' (an Israélite) (ll. 339–41) 'Ce Dieu . . .' (another) (ll. 342–7) 'Il renverse . . .' (another) (l. 348) 'Il prend . . .' (another) (l. 349)	18 bars (total)
Ritornello Chorus	Instrumental 'Le Dieu que nous servons' (ll. 350–2)	9 bars 9 bars

From their despair at the start of the scene, the girls progress to a call for resistance at the end; corresponding to this progression is a basic change in tonality (even if at that time the notions of well-defined tonalities, or of clear characteristic traits of different tonalities, were not formally identified). What strikes the reader is the shift to the major mode after l. 336 ('Le Dieu que nous servons'), and to a tonality which is simpler, less expressive, and partially chromatic. It should be stressed that it is because of the effect of the choir's delicate melody ('Tu vois nos pressants dangers', l. 359), in which Moreau goes evenly down from B major through the circle of fifths via E major and A major ending in D major (that is, the tonality which closes the first Act, as in the repetition of 'Tu vois nos pressants dangers', ll. 358 ff. / 370 ff.), that Act I has its own separate sense of unity, isolating it somewhat from from the rest of the drama. The first act therefore presents all the musical devices of the play, as well as all the important themes (see Table 2, p. 195).

From the strictly musical point of view, Act II is by far the least interesting. Consistent with its function as a catalyser of action, this act is the least contemplative, and so carries few musical passages. On the other hand, it is more dramatic than Acts I and III. The choir intervenes only once, at the end of the act just after the invitation extended by Esther to her husband the king and Aman his counsellor. The song of the young girls (in the recitative style) takes up the issue of the play and gives it a wider meaning;[17] at the end, taking up the hymn, the young Israelite maidens confirm their faith in God, the one true and all-powerful God:

> Que ma bouche, et mon cœur, et tout ce que je suis
> Rendent honneur au Dieu qui m'a donné la vie.
> > (Act II. 8, ll. 771ff.).

> Le bonheur de l'Impie est toujours agité.
> Il erre à la merci de sa propre inconstance.
> Ne cherchons la félicité,
> Que dans la paix de l'innocence.
> > (Act II. 8, ll. 798–801)

By confirming the permanence of faith and the defeat of impiety, the chorus of Act II has a function similar to those of Acts I and III. Thus all the acts conclude on an evocation of the same dichotomy. Furthermore, the emphasis is placed upon the importance of the role of the King who, despite all his power, is represented only as an instrument of God:

---

17 'Que vous semble, mes sœurs, de l'état où nous sommes? / D'Esther, d'Aman, qui le doit emporter? / Est-ce Dieu, sont-ce les hommes, ? Dont les œuvres vont éclater?' (Act II. 8, ll. 713–16).

Table 2

Ritornello	Prelude	Air/ Récitatif	Ritornello/ Chorus	Solo/Air	Rit./Symph./ Chorus	Duo	Chorus & Air	Overture
'Pleurons et gémissons'	only the basso continuo	'Arrachons, déchirons'	'Arrachons, déchirons'	'Quel carnage de toutes partes!'	'Le Dieu que nous servons'	'Dieu que la gloire couronne'/ 'Dieu qui veux bien'	'Tu vois nos pressants dangers'/ 'Arme-toi'	Overture
Interpretation chromatic 'passus duriusculus',	tonality: D minor	Change of style air/récitatif, two soloists	Chorus based on two parts previously sung by soloists	Figurative melody, example: 'Hélas'	Change of tonality: D major; (symbol of revolt?)	Duo ('vole'), more and more expressive > music in several parts	Very expressive style; more complex counterpoint; figurative bass melody; varied harmony: B major > E major > A major > D major (descending cycle of fifths)	Overture as frame of first act > as a 'musical display'

Dieu, de nos volontés arbitre souverain!
Le cœur des Rois est ainsi dans ta main
(Act II. 8, ll. 733 ff.).

The last scene of the second act is marked by the change in declamation and song, as the stage directions indicate. The aria-like melody ('Tel qu'un ruisseau docile', ll. 729 ff.) is most striking; it includes a number of ornaments and decorative insertions in the fluid movement of the bass continuo. In keeping with the dramatic character of the second act, the solo and choral interventions are shorter than elsewhere, so that the music reflects more immediately the emotions expressed in the text, as for example in: 'Malheureux! vous quittez le Maître des humains, / Pour adorer l'ouvrage de vos mains.' (ll. 742 ff.); sung by two voices, the imitative shifts of this passage reflect the underlying tension. The rapid succession of sung and spoken parts at the end of the second act, masked by an acceleration in the rhythmic language, anticipates the conclusion of the third act: arias which are detached from the musical context ('Dieu d'Israël, dissipe enfin cette ombre.' l. 744), choral parts written in a relatively free style ('Que les Démons', l. 769), *concertante* interludes (with the participation of the flutes), and the subtle accompaniment of the basso continuo, all serve to illustrate the deployment of the full range of available musical resources. Furthermore, the motifs and the rhythm of the first entr'acte, and the three-part imitative structure, recall very strongly the overture 'à la francaise' at the beginning of the play.[18]

In the third act, the chorus assumes a very important role by means of two essential contributions: the first is in Act III. 3, following the prophetic words delivered to Aman (ll. 921–5), and the second comes as the finale of the play. The significance of the first of these interventions lies in its length: all previous interventions of this length were in the form of an interlude between acts. The maidens of the choir begin by expressing the horror inspired in them by Aman;[19] then, in order to 'adoucir la rudesse' of the King (l. 957), they sing praises which, as the celebration of a happy people, have a utopian character. The function of the King is examined from the perspective of the ideal monarch, of a *princeps optimus*.[20] Among the songs of the

18 Describing this overture (like 'toutes les pages symphoniques' of the work) as 'puéril[e]', Bordes ('Les Chœurs d'*Esther* et d'*Athalie*', p. 73) mistakenly compares the work of Moreau to the bigger overtures 'à la française' which preceded the divertissements and opéra-ballets in earlier years at the court of Versailles.

19 For Jean Dubu, they present Aman as 'quasi-satanique', *Racine aux miroirs* (Paris: SEDES, 1992), p. 349.

20 See Bruno Singer, *Die Fürstenspiegel in Deutschland im Zeitalter des Humanismus und der Reformation*, in *Bibliographische Grundlagen und ausgewählte Interpretationem*, (eds) Jakob

chorus in Act III. 3 are four stanzas (ll. 969–84) which denounce
Calumny. Just as they are highlighted by their identity in a different
literary form, so too are they distinguished by Moreau's musical interpretation of them. Pushing pathos to a high point in the play, these stanzas
and those which follow them form the only really active intervention
by the chorus.

In these stanzas, Racine sketches the portrait of the ideal prince as
the enemy of Calumny; they are followed by five more stanzas which
offer an evocation of the princely qualities of *Caritas, Fides, Iustitia*,
concluding with *Prudentia*, all of which amounts to a summary of the
play's content and a commentary on the role of the King. By constructing an exemplary model which glorifies the King, while requiring
him to serve the qualities demanded of his rank, these stanzas have a
pedagogical value,[21] being a *speculum principis*. Through this general
address to all monarchs, Racine speaks directly to Louis XIV. The
repetitive nature of the stanzas clearly shows that this is the fundamental issue in the play. In the first two stanzas (ll. 969–76), Calumny
(representing unrest), is opposed to Justice (representing peace). In the
following two stanzas, emphasis is placed upon the discrepancy
between 'être' [being] and paraître ['seeming'], as in 'feinte douceur'
(l. 978) and 'fraude adroite et subtile' (l. 981). This is another way of
reinforcing the two key concepts of '*la vérité*' [truth] and *justice*; these
two words are sung by the choir in the same line just prior to the
sequence of stanzas (l. 968).

The King Assuérus is but the instrument of God, and he must
's'éveiller' [awake to this] (l. 1001).[22] The fundamental point is that the

---

Wimpfeling, Wolfgang Seidel, Johann Strum, Urban Reiger (Munich: Fink, 1980),
p. 32: 'Der "Princeps optimus" als Summe aller Tugenden, "als Idee vom Fürsten" –
was es im Mittelalter so nicht gibt, als "Utopie" es hängt wie die mit dem Humanismus aufkommenden utopischen Staatsromane, mit der neuen Rangstellung Platos
zusammen', [The 'princeps optimus' as the sum of all virtues, as 'the very idea of the
prince' – who does not exist in the Middle Ages – as utopia: this, like the novel of
the utopian state which emerges with humanism, is linked to the new status ascribed
to Plato].
21 See Gero von Wilpert, *Sachwörterbuch der Literatur*, 7., verbess. u. erw. Aufl (Stuttgart,
1989), p. 315: the exemplary mirror of princes 'wendet sich meist an Fürsten und
Adel direkt und entwirft in utop[isch]-didakt[ischer] Form reiner Theorie oder am
Beispiel e[iner] histor[ischen] Persönlichkeit das Idealbild des Herrschers mit seinen
Pflichten und Aufgaben und gibt Ratschläge zur besten Regierungsweise' [. . . is
directed for the most part immediately at princes and aristocracy, sketching in the
utopian–didactic form of pure theory or, through the example of an historical
personality, the ideal image of the ruler with his duties and tasks, and offering advice
on the best approach to government].
22 Thus the words of Assuérus after Esther's confession: 'J'étais donc le jouet [. . .]
Ciel, daigne m'éclairer.' (l. 1138).

true interests of the King are those of God Himself,[23] and in such a way that all the passages which praise God can also be read at a second level as praise for Louis XIV (see Caldicott, p. 118). It is upon the calumniator that all the blame falls.[24] The theme of the evil counsellor will be taken up again in *Athalie*.[25] The intervention of the choir in Act II. 3 has thus two major functions: first of all, it summarizes the conflict of the play by focusing upon the central royal figure; then it situates the action of *Esther* in a broader perspective by attributing more general moral principles and ideas to the functions of kingship. After this sequence of stanzas, the girls of the choir praise the just King and offer more advice, but this time to the king in his mortal specificity. In other words, after its excursion into general reflexion, the choir returns to the specific case of Assuérus and the detail of the play. The stanzaic form has the advantage of being easy to memorize, particularly because of the music which reinforces the weight of the words and their thematic insistence; it is thus the music which turns this distinctive sequence of stanzas into a form of meditation close to the *exercitia spiritualis*.[26]

23 This has already been observed in the Prologue of la Piété [Piety] which presents the King as the energetic servant of God; see Gilles Revaz, *La représentation de la monarchie absolue dans le théâtre racinien. Analyses sociodiscursives* (Paris: Editions Kimé, 1998), pp. 229 ff.: 'Esther représente la monarchie absolue en tant qu'elle est une monarchie de droit divin' [Insofar as it is a monarchy derived from Divine Right, Esther also represents the absolute monarchy].

24 Revaz, *La représentation de la monarchie absolue*, p. 227, 'd'un point de vue dramatique, il n'y a pas de conflit entre le Roi et la loi de Dieu. Toute la contradiction est en effet reportée sur le ministre: "charger" celui-ci plutôt que le Roi est un procédé assez répandu dans la littérature du dix-septième siècle, notamment chez Corneille. Le Roi échappe ainsi à la critique comme s'il était intouchable, au-dessus de la mêlée. Une telle image fait naturellement partie des procédés de représentation du pouvoir absolu' [from a dramatic perspective, there is no conflict between the King and the law of God. The whole contradiction is in fact carried over to the minister: to burden him rather than the King is quite a common procedure in the literature of the seventeenth century, particularly in the work of Corneille. The king thus escapes obloquy as if he were untouchable, above all the hurly-burly. This image is naturally one of the modes of representation of absolute power at the time].

25 For the role of Mathan, see especially *Athalie*, ll. 933–6.

26 On the role of song in Lenten meditation, see Marianne Sammer, *Die Fastenmeditation. Gattungstheoretische Grundlegung und kulturgeschichtlicher Kontext* (Munich: Tuduv, 1996), p. 91: 'Während des "chorus" erfolgt [. . .] letztlich die eigentliche geistliche Arbeit an der Seele des Zuschauers, denn in diesem Teil wird die Rückbindung des dargestellten Exempels an die Meditationsvorgabe vollzogen, vergleichbar einem Exerzitanden, der nach erfolgter 'meditatio' über seine Erfahrungen und Gefühlsregungen bei der geistigen Betrachtung einer imaginierten Situation Rechenschaft geben muß, ehe er zum zweiten und dritten Betrachtungspunkt schreitet, die für den jeweiligen Tag in den "Exercitia Spiritualis" vorgeschrieben sind. Dabei erfüllt der Gesang eine doppelte Aufgabe, denn über das Medium der Sprache erhält der Zuhörer die notwendigen Angaben zum Verständnis des Exempels, und über das Medium der Musik wird

The stanzas are arranged in the form of a strophic song accompanied by the basso continuo: the first and third are sung by a single voice, the second and fourth by the choir. To the simple harmony of G and D major, a melody is created which is easy to memorize, and which rarely stretches for more than an octave. It can be concluded from this that Moreau knowingly composed this 'exemplary mirror' in the form of a hymn. This is therefore a *cantique*, to be distinguished from the other sacred songs of the play, and it marks a major point of focus. What is particularly striking is the balanced 12-bar melody (4 + 4 + 4), as simple in style as popular song, and corresponding to the metric regularity of the verse. Each verse is set to two bars of music; after four bars there is a well-defined cæsura, after eight bars (that is, in the middle of the first group of stanzas) there is a half-cadence in the dominant D major. In bars 9 and 12, Moreau repeats the last two verses of each stanza to return from the dominant D major to the tonic G major.

[margin note: like a hymn - cantique]

The chorus comes in for the last time at the end of the play, following the *dénouement* of the Court intrigue. The whole play is arranged as a graduated progress in pathos, and it is in the very last choral contribution that the climax of this process is reached. The effect of pathos is underlined by an orchestral march, introducing the choir and preparing an appropriately solemn atmosphere. This is a musical device which is frequently used just before a decisive moment or before the final scene of a tragedy set to music. *Esther* finishes with a hymn, which begins with the words: 'Dieu fait triompher l'innocence, / Chantons, célébrons sa puissance' (Act III. 9, ll. 1200 ff.), thus evoking a prayer.[27]

[margin note: chorus at end of play → pathos]

verhindert, daß sich die Beschaffenheit der Affekte des Zuhörers während des belehrenden Teiles verändern oder an Intensität einbüßen' [It is during the 'chorus' that the real spiritual work on the soul of the spectator is finally accomplished, for in this part the link between the example/exemplum depicted and the preceding task of meditation is established, just as in the case of those who are following spiritual exercises and who must, after a successful 'meditatio', account for their experiences and emotions with respect to the mental contemplation of an imagined situation, before proceeding to the second and third stage of contemplation prescribed for the relevant day in 'Exercitia Spiritualis'. In the process, the song fulfils two tasks, for through the medium of language the listener receives the information necessary to understand the example/exemplum, while the medium of music prevents the didactic element from altering or diminishing the intensity of the emotional condition of the listener].

27 As Raymond Picard puts it, 'la méditation religieuse, entraînée par le chant, s'est peu à peu éloignée de l'action pour se faire plus générale; l'action elle-même ne semble plus qu'une occasion exemplaire où la gloire de Dieu éclate, où les méchants sont punis, etc . . . , et toute la pièce apparaît comme une prière qu'illustreraient quelques tableaux' [religious meditation, borne along by the singing, has moved us gradually away from the action to become more general; the action itself seems to be no more than an exemplary moment when the glory of God bursts forth and the wicked are punished, etc ..., and the whole play seems like a prayer illustrated by a series of paintings], Picard, *Œuvres*, 1, p. 1160, note on chorus of Act II. 8.

The chorus begins its last entry by summarizing the action of the play and representing Aman as an unworthy courtier, the King as a representative of God (and thus the incarnation of Good), and Esther as His instrument. The unbeliever who disturbs the just and proper order is eliminated. This summary is presented in the form of an *exemplum*, whose meaning is encapsulated in the following lines:

summary ≈ exemplum [margin note]

> On peut des plus grand Rois surprendre la justice.
> Incapables de tromper,
> Ils ont peine à s'échapper
> Des pièges de l'artifice
>
> (Act III. 9, ll. 1214–17).

The following passages of the chorus resemble a series of *cantiques* in that they are inspired directly by the Psalms, Psalm 36 on the fate of the just compared with that of the unbeliever, Psalm 78 on the persecutors of Israël, and the sequence of Psalms 102–105 offering praise and thanksgiving.[28] With the use of the doxology closing the fourth book of Psalms, incorporating the words of Psalm 105 ('Que son nom soit béni. Que son nom soit chanté./Que l'on célèbre ses ouvrages, /Au-delà des temps et des âges, /Au-delà de l'éternité, Act III. 9, ll. 1283–86), the end of the play also reminds us of a number of dialogues from the works of Giacomo Carissimi, Domenico Mazzocchi, and Marc-Antoine Charpentier. The play thus ends like a *cantique* expressing gratitude, and evokng sacred verse.

play ends like cantique, expressing gratitude + evoking sacred verse [margin note]

Like the last scene of the first act, the last scene of the third act has the characteristics of a free-form finale, clearly showing features of the oratorio. Numerous instruments increase the dynamic range, and a variety of vocal forces are used, solos, airs (sometimes two-part), songs, heavily ornamented, with basso continuo, and large choral movements. The whole scene relies upon the structure of the ritornello to affirm its unity. It is once more evident how Moreau links the different musical parts of the whole, and this unity of composition highlights the novelty of the score. He derives the the chorus's refrain 'Esther a triomphé des filles des Persans./ La Nature et le Ciel à l'envi l'ont ornée' (ll. 1228 ff. / ll. 1234 ff.) from the earlier song 'Dieu fait triompher l'Innocence' (l. 1200), transforming the initial melody in triple metre (*tempus perfectus*, traditionally reserved for the praise of God), into a

final free-form finale ≈ oratorio [margin note]

28 [The reader should remember that the numbering of the Psalms varies according to the edition / tradition / source from which they are taken, Hebrew (Protestant), Greek, or Latin Vulgate (Catholic), thus Psalm 105 of *The Jerusalem Bible* becomes Psalm 106 in *The New English Bible*, but still closing the Fourth Book of Psalms in both editions. See also notes to chapters by Viala and Caldicott, pp. 231 and 113].

duple metre melody (*tempus imperfectus*, reserved for praise of Esther), evidence that Moreau borrowed his principles of style from sacred music and the liturgy. The identification with sacred music becomes even more evident with the chorus's rendering of 'Que son nom soit béni', l. 1283). It can be said that there is at this point a true two-part polyphonic imitation. Imitation apart, the melody effects a circular movement concluding with a descending leap of a fifth (soh – fa – mi – fa – soh – doh), representing a highly effective stylistic device for heightening solemnity and pathos.[29]

We have here, in embryonic form, the principle of the great choral fugue as it was developed in Rome by Giacomo Carissimi and Domenico Mazzocchi in religious dialogues and oratorios. The same principle is regularly applied in the cantatas and oratorios of the eighteenth century, especially in the work of Handel. The same order of reflexion applies also to the content, where a number of parallels should be stressed between *Esther* and sacred music. The words which conclude the play refer specifically to the verses of the doxology, 'Sicut erat in principio et nunc et semper' [As it was in the beginning is now and ever shall be], sung or recited at the end of every reading of the Psalms.[30] The most significant feature in this line is the change from triple to duple metre in the last line of the play ('Au-delà de l'Éternité', l. 1286). The emphatic accentuation of the notion of eternity is probably designed to replace the final reinforcing word of the old doxology, 'Amen', thus drawing Esther nearer again to the art of the oratorio. The final chorus of Esther is the solemn, uplifting conclusion of a sacred drama; its technique is similar to that of the dialogue of *Lazaro* by Domenico Mazzocchi which also concludes with one brief word evoking the last word of the doxology.[31]

29 In musical rhetoric of the seventeenth century, the figure of *circulatio* was the expression of the perfect and beautiful; see Hartmut Krones, 'Musik und Rhetorik' in *Die Musik in Geschichte und Gegenwart*, vol. 6 (Kassel/Stuttgart: Bärenreiter / Metzler, 1997), col. 829.

30 For the question of parallels between God and the King, see Ludwig Finscher, 'Psalm', in *Die Musik in Geschichte und Gegenwart*, vol. 7 (Kassel/Stuttgart: Bärenreiter / Metzler, 2e ed., 1997), column 1887: 'Der Grand motet wird [um die Mitte des 17. Jahrhunderts] zum musikalischen Mittelpunkt der werktäglich in Gegenwart des Königs zelebrierten Messe basse solennelle, und die Texte des Grand motet sind vor allem die Psalmen; dahinter steht die in allen Monarchien latente und im französischen Absolutismus virulente Gleichsetzung des Herrschers mit dem rex David' [The Grand motet becomes (around the middle of the seventeenth century) the musical centre of the Solemn low mass, celebrated daily in the presence of the King, and the texts of the Grand motet are above all the Psalms; behind this lies the equation of the ruler with King David, an equation which is latent in all monarchies, and virulent in French absolutism].

31 Compare with Domenico Mazzocchi, *Sacrae concertationes*, ed. Wolfgang Witzenmann, Concentus musicus 3 (Cologne: Arno Volk, 1975), preface, p. ix.

In choosing the subject of his play,[32] Racine had to allow for the very young age of the pupils of Saint-Cyr; this was accomplished by reducing the lines of the biblical story to a struggle between the opposing forces of faith and impiety.[33] In doing this, he displays his two outstanding qualities of simplicity and concentration. The plot is totally free from ambiguity, and the manichean psychology has a specific purpose: through the near-immobility of the characters, Racine draws attention to the only one capable of action – God, and through Him His instrument the King.[34] The powerful God of the Jews confirms his covenant with the chosen people by opposing the silence of the God(s) of non-sacred tragedy. The music of Moreau subtly translates the content of Racine's text by investing the simplicity of plot with solemnity. By emphasizing the contemplative nature of the lyric verse, the music is able to accentuate the increasing dramatic tempo of the play;[35] this is because the chorus, representing almost a third of the whole text, is not reduced to the function of interlude, as it is, for example in *Athalie*, which is far more dramatic but less contemplative than *Esther*.[36] Because the chorus appears always at the end of each act in *Esther*, and never at the beginning, it is possible to follow a gradu-

32 The subject had already been adapted to the theatre a dozen times, for the most part with a more romantic turn, Rohou, p. 1085 [and Forestier, *Œuvres*, p. 1681, n. 2].
33 Rohou, *Théâtre*, p. 1091, 'La pièce est 'scandée par trois révélations – celle de l'édit d'extermination, celle de l'identité de l'homme qui a préservé Assuérus d'un complot, celle de la nationalité d'Esther' [the play is paced by three revelations – the declaration of extermination, the identity of the man who saved Assuérus from conspiracy, and the nationality of Esther]. Racine thus cuts out the story of Vasthi and the revenge of the Jews, thereby focusing the story on the conflict between the forces of good and evil. All references specific to the world of the Orient are also eliminated. On the Book of Esther, see René Jasinski, *Autour de l'Esther racinienne* (Paris: Nizet, 1985), pp. 95 ff.
34 See Jürgen Grimm, "Des Herrn Auge . . ." . Pathos als Mittel der Instrumentalisierung und Subversion im Theater des Hochabsolutismus', in Jürgen Grimm/ Werner Hofmann/Henning Kraus *et al.* (eds), *Sichtweisen. Das Pathos der Franzosen* (Weimar: Edition Weimarer Klassik, 1997), pp. 11–35.
35 See Jean Mesnard: 'La tragédie présente de grandes affinités avec la poésie lyrique, "lyrique" étant synonyme de "musical"' [Tragedy offers a considerable affinity with lyric verse, 'lyric' being synonymous with 'musical'], 'La musicalité du texte dans la tragédie classique', in Irène Mamczarz (ed.), *Les premiers opéras en Europe et les formes dramatiques apparentées* (Paris: Klincksieck, 1992), pp. 117–31 (p. 117). According to Philippe Sellier, Racine added passages from the Books of Lamentations, Psalms, and Proverbs in order to reinforce the sense of a work of contemplation, see *Racine. Théâtre complet*, ed. Philippe Sellier, coll. La Salamandre (Paris: Imprimerie Nationale, 1995), 2, p. 585. It can thus be seen that the exploitation of the original biblical episode is orientated towards lyric contemplation, with two main axes: (1) persecuted innocence; (2) the victory of the righteous.
36 As in *Esther*, the entr'actes of *Athalie* are marked by the hymns and moralities of the chorus, but the chorus is less tied to the action; indeed, it ceases to appear at all at the end of the play.

ated emphasis in each act. Above all, the singing of the Israëlite maidens reinforces the emotions felt by Esther herself, thereby contributing to the understanding of their audience. Furthermore, the contributions of the chorus create a certain sort of religious lyricism in the play which is more powerful than the purely dramatic aspect.[37]

maidens' singing reinforces Esther's emotion

With the examination of the relationship between spoken and musical theatre, we have reached the vexed question of genre. In the preface of 1689, Moreau called his *Esther* an 'ouvrage de musique', but Dangeau's *Journal* announced the work of Racine and Moreau as an opera (18 August 1688). The terms used by Moreau and Dangeau are equally vague because the language of the seventeenth century did not possess the criteria necessary to define the genre.[38] Nevertheless, these two sources indicate that *Esther* was identified as a tragedy with an inspiration and a purpose which were totally original in France at the time. From the point of view of text as well as of music, Racine's *Esther* can be called a collective religious exercise, a term used by Sammer to define oratorios in general.[39] In this regard, Tiersot quotes Charles Bordes in support of his contention that the melodies of Moreau heralded the work of Gluck.[40] That being said, the oratorio is a form which represents action without recourse to the scenic effects of theatre: it is a musical drama on a 'religious stage'.[41] The title page of *Esther* announces a 'tragedy', but the play does not have the accepted structure of a tragedy of the time. First of all, it has only three acts, and then the dramatic element is too simple. The human condition is not presented as complex because the play only contains non-Aristotelian characters who are either completely guilty or completely innocent. Furthermore, there is no conflict of values because the forces wrestling in the soul of the main character are symmetrically opposed. All in all, it would be more accurate to call the play a *cantique* in

totally original at the time

collective religious exercise

not a tragedy according to definition of time

too simple, no conflict of values

37 This runs counter to the precept of Aristotle: 'The treatment of the chorus': 'One should regard the chorus too as one of the actors' (*Poetics*, ed. Russel, 1456a), p. 116. The chorus of *Esther* is above all a witness which observes, explains, and judges the action on stage without being involved (except in Act III. 3). Its presence therefore underlines the contemplative character of the play, which is like an immense prayer.
38 On the problems posed by the definition of the term 'opera', see *Die Musik in Geschichte und Gegenwart*, vol. 7, 2ᵉ ed. (Kassel/Stuttgart: Bärenreiter / Metzler, 1997), col. 635s.
39 Sammer, *Die Fastenmeditation*, p. 131.
40 Tiersot, 'Les Chœurs d'*Esther* de Moreau', pp. 36 ff., but Bordes also places Moreau in the tradition of medieval mysteries, and also considers him a precursor of the oratorios of Felix Mendelssohn-Bartholdy ('Les Chœurs d'*Esther* et d'*Athalie*', pp. 69 and 73).
41 See Werner Oehlmann, *Reclams Chormusik- und Oratoriumsführer*, 5ᵉ ed. (Stuttgart: Reclam, 1987), p. 174.

action.[42] In this regard, it is therefore comparable to an opera, the new 'art d'état',[43] although not to Italian 'opera seria' in which the chorus played a negligible part. What makes it like opera is the co-existence of text, music, and stage performance, but *Esther* was not, and cannot be, considered an opera, because the formula adopted by Lully and Quinault is that the whole work should be sung.[44] It might also be remembered that *Esther* was a play written for a performance at carnival time, a fact which brings it nearer the religious meditation of Lent.[45]

The structure of *Esther* also derives from the college drama of the Jesuits.[46] This can be described as the public performance of didactic

42 See Jacques Truchet, 'Le chant demande des textes simples, pathétiques, tendres ou violemment contrastés: à la lecture, ils paraîtraient simplistes [Song requires simple, moving texts which are tender or sharply contrasting; they are texts which can appear over-simplistic on preliminary reading], *La tragédie classique en France* (Paris: PUF, 1975), pp. 150 ff.

43 See Fritz Reckow, 'Der inszenierte Fürst. Situationsbezug und Stilprägung der Oper im absolutistischen Frankreich', in Klaus Hortschansky (ed.) *Traditionen – Neuansätze. Für Anna Amalie Abert (1906–1996)* (Tutzing: Schneider, 1997), p. 421, 'Die Oper im Absolutismus ist [. . .] durch aktuellen Situationsbezug und politische Indienstnahme geprägt. Sie ist zur Bühne des absoluten Fürsten selbst geworden und ungeachtet der mythologischen oder romanhaften Sujets als eine Art 'idéologie concrétisée' eng mit der jeweiligen politischen, sozialen, militärischen Realität verknüpft [. . .]' [The opera under absolutism is marked by its relation to topical context and subordination to politics. It has become the stage for the absolute prince himself and is, regardless of mythological or fictional subject, intimately linked with the prevailing political, social, and military reality as a kind of "idéologie concrétisée"]. After Jean-Baptiste Lully obtained the royal authority in 1672 to found l'Académie royale de musique (after which the king later granted him the privilege to publish), the opera was centred at the Court, as much in its content as in its place of performance. For the significance of the royal authority granted to Lully, see the following: Robert M. Isherwood, *Music in the Service of the King. France in the Seventeenth Century* (Ithaca/London: Cornell University Press, 1973), pp. 180–7, 199–203; Manuel Couvreur, *Jean-Baptiste Lully. Musique et Dramaturgie au Service du Prince*, (Brussels: Vollar, 1992), pp. 263–75. Even after the death of Lully, French composers strove to emulate the form of tragedy in music created by Quinault and Lully (see Herbert Schneider, 'Frankreich', in *Die Musik in Geschichte und Gegenwart*, vol. 3, 2ᵉ ed. (Kassel/Stuttgart: Bärenreiter / Metzler, 1995), col. 737.

44 Truchet, *La tragédie classique en France*, p. 150.

45 According to Sammer, *Die Fastenmeditation*, p. 100, religious meditation, oratorios, and opera were originally genres linked to Lent and the liturgy. The religious musical dramas reflect doctrinal positions.

46 For the success of Jesuit college theatre, see L.-V. Gofflot, *Le théâtre au collège du moyen âge à nos jours. Avec bibliographie et appendices* (Paris: Champion, 1907), pp. 166–204; also Rudolf Rieks, *Drei lateinische Tragiker des Grand Siècle* (Munich: Bayerischen Academie der Wissenschaften, 1989), pp. 8–15, and Elida Maria Szarota, *Das Jesuitendrama im deutschen Sprachgebiet* (Eine Periochen-Edition). Texte und Kommentare, vol. 1: *Vita humana und Transzendenz*, part 1 (Munich: Fink, 1979) p. 6. Szarota (*ibid.*, p. 47) informs us that, written in Latin the college drama was arranged with prologue, separate acts, and frequently after each act, a chorus; it was a form mobilized in the doctrinal struggle between Catholics and Protestants.

themes, of the *exemplum* in the service of Christian *persuasio*.[47] From this point of view, the theatre becomes a means of education as a representation of the *polis scholastica*, the *polis regia*, and the *polis christiana*, in other words, a global view of social and political worlds of the time in the service of Christian propaganda.[48] With the arrival of opera in France, Jesuit theatre lost its prestige, and this is perhaps the reason why Racine created a genre half way between the two. In choosing the form of a lyric religious tragedy, offering interest to lovers of both opera and tragedy, Racine showed himself once more to be a chameleon. He knew how to adapt to the prevalent taste in exploiting the form of the opera while skilfully introducing the praise of God and the King. The theme of *Esther* is in the tradition nourished by 'Latin dramatic dialogue',[49] an important weapon of the Counter-Reformation in the hands of the Jesuits. In France, it was above all Henry Du Mont and Marc-Antoine Charpentier (a disciple of Giacomo Carissimi) who made the new form popular. These dialogues, initially called *Motette* or *Concerti*, and *Histoire* or *Historia* in France and Germany, were highly appreciated in the early 1600s, and their centre of diffusion was Italy, particularly the Collegium Germanicum in Rome.[50] The favourite themes were from the Old Testament, due in part to the dramatic structure of these texts, as distinct from the more reflective ones of the New Testament. The difference between these religious dialogues and Racine's *Esther* lies in the fact that Racine used the Book of Esther as an inspiration for his own themes whereas the dialogues of the earlier period (which were sometimes included in the liturgy) reproduced the language of the biblical texts themselves.[51] Racine's play is thus different, and one must conclude that it is a work apart, belonging to none of the genres mentioned above. In the service of courtly considerations,

47 'Als Mittel der religiösen "persuasio" dienen das Exempel, die Allegorie und vereinzelt das Emblem als eine der Allegorie verwandte Argumentationsform' [As a means of religious 'persuasio', the example/exemplum, the allegory and, in isolation, the emblem serve as a form of argumentation related to allegory] (Sammer, *Die Fastenmeditation*, 141). Racine's play aligns the two opposing principles of *virtus* and *vitium*, a characteristic feature of Jesuit college drama according to Szarota (*Das Jesuitendrama im deutschen Sprachgebiet*, pp. 44 ff.).
48 See Rieks, *Drei lateinische Tragiker*, p. 63 ff.
49 See Howard Smither, 'The Latin Dramatic Dialogue and the Nascent Oratorio', *Journal of the American Musicological Society*, 20 (1967), 403–33; Smither finds in the dramatic construction of biblical texts 'verbal exchanges comparable to those found in a drama' (p. 408). See also Frits Noske, *Saints and Sinners. The Latin Musical Dialogue in the Seventeenth Century* (Oxford: Clarendon, 1992).
50 Thomas Culley, *Jesuits and Music* (Rome: Jesuit Historical Institute, 1970), p. 272.
51 Indeed, so widespread was their incorporation into the liturgy that in two decrees, of 1657 and 1665, Pope Alexander VII commanded that only the Missel and the Breviary could be used for liturgical celebration; see Noske, *Saints and Sinners*, p. 6.

Racine and Moreau created a work of transition between the older sacred drama, represented by Jesuit theatre, and the oratorio.

Thirty years after the first performance of *Esther*, Handel created a new form of oratorio after settling in London where Italian opera was less popular. For his first oratorio, he chose the theme of *Esther*, and even today the influence that the work of Racine and Moreau may have had on this early piece remains to be examined, especially in relation to the chorus, a most important part of Handel's work.[52] Several scholars have examined connections between the works of the two composers.[53] The precise extent and nature of the collaboration between Racine and Moreau in their innovative new work will never be known, but it is important to remember that it was his loss of favour at Court which cost Moreau his opportunity for lasting fame. In the relatively brief period of his favour as the composer for La Maison Royale de Saint Louis, he wrote the chorus parts for *Jephté*, *Judith*, *Jonathas*, and *Débora*, not to mention a version of *Esther* destined for public performance outside Saint-Cyr, and now lost. Entitled *Concert spirituel où le peuple juif est délivré par Esther*, it has been suggested that this work already contained the elements of the oratorio as we now know it today.[54]

---

52 In his study of Handel, Arnold Schering makes reference to the earlier example of *Athalie*: '[Händel] vermied die breiten, wuchtigen Formen und versuchte es mit einer knapperen Anlage, indem er sich zwei Kunstgriffe der französischen Opernkomponisten zu eigen machte, nämlich Sologesänge pausenlos in Chöre übergehen zu lassen, wobei diese die thematischen Ideen jener weiterführen, und das Einstreuen von Soli in Chorensembles' [Handel avoided using large and unwieldy forms and instead tried out a lighter concept: he adopted two tricks of French opera composers: (1) he let arias blend into choruses without any break, where both were developing the same themes (like we find in 'O thou that tellest . . .'), and (2) he inserted arias into choral ensembles (which included trios and quartets, etc.)], Arnold Schering, *Geschichte des Oratoriums* (Leipzig: Breitkopf & Härtel, 1911), pp. 264 ff.

53 Bernd Baselt, 'Das biblische Thema im Schaffen Händels', in Klaus Hortschansky (ed.), *Traditionen–Neuansätze. Für Anna Amalie Abert (1906–96)* (Schneider: Tutzing, 1997), pp. 7–40, especially pp. 33–6.

54 See Madelaine Garros, 'Moreau', in *Die Musik in Geschichte und Gegenwart*, vol. 9 (Kassel/Stuttgart: Bärenreiter / Metzler, 1961), col. 569.

Appendix

Example 1

Example 2

Example 3

Example 4

12

Moreau as Teacher: The Impact of his Vocation on the Composition of Esther

GRÁINNE GORMLEY

In this chapter I shall explore Jean-Baptiste Moreau's career as a teacher and examine how this vocation informed and shaped the musical language of *Esther*. I shall analyse the work from this perspective and suggest how the music might be performed in light of this analysis.

In October 1999, a group of nine singers and six instrumentalists assembled in Trinity College Chapel, Dublin, to present what was probably the first performance in Ireland of Jean-Baptiste Moreau's music for Racine's tragedy, *Esther*.[1] As conductor of the performance, I was intrigued by this unusual work and curious to investigate the life and times of its creator, Jean-Baptiste Moreau, whose return from relative obscurity to a position of scholarly interest is due entirely to his association with Racine and their successful artistic partnership at Saint-Cyr. Like many minor composers, Moreau's life is poorly documented, with scant information on his activities before and after his brief tenure at Saint-Cyr.[2] Most of his compositions do not survive,

1 The singers were drawn from the choir of the Carmelite church, St Teresa's, Clarendon Street, Dublin: Maria O'Connell, Elizabeth Nolan, Sylvia O'Brien, Cliona McDonough, Meav Ni Mhaolchatha, Mary O'Sullivan, Joanna Griffin, Assumpta Lawless and Cora Newman. The instrumentalists were Thérèse Timoney and Sarah Moffat, baroque violin, Andrew Robinson and Mark Wilkes, viola da gamba, Richard Sweeney, theorbo and Desmond Earley, harpsichord.

2 Apart from brief biographies in general reference works, Moreau's life and works receive but a passing reference in texts devoted to the baroque period in France. No original material on Moreau's life came to light in the tercentenary year; in consequence, biographical material for this study has been culled and collated from biographical dictionary and encyclopaedia entries. On the other hand, the music was drawn from the original sources indicated in the body of the text above; in this regard, see also the following: Carol Uncley-Irwin, 'An Investigation of Moreau's incidental

which adds to the difficulty of analysing his compositional style, inter-
preting his musical language, and assessing his contribution to the
broader Baroque canon.

biography

Although he had enjoyed success as a composer in his collaborations
with Racine at Saint-Cyr, the greater part of Moreau's adult life was
devoted to the teaching of composition and singing. Moreau, who was
born in 1656, had received his early musical training at the cathedral
of Angers, his birthplace, and he went on to direct the choirs at the
cathedrals of Langres and Dijon in the early 1680s. He came to Paris,
where a *Te Deum*, performed at St Cosme in 1687 and a *divertissement*,
performed at court, helped to establish him in the French capital.[3] In
1688 Louis XIV invited him to serve as *musicien ordinaire* at Saint-Cyr,
the school which Mme de Maintenon, the king's morganatic wife, had
established in 1686 for the daughters of impoverished gentlemen.[4] At
Saint-Cyr, Moreau's duties would have been delegated by Guillaume
Gabriel Nivers (*c*.1632–1714), who was appointed the first head of
music at the school, a position he held until his death. Nivers was
principally involved in the preparation and performance of sacred
music for the various liturgies at Saint-Cyr; he conducted chants and
motets in the chapel and composed sacred music for the community.

esp. involved in secular aspects of Saint-Cyr, teaching singing

Moreau, on the other hand, appeared to be involved in the more
secular aspects of the curriculum at Saint-Cyr. His early training as a
singer and the experience he gained as director of the choir at two
important French cathedrals suggest that he was employed as a singing
teacher by Mme de Maintenon. This conjecture is supported by the
fact that there is no evidence that Moreau had received any training
or was active as a keyboard player, and that with only two compositions
to his credit at this point, it appears unlikely that he was employed
purely as a composer. While the curriculum at Saint-Cyr was dominated by religious instruction, the development of the feminine arts of

2 *cont.* music from Racine's play *Esther*', unpublished doctoral thesis, University of
Rochester, NY; Anne Piéjus, '*Esther*, un modèle paradoxal de théâtre musical pour
Saint-Cyr', *PFSCL*, 24. 47 (1997), 395–420; the liminal note by Anne Piéjus on the
extract of Moreau's music reproduced for illustration in Forestier, *Œuvres*, p. 1001. As
the editors have noted in their introduction, it would be difficult to speak highly
enough of the complex work of transcription for choral and instrumental parts
accomplished by Emmanuel Mandrin; this was the indispensable starting point.

3 The *Te Deum* was performed in thanksgiving for Louis XIV's recovery from illness;
this work and the divertissement, *Les bergers de Marly*, do not survive.

4 The Maison Royale Saint-Louis de Saint-Cyr was established in Saint-Cyr, a small
village just west of Versailles. A significant corpus of music composed for the 'usage de
l'église et communauté des dames et démoiselles à Saint-Cyr' is contained in the music
section of the Saint-Cyr library and includes compositions by, among others, Lalande,
Campra and Clérambault.

singing, dancing and drawing was encouraged. Thus Moreau probably taught singing and composed music suitable for performance by his young pupils, his greatest achievement being his musical settings for Racine's *Esther* (1689) and *Athalie* (1691).

In 1694, Moreau fell out of favour with the king. In an attempt to widen his circle of influence and establish himself outside the limited sphere of the school, where all performances were given before a private audience, Moreau had composed music for *Zaïre*, a divertissement with a text by Alexandre Laînez. His association with Laînez, whose libertine verse offended the now strictly religious Louis, resulted in his forfeiting the esteem of the king. Thus in 1694, Moreau was sent as superintendant of music to Languedoc, a position tantamount to exile. However he managed to sell his benefice and returned to Paris.

His association with Saint Sulpice, which began after his return to Paris in the early years of the eighteenth century, affirmed his reputation as a teacher, as he instructed many students who were to go on to make a significant impact on French musical life. Moreau's composition students included Jean-François Dandrieu (*c.*1682–1738), the celebrated harpsichord player and composer, and his sister, Jeanne-Françoise, also a gifted musician, and Louis-Nicolas Clérambault (1676–1749). Clérambault also studied singing with Moreau and went on to become organist and singing teacher at Saint-Cyr in 1714. Moreau's other vocal protégés included his daughter, Marie-Claude, who was considered a fine singer in her day, and Louise Couperin (*c.*1679–1728). Louise, daughter of François was, according to Titon du Tillet 'one of the most celebrated musicians of our time, who sang with admirable taste and who played the harpsichord perfectly'. Interestingly, she was also taught by Michel Pignolet Monteclair (1667–1737), who was Moreau's earliest recorded student. Monteclair studied with Moreau between October 1681 and February 1682, while Moreau was *maître de musique* at the cathedral at Langres, his first appointment. Moreau wrote a manual on vocal technique entitled *L'Art Melodique* which, unfortunately, is lost.

Clearly Moreau was a gifted and influential teacher whose pupils included some of the most impressive performers and composers to emerge from the early decades of the eighteenth century. His pedagogical career, from his time in Langres to his association with Saint Sulpice spanned over fifty years. His compositional career, on the other hand, was considerably shorter. His earliest composition, a *Te Deum*, dates from 1687, and his last, a setting of Duché de Vancy's *Débora*, was written in 1706. The only compositions to survive are those written during his tenure at Saint-Cyr and in association with

Racine. Although Moreau did work with other writers, including Alexandre Laînez, Abbé Boyer and Duché de Vancy, there is little to suggest that these partnerships produced works comparable to the artistic achievements of the Moreau/Racine partnership. Moreau had composed music for Duché de Vancy in 1688, when he set *Jonathas*, the only Moreau/de Vancy work that was actually staged at Saint-Cyr. Because no copy of *Jonathas* survives, it is impossible to assess the merits of their creative endeavour. However, given the fact that their subsequent collaborations – *Absalon*, in 1702 and *Débora*, in 1706 – did not receive a public performance, and that *Jonathas* was not revived, suggests that theirs was not an especially successful creative partnership.

The year 1688 was to have a lasting significance in Moreau's life, for it was during this year that he met Jean Racine. At the request of Mme de Maintenon, who encouraged play-acting among her pupils, Racine and Moreau produced *Esther* in 1689, to universal acclaim. *Athalie* followed in 1691, and Moreau then composed four settings of Racine's *Cantiques Spirituels* which were published in a collection entitled *Cantiques chantez devant le Roy* in 1695.[5] *Esther* marked the pinnacle of Moreau's career. The king's presence at several performances ensured that production values were high. Bérain, who designed productions at Louis's court, designed the sets and costumes, and Moreau conducted an orchestra that included Nivers at the harpsichord. The exiled James II attended one of the last performances of the season and was reported to be enthusiastic in his praise.

In summary, Moreau was not a prolific composer. Before his serendipitous meeting with Racine, he had composed only three works. When he wrote the music for *Esther*, Moreau's principal function at Saint-Cyr would appear to have been as a teacher rather than as a composer, yet Racine collaborated with him to produce two works of great significance in their oeuvres. I shall now examine how Moreau's talents as a teacher rather than as a composer shaped and informed the musical language of *Esther*, and suggest how the music might be performed in light of this analysis.

Moreau's music was written to be performed by his singing students, who were probably aged between twelve and eighteen years. In crafting the music for *Esther*, Moreau had to take into account the physical immaturity and lack of experience of his pupils. Adolescence represents a delicate stage in the development of the voice. The diaphragm is not fully developed, the lungs are not functioning at full

5 The collection includes four settings by Pascal Collasse (1649–1709), composer and secretary to Lully, four settings by the organist of Notre Dame de Versailles, Jean-Noel Marchand (1660–1710), and one setting by Michel Richard de Lalande (1657–1726).

capacity and the outer limits of the vocal range have yet to be defined and developed. Incorrect placement and ignorance of a proper breathing technique at this stage can have a significant impact on the future development of the instrument. Add to this the constricting clothing fashionable in Moreau's day, and the challenge to produce a full, even, rounded tone is even greater.

While teenage girls can certainly produce a pleasant sound, they do not, generally, produce a very big sound. While we can but imagine what Moreau's students sounded like, the gentle scoring he employs for the majority of the airs, the carefully shaped phrases and the balance he strikes between solo and ensemble writing suggest that he was keenly aware of the strengths and limitations of his performing forces. As well as the physiological make-up of his students, Moreau had to consider their intellectual ability, and their capacity to study, rehearse and perform, in the presence of the king, a play written by France's greatest living playwright. And he had to consider their ability to read, interpret and execute his musical score. Moreau's composition reveals a sensitivity to the technical shortcomings of his protégés, with vocal writing that eschews complexity in favour of simple, unforced melodic lines. For the greater part of the piece, he does not stretch the voice beyond its natural range, and confines his musical vocabulary to formal structures that remain within the technical capacity of his young performers. Thus, his airs feature stepwise and triadic movement, with melodic leaps that reinforce rather than challenge the tonality, short phrases that do not require a sophisticated breathing technique, and an instrumental accompaniment that provides sympathetic support throughout. On the rare occasion when Moreau does extend his vocabulary, it is for a particular dramatic effect, as we shall see.

While we were indeed fortunate to have at our disposal a new edition of *Esther* – the work of the French organist, conductor and musicologist, Emmanuel Mandrin – several aspects of the work's structure presented musical and interpretative challenges which were not immediately satisfied by a close study of the score. According to the *dramatis personae*, Moreau's music is intended to be sung by the *Choeur de Jeunes Filles Israélites*, that is, a chorus of young girls. However, this group only functions as a chorus, in the literal sense, for less than a third of the play. For the greater part of the drama, Racine's text is communicated by solo vocal lines – *Une des Israélites, Une Autre, La Même* – and, less often, by two soloists in duet – *Toutes Deux, à deux*. The difficulty, then, in preparing the performance was to ascertain how these solo lines should be distributed among the choir. How many soloists had Moreau used? Who sang what? As we rehearsed the music in each scene, a pattern appeared to emerge from within the vocal textures that suggested an organized rather than an arbitrary distribution of the solo airs and recitatives.

The Chorus of Israelite girls appears in five scenes: Act I. 2 and 5; Act II. 8; Act III. 3 and 9. Table 1 shows how the solos, duets and choruses are distributed within each scene:

Table 1.

Esther	Act I. 2	Act I. 5	Act II. 8	Act III. 3	Act III. 9
Chorus	34 bars	95 bars	91 bars	54 bars	185 bars
Solos	52 bars	177 bars	206 bars	174 bars	292 bars
Duets	4 bars	19 bars	14 bars	16 bars	30 bars

It is clear from the table that solo writing prevails, particularly in the only appearance by the singers in Act II, where solos account for two thirds of the musical content. Although the ensemble writing increases, as might be expected, in the Finale, soloists continue to dominate the musical landscape. Moreau's pupils probably varied considerably in standard, ability and talent and the ratio of solo to ensemble singing suggests that he decided to feature his best singers in the solo parts, reserving the choral singing for a competent group of less able, less experienced singers. The relative simplicity of the ensemble music compared with the solo music supports this theory. Furthermore, a clear pattern throughout the solo lines points to five soloists being featured in the play. The soloists may be defined as follows: Singer A and Singer B, sopranos, who sing either in duet or in sequence throughout, in recitatives and airs in declamatory style; Singer C, soprano, who features in minor key airs and recitatives, dominates the early scenes, and represents the sadness and dejection of the Israelites in exile; Singer D, the only mezzo-soprano among the soloists, who injects a masculine presence into the feminine forces, with a series of dark, aggressive airs in which she denounces the ungodly; and Singer E, soprano, who sings throughout in major keys, dominates the central scenes and represents the Israelites hope and desire for deliverance through a series of airs that extol the virtues of the king and the glory of god.

Singer A and Singer B

The *Choeur de Jeunes Filles Israélites* first appears in Act I. 2, where they perform just 90 bars of music; this figure increases to 507 bars for the Finale to Act III. The scene opens with *Une des Israélites*, Singer A, and

Une autre, Singer B. Here, in the first musical constituent of the drama, Singers A and B sing, according to the stage direction, from the back of the theatre. This suggests several things: first, that they have good vocal projection and can be heard clearly by the audience; second, that they have the confidence to begin Act I. 2, in this rather exposed fashion, without significant instrumental support; and lastly, that their voices blend particularly well. Singer A has a slightly higher range than Singer B and takes the upper part in their short duet in this scene. In fact Singer A's music throughout favours the upper tessitura, while Singer B's favours the mid-to-lower range. This first dialogue moves homophonically and homorhythmically in parallel thirds, the interval Moreau favours for much of the choral writing in the play (Example 1, p. 225). The acoustical quality of the third, and its significance in affirming the major or minor tonality of the musical phrase, can be difficult to tune, and requires a good balance between the upper and lower voices to give equal weight to the upper and lower constituents of the interval. The successful execution of musical writing of this kind requires singers with similar voices, voices which complement each other in aspects of colour, timbre, resonance and articulation. Singers A and B appear together often throughout the play, frequently in duet, which suggests that Moreau selected them from among his pupils because of the vocal quality they shared.

When not singing duets together, Singers A and B usually sing in sequence, which is then repeated by the Chorus. This section, the only musical structure in the play to feature compound duple time, again emphasizes their confident delivery as, once more, they set the scene, both musically and dramatically for the Chorus. Singer A continues with an extended recitative, 'Quel carnage de toutes parts!' (Act I. 5, ll. 316–24), a declamatory, dramatic passage which requires clear articulation and a strong rhythmic sense, as the accompaniment here is minimal. Singer B sings the more reflective, plangent 'Des offenses d'autrui' (ll. 332–5), which echoes the loss of the Israelite people to the force of the enemy, as expressed by Singer A.

Between these two sections, however, is a passage which does not fit the characteristics noted in the soloists to this point. Racine indicates in the text that the air 'Hélas! si jeune encore' (Act I. 5, ll. 325–31), should be sung by *Une Des Plus Jeunes Israélites*. Obviously, the dramatic affect of these lines would be diminished if it were performed by one of Moreau's featured soloists, older, more mature girls, closer to womanhood than childhood, and so Moreau probably selected a girl from among his younger pupils to sing this simple air. Racine again requires a young, vulnerable presence later in the scene for the lines

'Dieu, qui veux bien que de simples enfants / Avec eux chantent tes
louanges' (Act I.5, ll. 357–8), and Moreau sets this text as a simple six-
bar duet for two young voices. This brief contribution from these very
young performers enriches the dramatic rather than the musical thrust
of the play. Their insertion into Moreau's musical landscape upsets the
balance he had achieved between his soloists to this point. However,
their presence among the older girls on stage serves Racine's purpose
in highlighting the vulnerability of the exiled Israelites.

young singers (2) highlight vulnerability of exiled Israelites

Singers A and B continue in declamatory mode in scene 5, as they
extol the virtues of their victorious God. Their duet, 'O dieu que la
gloire couronne' (ll. 353–6), is written in the same style – parallel thirds –
as their duet earlier in the act. They are next featured in Act II.8,
in another duet, 'Malheureux! vous quittez le maître des humains'
(ll. 742–3). According to Racine's text, this should be performed by *Le
Choeur*. However, Moreau clearly wishes to feature Singers A and B in
this scene, and writes a duet that mirrors the style of their first duet,
but extends the musical vocabulary by featuring imitative writing and
more elaborate cadential figures. Singers A and B do not perform as
soloists in this scene, which, as we shall see, is dominated by Singer E.
Their contribution to Act III. 3 is again brief, with two short phrases
beginning 'La veuve en sa défense' (ll. 995–6), which leads into 'Et les
larmes du juste implorant son appui/Sont précieuses devant lui
(ll. 997–8), which they sing together in unison.

Moreau reserves one of his most interesting compositional devices
for Singers A and B in the final scene of the play. Using the passage
'Esther a triomphé des filles des Persans/La nature et le ciel à l'envi
l'ont ornée (Act III, 9, ll. 1228–9) as his focus, he constructs a series of
short recitatives, airs and a duet around this triumphant chorus. After
the Chorus sings 'L'aimable Esther a fait ce grand ouvrage' (l. 1223),
Singer A sings the air 'De l'amour de son Dieu (ll. 1224–7). 'Esther a
triomphé' is then sung in unison by Singer A and Singer B. Then
follows a short air from Singer B, 'Tout ressent de ses yeux les charmes
innocents' (ll. 1230–1). The soloists repeat 'Esther a triomphé,' and
Singer A continues with the more elaborate air 'Les charmes de son
coeur'. The Chorus then sings 'Esther a triomphé'. According to
Racine's text, the play should continue with the air 'Ton Dieu n'est
plus irrité' (Act III. 9, ll. 1236–45). However Moreau instead combines
the earlier solo texts, 'Tout ressent de ses yeux' and 'Les charmes de
son coeur' in a duet which recalls the imitative features of their earlier
duets. This works most effectively, because although each textual passage begins differently, each ends with a line that is common to both
passages but for one word, 'Jamais tant de beauté (vertu) fut-elle

A + B have strong piece at end of play

couronnée' (ll. 1231–3), which provides Moreau with the opportunity to
bring his soloists together for the final cadence.

Moreau repeats this interesting structural device around the text
'Repassons les monts et les mers;/Rassemblez-vous des bouts de
l'univers' (ll. 1244–5). These lines, which close the air 'Ton Dieu n'est
plus irrité', are repeated by the Chorus; this is not indicated in
Racine's text. Moreau also alters the performing forces of the next
air 'Rompez vos fers,/Tribus captives' (ll. 1246–50), and indeed rear-
ranges some of the text in an attempt to mirror the chorus/solo/
duo/chorus construct of the previous complex. Thus Singer A sings 'Je
reverrai ces campagnes si chères' (l. 1251), with Singer B singing 'J'irai
pleurer au tombeau de mes pères' (l. 1252). They then sing the previous
text 'Rompez vos fers,/Tribus captives' (ll. 1246–8) as a short, imitative
duet, with the Chorus concluding this section with a repeat of
'Repassons les monts et les mers'. This additional material for Singers
A and B allows Moreau to maintain the vocal balance between solo,
chorus and duet which he established in Act I.

Their contribution to the play concludes with two airs, Singer A's
'Révélez, révélez les superbes portiques (ll. 1255–60), followed by
Singer B's 'Dieu descend et revient habiter parmi nous' (ll. 1261–4).
These airs reinforce the impression made by these singers in terms of
vocal range, dramatic context and musical personality.

While Singer A and Singer B have the least amount of solo singing
to perform, what they do sing is of great importance within the drama.
The first musical entry is theirs, and with it the responsibility to give a
confident, secure performance that will encourage the other performers
and establish Moreau's personality within Racine's play. Frequently,
their entries signal a change of metre, for example, the 'Arrachons'
section in 6/8 time, and in many cases they establish, both musically
and dramatically, what will become central to the Chorus's participation in several scenes, for example, Singer A sings through the upper
part of the 'Arrachons' chorus before they sing it, both Singers sing
'Esther a triomphé' before the Chorus sings it. In selecting Singer A
and Singer B, Moreau had to consider several factors: the size of the
voice, the range, the technical ability and musicianship of each singer
and, most importantly, the particular colour and personality of each
voice. He probably tried several different combinations of singers
before he was satisfied that he had found a well-matched pair. I would
suggest that Moreau possibly used two sisters in these roles, as I have
observed that siblings often share similar and, occasionally, identical
vocal characteristics.

Singer C

Marginalia (handwritten):
C: signif presence in every scene

1st air...

singing has plangent quality

(plaintive yearnings) see p.224

note difficulty of her pieces

+ intensity

Singer C has a significant musical presence in every scene. She sings more than half of the music, 48 bars, in the first scene alone and continues to have a striking musical presence throughout the play. Her music is characterized by dramatic recitatives, airs in minor keys (often accompanied by full orchestra), and an important solo role within the choral textures. During her first appearance in Act I. 2, for example, she sings the plaintive 'Déplorable Sion' (Act I. 2, ll. 132–40), and intersperses the chorus 'O rives du Jourdain!' (ll. 141–5) with passages of recitative. In this early scene, she utilizes her full range, b-flat–a″, and establishes the plangent quality that will be a feature of her singing in the play.

Sung at the request of Queen Esther, the air 'Déplorable Sion' presents several challenges for the performer. The first eight bars are slightly unsettling with changes of metre every other bar and a significant amount of text to articulate, hence the use of semiquavers, which can be difficult to project. Moreau repeats the last three lines of Racine's nine-line text to extend the musical structure and, I suggest, to draw attention to the textual references to songs, 'Si dans mes chants ta douleur retracée', and to the voice, 'Puissé-je demeurer sans voix'. Curiously, this line, which is seventh in the nine-line text, is presented again to close the air, the final cadence occuring on the words 'sans voix'. Apart from the dramatic implications of the repeated lines, the repetition allows Moreau to extend the air and create a more substantial piece for Singer C in this, her first scene. The recitatives that follow serve to further define her presence in the drama; the first recitative, though only four bars long, moves through the keys of C, F and B-flat major, creating a feeling of tension and uncertainty. The second, sung in her lower range, wanders again through a variety of keys, as she sings of her desire to see her homeland once more.

This intensity is again brought to bear on Act I. 5. Singer C opens the scene with the plaintive 'Pleurons et gémissons' (Act I. 5, ll. 293–300), which begins with an orchestral ritornello. When Singer C enters in bar 5, her air is accompanied by a counter-melody played by the second violins. (Example 2, p. 226). This air, with its many references to tears, crying, sobbing and sadness, is one of the most carefully orchestrated in the entire drama, with Moreau at pains to exploit the affecting text. As in the earlier scene, he repeats the last three lines of Racine's text, giving an especially effective treatment to line 6, 'Pleurez, mes tristes yeux'. This scene continues in the same way as scene 2, with Singer C interspersing the chorus, 'O mortelles alarmes!' (l. 301) with recitatives.

Singer C next appears in Act II. 8, with another affecting air, 'Dieu d'Israël, dissipe enfin cette ombre'. (Act II. 8, ll. 744–9). (Example 3, p. 226). This, like the previous air, is in a minor key, C minor, and opens with a short ritornello, this time featuring two flutes. (Flutes are used in one other air, later in the drama, an air that also features Singer C.) This setting of Racine's six-line text is simpler than the previous airs. Rather than composing additional musical phrases to support the repetition of text, Moreau simply repeats the second half of the air as it is, ABB.

The final air in Act III. 3, 'Détourne. roi puissant, détourne tes oreilles' (Act III. 9, ll. 999–1005), is sung by Singer C. In G minor, this setting of the ten-line rallying cry marks a return to the style of Singer C's airs in Act I. 2. The tonality is again unsettling, with chromatic movement in the vocal and continuo parts. Each line of text is given a separate musical treatment, which must have made it difficult for Singer C to memorize, but of course this approach gave equal weight to all the text.

In the Finale, Singer C is again joined by the flutes for the air 'Il s'apaise, il pardonne' (Act III. 9, ll. 1272–9), another air in C minor, triple metre. The second violins again provide a counter-melody. This air is perhaps Moreau's finest creation in *Esther*, and one that could be effectively performed as a solo air outside the context of the play. At 76 bars, it is the longest air in the play, but also the most balanced, with a series of short ritornelli and longer vocal phrases providing the perfect musical setting for Racine's seven-line text. In binary form, Moreau extends the B section by repeating the last line 'Ah! qui peut avec lui partager notre amour?'

By giving Singer C the first and last airs in the play, Moreau accords her a position of importance among his performing forces. It is clear that he took some time over her airs and recitatives, electing to repeat sections of the text so that he could provide her with longer, more elaborate pieces, awarding her the only airs with flute accompaniment, allowing her to dominate the earlier scenes. His strong leaning towards minor tonality in his compositions for Singer C suggests two things: first, that she had good intonation and was able to negotiate the sometimes difficult shifts between major and minor keys; and second, that her vocal colour was darker than the other sopranos and suited the sombre settings Moreau selected for her. Given that she was able to project above the counter-melodies that feature in two of her most noteworthy airs, she clearly had a bigger, more resonant voice than the other sopranos. Her central musical role in each scene suggests that she was a confident performer, with the poise and presence to give a dramatic and convincing performance. She was probably one of Moreau's best pupils.

Singer D

Singer D first appears in Act I. 5, and is perhaps the most distinctive and arresting of Moreau's performers. Unlike the other soloists, she is a mezzo-soprano, with a vocal range that extends from g–f'. Moreau exploits her range to dramatic effect throughout the play, her darker tone adding a masculine presence to his feminine forces. And indeed if Moreau had been writing for mixed voices, Singer D's airs and recitatives would surely have been created for a baritone or bass soloist. Her first air, 'Arme-toi, viens nous défendre' (Act II. 5, ll. 363–8), begins with a stirring, march-like ritornello in D major, and her melody, based on a series of rising fourths, is mirrored throughout at the octave by the basso continuo. This doubling is a feature of most of Singer D's music, as is the upper string accompaniment throughout, and the effect is to add weight to her voice, to distinguish her from the other singers and to emphasize the dramatic impact of the text. Another characteristic of Singer D's music in this scene is Moreau's departure from a purely syllabic word-setting to the use of melismas in the vocal line. In this air, the melisma on the word 'chasse' is not only an example of creative word-painting, but also an opportunity for the singer to show off. (Example 4, p. 227).

Singer D appears to have an even-toned and pliant instrument that sounds equally well in the upper and lower tessitura. Moreau demands great vocal agility from her, as the music moves swiftly from head to chest voice. She also appears to have excellent breath control, vital in negotiating the final phrase of her first air.

In Act II. 8, the air 'Le bonheur de l'impie est toujours agité' (ll. 798–801) features Singer D in similar mode. Again she is doubled at the octave by the basso continuo, with the upper strings playing a contrasting accompanying figure above. Although the strong rhythmic pulse at the beginning of the air echoes the style of 'Arme-toi', the second half of the air is more reflective, featuring gently shaped phrase with step-wise movement as she sings 'Ne cherchons la félicité que dans la paix de l'innocence', words that require gentle, less aggressive treatment. The text of her next air 'Nulle paix pour l'impie' (Act II. 8, ll. 814–17) has an obvious resonance with her previous air, and Moreau sets it to the same music, with some slight melodic and rhythmic changes to facilitate the new text.

Moreau's most vivid writing for Singer D occurs in Act III. 3 when, after the simple, strophic *Cantique*, Singer E launches into an unaccompanied quasi-recitative, nine bars long, which describes how Aquilon blew away the clouds and chased away the thunder and lightning (ll. 985–8). Another composer might have composed a dense, dramatic accompaniment to evoke the images presented in the text. But Singer D clearly has the presence, both vocally and personally, to deliver this electrifying solo a capella. (Example 5, p. 227). And the effect is remarkable, after so much accompanied singing. Several characteristics of Singer D's music to date feature here, for example, her vocal range, a–d", and a melisma on 'orages'. She continues with a short air, 'Un Roy sage, ennemy du langage menteur', with full string accompaniment, which again draws attention to her supple delivery throughout her range.

Singer D's final contribution to this scene is the air 'Détourne, roi puissant' (Act II. 4, ll. 999–1005). Although it begins with an elaborate ritornello, the solo part, unlike the earlier movements, is accompanied only by basso continuo. While Moreau does include several of the characteristics we have come to associate with Singer D (word-painting, for example, a downward leap on 'plonger', the lengthening of note-values for 'sommeilles', and a significant use of the lower part of her range), Racine's text, with its stark image of the blood of the innocents and its appeal to the King not to listen to false counsel, demands a different musical treatment from Moreau. The doubling of the voice at the octave does not begin until Bar 7 of the vocal part, the effect being to highlight the repetition of the words 'de tout conseil barbare et mensonger'. The customary melismatic writing is absent, the text being delivered without decoration. Again, the masculine element comes to the fore in Moreau's writing for Singer D, as she uses her chest-voice for much of this low-lying music.

In the Finale to *Esther*, Singer D appears briefly to sing an air which has textual associations with an earlier scene. 'J'ai vu l'impie adoré sur la terre' (Act II. 9, ll. 1208–13), recalls her airs in Act II. 8, 'Le bonheur de l'impie' and 'Nulle paix pour l'impie', although the musical treatment is quite different. In this scene, the musical language revives some of Moreau's ideas from Singer D's music in Act III. 3, specifically, the accompaniment of lower strings only and melodic figures that echo 'Détourne roi puissant', and the melisma and word-painting on 'le tonnerre' which is like an extended version of Moreau's treatment of 'orages' in 'D'un souffle d'Aquilon' (Act III. 3, ll. 985–8).

Singer D provides a welcome contrast to the other soloists through the distinctive musical language that characterizes her contribution. Moreau creates in her a masculine presence that sets her apart from the other singers, yet helps to affirm the male presence within the dramatis personae. The darker timbre of her voice, her confident technique, the dramatic and vigorous style of her music, all combine to create an impression of virility and strength. That this is achieved by a girl is a creative triumph for Moreau. Clearly, Singer D was one of his best students, possibly a little older, given the significance of her part, her regular interaction with the full orchestra and the musical and dramatic challenges of the role.

Singer E

Singer E does not make her first appearance until Act II. 8, when she performs the first air, 'Un moment a changé ce courage inflexible' (ll. 723–6). (Example 6, p. 228). This and the following air reveal some of the distinctive aspects of Moreau's writing for Singer E. Firstly, she always sings in a major key. Secondly, both the vocal line and the continuo feature running quavers and semiquavers. And lastly, the texts are either pastoral or in praise of God and the king. Her airs contrast sharply with Singer C's, whose angular, dramatic phrases and brooding tonality are balanced here by Singer E's light, regular phrases and uplifting texts.

Her second air, 'Tel qu'un ruisseau docile' (Act II. 8, ll. 729–34), a flowing air that favours the upper tessitura, closes with a repetition of the final line of text, 'Le coeur des rois est ainsi dans ta main!'. Moreau draws attention here and throughout Singer E's repertoire to any mention of kingship; as the play progresses, these allusions to the strength, wisdom and power of Assuerus, the monarch within the drama, transcend the action on stage and allow Racine and Moreau to honour their king, Louis, whose presence in the audience has elevated their simple play for schoolgirls into an elegant courtly ritual.

'Que ma bouche et mon coeur' (Act II. 8, ll. 771–7), in F major, triple metre, is another delicate, gentle air for Singer E in this scene. Again the upper tessitura is featured, and the ABA form of the text is mirrored in the music. Another air in F major follows the chorus 'Heureux dit-on' (l. 790). This air, 'Pour contenter ses frivoles désirs' (ll. 794–7), is similar in affect to the previous airs. At the end of her first air, Singer E sang of 'Cet Esprit de douceur' (l. 726). Her next air begins with the words 'O douce paix' (l. 802), which emphazises Singer E's association with all that is gentle, sweet and mild. The air itself is an ethereal, shimmering creation, which focuses on the upper part of Singer E's range. This twenty-bar section is then developed by the Chorus, using the same text. Singer E continues with another air

in F major, 'La gloire des méchants' (ll. 818–21). Moreau extends the
air by repeating the final line 'Il renaîtra, mon Dieu, plus brillant que
l'aurore', highlighting her association with God.

In Act III. 3, Singer E returns with another simple air, this time in
G major, 'Que le peuple est heureux (ll. 960–3), which includes further
references to the king, 'Lorsqu'un roi généreux' and 'heureux le roi lui-
même'. She continues with a strophic setting that alternates a solo voice
with the full chorus, again in G major, which Moreau entitles *Cantique*
(ll. 968–84). This is a simple, dance-like setting which again highlights
Singer E's light, fluid instrument.

Singer E's next air is perhaps the most overt in its praise of the
monarch. 'J'admire un roi victorieux' (Act III. 3, ll. 989–94), again in
G major, lauds the valour and wisdom of the king, and easily
transcends the action on stage to become a paean to Louis himself
(Example 7, p. xxx). In the final scene, she sings 'Il a vu contre nous
les méchants s'assembler' (ll. 1202–7), which marks the return of the
pastoral elements of her airs in Act II. 8, with phrases such as 'comme
l'eau sur la terre' and 'du haut du ciel', recalling 'le ruisseau docile' in
the earlier scene. She continues in C major with the air 'On peut des
plus grand rois surprendre la justice' (ll. 1214–20), another air that
extols the virtues of the king. A short air 'De l'amour de son Dieu son
coeur s'est embrasé' (ll. 1224–7) within the 'Esther a triomphé' section
of this final scene, and Singer E concludes her performance in the
play with two airs, songs of praise to God for the deliverance of the
Israelites. The first, in G major, is the delightful, buoyant 'Ton Dieu
n'est plus irrité' (ll. 1237–40)', the only one of Singer E's airs to begin
with a ritornello, a device used, perhaps, to separate the temporal
majesty of Esther from the spiritual majesty of God. The second, in
C major, 'Que le seigneur est bon' (ll. 1265–71) epitomizes Singer E's
airs, with its charming naiveté and innocence. Once more she sings of
'la douceur', this time in the phrase 'Heureux qui dès l'enfance en
connaît la douceur', and comes across at her most childlike in the
phrase 'Jeune peuple, courez à ce maître adorable'.

When Singer E appears for the first time in Act II, the sadness
and wretchedness of the Israelites in captivity, as evoked in particular
by Singer C, has been replaced by a feeling of optimism. Esther has
invited the king and Aman to dine with her, and hopes to persuade
the king to spare her people. Singer E, in her series of major key airs,
focuses on the power and goodness of God, on peace and eternal
light, 'O douce paix, O lumière éternelle' (Act II. 8, ll. 802–3), phrases
which are echoed by the Chorus. This pairing of Singer E and the
Chorus occurs again in Act III. 3, with a chorus similar in effect, 'O
repos! O tranquillité!' (ll. 964–8).

Although she does not appear until Act II, Singer E has the greatest
amount of solo singing in the entire play. However, her airs and recitatives, though numerous, are relatively easy to learn and execute, given
that Moreau's writing for her features stepwise or triadic movement
and regular rhythmic patterns, and is firmly based in a major key.
His writing exploits the upper tessitura, with most of Singer E's airs
venturing frequently above the stave, which suggests a voice with an
even, flexible tone and a bright timbre. She is often heard either just
before or just after Singer D, for example, Act II. 8, 'Pour contenter ses
frivoles désirs ses frivoles' (ll. 794–7), is followed by 'Le bonheur de
l'impie' (ll. 798–801). The juxtaposition of these soloists suggests that
Singer E has a lighter, more fluid vocal presence to contrast the dark,
weighty tones of Singer D. Her association throughout with major
rather than minor tonalities, with dance-like melodies and gently
shaped accompaniments, also highlights the strong contrasts that exist
between Singer E and Singer C, whose plaintive yearnings are balanced
by the buoyant, joyful melodies in Singer E's repertoire. Her central role
in the play suggests that she was another of Moreau's better students.
Her airs are among the most attractive in the play, and are most effective when executed by a small, well-focused voice, with a light vibrato
(based on the fact that she is only ever heard with continuo accompaniment) and with a well-developed upper register. I would also surmise
that she was perhaps the youngest of the five soloists, her youthful
presence complementing the naïveté and simplicity expressed in her airs.

There are obvious advantages to defining the solo vocal roles and
assigning the recitatives and airs to five specific singers. From a purely
practical standpoint, the performers at the recent Irish premiere found
the simple, consistent labelling system, using the first five letters of the
alphabet, much easier to follow than the original, seemingly arbitrary
designation of solos to *Une des Israélites*, *Une autre*, etc. From my perspective as conductor, the defining of the solo roles thus facilitated the
selection of the most suitable singers from within the ensemble to assume
these important roles. The other significant benefit derived from the
application of this performing model is that clearly defined characters
emerge from within the *Chœur des Jeunes Filles Israélites*, personalities
whose musical input complements the drama being enacted in verse by
Queen Esther and her suite: Singers A and B, whose pairing in the
early scenes establishes the dramatic and musical thrust of the Chorus's
presence; Singer C, whose melancholy airs evoke the sadness of the
exiled Israelites; Singer D, the aggressive, masculine presence within the
all-female cast; and Singer E, whose brighter vocal timbre embodies
Virtue's triumph over the forces of Evil.

Appendix

Example 1

Example 2

Example 3

Example 4

Example 5

Example 6

Une des Israélites (Singer E)

Un mo-ment a chan-gé ce cou-rage in-fle-xi-ble, Le li-on ru-gis-

sant est un a- — -gneau pai-si- — -ble.

Example 7

Une Autre (Singer E)

J'ad-mire un Roy vic-to-ri-eux, Que sa va-leur con— -duit tri-om-phant en tous

lieux, tri-om-phant_____ en tous lieux;

13

Racine and the Three Vanities

ALAIN VIALA

After three centuries of Racinian criticism, and in particular after the profusion of works produced during the tercentenary year, has everything not been said, done, seen or heard? One could indeed be forgiven for thinking that interpretation of Racine's work has, quite literally, been played out, all the more so since in the autumn of 1999 the *Théâtre du Nord-Ouest* in Paris staged a season of Racine's entire theatrical *œuvre*. However, if one rejects the rhetorical 'everything has been said and we're too late because people have been commenting on Racine's work for three hundred years', then my opening question takes on a fuller, more productive meaning. It indicates that even if the tasks of learned philology may, to a greater or lesser degree, be settled, interpretations are constantly being revisited and a 'border zone' where both interpretation and philology meet is still open.[1] By 'border zone' I refer to all those procedures which link historical data, i.e. 'facts', to interpretative textual analyses, i.e. 'readings'. As these procedures allow us to contextualize, they are, in part, linked to philology. However, they also permit us to draw out interpretations, and as such they are part of criticism, and must necessarily be seen as partly subjective.

In order to play my part, as it were, in this subjectivity it would be useful to follow the gestation of these 'border zone' links. In 1999, I participated in a discussion on literary history and topology.[2]

[handwritten margin notes: "has all been done+said?"; "no — interps are constantly being rerouted"; "I still a 'border zone' = procedures linking historical fact + interp"]

1 Amongst 1999 publications two examples of such philological stabilization are Georges Forestier's Pléiade edition (referred to throughout this volume) and J. Lesaulnier's edition of *Abrégé de l'histoire de Port-Royal.*
2 This was at the occasion of the *viva voce* for A. Boissinot's doctoral thesis, 'Littérature et argumentation', Université de Paris–VIII, Saint-Denis, June 1999.

Furthermore, throughout the year of the tercentenary, I also had the opportunity to see that, as far as Racine and associated subjects are concerned, critical reflection on rhetorical issues was developing.[3] And whoever says rhetoric says, amongst other things, topoi or common-places. The developing critical areas of contextualization and topology appear to me to be of great importance to the study of Racine. They are growth areas of research, and it is perhaps the historical status of the 'classic', with its privileged area of exploration, which allows new interrogations to develop. In the context of this chapter, this means asking whether or not a Racinian subject exists. The answer is most certainly yes, but how can it be defined? Or rather, how can one avoid slipping once more into vague thematic study? A recent conference, as well as current and ever more probing research, have led me to suggest the subject of vanity.[4] In this instance, I understand 'vanity' not as a theme, but 'vanitas' as a topos within the global discourse of the culture of a given period.

The existence of 'vanity' within such a global discourse does not mean it is omnipresent or evenly distributed. When speaking of *lieux communs* the least we must do is to situate them, and to establish by whom, in fact, they are shared. Therefore, we must specify that, as part of the subject, vanity belongs above all to the domain of painting and fine art, and, more precisely, it refers to a specific genre: the 'vanitas' [or in English, the still-life] as the representation of inevitable death. Literature has no corresponding genre, but one could argue that vanity exists as an attracting pole present in different genres, or as a discourse which is at work in them. And of the various genres solicited, tragedy, with its fatal ending, is an obvious case.[5] Consequently, it is possible to imagine the subject of vanity in tragedy, and particularly in Racinian tragedy. To my knowledge this has not yet been done in this specific

3 With regard to studies relevant to Racine in this area, I refer in particular to the work which succeeded Peter France's pioneering *Racine's Rhetoric* (Oxford: Clarendon, 1965), such as Michael Hawcroft's *Word as Action: Racine, Rhetoric and Theatrical Language* (Oxford: Clarendon, 1992) and more recently his *Rhetoric: Readings in French Literature* (Oxford: Oxford University Press, 2000), in addition to Gilles Declercq's *L'Art d'argumenter: structures, rhétoriques, et littératures* (Paris: Editions Universitaires, 1995), *Racine. Une rhétorique des passions* (Paris: PUF, forthcoming), and 'Le Lieu commun dans les tragédies de Racine: topique, poétique et mémoire à l'âge classique', *XVIIᵉ siècle*, 150 (1986), 43–60. More general studies on rhetoric include *L'Histoire de la rhétorique dans l'Europe moderne, 1450–1950*, edited by Marc Fumaroli (Paris: PUF, 1999) and Pierre Zoberman's *Cérémonies de la parole* (Paris: Champion, 1999).
4 I refer to the conference 'La Vanité au XVIIᵉ siècle', organized by A.-E. Spica and held in Metz in 1999; mention should also be made of the current research of K. Lanini.
5 At the conference in Metz mentioned above, B. Donné presented a paper entitled 'Tragédie et vanité'.

way, but to attempt this now (as if an already established framework could exist before extensive knowledge of the subject has been established), would be an exercise in delusion. It would obviously be better to begin with an examination of the texts in light of this question, in order to establish first of all what they say about vanity. If the texts have something to offer on this particular subject, they may also contribute to working premises for the reconstruction of the historical context of the text's production. Consequently, in this chapter, rather than 'explaining' Racine's texts, I would like to attempt a close 'questioning' of them.

*   *   *

In order to question the texts, the particulars of my approach need to be made more precise. In short, the notion of 'vanitas' needs to be clarified. Needless to say, the term does not correspond here to the modern and common meaning which describes the vanity of the vain, a character trait describing a tendency towards inordinate and misplaced pride. I refer rather to the original sense of *vanitas vanitatum* [vanity, vanity, all is vanity] and *omnia vanitas* as interpreted in the Old Testament book of Ecclesiastes.[6]

In particular, 'vanitas' designates objects, that is paintings which depict the inevitable death of mortal beings in an allegorical and symbolic manner. In this respect, vanity is most frequently presented as a skull surrounded by various objects according to the symbolism the artist has chosen to develop. In order to provide a precise and technical definition, one may say, therefore, that the appreciation of 'vanity' is a question of aesthetics. However, vanity also evokes the sense of abandonment which engulfs man when he contemplates his mortality, and for this reason can be said to have an ontological dimension. In Western tradition, the very thought of this abandonment links vanity to anxiety, and to the notion of punishment; anxiety because, according to the Bible, man was banished to this world against his wishes, and

6 [Ecclesiastes, i. 2. The key term 'vanité' is retained in modern French versions, such as *La Bible de Jérusalem* ('Vanité des vanités', dit Qohélet, 'vanité des vanités, tout est vanité'), but it has disappeared from successive English versions, becoming 'emptiness' in *The New English Bible* (Cambridge: Cambridge University Press, 1970), and then 'futility' in *The Revised English Bible* (Cambridge: Cambridge University Press, 1989). It is the American edition which returns to tradition with the restoration of 'vanity', in the *New Revised Standard Version* (English edition published by Collins, 1989). Information gratefully acknowledged from Kevin Cathcart, Professor of Near Eastern Languages, University College Dublin. This brief excursion is a useful reminder of the importance to Racine himself of the provenance of his biblical sources, whether Latin, Greek, or Hebrew.]

punishment because his banishment resulted from original sin. In short, man's mortality is the punishment for his original transgression. It is the price to pay for the possibility of being reunited with God yet, at the same time, holds the equal risk for man of being eternally damned. This explains the ontological dimension of vanity.

As vanity describes a type of religious contemplation and a vision of the world which aims to elicit a particular emotion, it is also linked to a type of anthropology. As it unites these different levels of perception, it may be viewed as a topos. As such, having the properties of a commonplace, vanity also represents a place that could not be more common to all of us, and for this reason is undeniably a matter for topological study.

Empirical observation suggests that these interpretations of 'vanitas' abound in the seventeenth century.[7] A common and pragmatic classification of literary history prompts one to link this to baroque sensitivity. However, the importance of vanity in Philippe de Champaigne's paintings or in Pascal's *Pensées* also suggests that the usefulness of classification is illusory, and its heuristic value limited.[8] One could even argue that where it arises, the baroque is linked to the tradition of *memento mori*, associated with *artes moriendi*, and therefore with the idea that, provided one had a *good* death, leaving this earthly life (mortal, thus vain) could mean gaining a heavenly life where eternal beatitude guaranteed fulfilment. And yet, on the other hand, vanities proper may be seen no longer as a means to conquer death, but as an admission of the anxiety it causes. As with Pascal, they can be seen as a repetition of the certainty that 'le dernier acte est sanglant' and that 'un roi sans divertissement est un homme plein de misères'.[9]

It is important to remember that vanity refers to a void. For this reason, and forgive the truism, it is the opposite of the pleasant sensations of fulfilment and satisfaction. The feeling of satisfaction results from the perception that our desires are met, fulfilled, satiated. In 'classical' (the term is retained for practical reasons) Christian anthropology, desires are the manifestation of man's intrinsically corrupt nature, or his libido. Therefore, as a specific discourse, vanity expresses

---

7 K. Lanini originally proposed these ideas in 'Le Discours de vanité chez Pascal', D.E.A. thesis, Université de Paris–III, 1998.

8 It would be tempting to link vanity to the theology of both the Jansenists or more broadly the Augustinians. However, apart from the fact that this is not my intention here, it seems to me that before attributing vanity to any one person or group, its status as a topos, unevenly distributed amongst individuals and groups, must be established. This is one of the conceptual issues in the process of contextualization.

9 Blaise Pascal, *Pensées*, ed. Michel Le Guern (Paris: Gallimard, 1977), fragments 154 and 127, respectively.

the 'impasse libidinale'. This can be illustrated by the following short example. To say that 'Pour grands que soient les rois, ils sont ce que nous sommes et meurent comme nous' [no matter how great kings are, they are as we are, and die like us] is a cliché used habitually to deny worldly manifestations of grandeur. However, to say as Pascal does, that 'un roi sans divertissement est un homme plein de misères' is to point towards the fact that the libido is never satisfied. Not only are satisfactions (wealth, power, etc.) without any true value, but desire itself is an illusion, or vain. Strictly speaking, vanity is not only a call to reject 'things' which provide satisfaction, but a command to renounce desires themselves.

*   *   *

Racine wrote his preface to *La Thébaïde* in hindsight, and in doing so he becomes at once the reader and critic of his first play:

> La Catastrophe [en] est peut-être un peu trop sanglante. En effet il n'y paraît presque pas un Acteur qui ne meure à la fin.
>
> [The ultimate conclusion is perhaps too gory. Indeed, there is hardly anyone left alive the end.][10]

As this is theatre, there is a double statement explaining the different levels at which ethics function. The first level is the relationship between the text and the stage, where the 'ethos' of the characters is constructed. On another level, the relationship between the spectators and the stage (or the text and the readers) creates the space of pathos or the emotions of the audience. This is the space of aesthetics. Here, meaning is established in the relationship between the gaze of the public and their perception of the characters: what they do and who they are, which in the audience's mind is the product of what they say and do. The comment, 'un peu trop sanglante', belongs to the impressions which Racine, as reader of his own work, has of his own play. First and foremost amongst the deaths which accumulate on stage are those of Etéocle and Polynice, who kill each other for power, thus under the impetus of *libido dominandi*. However, neither of these characters benefits from death. Créon, who also dies and who incites Etéocle and Polynice to commit the crime, is also motivated by *libido dominandi*. Indeed, through the character of Créon we see a link established between the separate libidos of power and of love. Créon loves Antigone as much as the throne and sacrifices everthing for her, but in vain. Thus the spaces which create the desire for love are destroyed by the desire

10 Forestier, *Œuvres*, p. 119.

for power. The type of love I refer to is the physical love which links Antigone and Hémon, and which is crushed by civil war. However, love in the play also refers to family love: maternal in the case of Jocaste, brotherly as should have existed between Etéocle and Polynice, and sisterly in the case of Antigone. The character of Ménécée, who dies in vain having sacrificed herself for family and country, symbolizes the failure of love which is *généreux*, altruistic and benevolent. Each death in the play is emblematic of the failure of a libido whether it be power or love. They who desire, die. The 'catastrophe trop sanglante' stems from this: *La Thébaïde* can be said, therefore, to be a tragedy of vanities.

It is frequently claimed that the first work sows the seeds for those that follow. This may be true in general, but in the case of Racine, and from the point of view of this chapter, it is far from true. Perhaps because Racine was sensitive to the difficulties that this 'catastrophe trop sanglante' could pose, perhaps because *La Thébaïde* was not a success, a fact which he perhaps tries to explain in the extract from the preface I have just quoted. In the following play he explores another direction. In *Alexandre le Grand*, almost as though the play were a counter-test, desires are triumphant. Alexandre conquers the world and Cléofile, and Porus conquers respect, *gloire* and Axiane. We are presented with a universe where *générosité* is successfully attained. Here, death has meaning: it is not vain, as long as one dies (Axiane's words) 'en Roi' (*Alexandre le Grand*, Act IV. 1, l. 1032). Even Taxile, the only character who dies, has some dignity in death, albeit of little benefit. After the temptation of the absolute tragedy of universal vanity, this work displays the temptation of *héroïsme galant*.

If, then, in Racine's theatre there is a dimension of vanity, it is not unique, constant or uniform. It is important then in this case, as in others, to pay careful attention to differences between the plays. Like Ménécée, Alexandre and Porus illustrate the opposite values of vanity which are *gloire* and *générosité*. *Générosité* gives meaning to life and *gloire* gives meaning to death, because in the fullest meaning of the term, *gloire* ensures posterity and immortality and therefore allows an escape from the silence of the tomb. Consequently, the critic who wishes to establish the presence, forms and meanings of vanity in Racine's work must also consider the meaning which the 'soins de gloire' and the acts of *générosité* of the characters held for his audiences.

Having established these two pointers, that vanity is not omnipresent and that it must be imagined in its relation to *gloire* and *générosité*, one could examine the entire corpus. One could illustrate, for example, how Pyrrhus, Oreste and Hermione represent deadly and vain desires in contrast to Andromaque, who no longer has any, and who, alone, finally emerges triumphant. One could also examine how in *Britannicus*, Néron, Agrippine and even Britannicus, not to mention Narcisse, are all led by their libido. The exception, of course, is Junie who 'sans mourir, [. . .] est morte pour lui', i.e. for Néron (*Britannicus*, Act V. 8, l. 1742). This sentence is revealing with its reference to death 'in this world', and implicitly to the creatures of desire whose very desires perturb and derange them. (Néron, like Oreste, ends up lost and distraught.)[11] However, given the limits of this chapter, such a panorama would be superficial. I have chosen, rather, to indicate the hypothesis and to examine two cases in closer detail.

*   *   *

As vanity and *générosité* are dialectically linked, a detail of *Bérénice* attracts attention. In the great tirade of the play's *dénouement*, there is an unusual occurrence. Bérénice begins her tirade with a cry, 'Arrêtez. Arrêtez. Princes trop généreux' (*Bérénice*, Act V. 7, l. 1481). Then, thirty lines later she says to Antiochus, 'Vivez, et faites-vous un effort généreux' (l. 1510). In the first quotation, 'Princes' is in the plural and refers to Antiochus as well as Titus. Given that Bérénice asks Antiochus to 'faire un effort généreux', must we assume that she finds him alternatively 'trop généreux' and then not magnanimous enough? And although she had not used the same term when speaking to Titus, when forbidding him to kill himself (as he had threatened to do in lines 1432–4), she was, in substance asking him the same thing. In short, having first forbidden an excess of magnanimity, Bérénice then demands more magnanimity. Consequently, are we to think that the character is so upset there is confusion in her words (or rather, because we are dealing with literature, that Racine cleverly creates linguistic confusion in her in order to let the public know she is very upset)? Or must we suppose that Racine was careless? Or is he exploiting two different connotations of the same term? Titus and Antiochus have announced their willingness to die for Bérénice. She answers that such generosity, to sacrifice life in the name of love, is vain. She requests a conversion, a change of their system of values, asking them to sacrifice the satisfaction of love rather than sacrifice life. In so doing, Bérénice requests an act of transcendence.

According to Racine's text, Titus does not have to conquer the throne any more than he has to conquer Bérénice – their love is

---

11 See *Britannicus*, ll. 1777–8, and *Andromaque*, ll. 1689–92.

reciprocal. He is the successor to the throne by heredity, and his power does not result from any action, less still from any manoeuvre, on his part. Titus had not desired power, nor was he motivated by *libido dominandi*, the Roman people desired him.[12] This portrait of Titus makes him, of all Racine's monarchs, the only one who holds an initial hereditary right of succession.[13] Consequently, his decision to give up Bérénice is a struggle against the only desire that motivates him, amorous desire. The real transcendence of this play lies here: how does one transcend love? When Bérénice is won over by his argument, she succeeds in reversing the values of love. Firstly she says:

> Bérénice, Seigneur, ne vaut point tant d'alarmes,
> Ni que par votre amour l'Univers malheureux,
> Dans le temps que Titus attire tous ses vœux,
> Et que de vos vertus il goûte les prémices,
> Se voie en un moment enlever ses délices.
>
> (*Bérénice*, Act V. 7, ll.1496–1500).

And then, in her final words, she adds:

> Adieu, servons tous trois d'exemple à l'Univers
> De l'amour la plus tendre, et la plus malheureuse,
> Dont il puisse garder l'histoire douloureuse.
>
> (*Bérénice*, Act V. 7, ll. 1514–16).

The same terms are repeated but are distributed differently: the 'univers malheureux' is divided into a 'univers' of the audience and a 'malheur exemplaire' which is that of 'l'amour la plus tendre'. In the first instance, the universe is the subject and recognizes Titus's *gloire* in the political order. In the second instance, where the word 'univers' is used as a complement, it is a question of conquering one's self-respect in order to attain another *gloire*, because if the sacrifice is remembered, *gloire* will be achieved. The price for such *gloire* is to transcend love, to reach an absolute of 'tendresse'. It is the sublime message of the *Carte de Tendre*, which, as I have noted elsewhere, provides one of the codes to Racine's language.[14] So, *générosité* no longer means to die in the name of desire, which would demonstrate supreme strength of desire, but to live beyond desire.

[margin note: gloire attained when one transcends love → tendresse]

[margin note: living beyond desire]

12 As if to prove he does not desire power, Titus comments 'je me souviens à peine / Si je suis Empereur' (*Bérénice*, ll. 1392/1394).

13 For a study of the Machiavellian imagery of Racine's tragedies, see Alain Viala, 'Péril, conseil et secret d'État dans les tragédies romaines de Racine: Racine et Machiavel', in 'Les Tragédies romaines de Racine: *Britannicus, Bérénice, Mithridate*', *Littératures classiques*, 26 (1996), 91–113.

14 Alain Viala, 'Racine et la Carte de Tendre', *La Licorne*, special no. *Racine poète*, 50 (1999), 369–87.

Other Racinian tragedies also reveal the emptied (vain) desire of their object. For example, Néron fails to win Junie, Agrippine fails to win power, Roxane wins neither Bajazet nor the throne. Here the object is neither absent nor abolished: it is desire itself which is at stake. Supreme *générosité* is to renounce desires in the name of that which gave rise to those desires. Thus, Bérénice invites her two suitors to abandon one form of *générosité* in favour of another. As I suggested above, artists painting the Vanities included symbolic objects which signified the type of vanity they wished to represent (arms or a crown for the vanity of power for example). In the same way one could suggest that *Bérénice* and its eponymous heroine represent a 'vanité au cœur', if we can call it that.

*　　*　　*

There are also 'vanités aux livres'. *Athalie* provides a scene quite different from the one we have just examined. Here there is no question of amorous libido. Religious faith and the law find themselves in opposition. Earthly law, linked to the desire for power, is opposed to faith, which does not represent desire but the certainty of knowledge. Athalie is presented as:

> [. . .] Reine éclairée, intrépide,
> Elevée au-dessus de son sexe timide,
> Qui d'abord accablait ses ennemis surpris,
> Et d'un instant perdu connaissait tout le prix.
> (*Athalie*, Act III. 3, ll. 871–4).

These words are pronounced by Mathan, who at this point in the play is speaking in confidence, thus sincerely. He is a Machiavellian character, therefore lucid, and establishes an authentic reference point. In this way he confirms the validity of Athalie's statement (Act 2. 5, ll. 465–84) regarding the successes of her reign. We have, therefore, an image of a woman whose desire for power is so well controlled and mastered that it has enabled her to transcend her female identity; in short, she is 'élevée au-dessus de son sexe'. Athalie acts in this way because she has acquired positive knowledge regarding action and political science: she knows the price of time. The play is the account of her downfall and the failure of both this power reincarnated as Machiavellian realism and the knowledge which is the means to this power. In the character of Athalie the two libidos of *dominandi* and, at its service, *sciendi*, are at stake. This a rare occurrence in Racine's work, and only Agrippine shares these characteristics with Athalie.

Needless to say, in biblical tragedy, the social order is determined by faith alone. If Joad wants to put Joas in power, it is not because the latter is a better king but because a pious king is needed. Furthermore, by reinstating the descendant of David, the lineage which will be Christ's is restored. The spectator is familiar with the biblical plot and is, therefore, aware of these facts. However, the character does not know the story in these terms. There is, therefore, a paradox in the character of Joad. He holds the truth yet repudiates material truth. In other words, he represents the paradox of the prophet. He can foresee the future but this very fact illustrates the vanity of knowledge, and even more so, the vanity of wanting to know. One must believe and nothing more. When Joad prophesies, a piece of knowledge is given to him, yet he pronounces it in an interrogative mode, a sign that he does not understand it, and cannot transform it into positive truth.

> Comment en un plomb vil l'or pur s'est-il changé?
> Quel est dans le Lieu saint ce Pontife égorgé?
> (*Athalie*, Act III. 7, ll. 1142–3).

Here, the double statement mentioned above is at its most effective because the spectators, who are familiar with the biblical story, know the answers to Joad's questions. They know that 'l'or pur changé en plomb vil' refers to Joas, who will become an infidel. They are also aware that the 'pontif égorgé' is Zacharie, whom Joas will have killed. Joas will reject the very religion that has allowed him to achieve power. However, this knowledge is not revealed to Joad. The prophecy becomes a question, which in turn becomes an assertion, indeed an injunction. By the time his speech ends, it is no longer a prophecy but a prayer. The veil thrown over the half-hidden truth helps to maintain the focus of the tragedy: would a father act unhesitatingly to bring to the throne a king who is obliged to renounce his faith and have his son killed? In another light, this would be a thematic revival of similar questions which emerged in *Iphigénie*. However, this is not what is at stake here. Joad cannot use this knowledge and his prophetic vision is used to announce something else. It is used to tell the spectators that knowledge amounts to nothing and that when confronted with divine, impenetrable intentions, it is vain to desire positive knowledge (i.e. the denial of Athalie by Joas is tied to a logic which leads to redemption, and is beyond human comprehension). Human knowledge is vain when faced with 'true' knowledge. Knowledge is vain when faced with faith.

What *Athalie* brings to our understanding of the question is the evidence that the monarchy of Divine Right is not an end but a means. The play highlights, therefore, that History does not have a 'meaning'.

Meaning belongs to an entirely different domain, that of Providence, which surpasses and renders useless the illusory knowlege of the earthly domain. In the same way that all power is vain when faced with divine will, all knowledge is vain when confronted with providential intentions which are part of religious faith. In a 'vanité aux livres' it is never the Bible which is the symbolic book of the vanity of *libido sciendi*. On the contrary, it is historical and political tomes which play that role. 'The Book', the Bible, is the one which says *et omnia vanitas* and clarifies that this results from man's original sin of yielding to his many libidos, primarily to curiosity, to *libido sciendi*.

* * *

Undoubtably there is more than enough material both to broaden this analysis and to examine other plays. For example, an obvious development would be to study the role of the sycophant, a character who plays with desires and thus acts as a catalyst for vanity. However, as this is beyond the scope of this chapter, I shall concentrate rather on drawing a number of propositions from the hypotheses already examined.

Firstly, Racinian tragedy has in its subject a topic of vanity. However, it is not present in all the plays, nor does it 'explain' those where it is present. Vanity is not a system but an element in a system, and it is significant as such. Secondly, the topic of vanity is represented, albeit infrequently and with varying importance, in three domains: power, love and knowledge. The three forms of libido then, *dominandi, amandi, sciendi*, are represented in the plays. While the desires for power and for love are more prominent than the desire for knowledge, nonetheless all three are present. Consequently, one can say, as a third proposition, that Racinian tragedy is a tragedy of the three vanities.

A corollary of this third proposition is that, although minor, the desire for knowledge touches on an area which is of particular importance where Racine is concerned: the question of historical knowledge. The paradox of the royal historiographer is that by writing a history which was intended to give meaning and *gloire* to his own actions, he contributed (if unconsciously) to an image of historical knowledge which was vain. In doing so, he also contributed to a human history which was vain when opposed to the almighty power of a sacred history, impenetrable to rational minds.[15]

15 Hence the ambivalences in his historical writing. See the proceeedings of the London 1999 conference *Racine et l'histoire*, particularly D. Ribard's article, 'Histoire et la *vie*'.

If the critic can draw the above conclusions, then the process of contextualization outlined at the beginning of this study is indeed possible. It is made possible by comparing theatrical images, not of general and potentially vague themes, but of the contemporary historical forms of these three dimensions of human action. This allows me to formulate my third proposition within the following categories: Racine's theatre reveals the vanity of Machiavellian realism, of *héroïsme galant* and of historical and political knowledge.

On that basis, a fourth proposition is then feasible. Not only does tragedy offer cathartic *pitié* and *terreur* to the spectator, it also provokes the feeling of the vanity of all desire. Rather than opposing the dream of satisfaction with dissatisfaction, which is a lesser form of satisfaction or satisfaction unattained, tragedy opposes it with the certainty of inevitable deprivation. In other words, it is not so much the fear of death and the beyond that tragedy evokes, but the certainty that desires, and therefore life, are vain. This is vanity as described by Pascal, where desire itself is vain, and the meaning of this goes beyond the widespread commonplace according to which the satisfactions of this world are a delusion. To live whilst being aware of the vanity of doing so, is to confront with dignity *la tristesse* or the immanence of death. Consequently, *la tristesse majeustueuse* (as mentioned in the preface to *Bérénice*[16]) could be considered as a specific form of the tragic sentiment, which Racine, at times, achieves and elicits in his work.

16 Forestier, *Œuvres*, p. 450.

Index

headaches

Rekopis
Znaleziony
W Saragossa
1955